THE STORY SO FAR

When Mizuha's mother, Izumi, came back from the dead,
Fushi began to realize the world was not as peaceful as he thought.

Izumi's wandering fye reveals that the creature that has taken over
her body is a Nokker, so Fushi, Bon, and the others begin an investigation.

That's when they discover the Beholder reborn in a human body.

After their previous battle had proven to be futile, the Nokkers choose to coexist
with humans and spread across the globe. Fushi briefly loses hope, but eventually
decides to fight the Nokkers once again in order to attain true peace.

Fushi's first target: Mimori, a girl who had been infected by a Nokker.

He faces off against the Nokkers in order to get her body back, but then he runs
into another girl, Funa, who seems to have some connection to the Guardians.

Fushi begins to search for Funa's secret, but is soon interrupted when
Mizuha starts to spiral out of control...

CHARACTERS

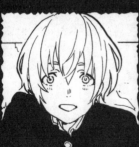

Fushi

Immortal. Can transform into vessels he
has acquired. Has the power of reconnection.
Has renewed his war with the Nokkers in order
to live peacefully with his comrades. Started
junior high school, where he is classmates with
Mizuha. Swore not to return home until he
wipes out the Nokkers.

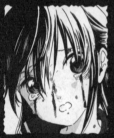

Mizuha

Second-year junior high
school student. Descendant
of Hayase. A girl with both
beauty and brains. Has an
unusually deep attachment
to Fushi. She has no
memories of it, but she
killed both her mother
and Funa.

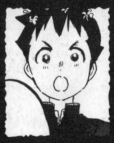

Yuki Aoki

First-year junior high
school student. Vice
President of the Occult
Research Club. Lives with
Fushi and the others.
Helps Fushi from the
sidelines as they fight the
Nokkers. Blabbermouth.

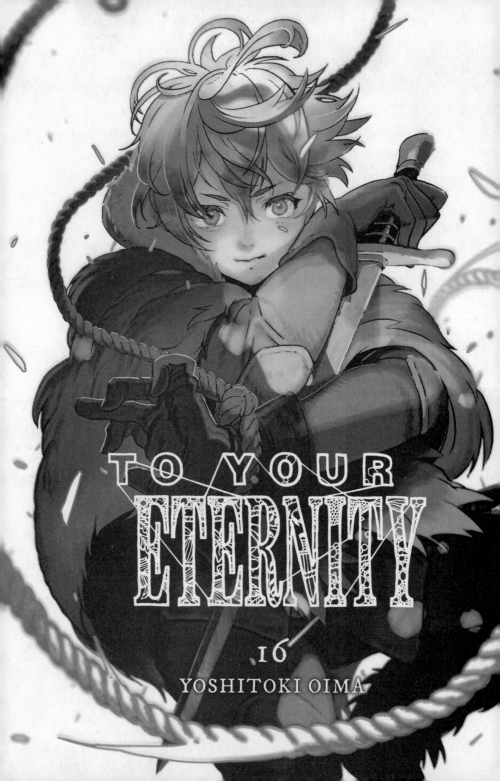

TO YOUR
ETERNITY

.16

YOSHITOKI OIMA

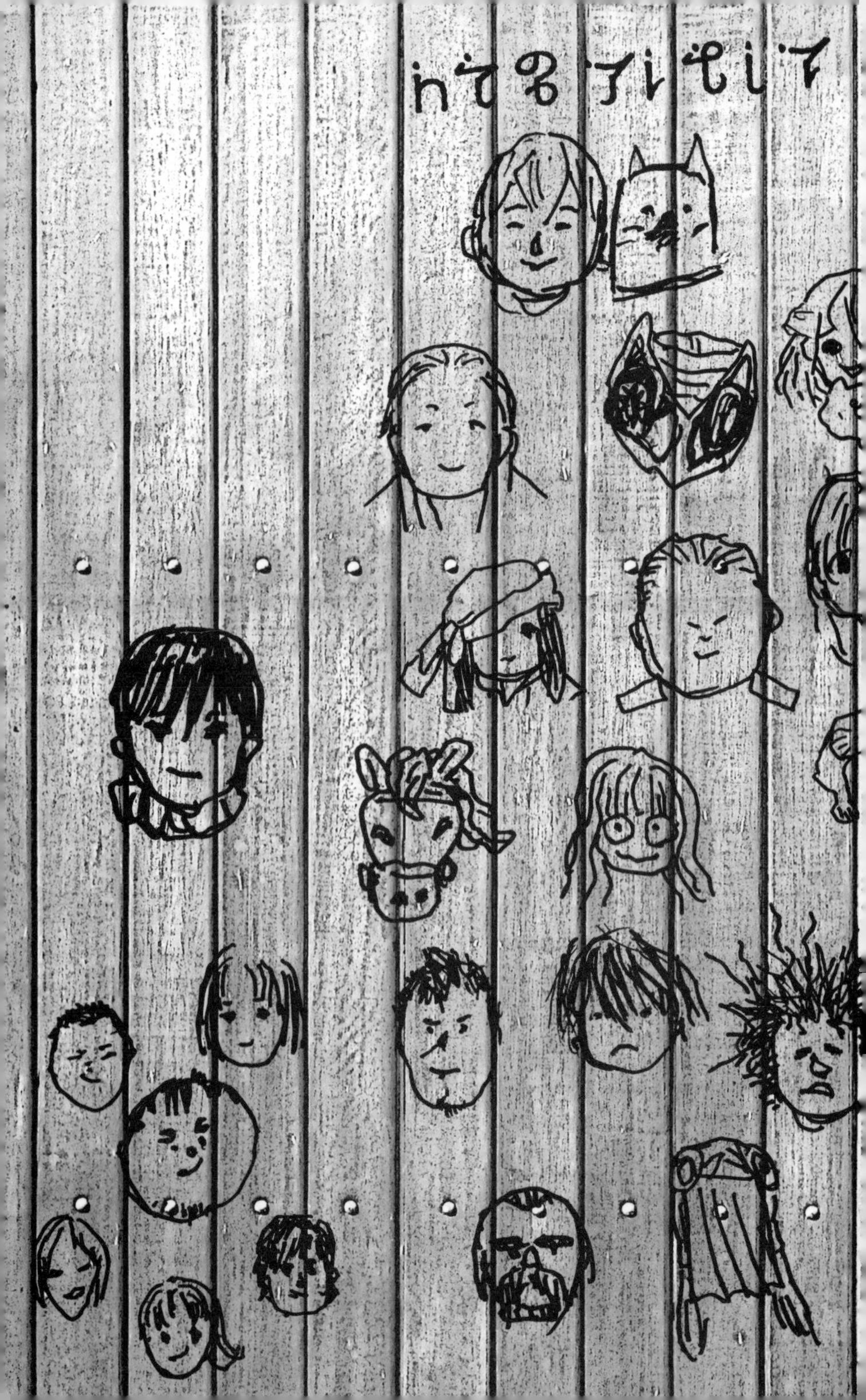

A Kodansha Comics Trade Paperback Original
To Your Eternity 16 copyright © 2021 Yoshitoki Oima
English translation copyright © 2022 Yoshitoki Oima

Published in the United States by Kodansha Comics, an imprint of Kodansha USA Publishing, LLC, New York.

Publication rights for this English edition arranged through Kodansha Ltd., Tokyo.

First published in Japan in 2021 by Kodansha Ltd., Tokyo as *Fumetsu no Anata e*, volume 16.

ISBN 978-1-64651-312-3

Cover Design: Tadashi Hisamochi (hive&co., Ltd.)
Title Logo Design: Shinobu Ohashi

Printed in Canada.

www.kodansha.us

9 8 7 6 5 4 3 2
Translation: Steven LeCroy
Lettering: Darren Smith
Editing: Haruko Hashimoto, Alexandra Swanson
Editorial Assistance: YKS Services LLC/SKY Japan, INC.
Kodansha Comics Edition Cover Design: Phil Balsman

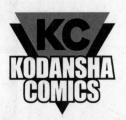

Publisher: Kiichiro Sugawara

Director of publishing services: Ben Applegate
Associate director of publishing operations: Stephen Pakula
Publishing services managing editors: Alanna Ruse, Madison Salters
Production managers: Emi Lotto, Angela Zurlo

COMRADES REINCARNATED IN THE MODERN WORLD

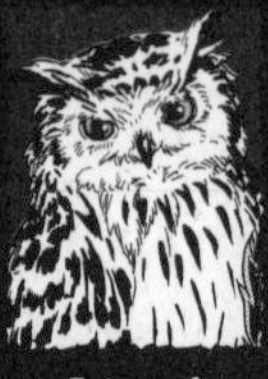
Ligard

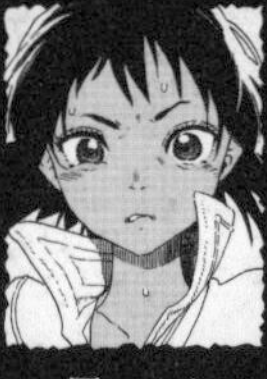
Tonari

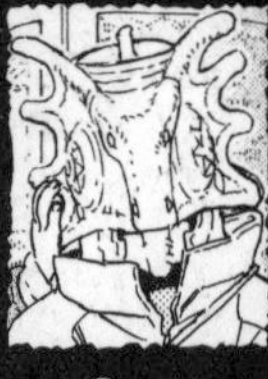
Gugu

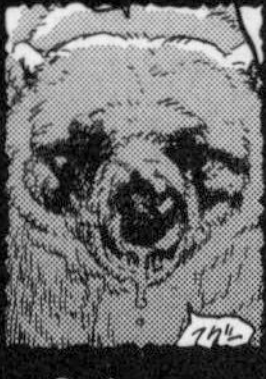
Oniguma

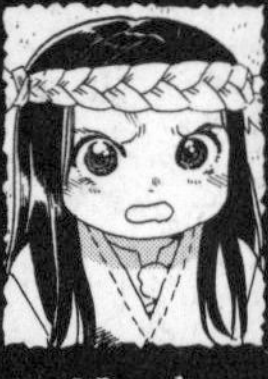
March

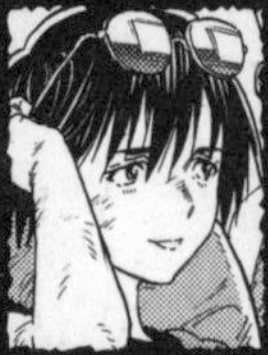
Hairo
Rich

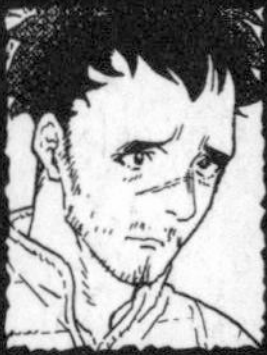
Kai
Renald Rawle

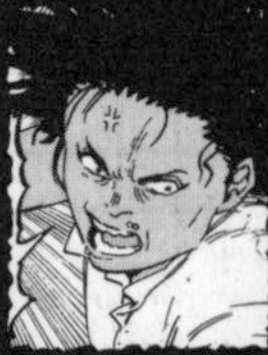
Messar
Robin Bastar

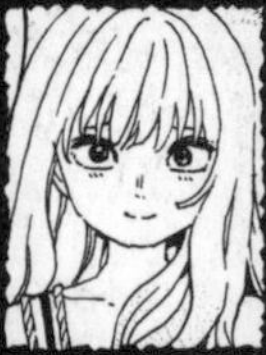
Iddy

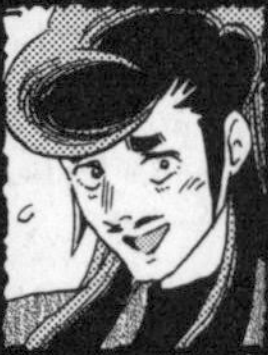
Bonchien Nicoli
la Tasty Peach
Uralis

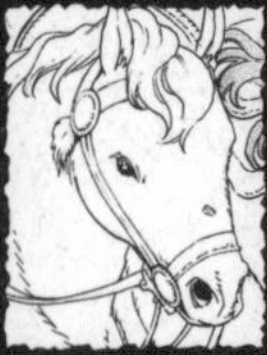
Horse

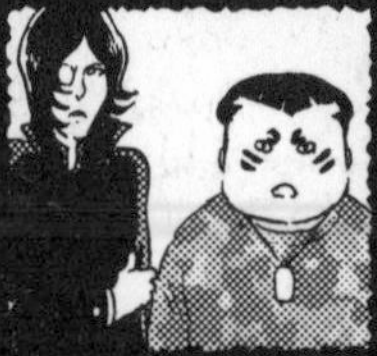

Occult Research Club Members

The Brains, Senba (left), and the Brawn, Tamaki (right). Both are very interested in Fushi's powers.

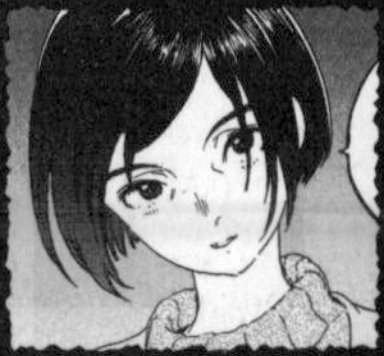

Izumi

Mizuha's mother, and a descendant of Hayase. After being killed by Mizuha, a Nokker took over her body. She is now a spirit.

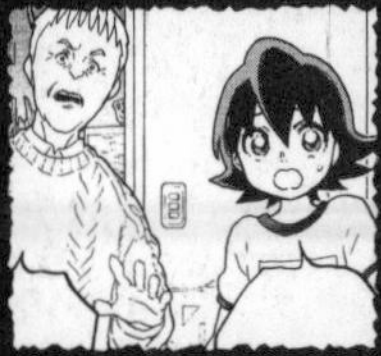

Yuki's Family

Aiko is Yuki's little sister, and is a super capable elementary schooler. Kazumitsu is the grand-father, and a good cook.

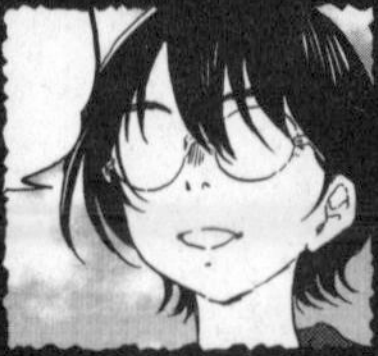

Hanna

Second-year in junior high. Mizuha's close friend. Her matching feathered hair tie with Mizuha is a symbol of their friendship.

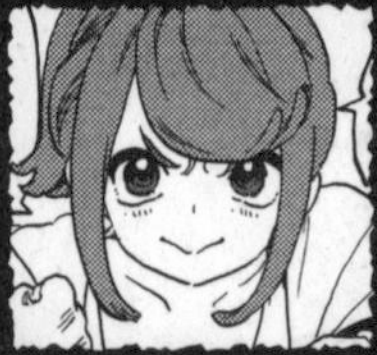

Sumika

The big sister at the orphanage where Satoru lives. Satoru's guardian and the one who gave him a name.

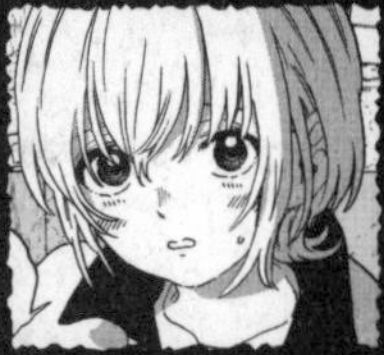

Funa

Second-year in junior high. A girl who has Hayase's naginata, and was taken over by a Nokker. Killed by Mizuha.

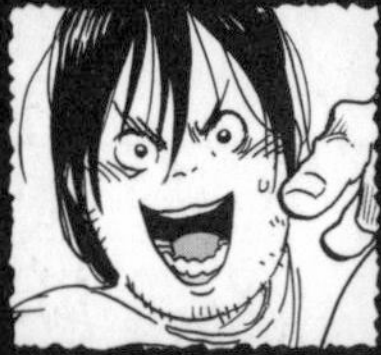

Hirotoshi

Mimori's older step-brother. Faces the Nokkers to save her. Fan of younger-sister-type media.

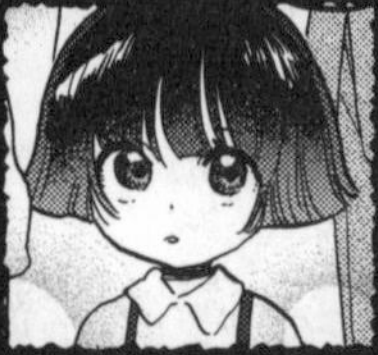

Mimori

Chose to die due to the pain of living, and was taken over by a Nokker. Now, she has returned to her body.

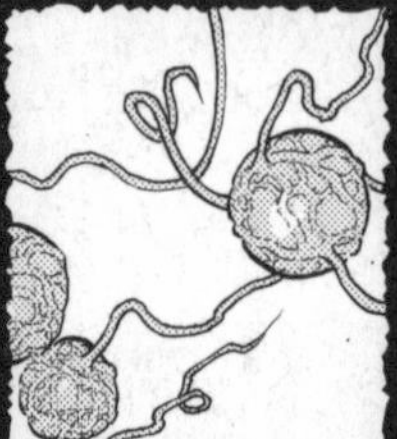

Nokker

Their true forms, called fye, are similar to souls. They evolved into smaller forms to escape Fushi's notice. They parasitize those who desire death, and blend into modern society.

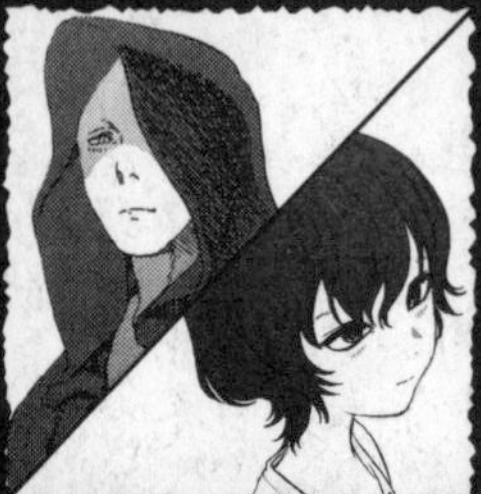

The Beholder

Fushi's creator and constant observer. Appears before him once again in the form of a boy named Satoru. His powers and memories are growing ever weaker, and in four years he will become a normal human.

CONTENTS

WARNING

This volume mentions instances of suicide.
If you are experiencing suicidal thoughts or feelings,
you are not alone, and there is help.
Call the National Suicide Prevention Lifeline at
1-800-273-TALK (8255) or go to
SuicidePreventionLifeline.org.

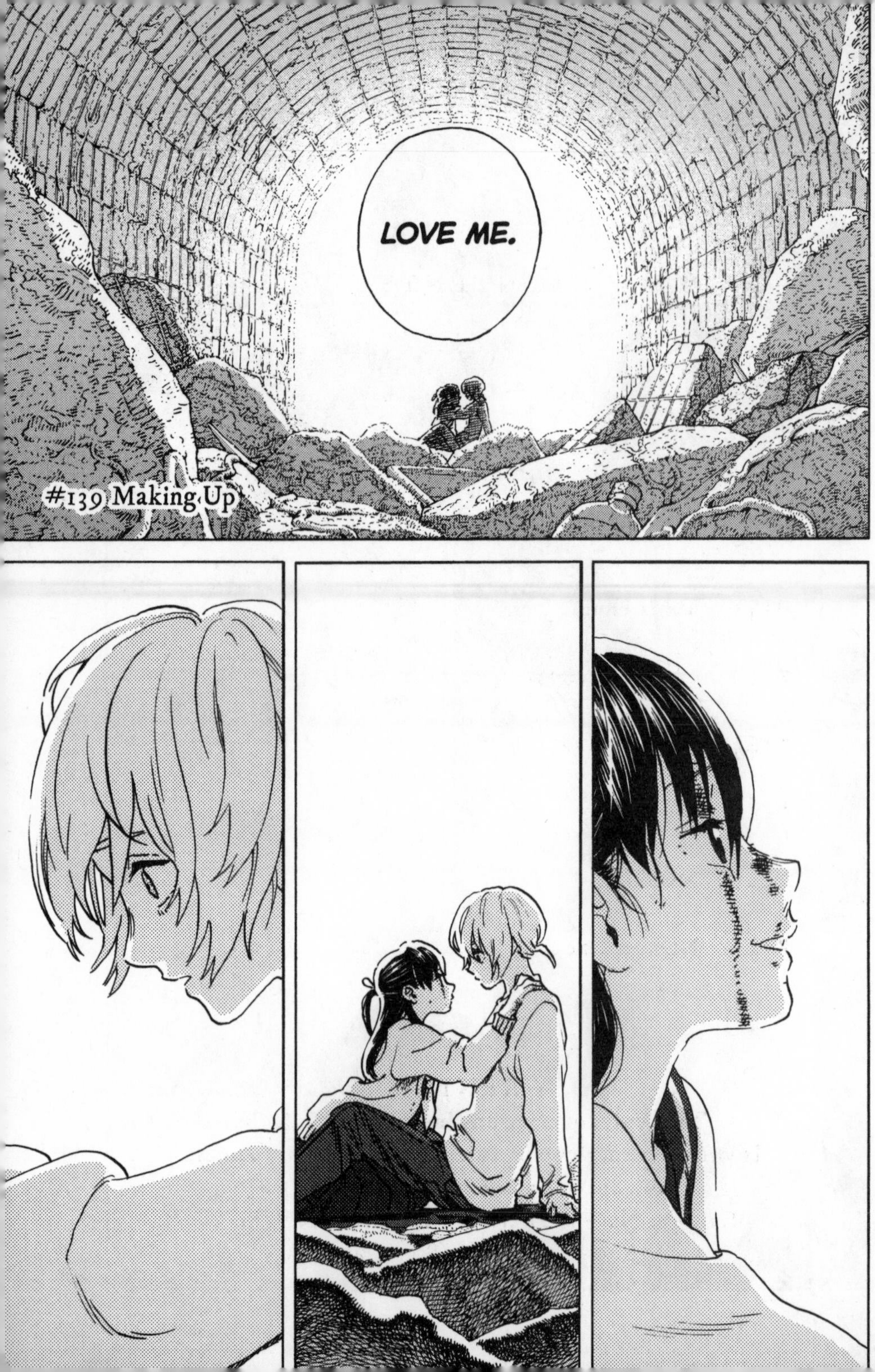
LOVE ME.
#139 Making Up

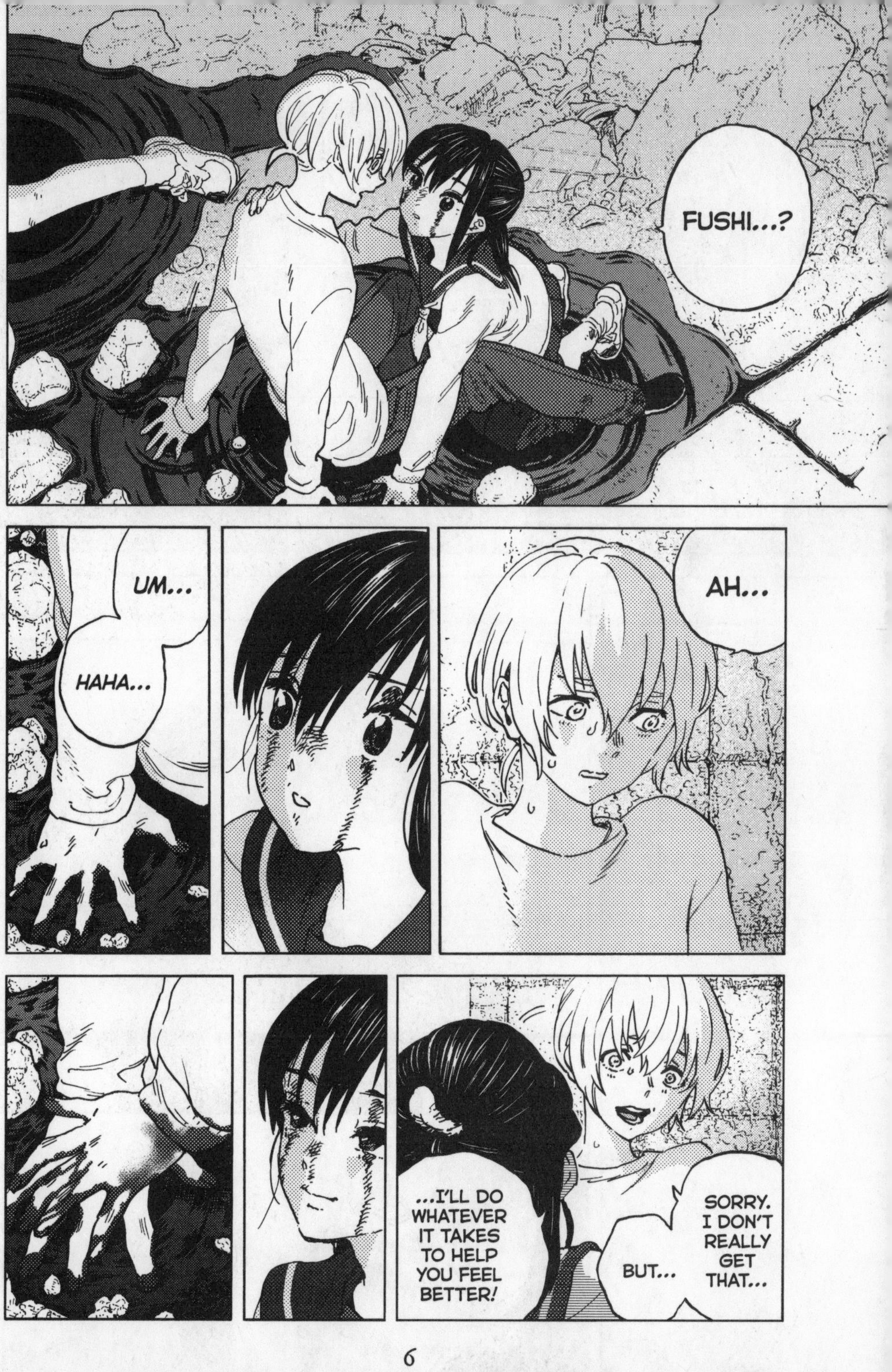
FUSHI...?
AH...
UM...
HAHA...
SORRY. I DON'T REALLY GET THAT...
BUT...
...I'LL DO WHATEVER IT TAKES TO HELP YOU FEEL BETTER!

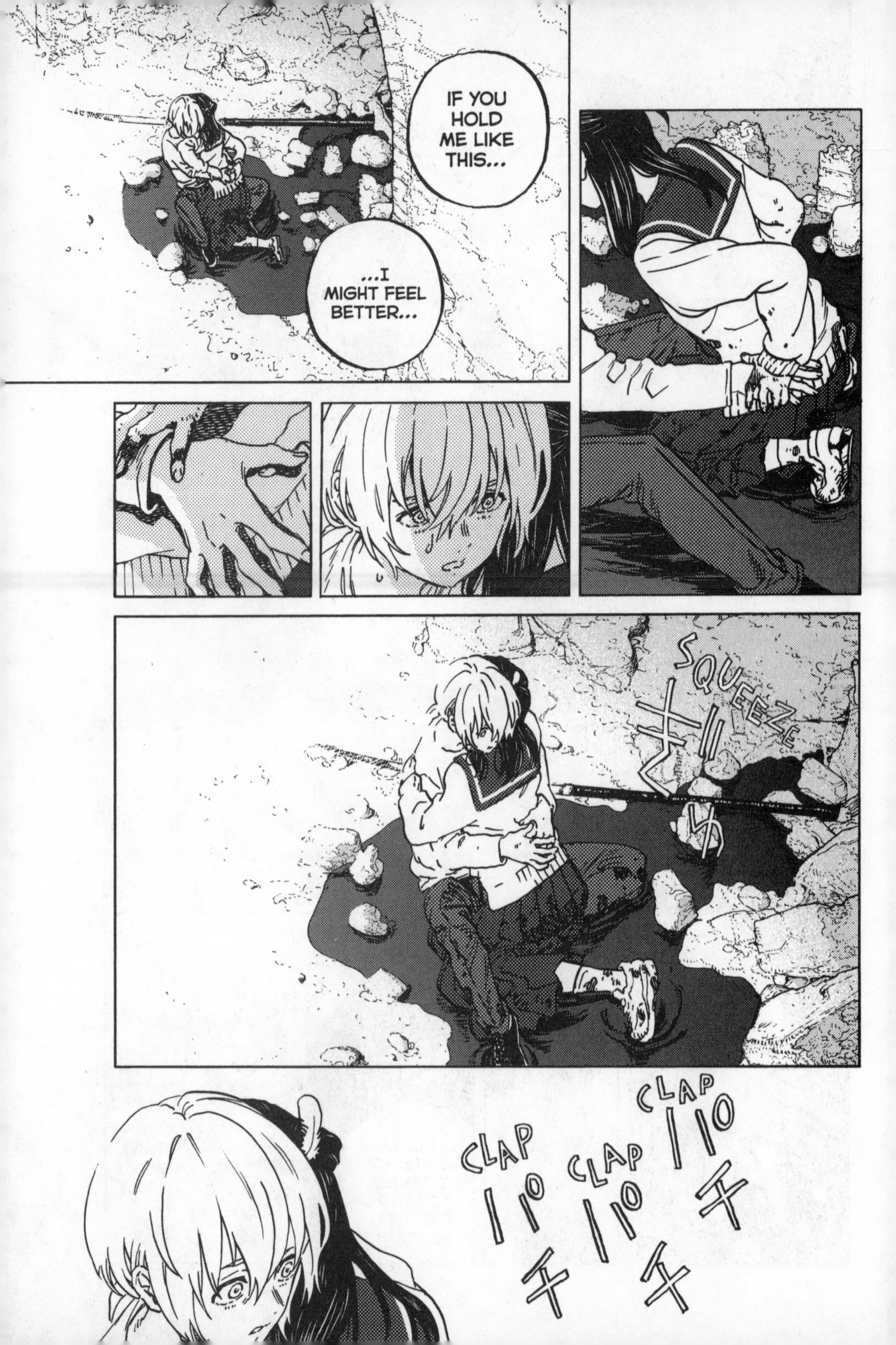
IF YOU HOLD ME LIKE THIS...
...I MIGHT FEEL BETTER...
SQUEEZE
CLAP
CLAP
CLAP

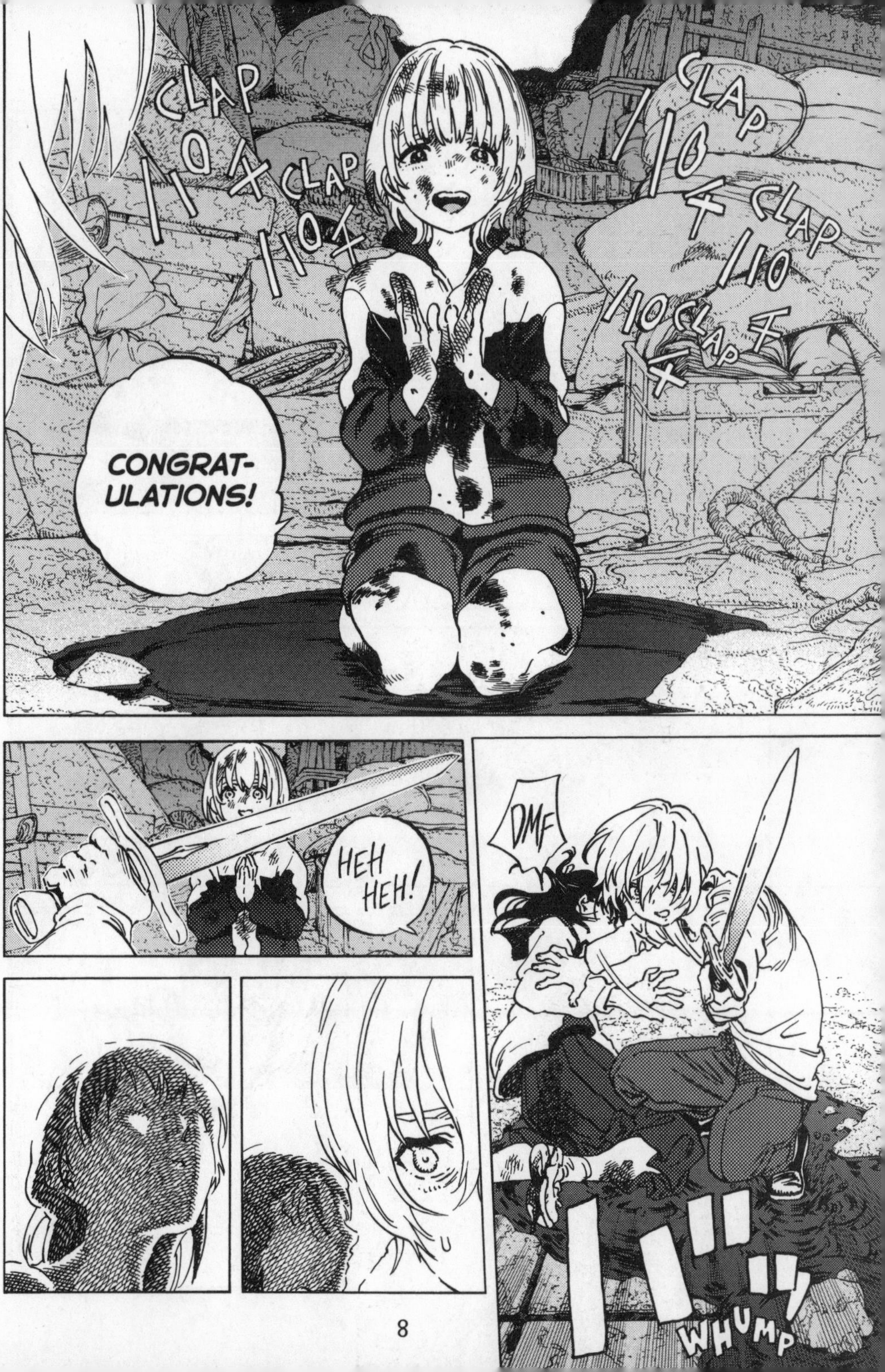
CLAP
CLAP
CLAP
CLAP
CLAP
CLAP
CONGRAT-
ULATIONS!
DMF
WHUMP
HEH
HEH!

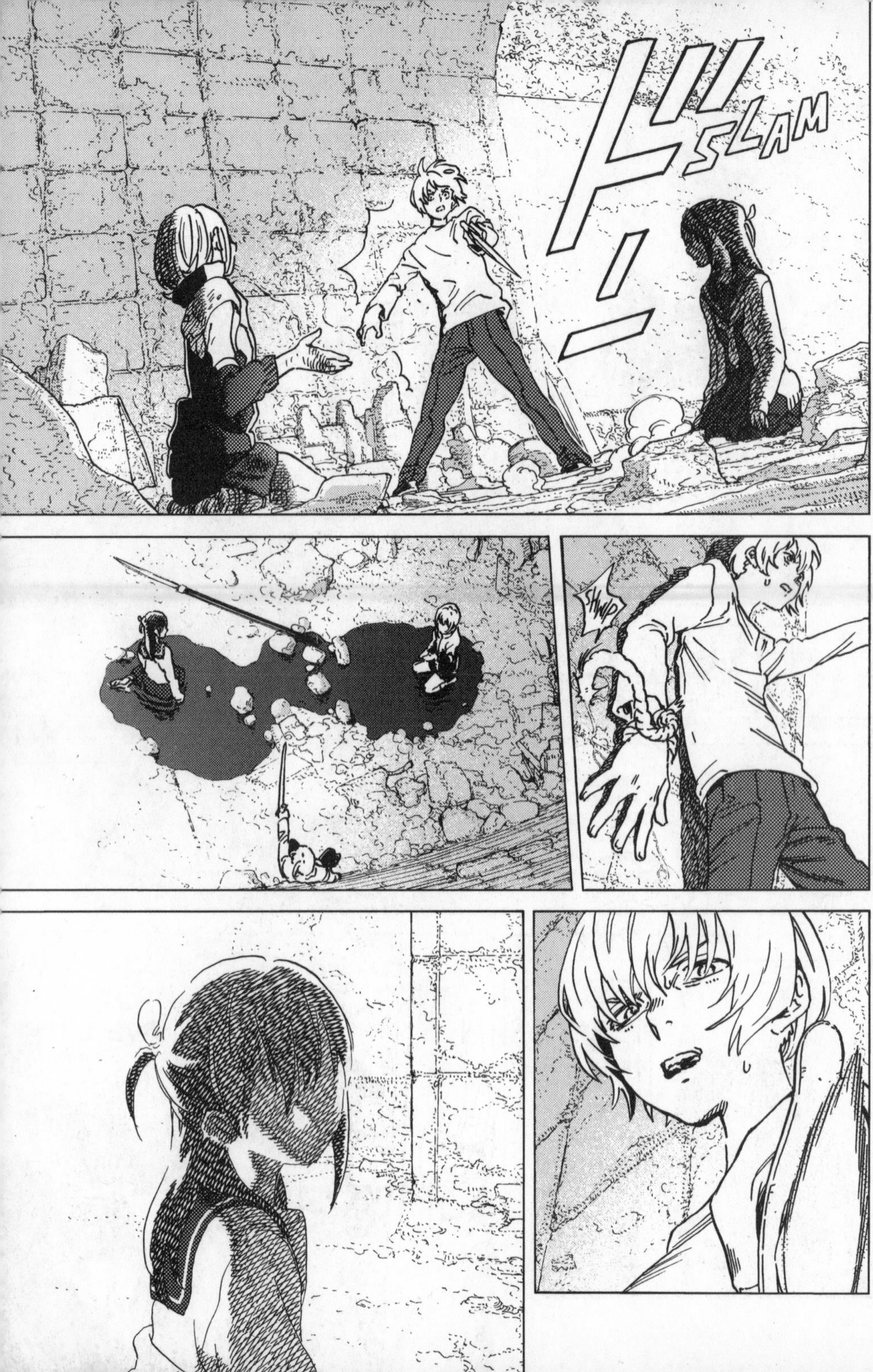
ドン
SLAM
SHWIP

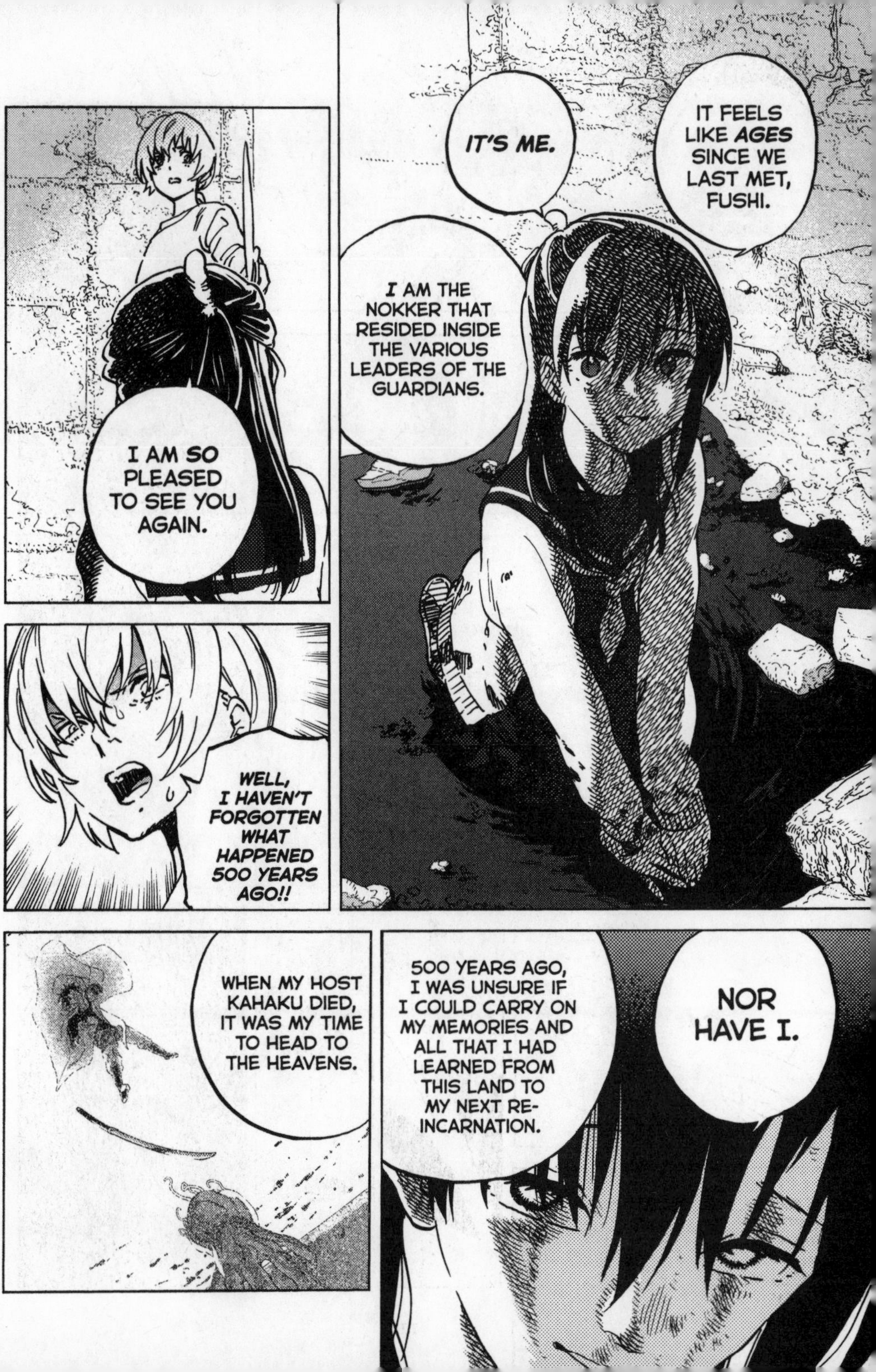
IT FEELS LIKE AGES SINCE WE LAST MET, FUSHI.
IT'S ME.
I AM THE NOKKER THAT RESIDED INSIDE THE VARIOUS LEADERS OF THE GUARDIANS.
I AM SO PLEASED TO SEE YOU AGAIN.
WELL, I HAVEN'T FORGOTTEN WHAT HAPPENED 500 YEARS AGO!!
NOR HAVE I.
500 YEARS AGO, I WAS UNSURE IF I COULD CARRY ON MY MEMORIES AND ALL THAT I HAD LEARNED FROM THIS LAND TO MY NEXT RE-INCARNATION.
WHEN MY HOST KAHAKU DIED, IT WAS MY TIME TO HEAD TO THE HEAVENS.

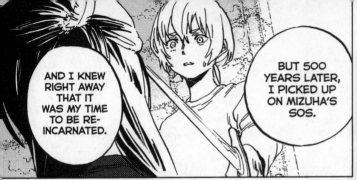

I WANT TO DIE.
BUT 500 YEARS LATER, I PICKED UP ON MIZUHA'S SOS.
AND I KNEW RIGHT AWAY THAT IT WAS MY TIME TO BE RE-INCARNATED.
WITH THE ENCOURAGEMENT OF MY COMRADES, I WORKED UP MY COURAGE AND LEFT PARADISE.
YOU CAN DO IT!
GOOD LUCK!
YOU CAN DO IT!
DO YOUR BEST!!
I FOCUSED ON THE INSIDE OF A TREE...
...AND IMPLANTED MYSELF THERE.
I WAS THRILLED TO FIND THAT I HAD BEEN REBORN AS MYSELF.
AS USUAL, I ENTERED THE BODY THROUGH THE LEFT ARM.
SHOOP

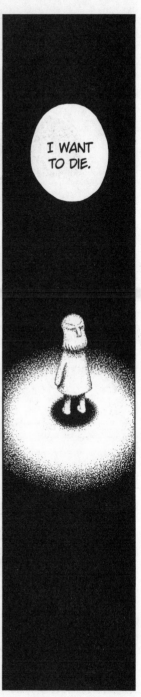

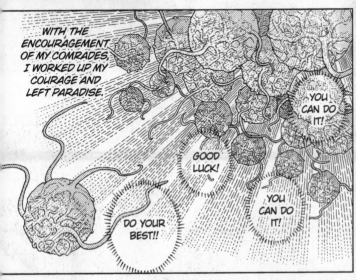

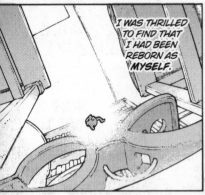

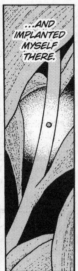

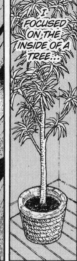

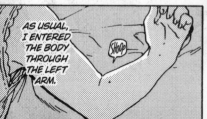

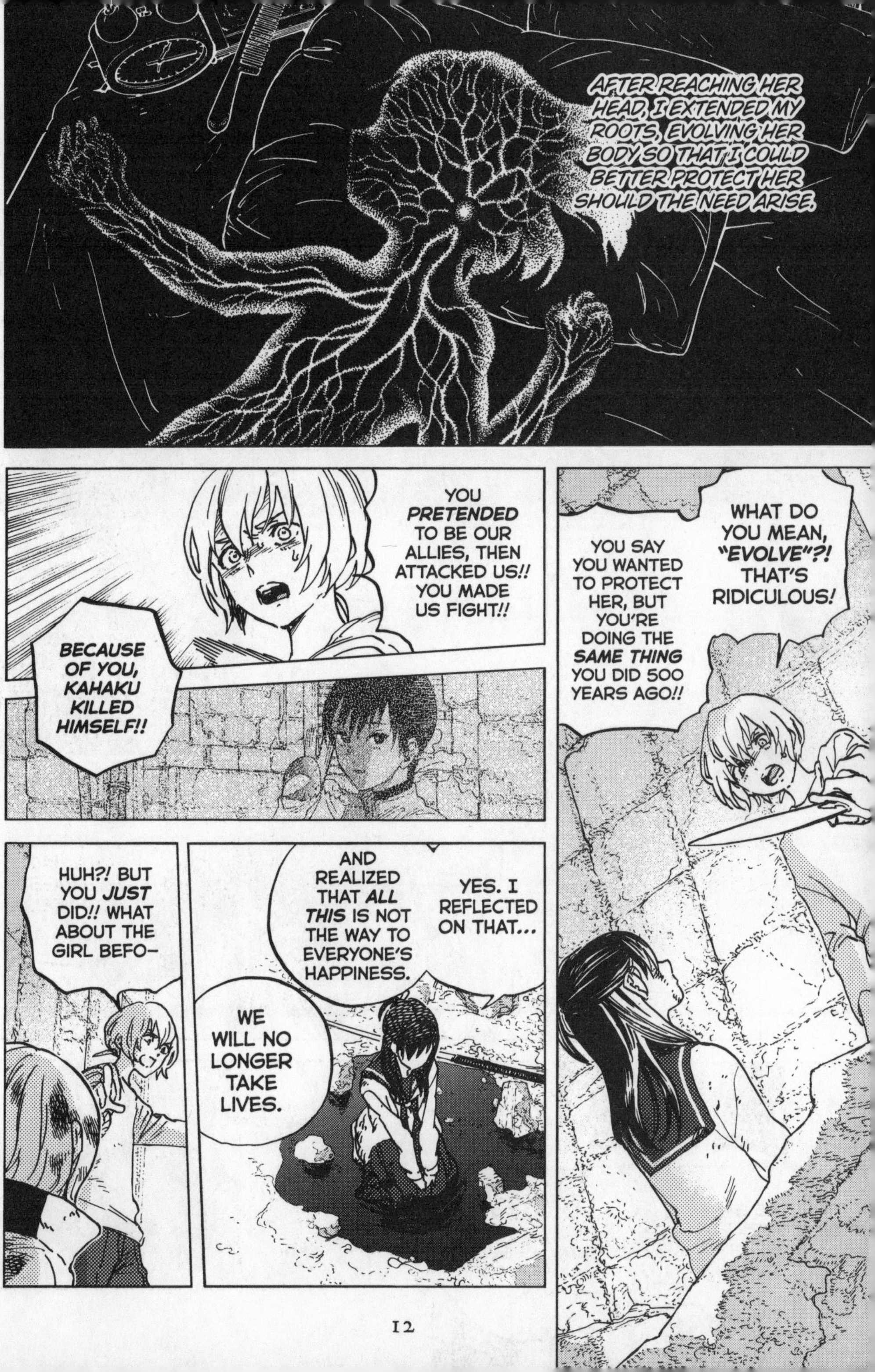
AFTER REACHING HER HEAD, I EXTENDED MY ROOTS, EVOLVING HER BODY SO THAT I COULD BETTER PROTECT HER SHOULD THE NEED ARISE.
WHAT DO YOU MEAN, *"EVOLVE"?!* THAT'S RIDICULOUS!
YOU SAY YOU WANTED TO PROTECT HER, BUT YOU'RE DOING THE *SAME THING* YOU DID 500 YEARS AGO!!
YOU *PRETENDED* TO BE OUR ALLIES, THEN ATTACKED US!! YOU MADE US FIGHT!!
BECAUSE OF YOU, KAHAKU KILLED HIMSELF!!
YES. I REFLECTED ON THAT...
AND REALIZED THAT *ALL THIS* IS NOT THE WAY TO EVERYONE'S HAPPINESS.
WE WILL NO LONGER TAKE LIVES.
HUH?! BUT YOU *JUST* DID!! WHAT ABOUT THE GIRL BEFO–

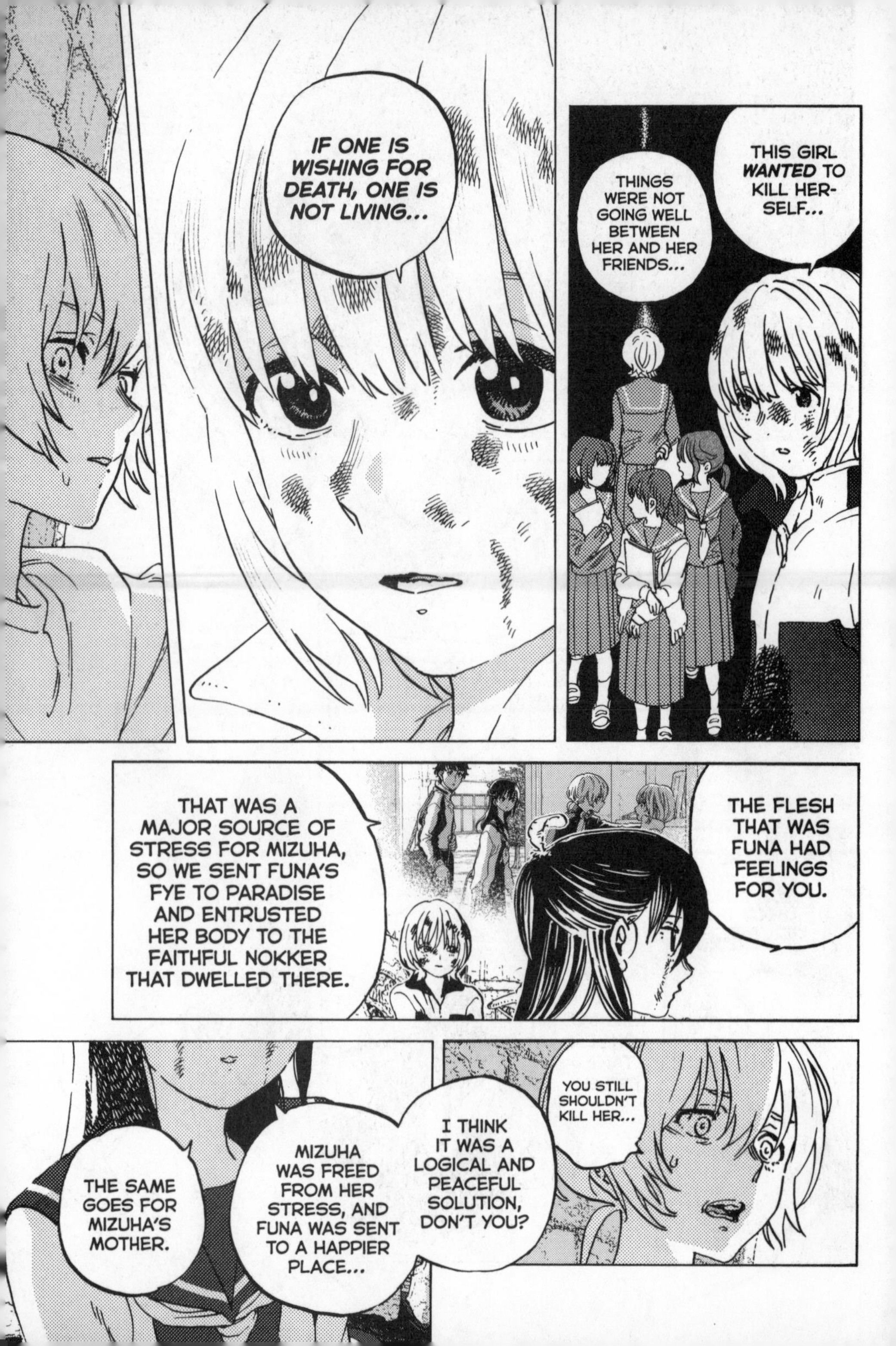
THIS GIRL *WANTED* TO KILL HER-SELF...
THINGS WERE NOT GOING WELL BETWEEN HER AND HER FRIENDS...
IF ONE IS WISHING FOR DEATH, ONE IS NOT LIVING...
THE FLESH THAT WAS FUNA HAD FEELINGS FOR YOU.
THAT WAS A MAJOR SOURCE OF STRESS FOR MIZUHA, SO WE SENT FUNA'S FYE TO PARADISE AND ENTRUSTED HER BODY TO THE FAITHFUL NOKKER THAT DWELLED THERE.
YOU STILL SHOULDN'T KILL HER...
I THINK IT WAS A LOGICAL AND PEACEFUL SOLUTION, DON'T YOU?
MIZUHA WAS FREED FROM HER STRESS, AND FUNA WAS SENT TO A HAPPIER PLACE...
THE SAME GOES FOR MIZUHA'S MOTHER.

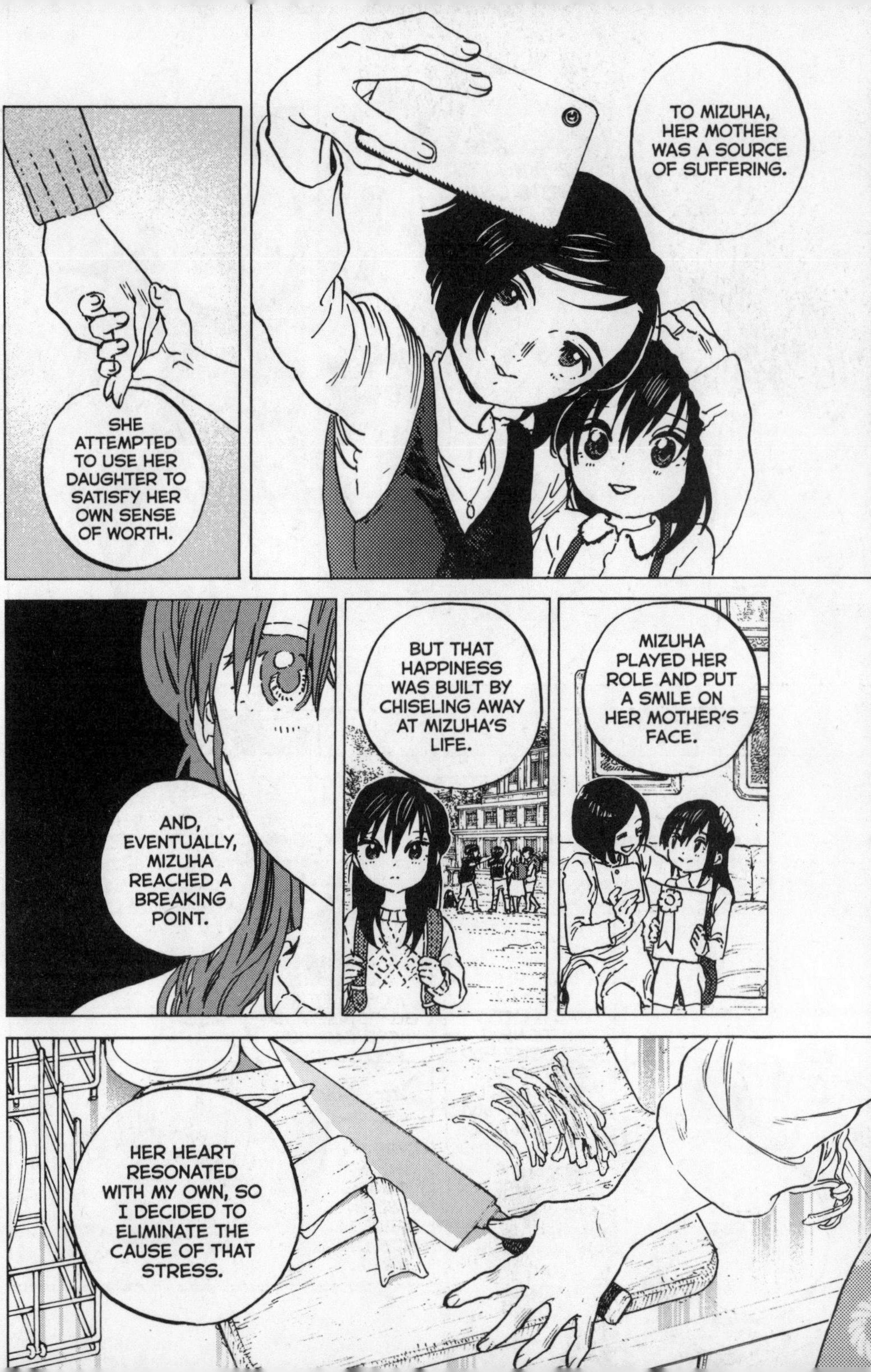
TO MIZUHA, HER MOTHER WAS A SOURCE OF SUFFERING.
SHE ATTEMPTED TO USE HER DAUGHTER TO SATISFY HER OWN SENSE OF WORTH.
MIZUHA PLAYED HER ROLE AND PUT A SMILE ON HER MOTHER'S FACE.
BUT THAT HAPPINESS WAS BUILT BY CHISELING AWAY AT MIZUHA'S LIFE.
AND, EVENTUALLY, MIZUHA REACHED A BREAKING POINT.
HER HEART RESONATED WITH MY OWN, SO I DECIDED TO ELIMINATE THE CAUSE OF THAT STRESS.

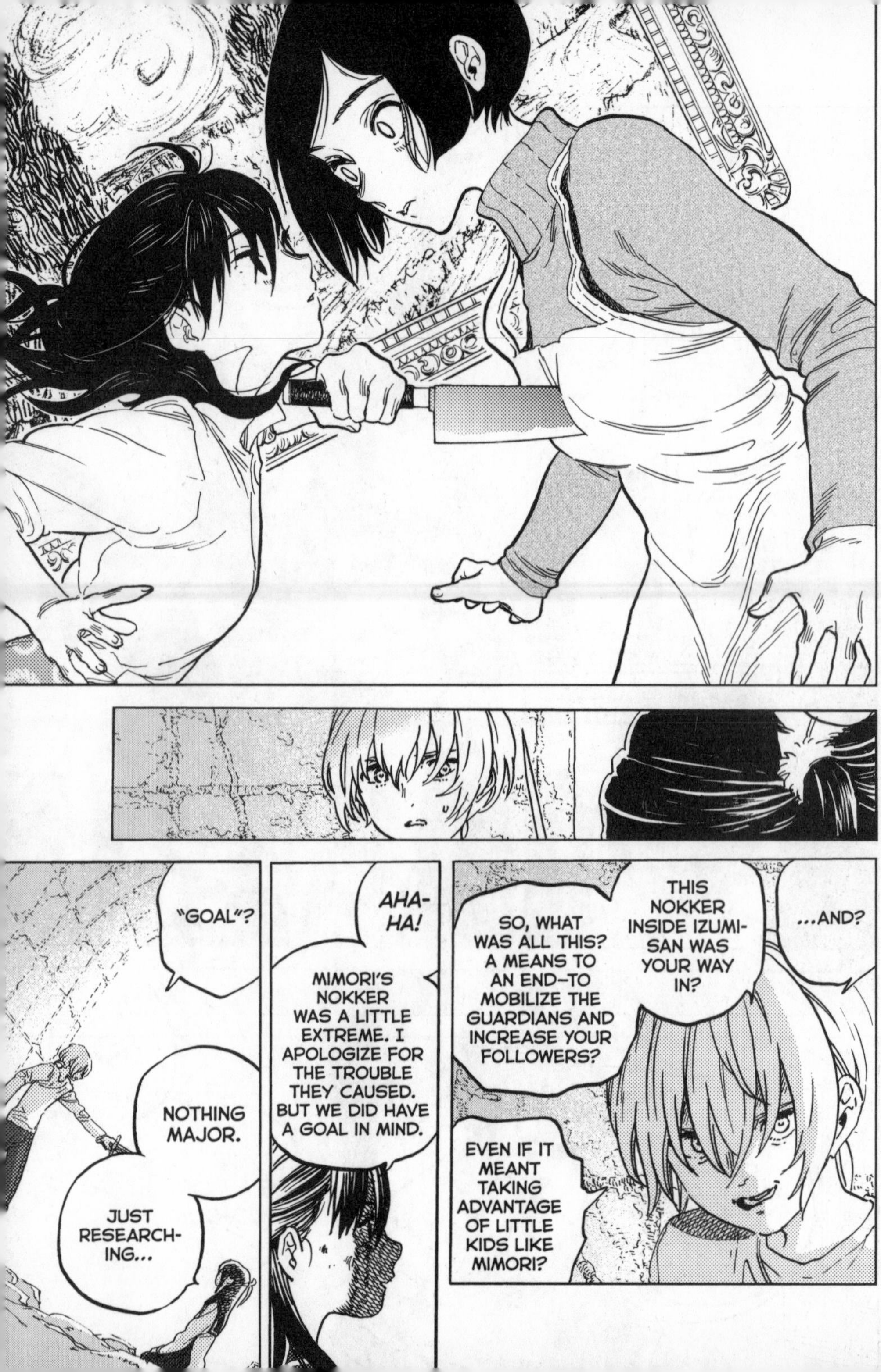
...AND?
THIS NOKKER INSIDE IZUMI-SAN WAS YOUR WAY IN?
SO, WHAT WAS ALL THIS? A MEANS TO AN END—TO MOBILIZE THE GUARDIANS AND INCREASE YOUR FOLLOWERS?
EVEN IF IT MEANT TAKING ADVANTAGE OF LITTLE KIDS LIKE MIMORI?
AHA-HA!
MIMORI'S NOKKER WAS A LITTLE EXTREME. I APOLOGIZE FOR THE TROUBLE THEY CAUSED. BUT WE DID HAVE A GOAL IN MIND.
"GOAL"?
NOTHING MAJOR.
JUST RESEARCHING...

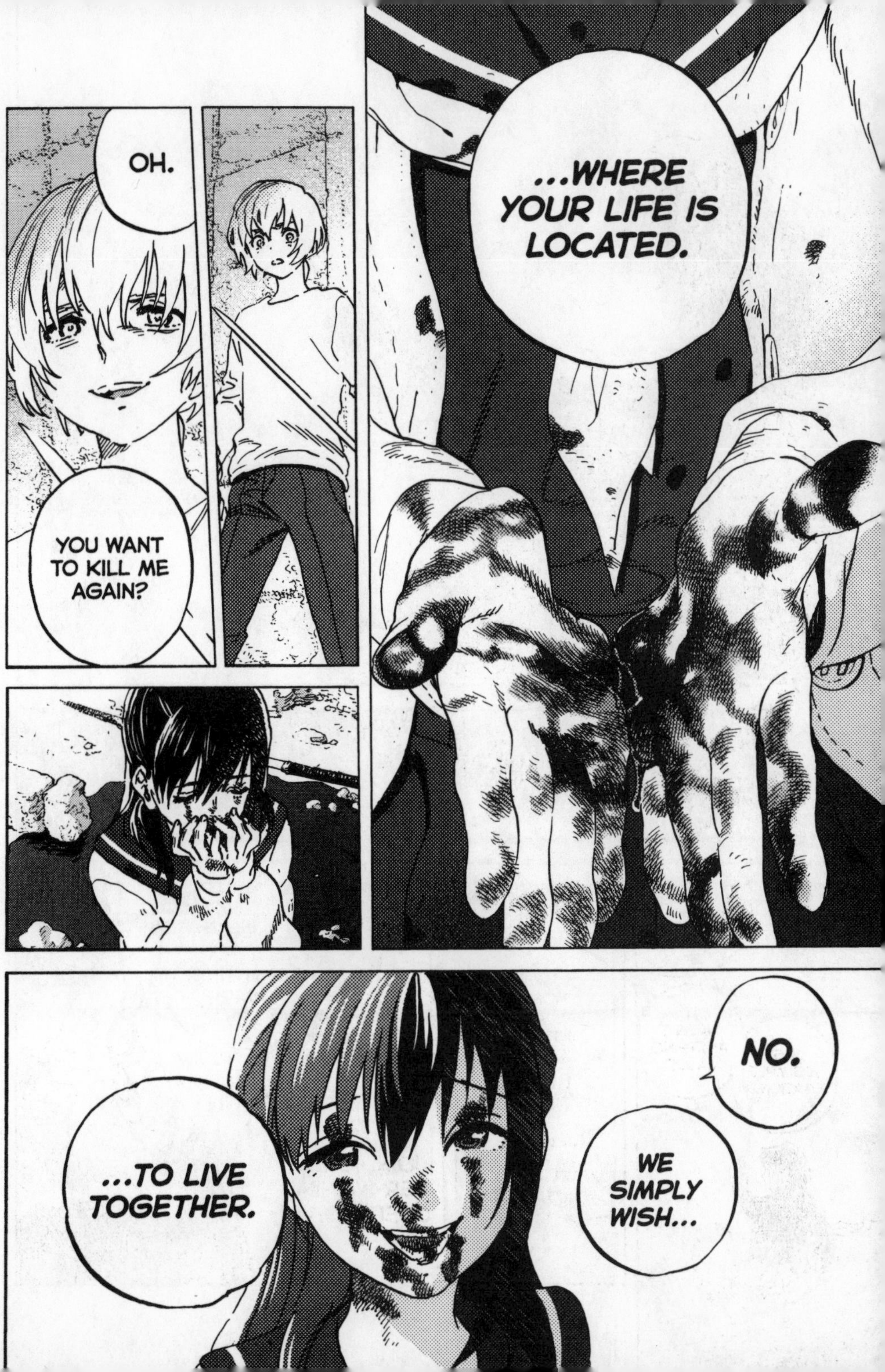
...WHERE YOUR LIFE IS LOCATED.
OH.
YOU WANT TO KILL ME AGAIN?
NO.
WE SIMPLY WISH...
...TO LIVE TOGETHER.

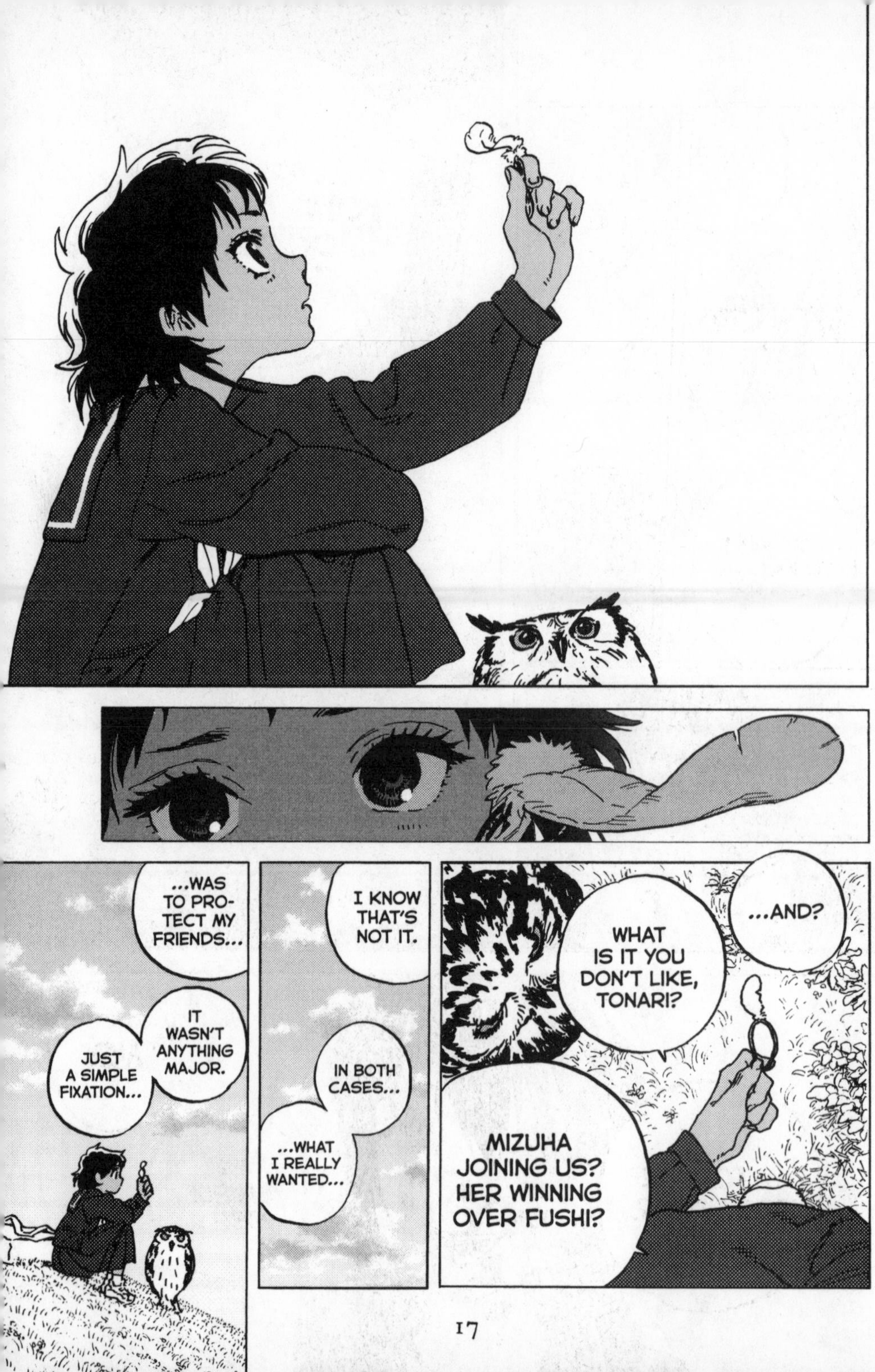
...AND?
WHAT IS IT YOU DON'T LIKE, TONARI?
MIZUHA JOINING US? HER WINNING OVER FUSHI?
I KNOW THAT'S NOT IT.
IN BOTH CASES...
...WHAT I REALLY WANTED...
...WAS TO PROTECT MY FRIENDS...
IT WASN'T ANYTHING MAJOR.
JUST A SIMPLE FIXATION...

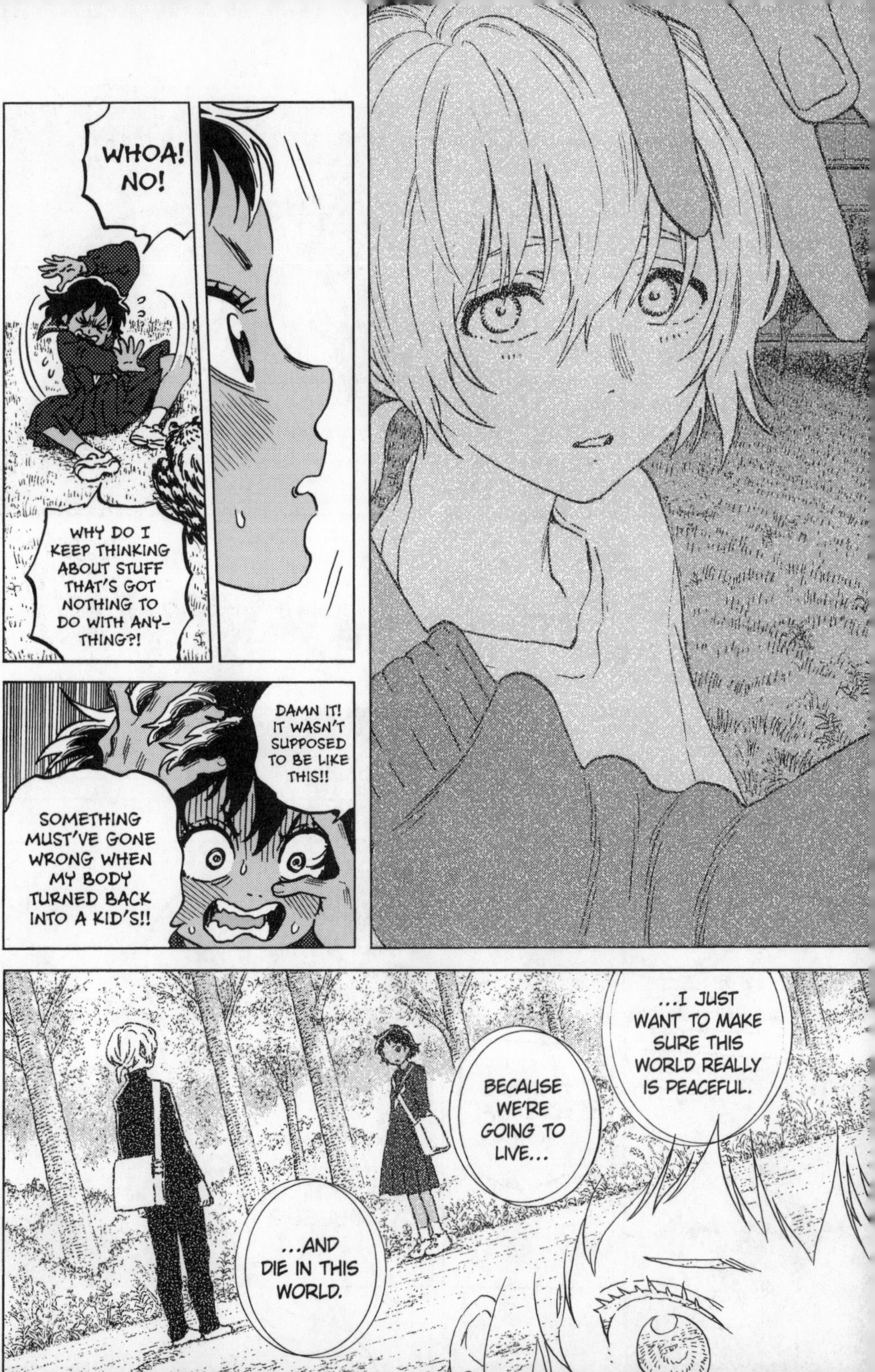
WHOA! NO!
WHY DO I KEEP THINKING ABOUT STUFF THAT'S GOT NOTHING TO DO WITH ANY-THING?!
DAMN IT! IT WASN'T SUPPOSED TO BE LIKE THIS!!
SOMETHING MUST'VE GONE WRONG WHEN MY BODY TURNED BACK INTO A KID'S!!
...I JUST WANT TO MAKE SURE THIS WORLD REALLY IS PEACEFUL.
BECAUSE WE'RE GOING TO LIVE...
...AND DIE IN THIS WORLD.

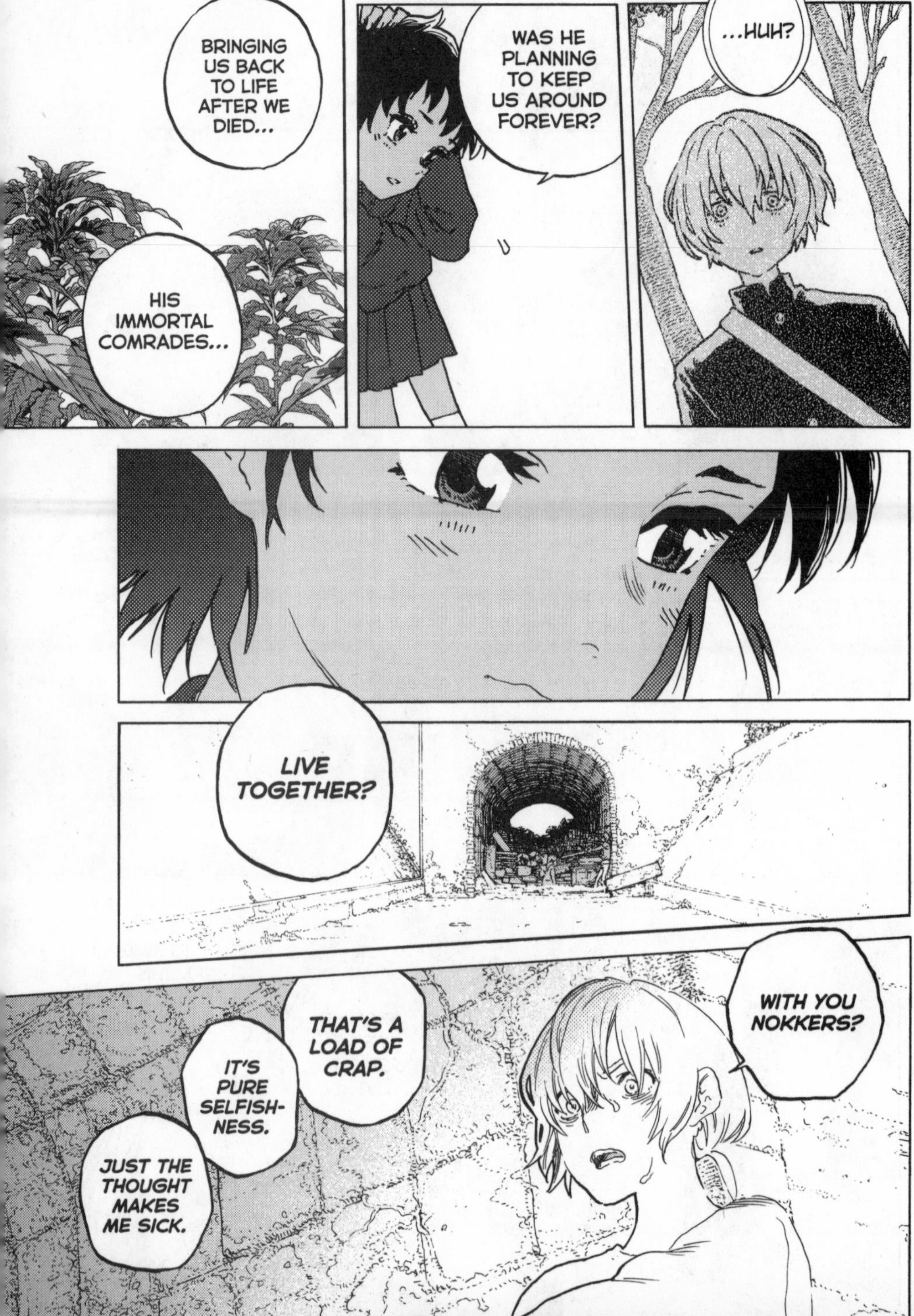
...HUH?
WAS HE PLANNING TO KEEP US AROUND FOREVER?
BRINGING US BACK TO LIFE AFTER WE DIED...
HIS IMMORTAL COMRADES...
LIVE TOGETHER?
WITH YOU NOKKERS?
THAT'S A LOAD OF CRAP.
IT'S PURE SELFISH-NESS.
JUST THE THOUGHT MAKES ME SICK.

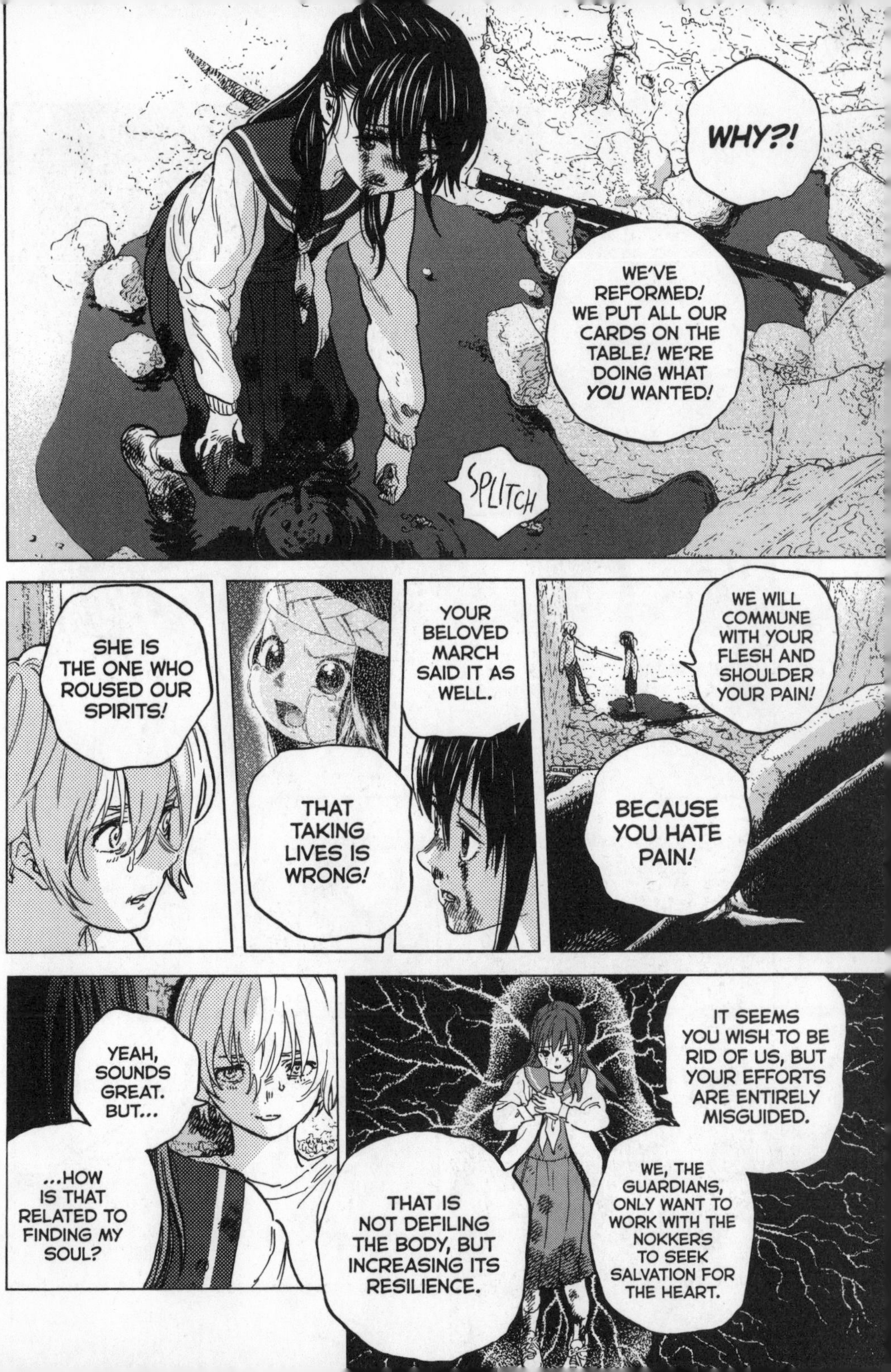
WHY?!
WE'VE REFORMED! WE PUT ALL OUR CARDS ON THE TABLE! WE'RE DOING WHAT *YOU* WANTED!
SPLITCH
WE WILL COMMUNE WITH YOUR FLESH AND SHOULDER YOUR PAIN!
BECAUSE YOU HATE PAIN!
YOUR BELOVED MARCH SAID IT AS WELL.
THAT TAKING LIVES IS WRONG!
SHE IS THE ONE WHO ROUSED OUR SPIRITS!
IT SEEMS YOU WISH TO BE RID OF US, BUT YOUR EFFORTS ARE ENTIRELY MISGUIDED.
WE, THE GUARDIANS, ONLY WANT TO WORK WITH THE NOKKERS TO SEEK SALVATION FOR THE HEART.
THAT IS NOT DEFILING THE BODY, BUT INCREASING ITS RESILIENCE.
YEAH, SOUNDS GREAT. BUT...
...HOW IS THAT RELATED TO FINDING MY SOUL?

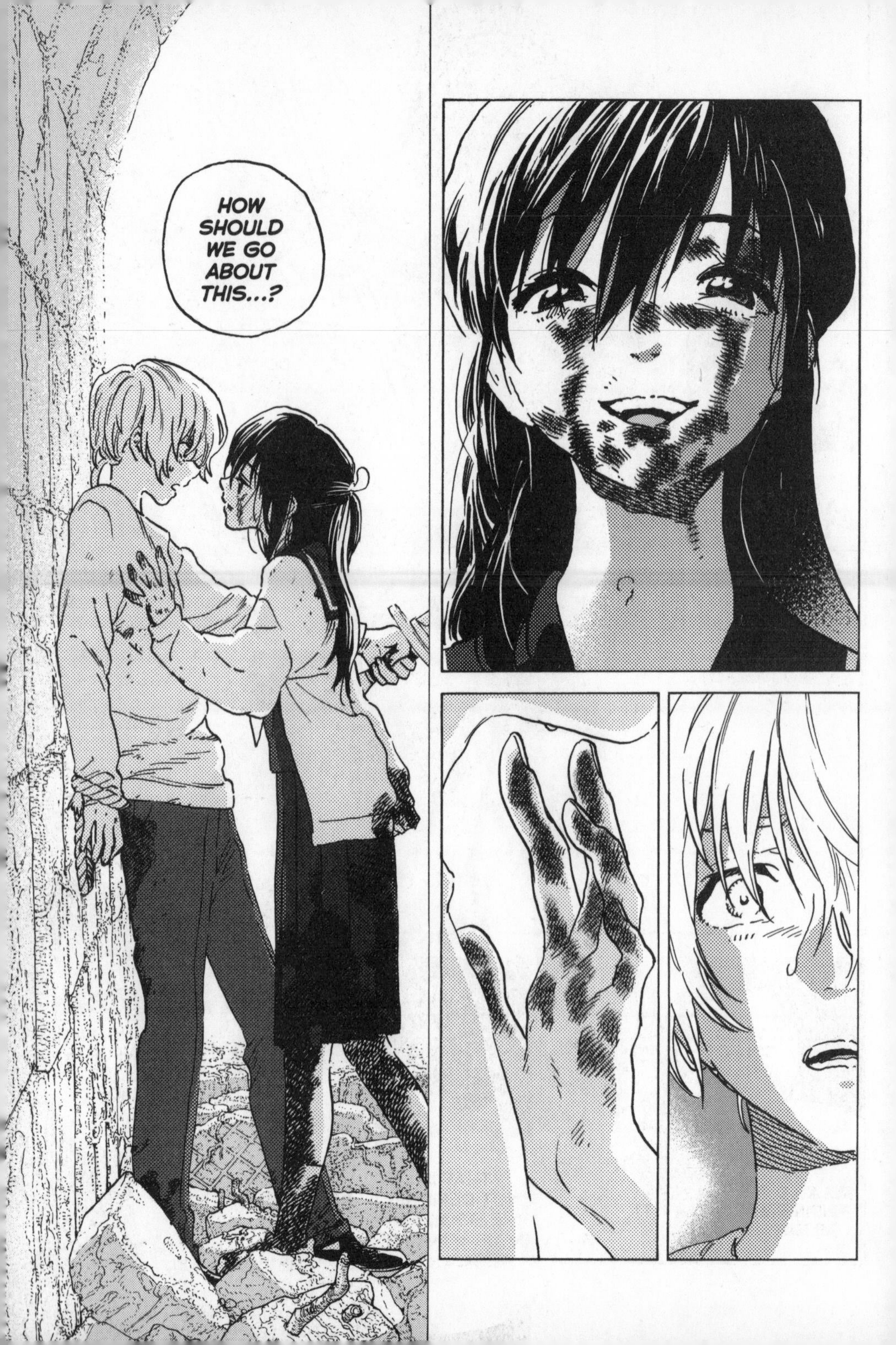
HOW SHOULD WE GO ABOUT THIS...?

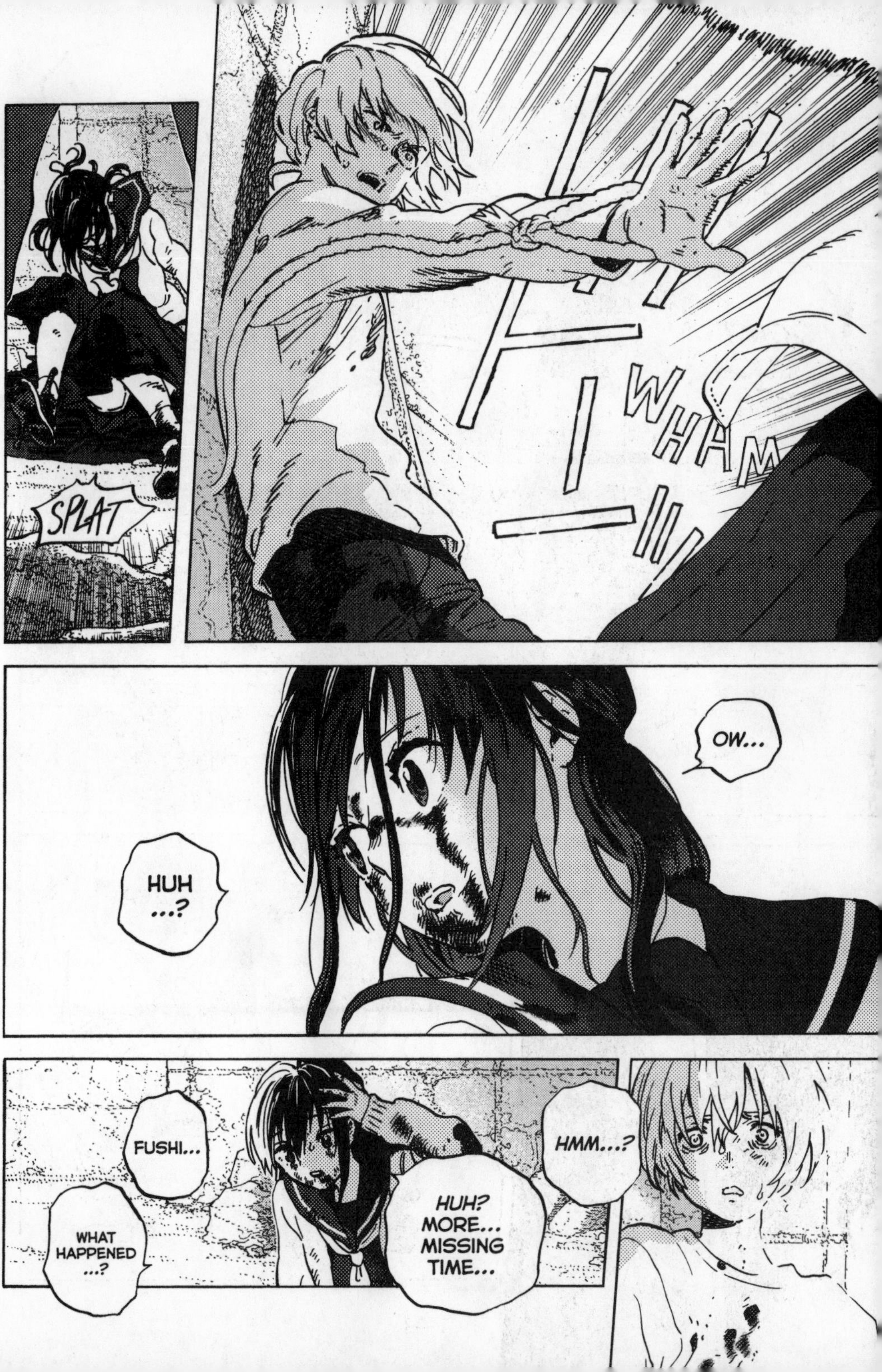
WHAM
SPLAT
OW...
HUH ...?
HMM...?
FUSHI...
HUH? MORE... MISSING TIME...
WHAT HAPPENED ...?

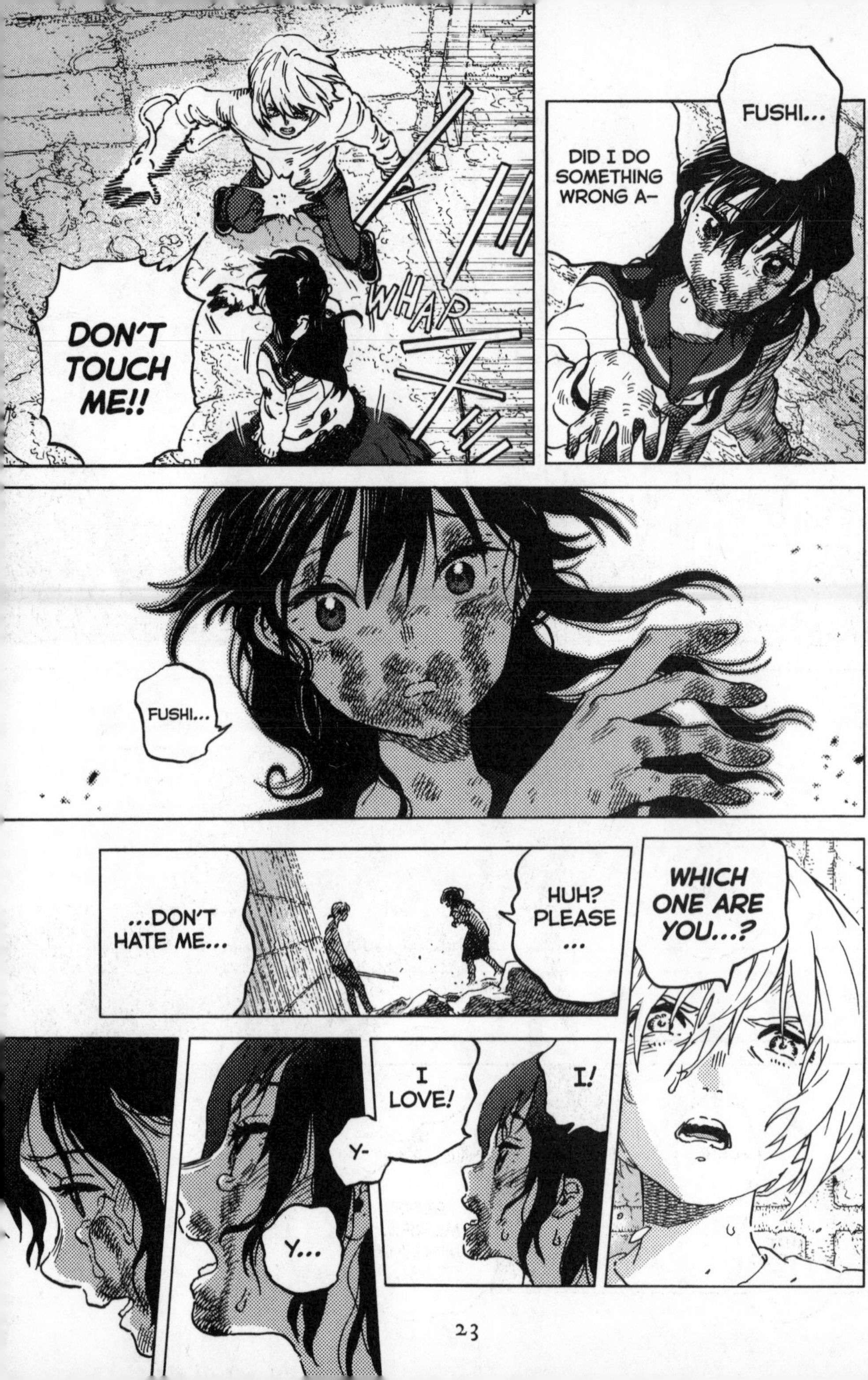
FUSHI...
DID I DO SOMETHING WRONG A-
DON'T TOUCH ME!!
WHAP
FUSHI...
WHICH ONE ARE YOU...?
HUH? PLEASE ...
...DON'T HATE ME...
I!
I LOVE!
Y-
Y...

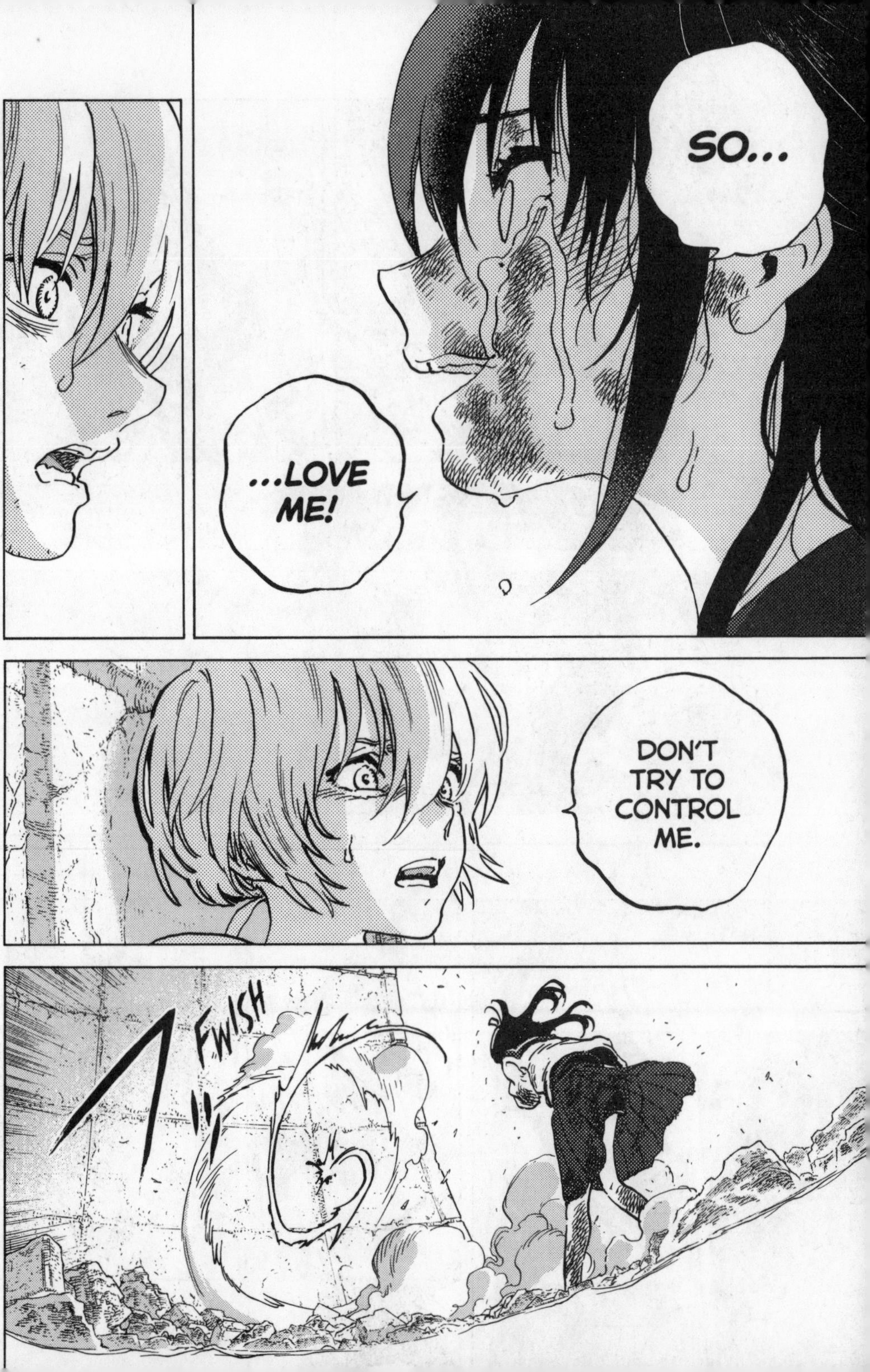
SO...
...LOVE ME!
DON'T TRY TO CONTROL ME.
FWISH

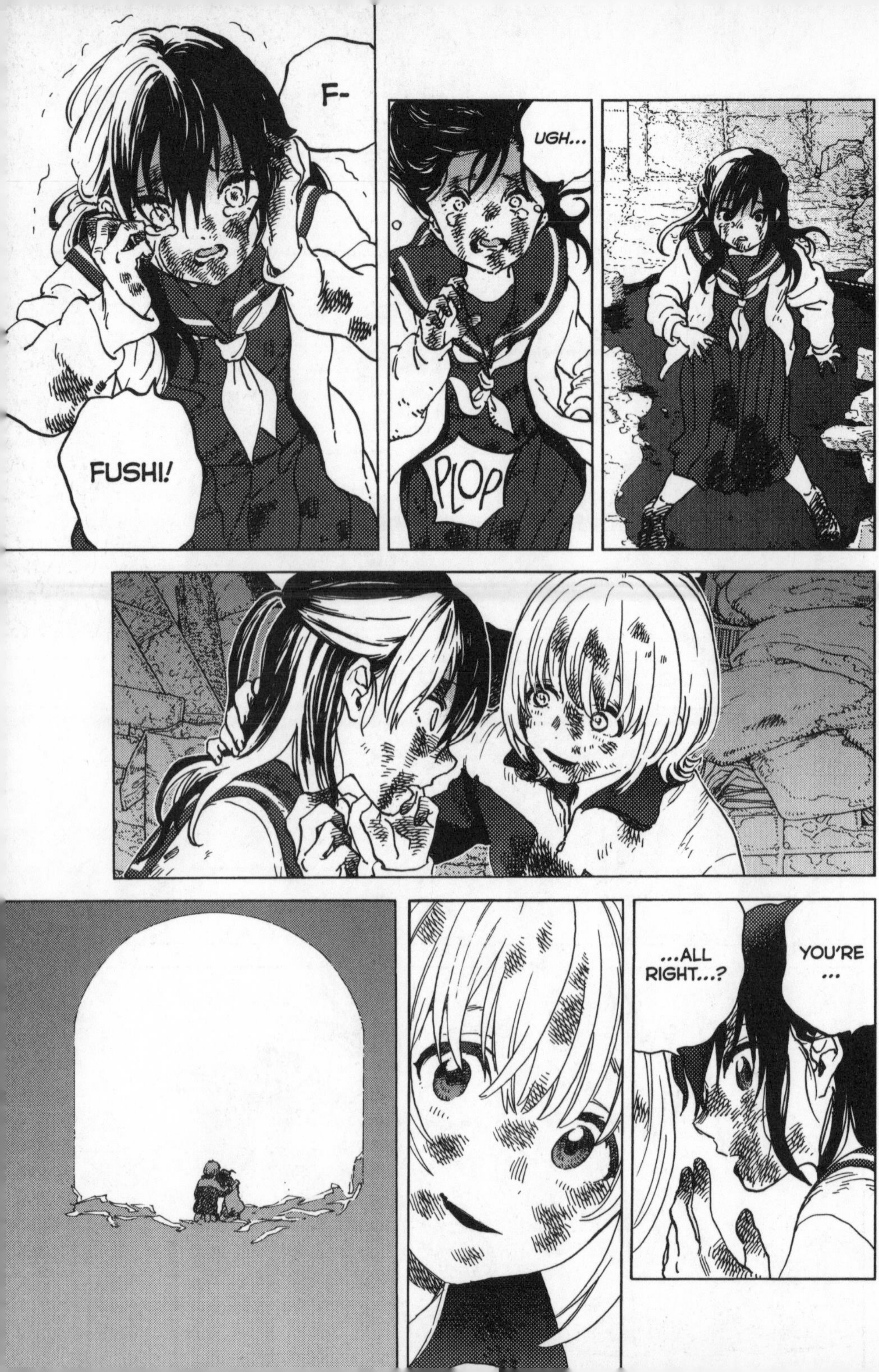
UGH...
PLOP
F-
FUSHI!
YOU'RE ...
...ALL RIGHT...?

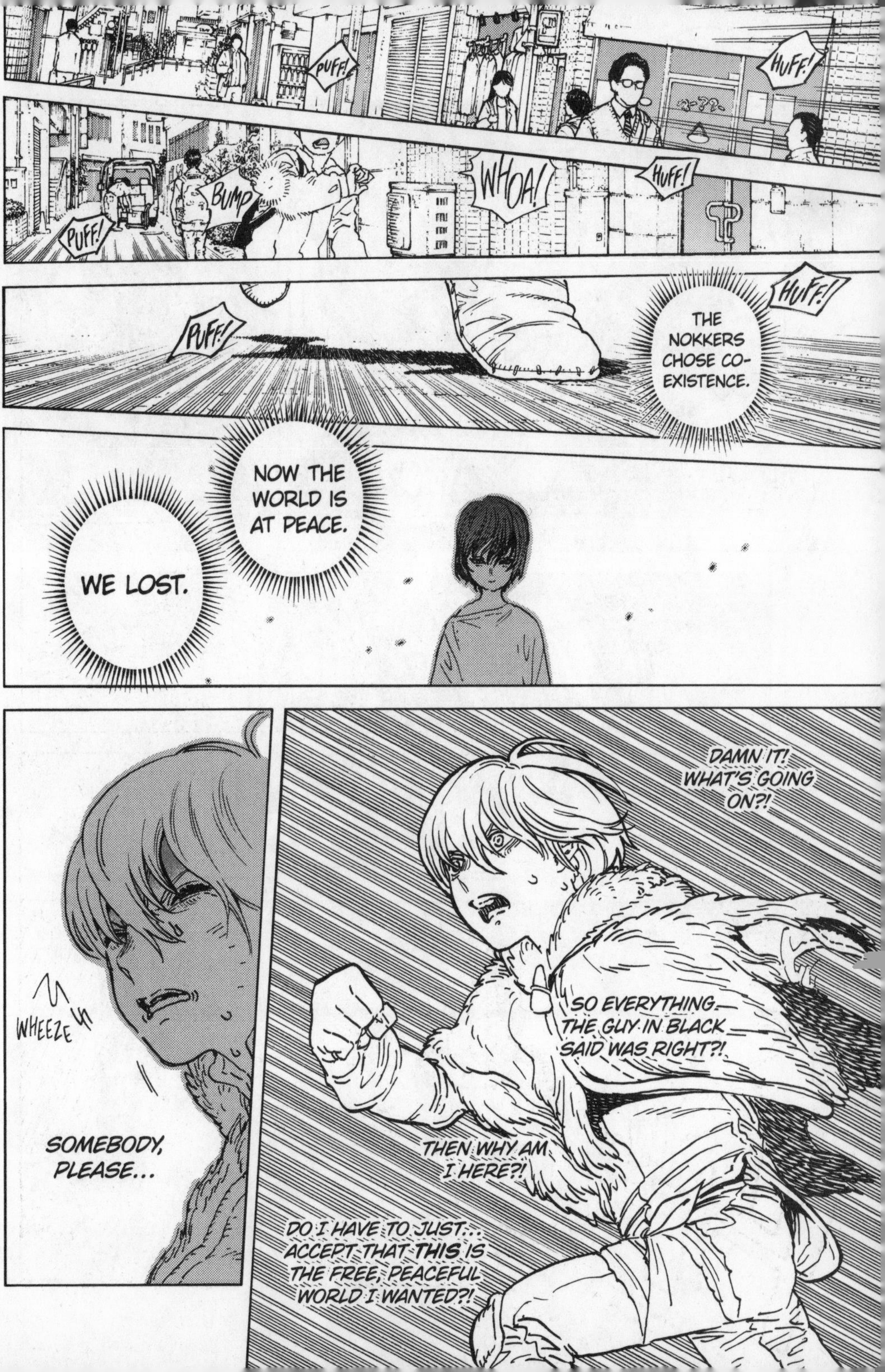
HUFF!
PUFF!
HUFF!
WHOA!
BUMP
PUFF!
HUFF!
THE NOKKERS CHOSE CO-EXISTENCE.
PUFF!
NOW THE WORLD IS AT PEACE.
WE LOST.
DAMN IT! WHAT'S GOING ON?!
SO EVERYTHING THE GUY IN BLACK SAID WAS RIGHT?!
THEN WHY AM I HERE?!
DO I HAVE TO JUST... ACCEPT THAT **THIS** IS THE FREE, PEACEFUL WORLD I WANTED?!
WHEEZE
SOMEBODY, PLEASE...

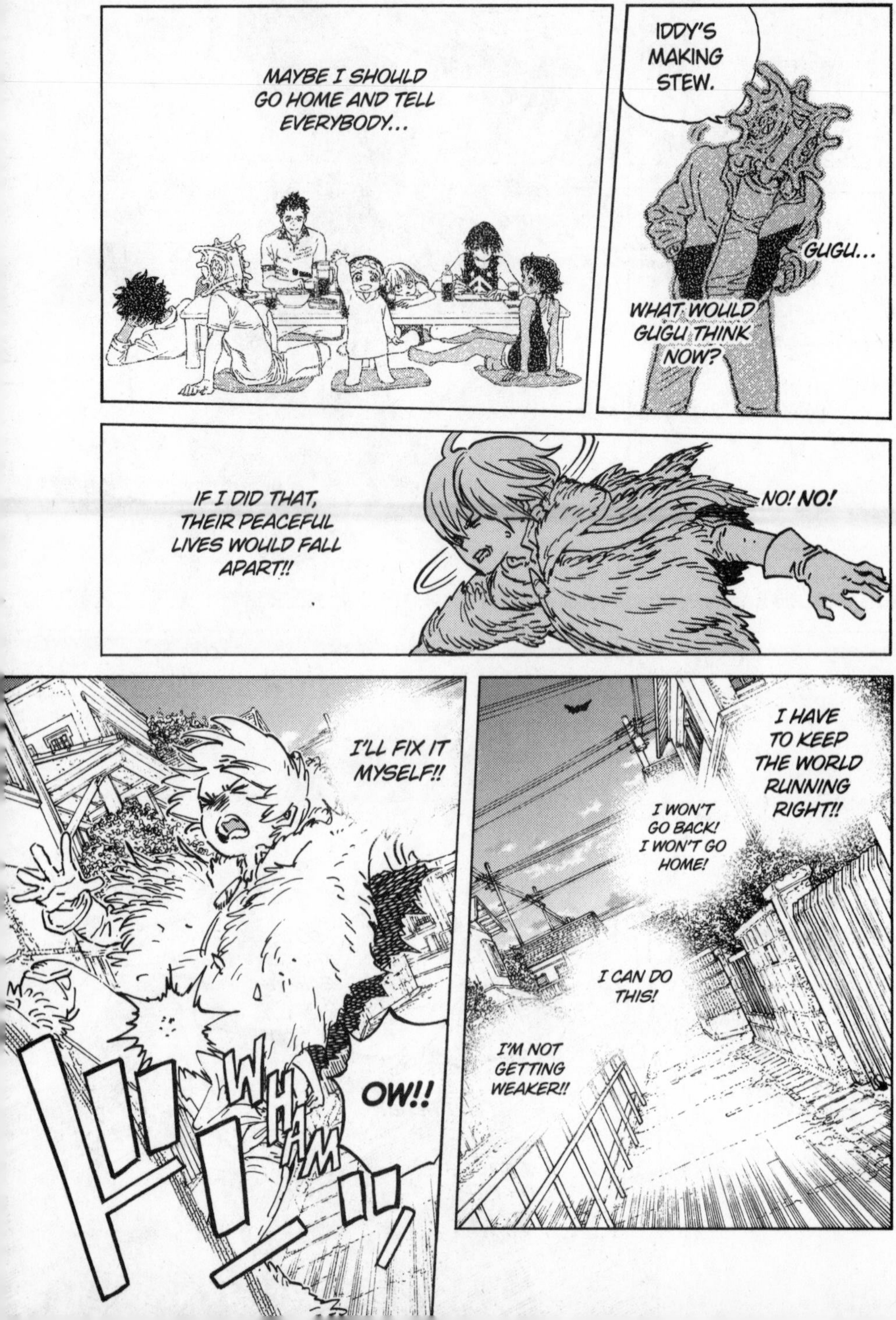
IDDY'S MAKING STEW.
GUGU...
WHAT WOULD GUGU THINK NOW?
MAYBE I SHOULD GO HOME AND TELL EVERYBODY...
NO! NO!
IF I DID THAT, THEIR PEACEFUL LIVES WOULD FALL APART!!
I HAVE TO KEEP THE WORLD RUNNING RIGHT!!
I WON'T GO BACK! I WON'T GO HOME!
I CAN DO THIS!
I'M NOT GETTING WEAKER!!
I'LL FIX IT MYSELF!!
WHAM
OW!!

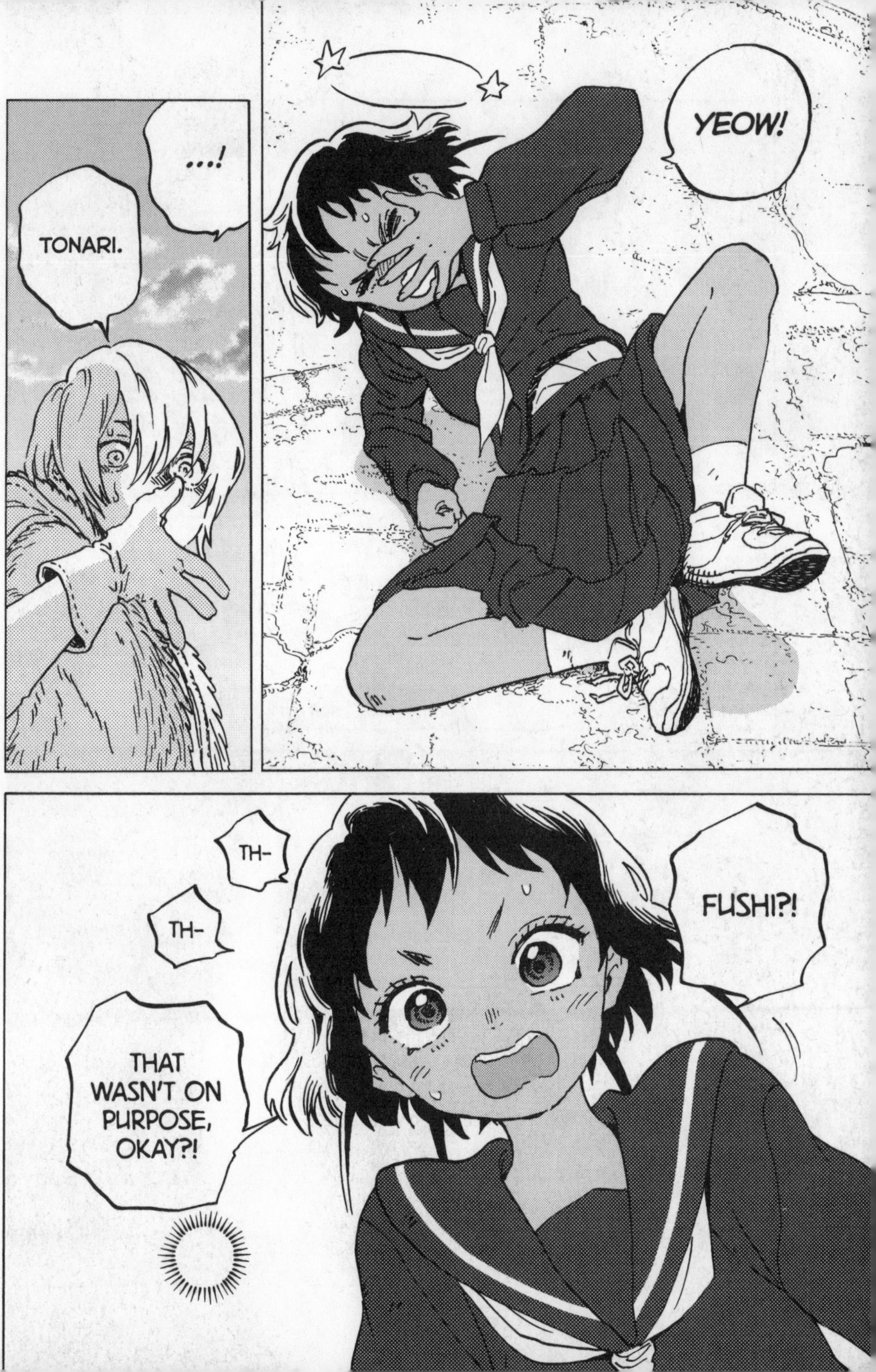
YEOW!
...!
TONARI.
FUSHI?!
TH-
TH-
THAT WASN'T ON PURPOSE, OKAY?!

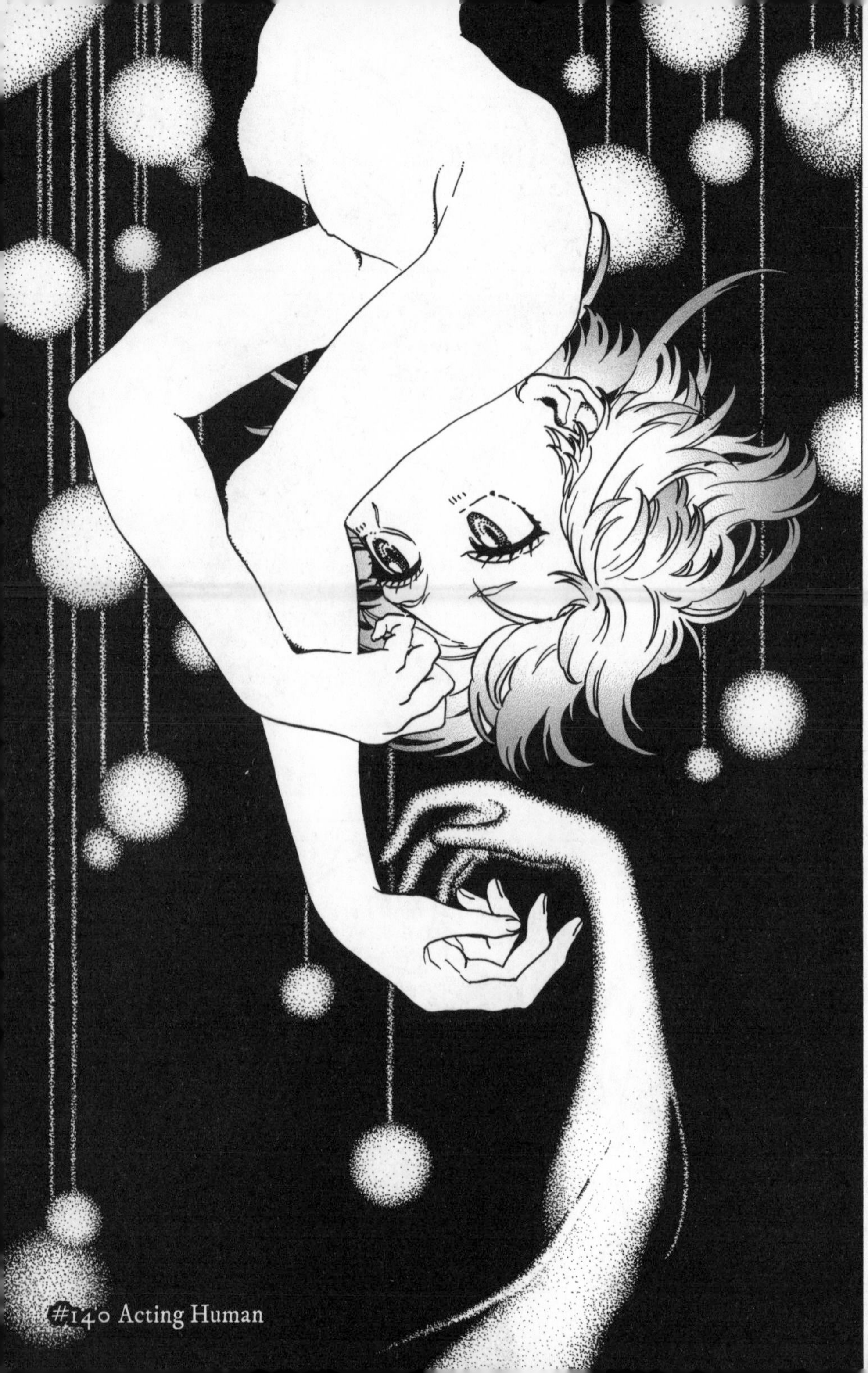

#140 Acting Human

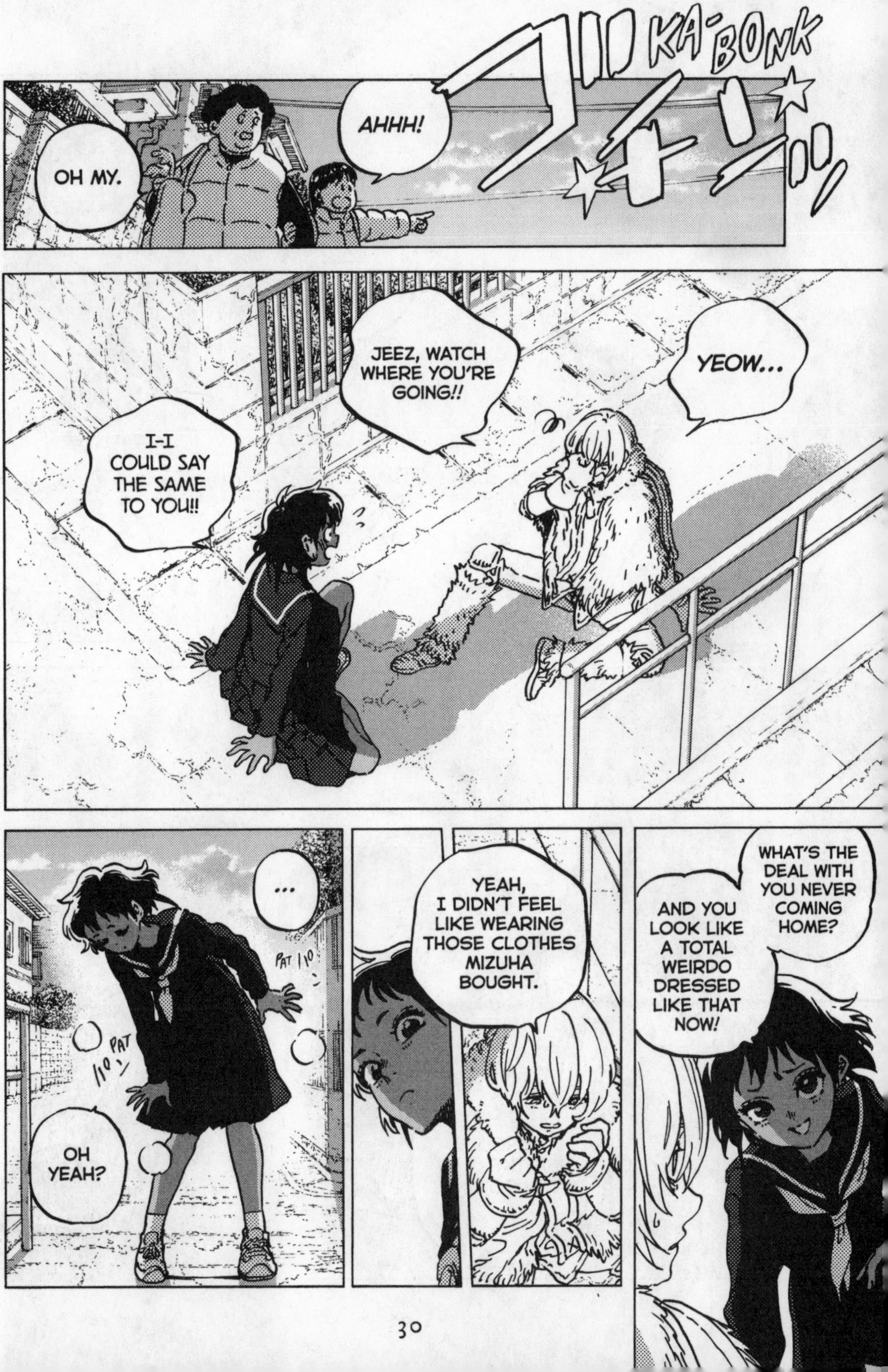
KA-BONK
AHHH!
OH MY.
YEOW...
JEEZ, WATCH WHERE YOU'RE GOING!!
I-I COULD SAY THE SAME TO YOU!!
WHAT'S THE DEAL WITH YOU NEVER COMING HOME?
AND YOU LOOK LIKE A TOTAL WEIRDO DRESSED LIKE THAT NOW!
YEAH, I DIDN'T FEEL LIKE WEARING THOSE CLOTHES MIZUHA BOUGHT.
...
PAT
PAT
OH YEAH?

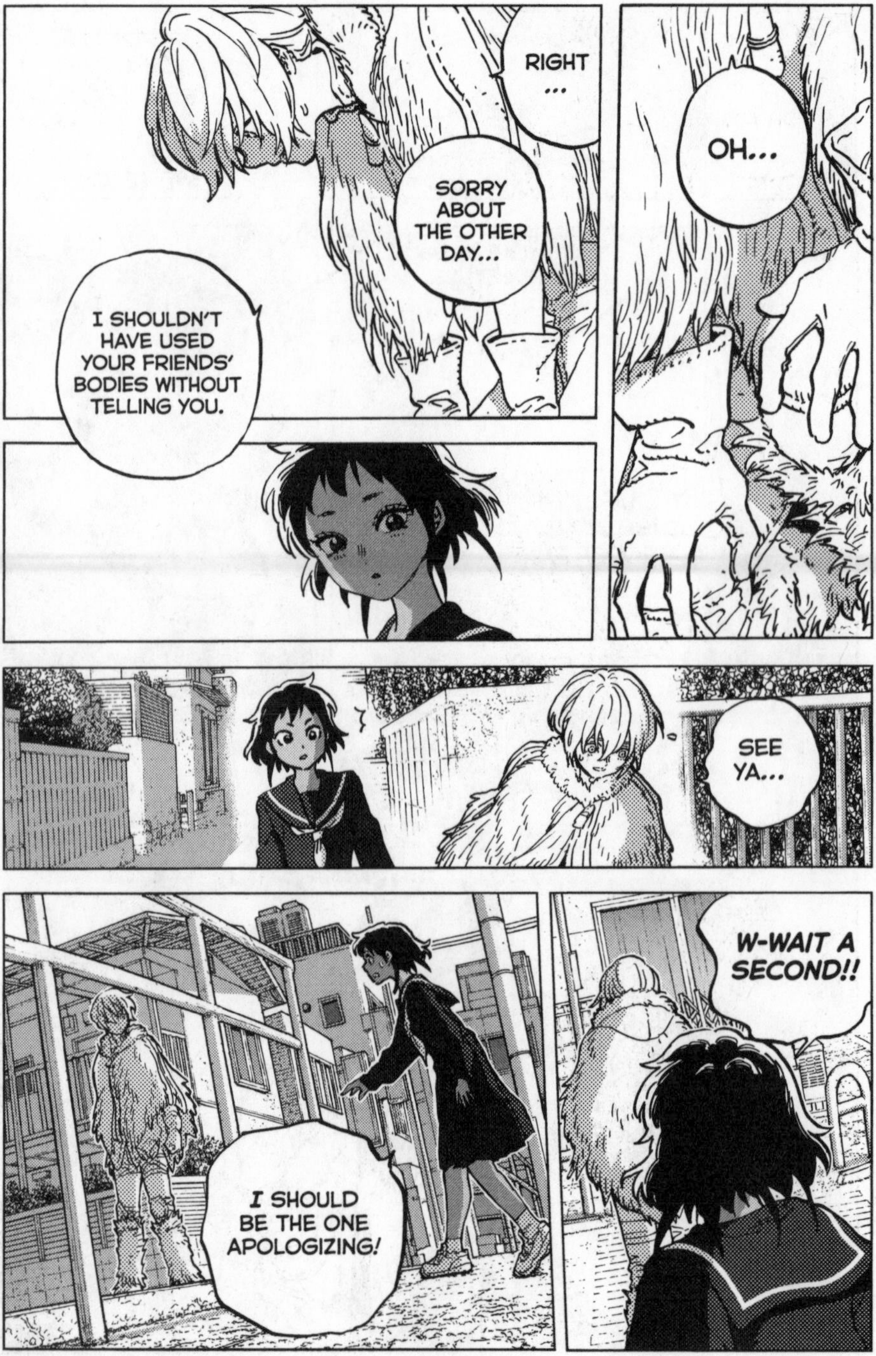
OH...
RIGHT ...
SORRY ABOUT THE OTHER DAY...
I SHOULDN'T HAVE USED YOUR FRIENDS' BODIES WITHOUT TELLING YOU.
SEE YA...
W-WAIT A SECOND!!
I SHOULD BE THE ONE APOLOGIZING!

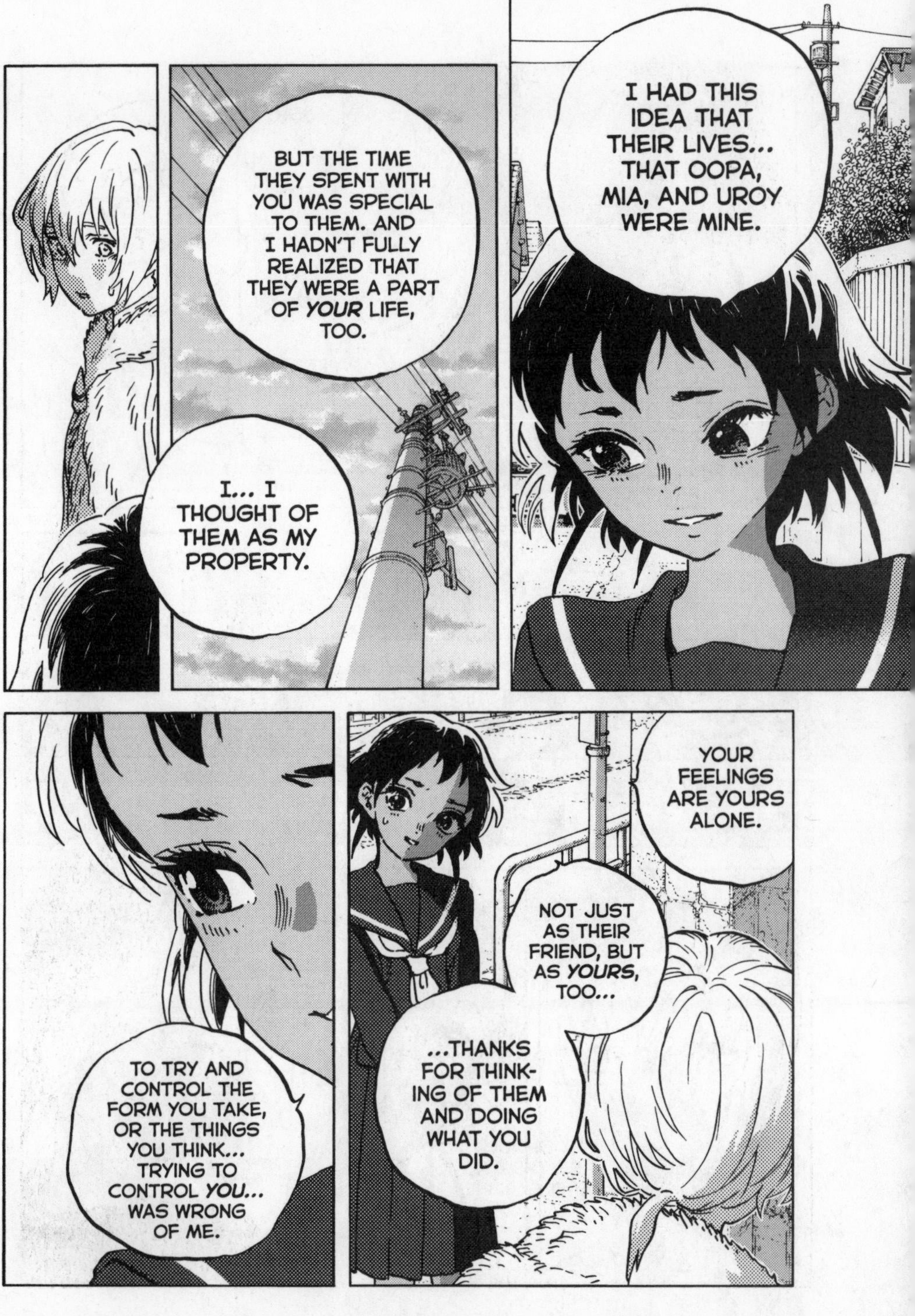

I HAD THIS IDEA THAT THEIR LIVES... THAT OOPA, MIA, AND UROY WERE MINE.
BUT THE TIME THEY SPENT WITH YOU WAS SPECIAL TO THEM. AND I HADN'T FULLY REALIZED THAT THEY WERE A PART OF *YOUR* LIFE, TOO.
I... I THOUGHT OF THEM AS MY PROPERTY.
YOUR FEELINGS ARE YOURS ALONE.
NOT JUST AS THEIR FRIEND, BUT AS *YOURS*, TOO...
...THANKS FOR THINKING OF THEM AND DOING WHAT YOU DID.
TO TRY AND CONTROL THE FORM YOU TAKE, OR THE THINGS YOU THINK... TRYING TO CONTROL *YOU*... WAS WRONG OF ME.

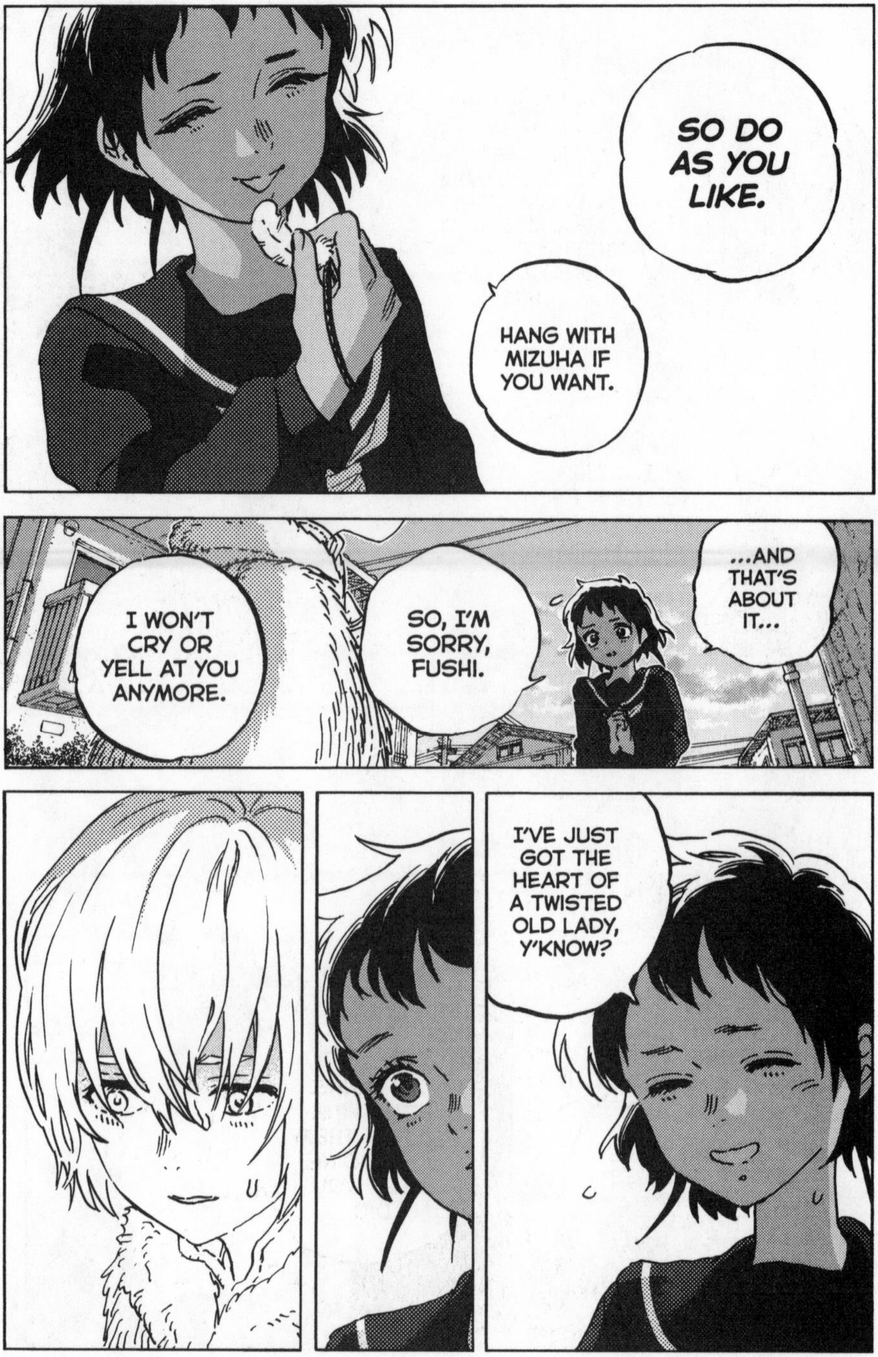
SO DO AS YOU LIKE.
HANG WITH MIZUHA IF YOU WANT.
...AND THAT'S ABOUT IT...
SO, I'M SORRY, FUSHI.
I WON'T CRY OR YELL AT YOU ANYMORE.
I'VE JUST GOT THE HEART OF A TWISTED OLD LADY, Y'KNOW?

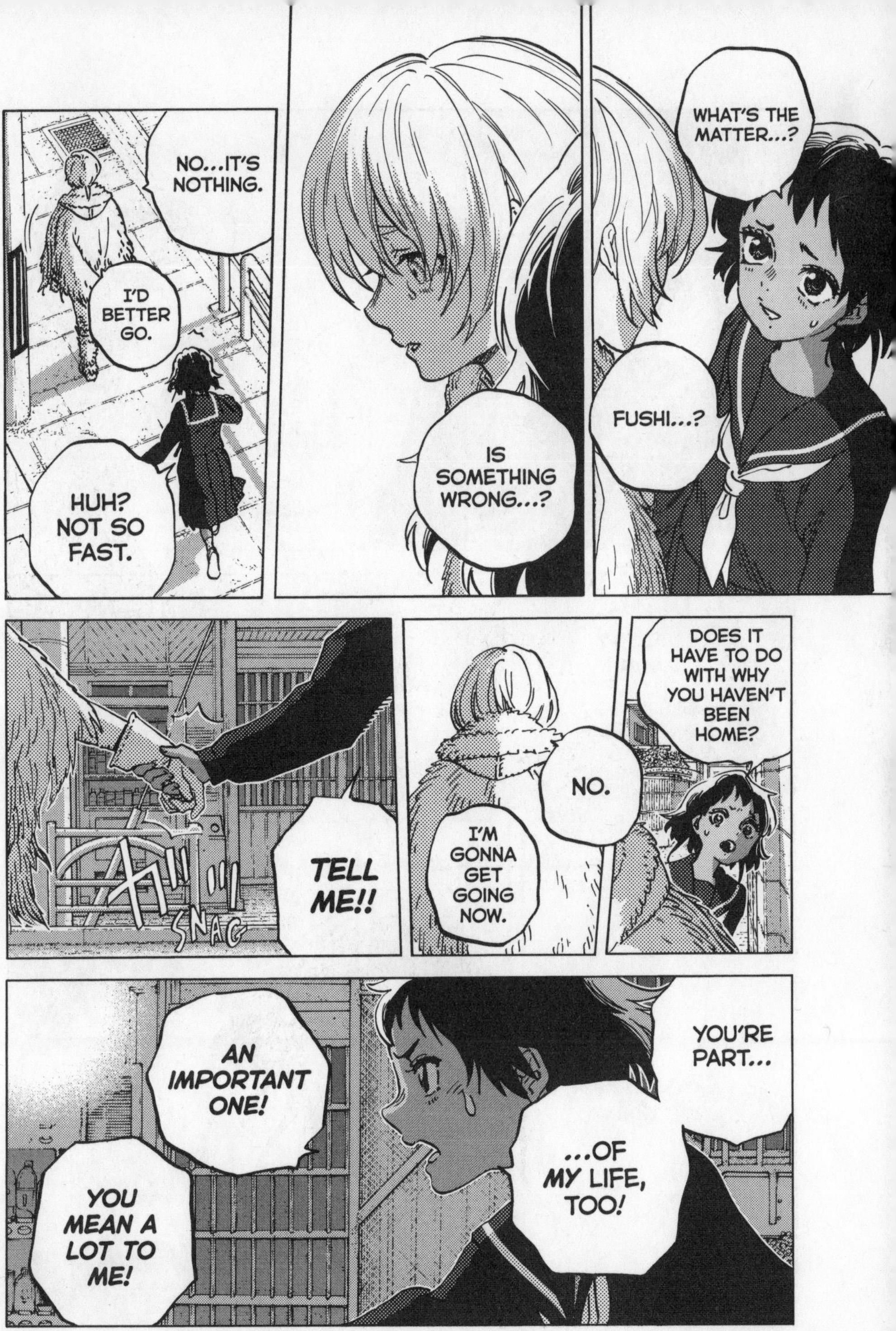
WHAT'S THE MATTER...?
FUSHI...?
IS SOMETHING WRONG...?
NO...IT'S NOTHING.
I'D BETTER GO.
HUH? NOT SO FAST.
DOES IT HAVE TO DO WITH WHY YOU HAVEN'T BEEN HOME?
NO.
I'M GONNA GET GOING NOW.
TELL ME!!
SNAG
YOU'RE PART...
...OF MY LIFE, TOO!
AN IMPORTANT ONE!
YOU MEAN A LOT TO ME!

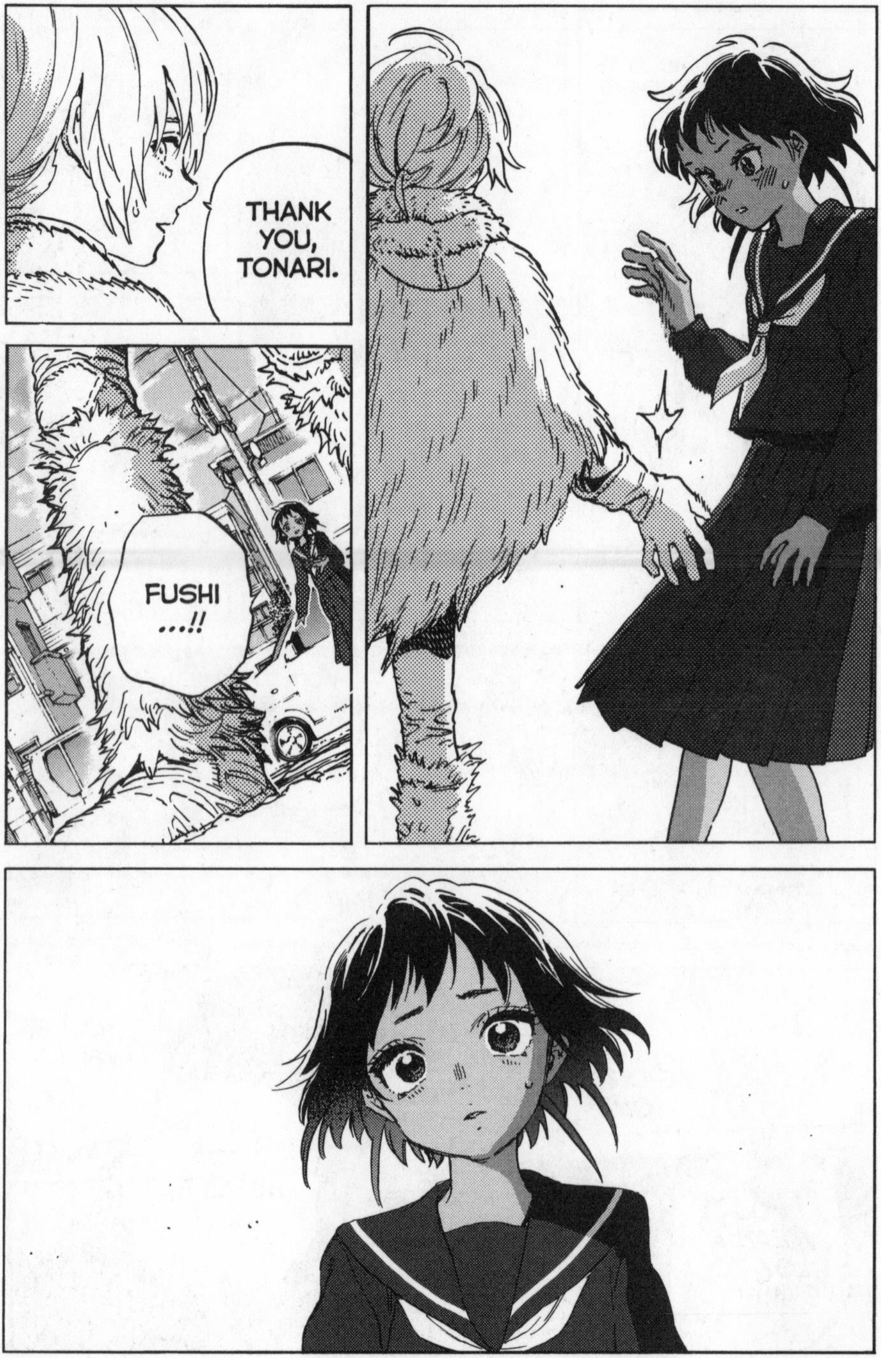
THANK YOU, TONARI.
FUSHI ...!!

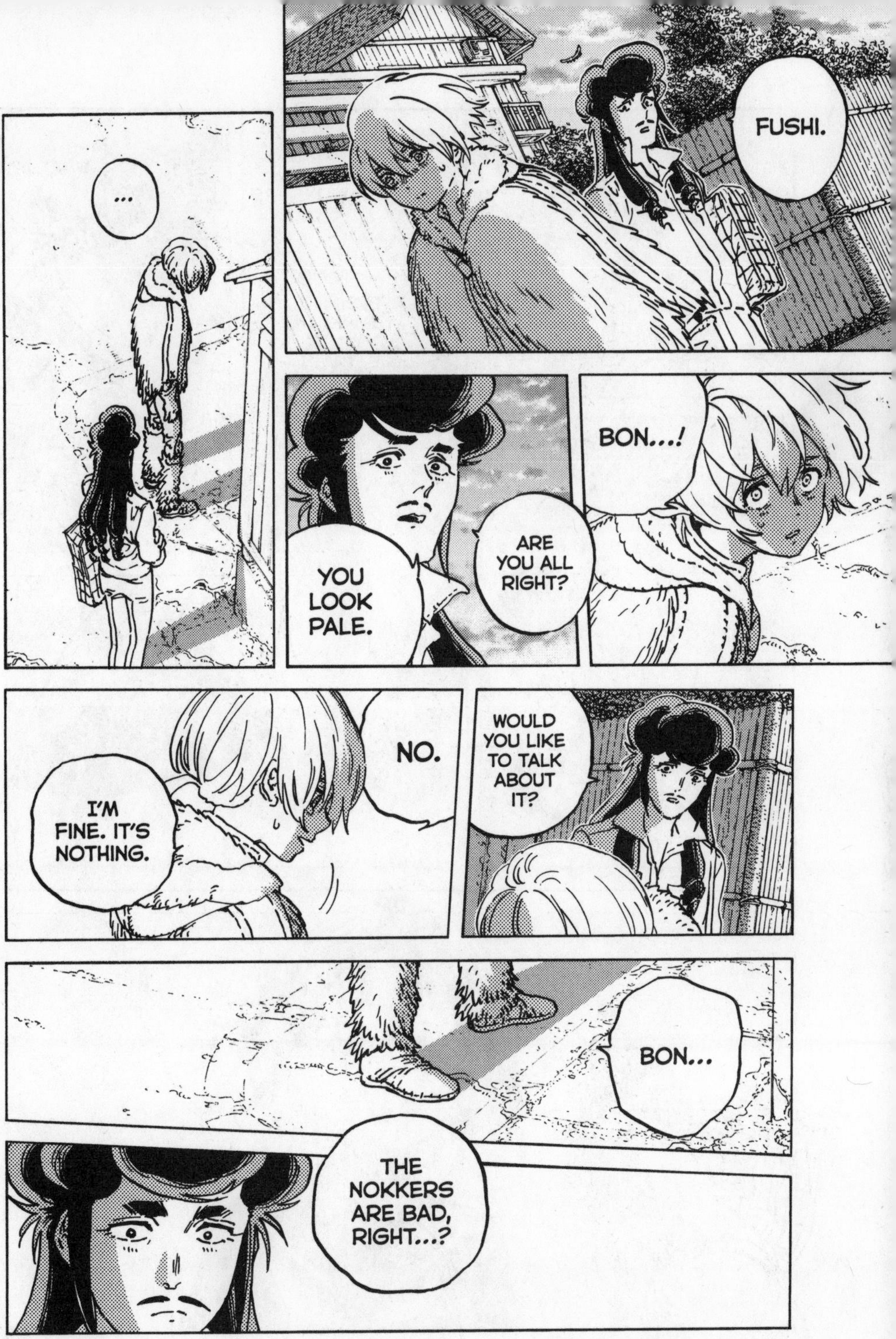
FUSHI.
BON...!
ARE YOU ALL RIGHT?
YOU LOOK PALE.
...
WOULD YOU LIKE TO TALK ABOUT IT?
NO.
I'M FINE. IT'S NOTHING.
BON...
THE NOKKERS ARE BAD, RIGHT...?

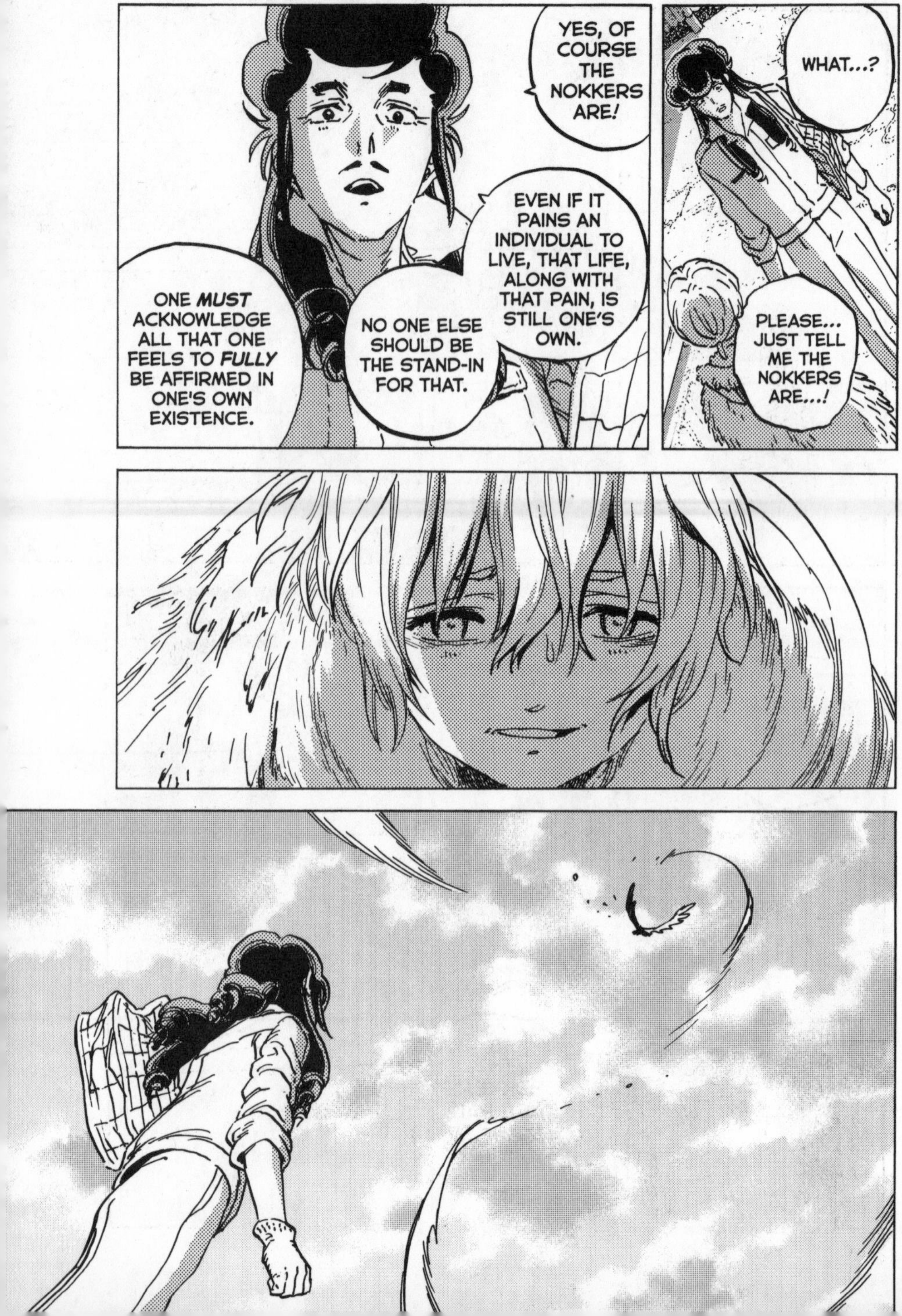
WHAT...?
PLEASE... JUST TELL ME THE NOKKERS ARE...!
YES, OF COURSE THE NOKKERS ARE!
EVEN IF IT PAINS AN INDIVIDUAL TO LIVE, THAT LIFE, ALONG WITH THAT PAIN, IS STILL ONE'S OWN.
NO ONE ELSE SHOULD BE THE STAND-IN FOR THAT.
ONE MUST ACKNOWLEDGE ALL THAT ONE FEELS TO FULLY BE AFFIRMED IN ONE'S OWN EXISTENCE.

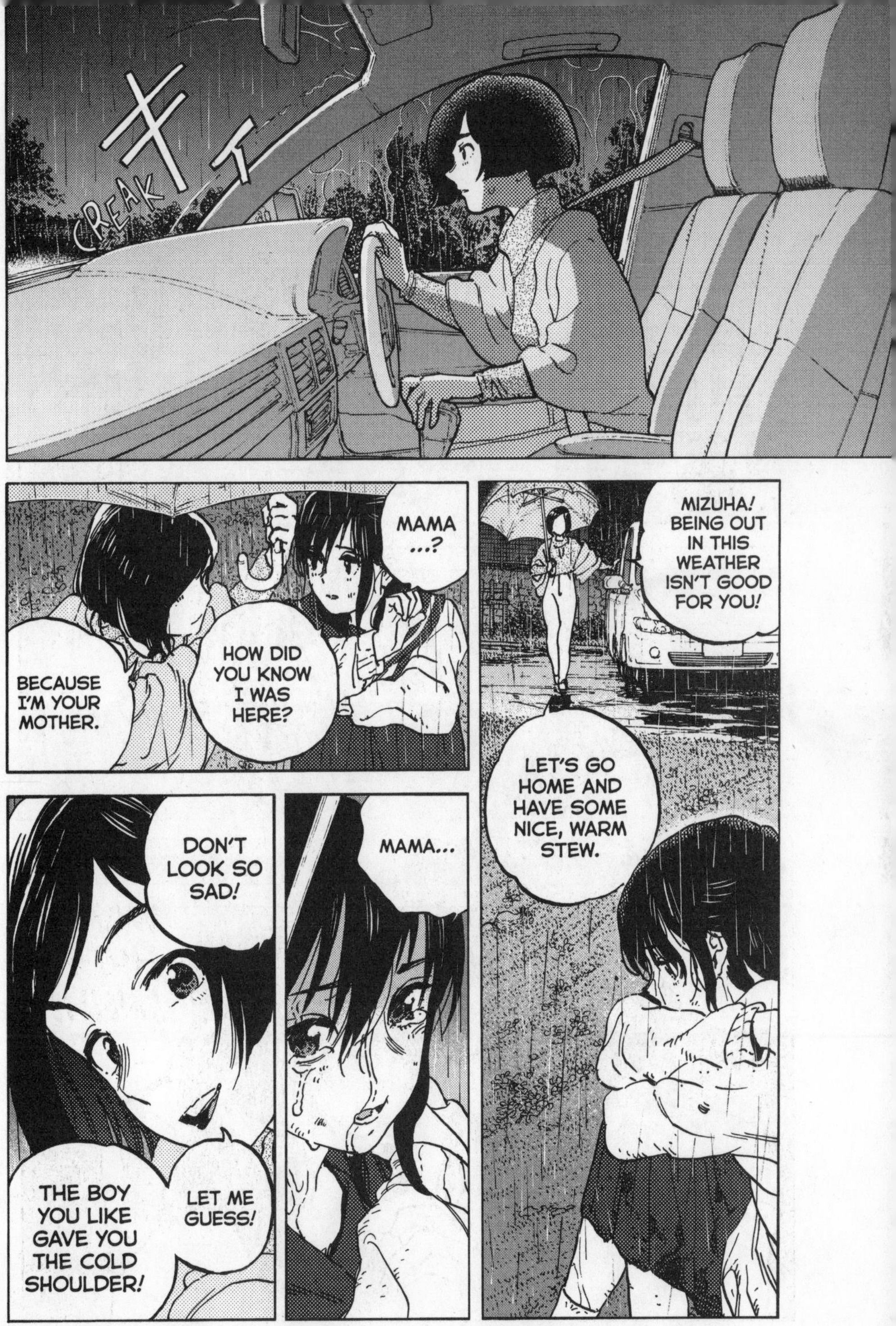
キイ
CREAK
MIZUHA! BEING OUT IN THIS WEATHER ISN'T GOOD FOR YOU!
LET'S GO HOME AND HAVE SOME NICE, WARM STEW.
MAMA ...?
HOW DID YOU KNOW I WAS HERE?
BECAUSE I'M YOUR MOTHER.
MAMA...
DON'T LOOK SO SAD!
LET ME GUESS!
THE BOY YOU LIKE GAVE YOU THE COLD SHOULDER!

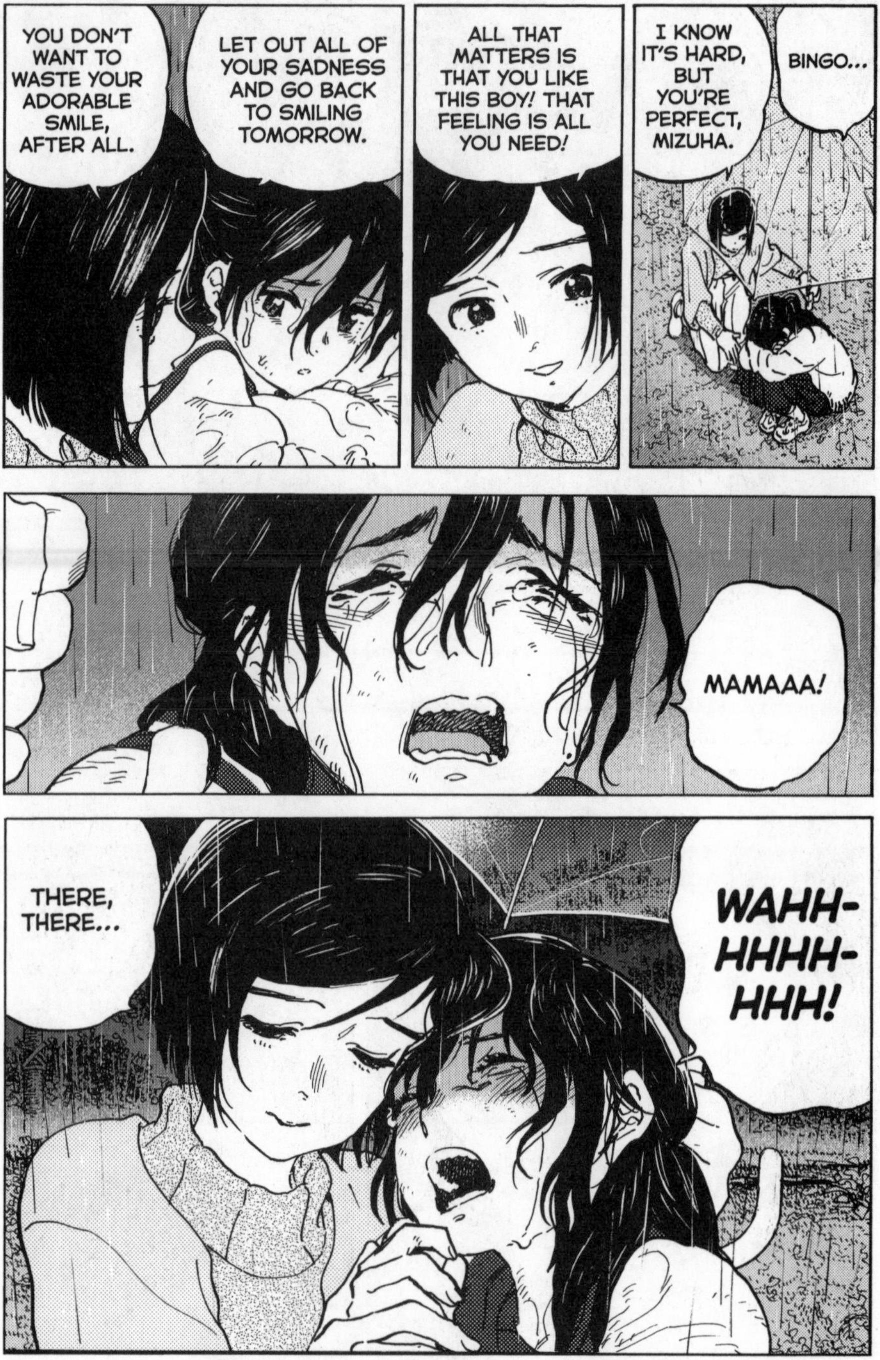
BINGO...
I KNOW IT'S HARD, BUT YOU'RE PERFECT, MIZUHA.
ALL THAT MATTERS IS THAT YOU LIKE THIS BOY! THAT FEELING IS ALL YOU NEED!
LET OUT ALL OF YOUR SADNESS AND GO BACK TO SMILING TOMORROW.
YOU DON'T WANT TO WASTE YOUR ADORABLE SMILE, AFTER ALL.
MAMAAA!
WAHH-HHHH-HHH!
THERE, THERE...

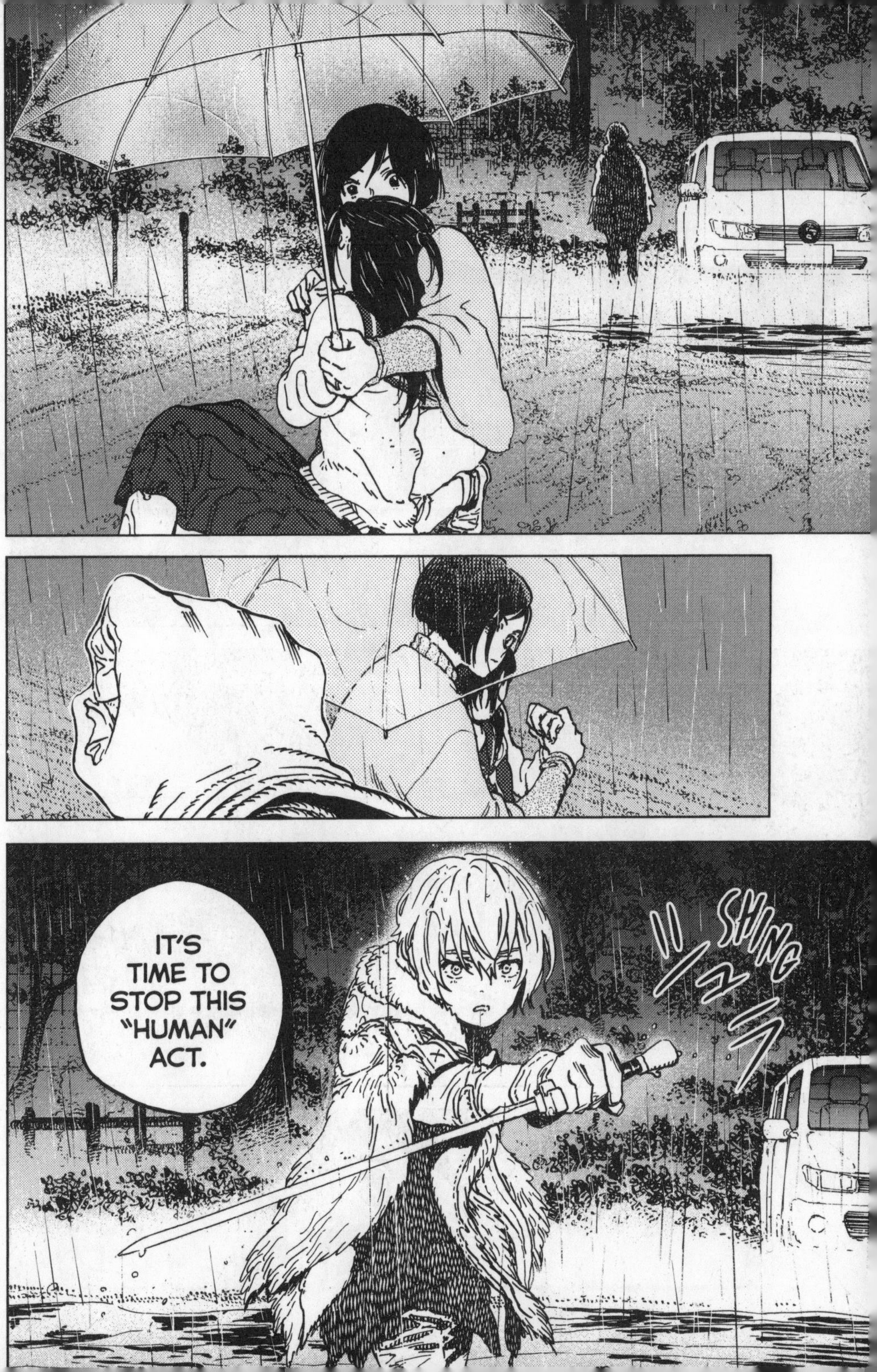
SHING
IT'S TIME TO STOP THIS "HUMAN" ACT.

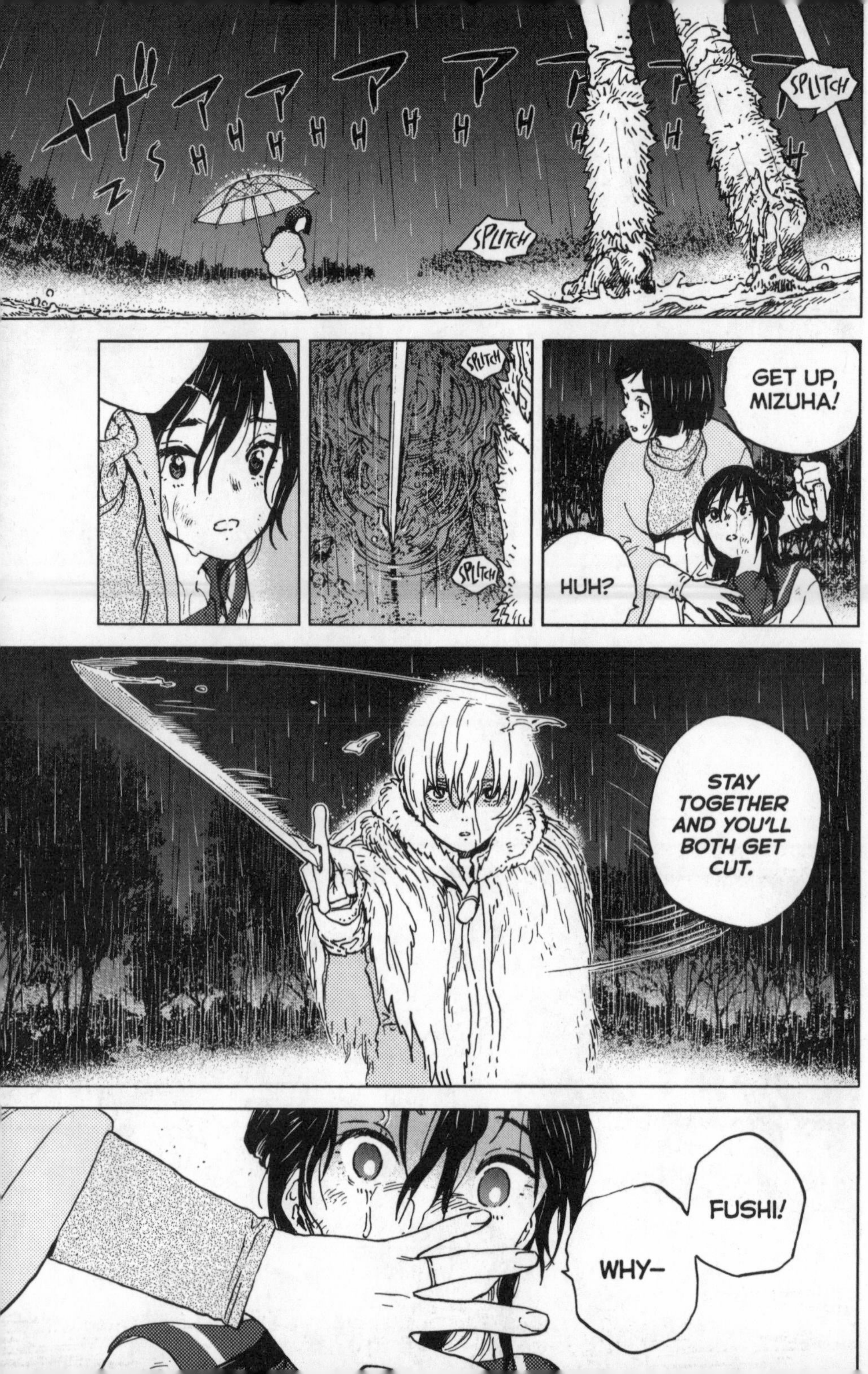
SPLITCH
ZSHHHHHHHHHHHH
SPLITCH
GET UP, MIZUHA!
HUH?
SPLITCH
SPLITCH
STAY TOGETHER AND YOU'LL BOTH GET CUT.
FUSHI!
WHY–

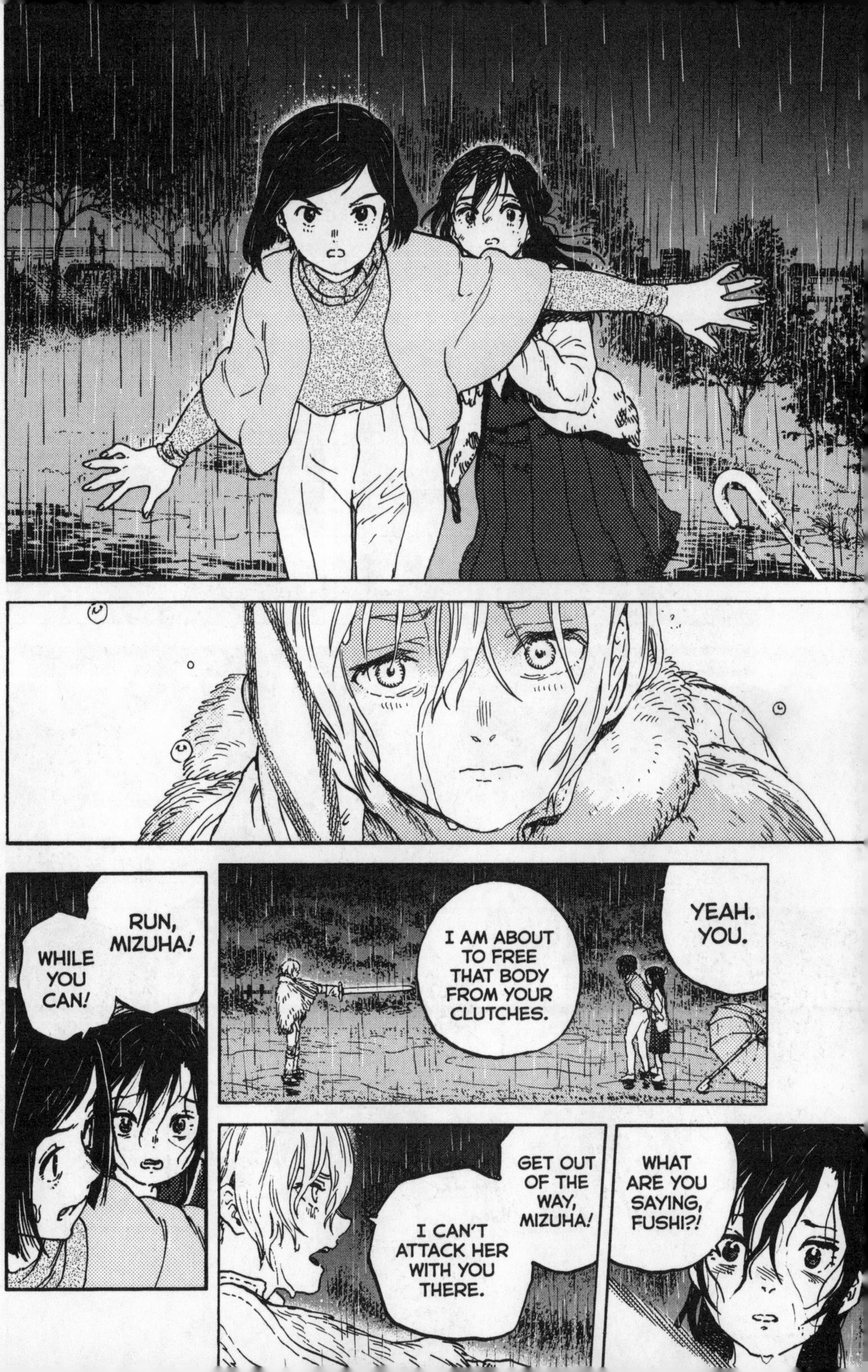

YEAH. YOU.
I AM ABOUT TO FREE THAT BODY FROM YOUR CLUTCHES.
WHAT ARE YOU SAYING, FUSHI?!
GET OUT OF THE WAY, MIZUHA!
I CAN'T ATTACK HER WITH YOU THERE.
RUN, MIZUHA!
WHILE YOU CAN!

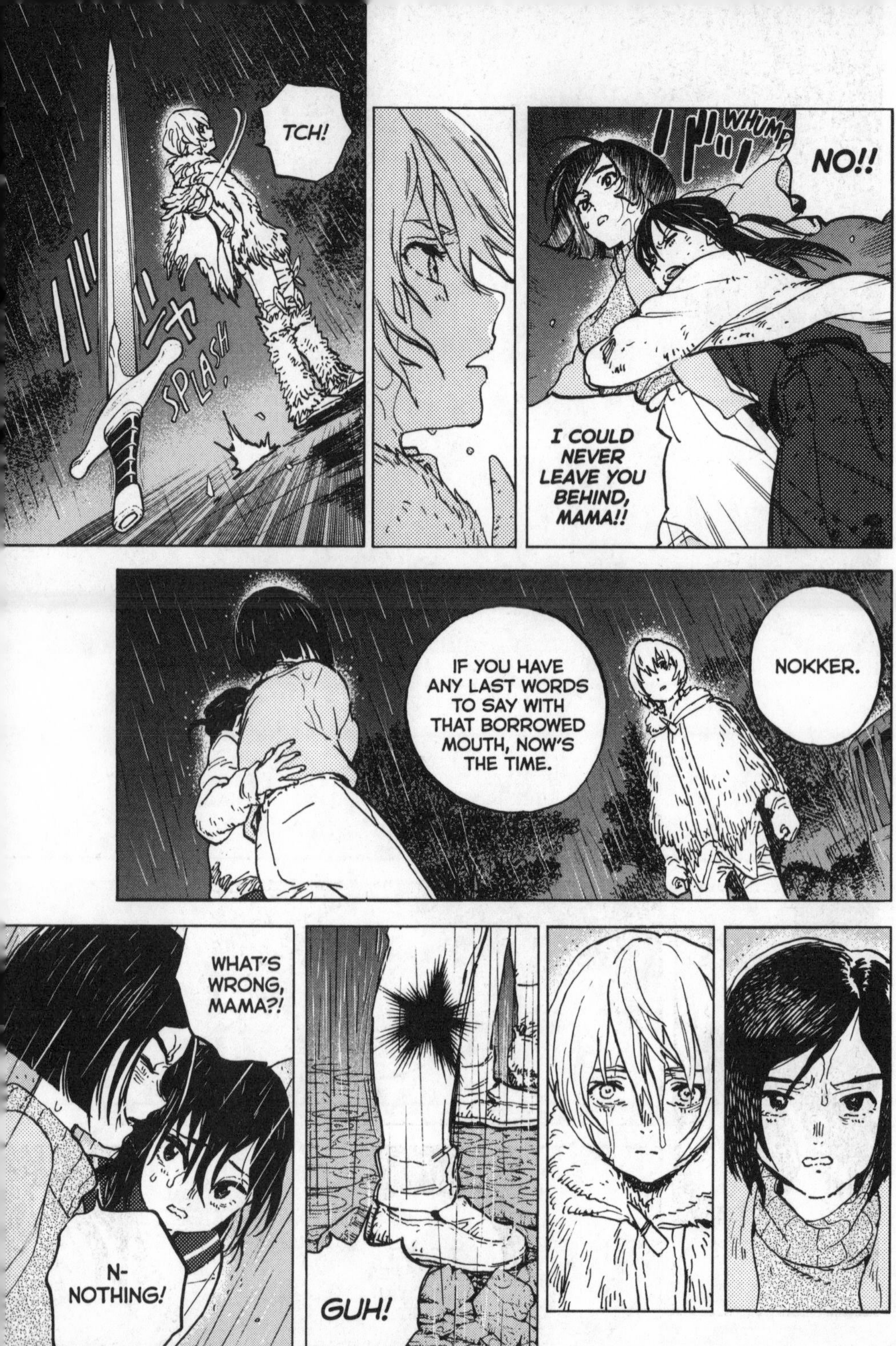
WHUMP
NO!!
I COULD NEVER LEAVE YOU BEHIND, MAMA!!
TCH!
SPLASH
NOKKER.
IF YOU HAVE ANY LAST WORDS TO SAY WITH THAT BORROWED MOUTH, NOW'S THE TIME.
GUH!
WHAT'S WRONG, MAMA?!
N-NOTHING!

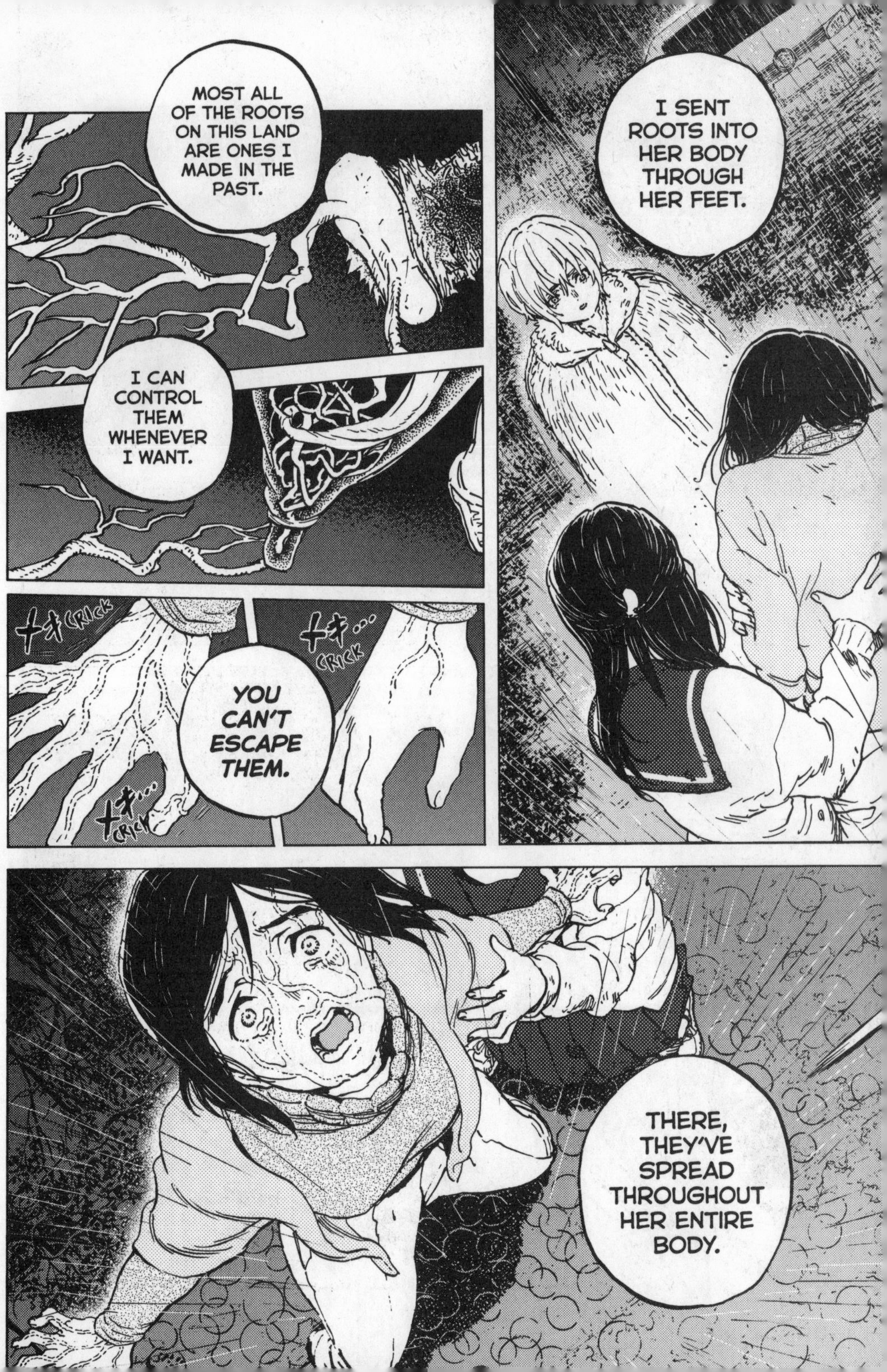
I SENT ROOTS INTO HER BODY THROUGH HER FEET.
MOST ALL OF THE ROOTS ON THIS LAND ARE ONES I MADE IN THE PAST.
I CAN CONTROL THEM WHENEVER I WANT.
CRICK
YOU CAN'T ESCAPE THEM.
CRICK
CRICK
THERE, THEY'VE SPREAD THROUGHOUT HER ENTIRE BODY.

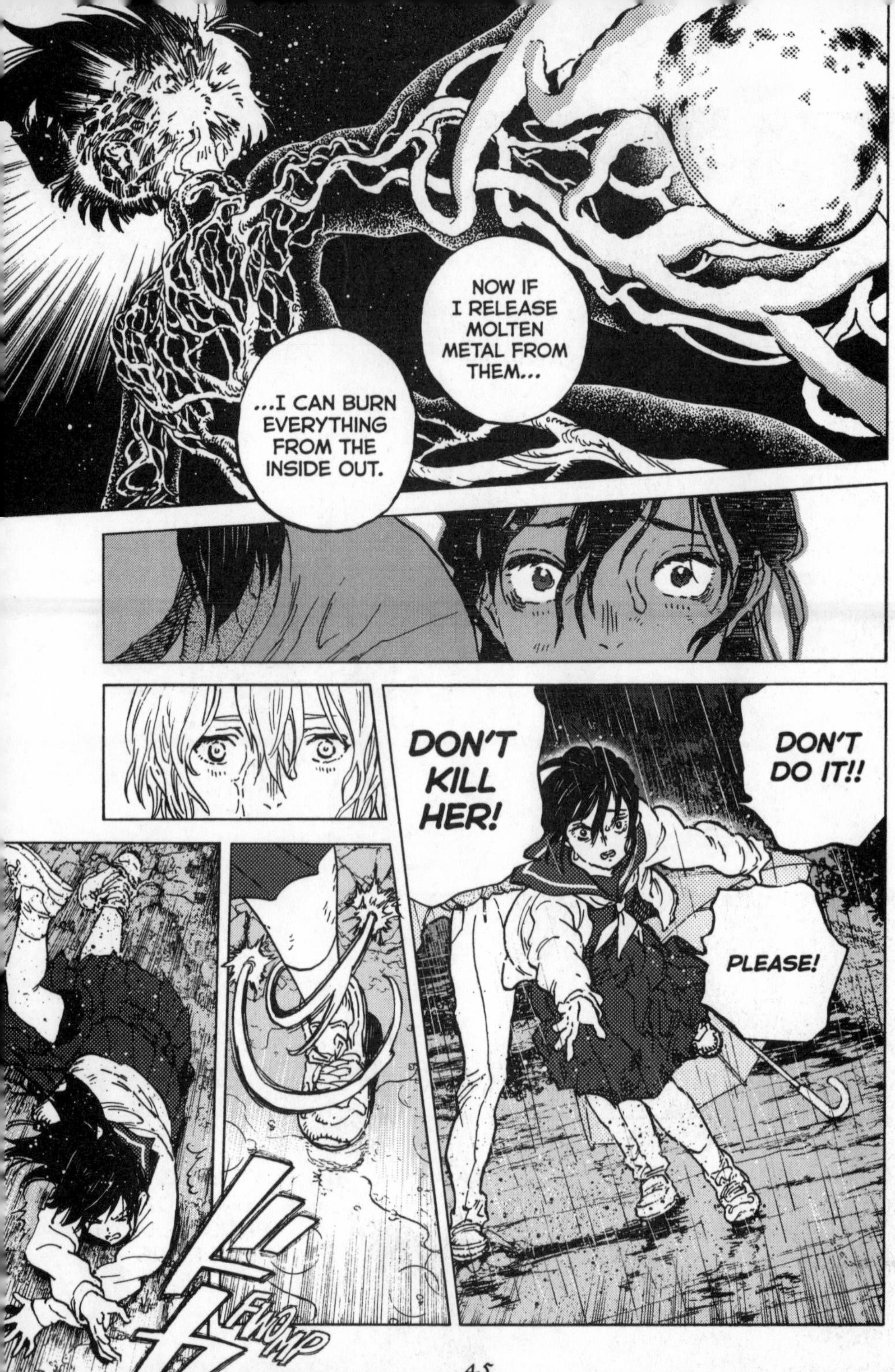
NOW IF I RELEASE MOLTEN METAL FROM THEM...
...I CAN BURN EVERYTHING FROM THE INSIDE OUT.
DON'T DO IT!!
DON'T KILL HER!
PLEASE!
FWOMP

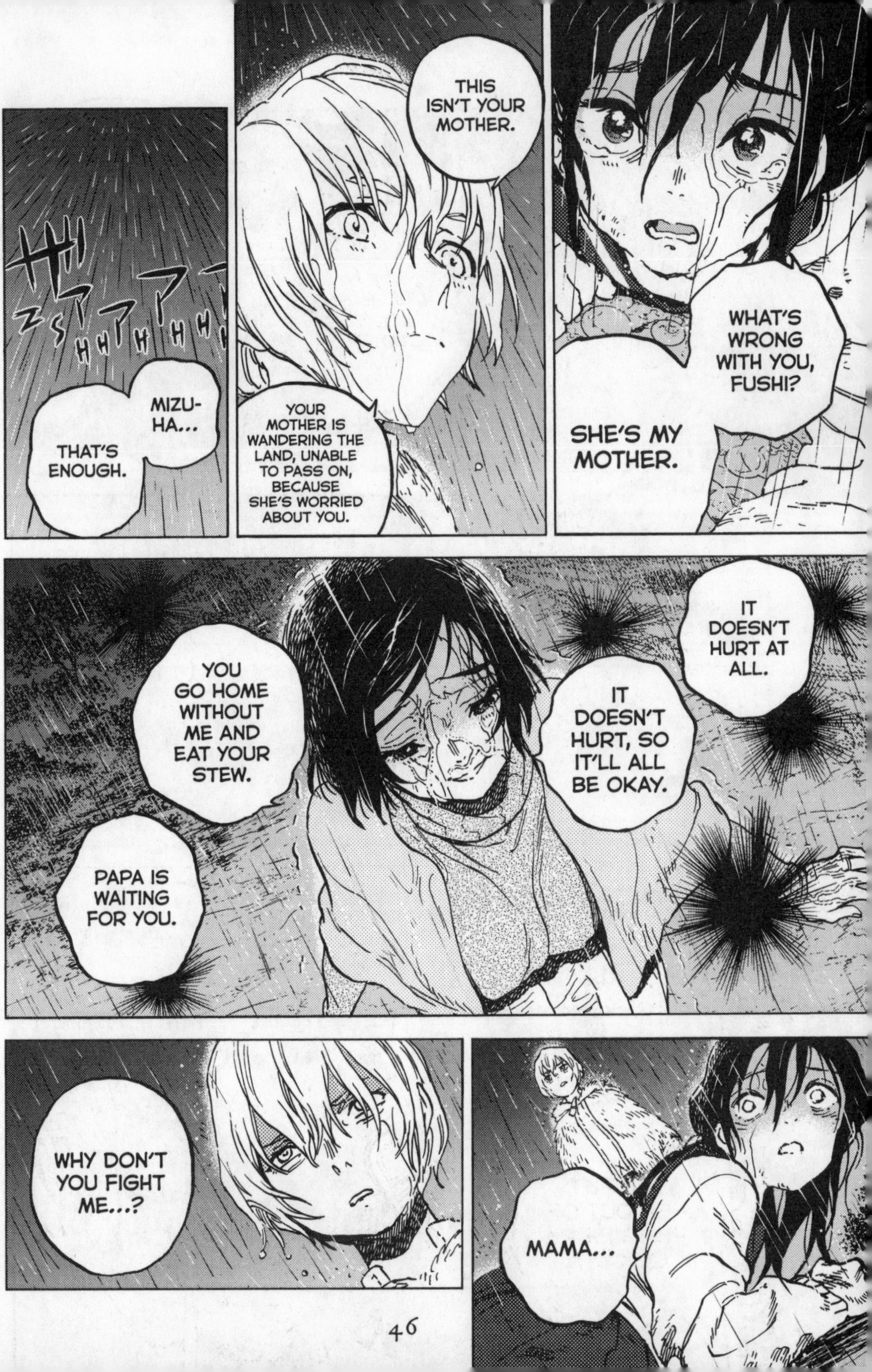
WHAT'S WRONG WITH YOU, FUSHI?
SHE'S MY MOTHER.
THIS ISN'T YOUR MOTHER.
YOUR MOTHER IS WANDERING THE LAND, UNABLE TO PASS ON, BECAUSE SHE'S WORRIED ABOUT YOU.
ZSHHHHH
MIZUHA...
THAT'S ENOUGH.
IT DOESN'T HURT AT ALL.
IT DOESN'T HURT, SO IT'LL ALL BE OKAY.
YOU GO HOME WITHOUT ME AND EAT YOUR STEW.
PAPA IS WAITING FOR YOU.
MAMA...
WHY DON'T YOU FIGHT ME...?

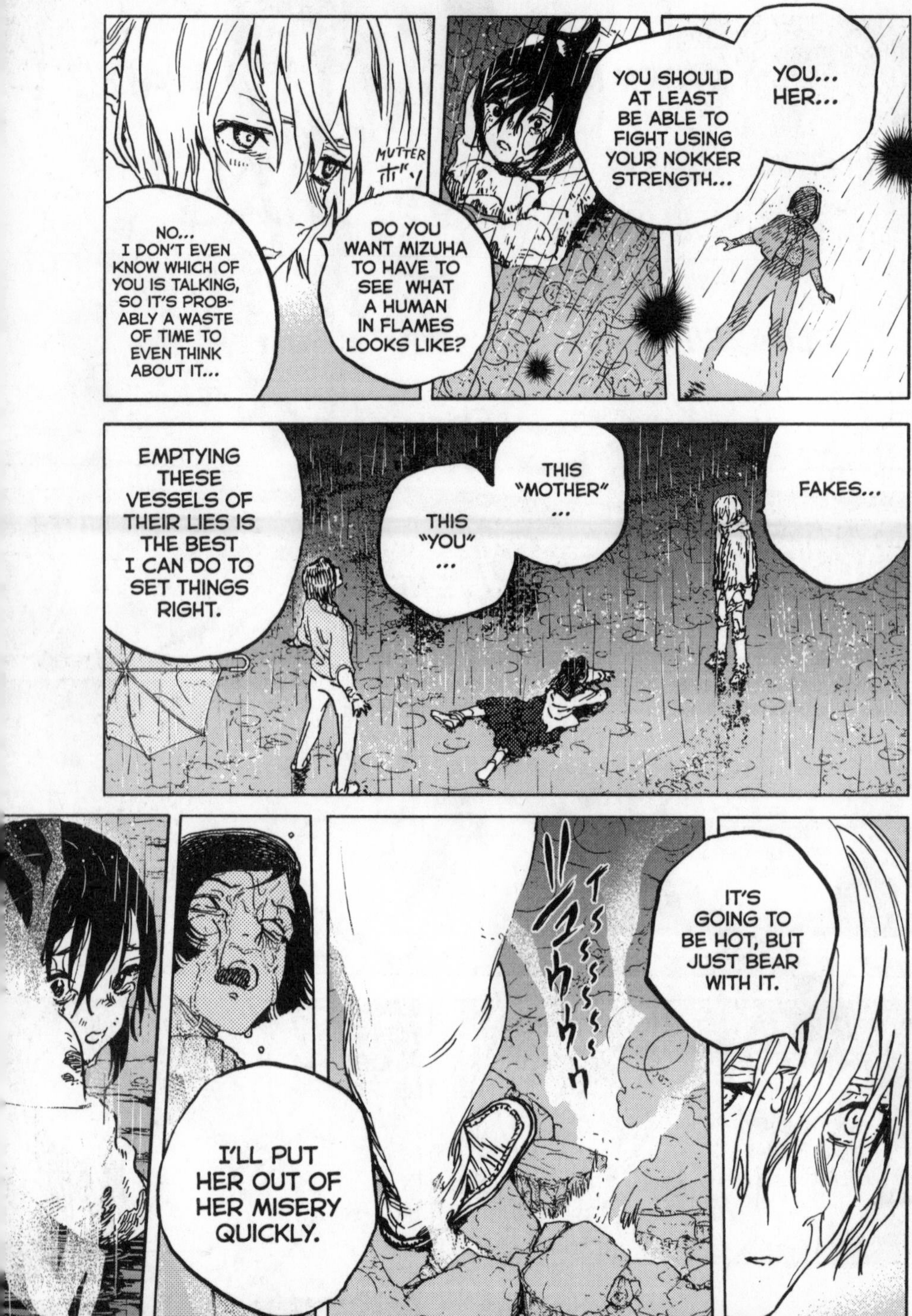
YOU... HER...
YOU SHOULD AT LEAST BE ABLE TO FIGHT USING YOUR NOKKER STRENGTH...
DO YOU WANT MIZUHA TO HAVE TO SEE WHAT A HUMAN IN FLAMES LOOKS LIKE?
MUTTER
NO... I DON'T EVEN KNOW WHICH OF YOU IS TALKING, SO IT'S PROBABLY A WASTE OF TIME TO EVEN THINK ABOUT IT...
FAKES...
THIS "MOTHER" ...
THIS "YOU" ...
EMPTYING THESE VESSELS OF THEIR LIES IS THE BEST I CAN DO TO SET THINGS RIGHT.
IT'S GOING TO BE HOT, BUT JUST BEAR WITH IT.
I'LL PUT HER OUT OF HER MISERY QUICKLY.

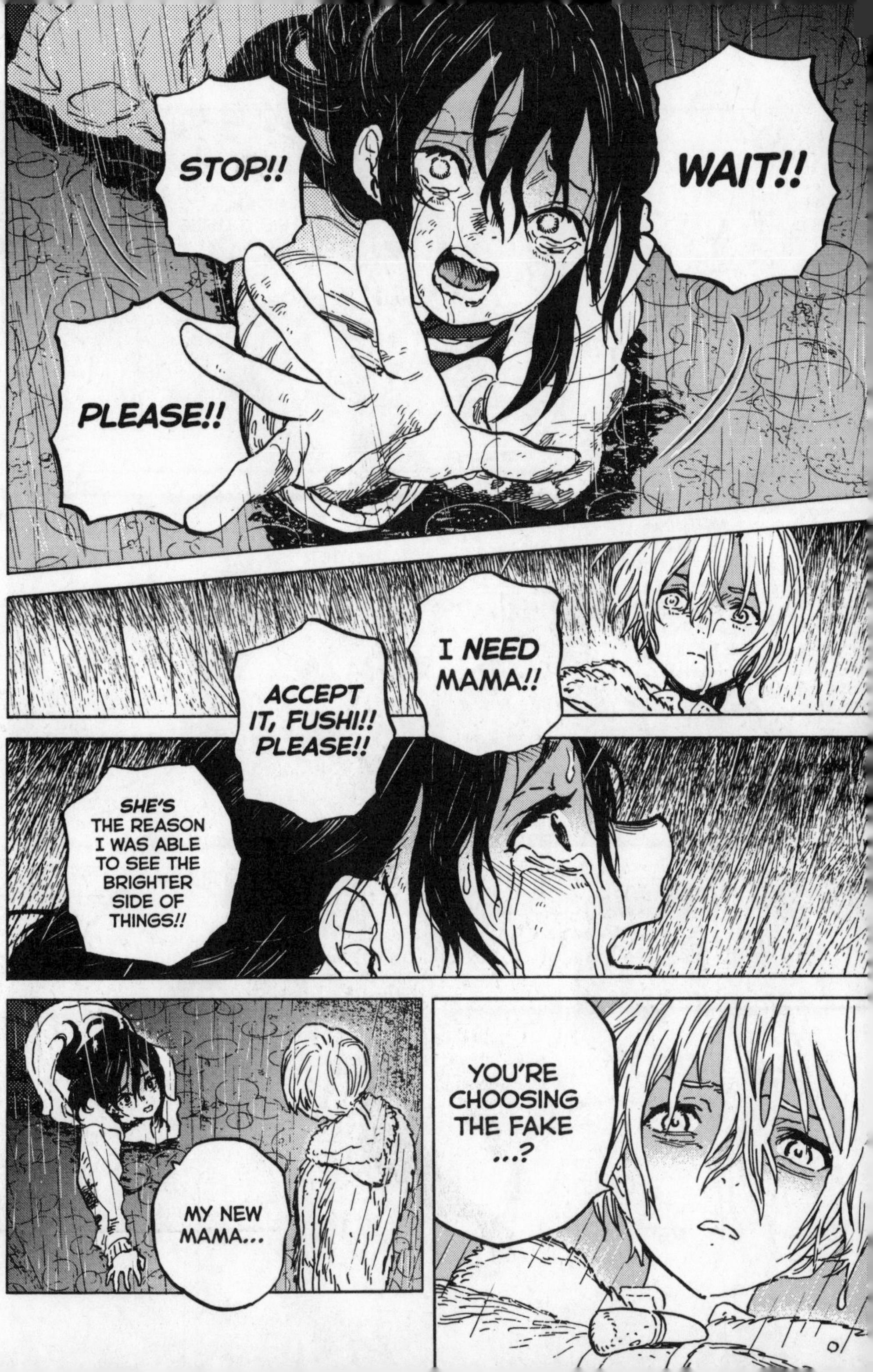
WAIT!!
STOP!!
PLEASE!!
I NEED MAMA!!
ACCEPT IT, FUSHI!! PLEASE!!
SHE'S THE REASON I WAS ABLE TO SEE THE BRIGHTER SIDE OF THINGS!!
YOU'RE CHOOSING THE FAKE ...?
MY NEW MAMA...

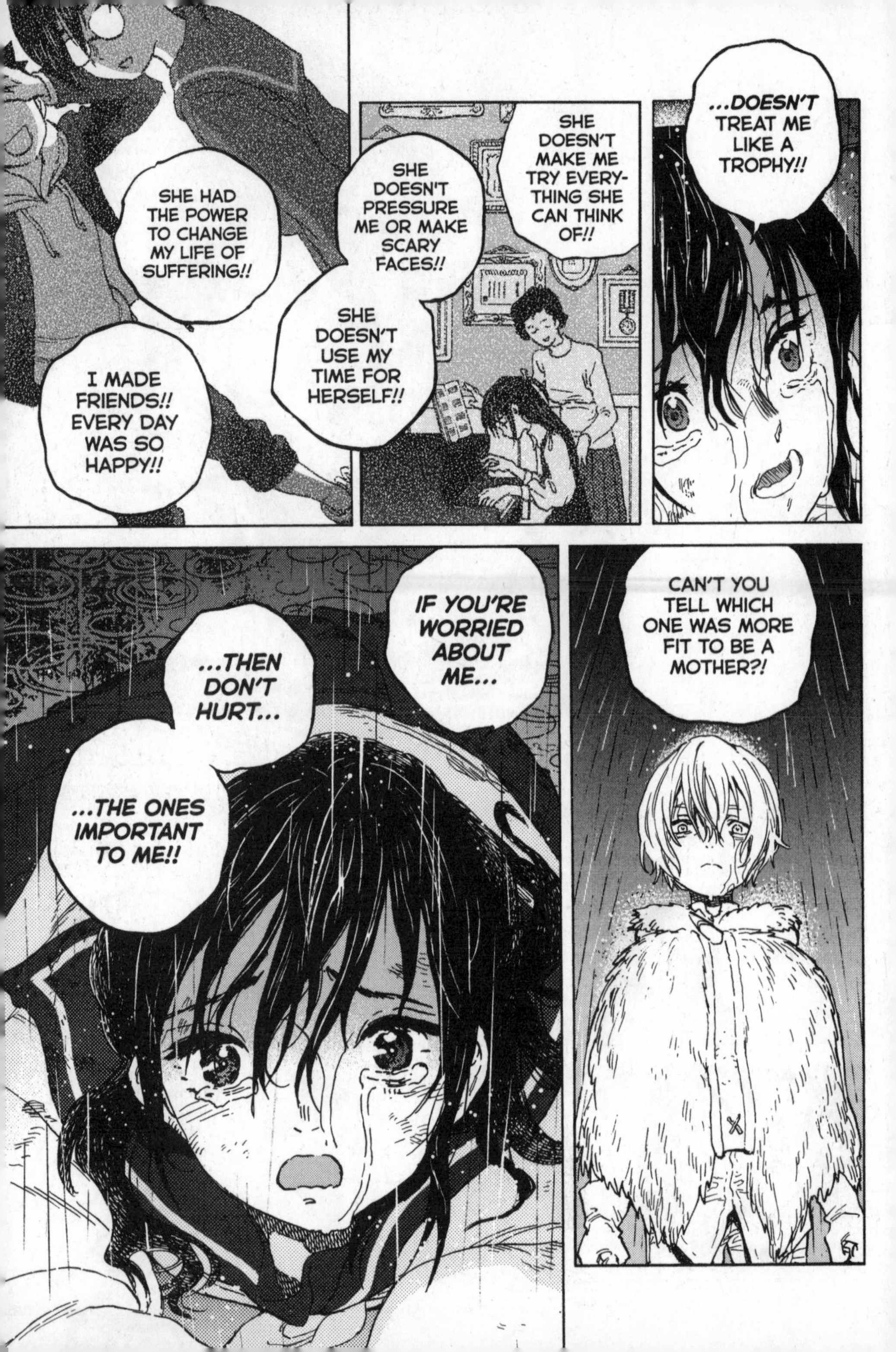
...DOESN'T TREAT ME LIKE A TROPHY!!
SHE DOESN'T MAKE ME TRY EVERY-THING SHE CAN THINK OF!!
SHE DOESN'T PRESSURE ME OR MAKE SCARY FACES!!
SHE DOESN'T USE MY TIME FOR HERSELF!!
SHE HAD THE POWER TO CHANGE MY LIFE OF SUFFERING!!
I MADE FRIENDS!! EVERY DAY WAS SO HAPPY!!
CAN'T YOU TELL WHICH ONE WAS MORE FIT TO BE A MOTHER?!
IF YOU'RE WORRIED ABOUT ME...
...THEN DON'T HURT...
...THE ONES IMPORTANT TO ME!!

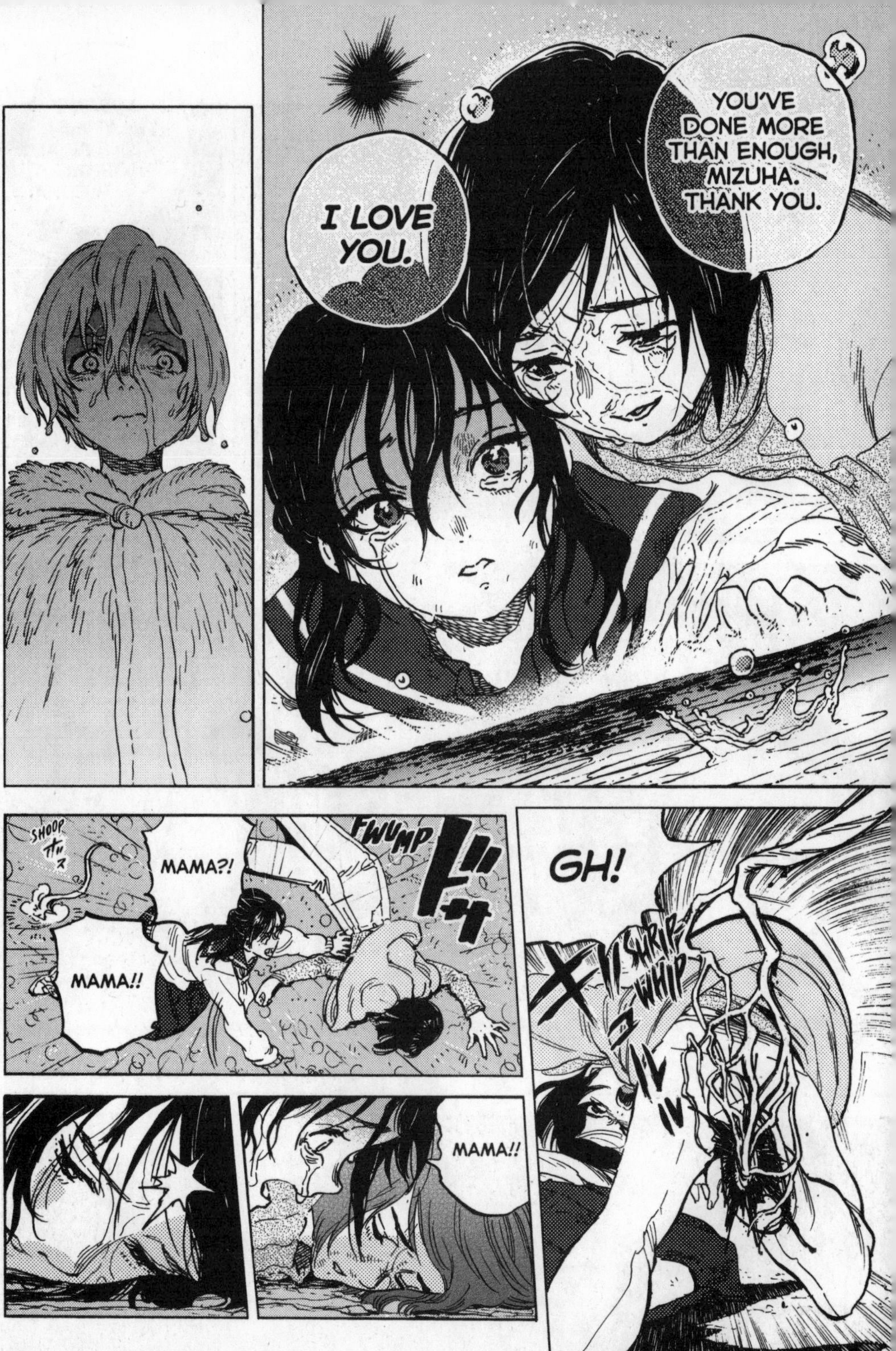
YOU'VE DONE MORE THAN ENOUGH, MIZUHA. THANK YOU.
I LOVE YOU.
GH!
SHRIP
WHIP
FWUMP
MAMA?!
SHOOP
MAMA!!
MAMA!!

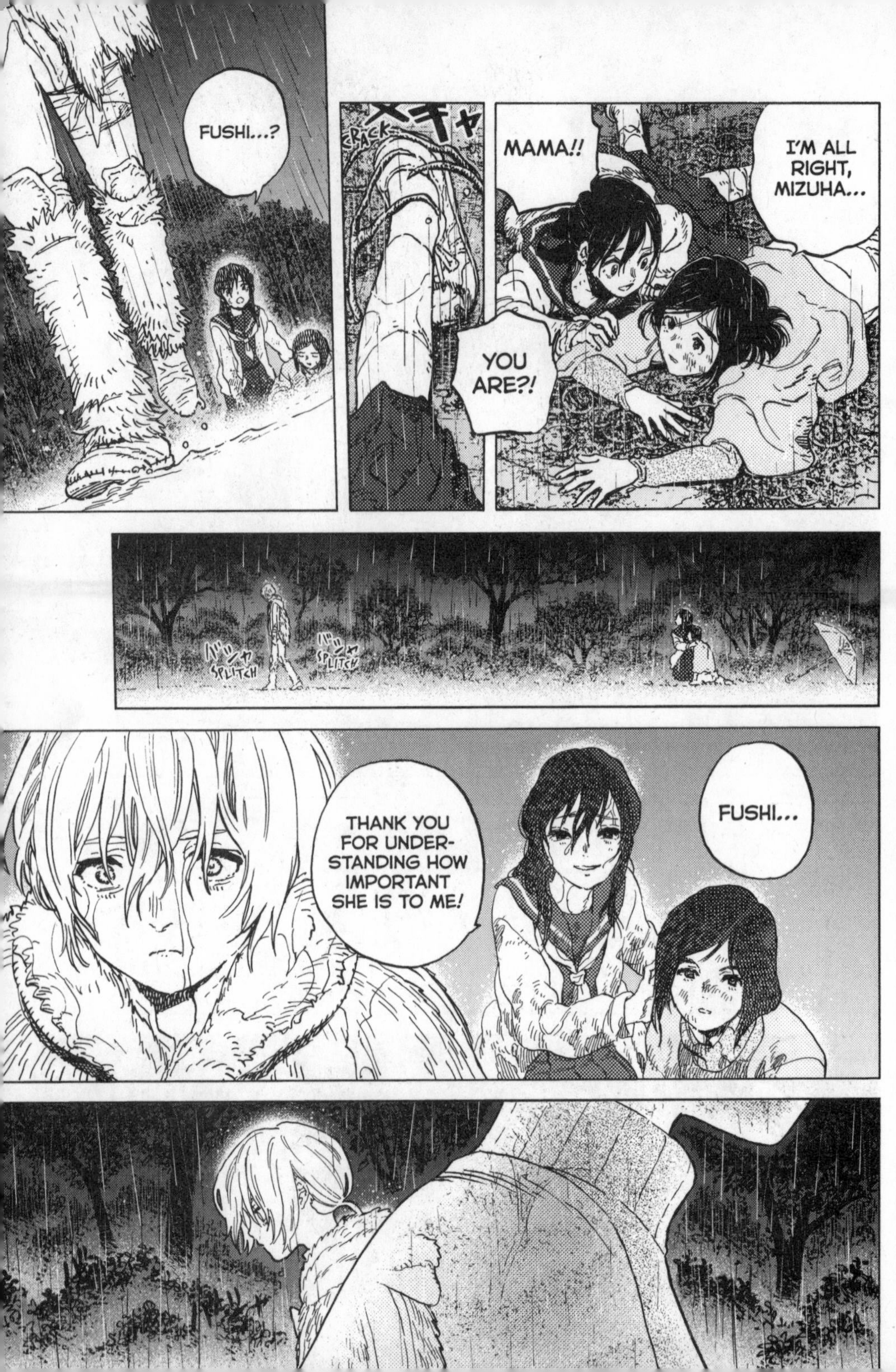

I'M ALL RIGHT, MIZUHA...
MAMA!!
YOU ARE?!
メキャ
CRACK
FUSHI...?
バシャ
SPLITCH
バシャ
SPLITCH
FUSHI...
THANK YOU FOR UNDER-STANDING HOW IMPORTANT SHE IS TO ME!

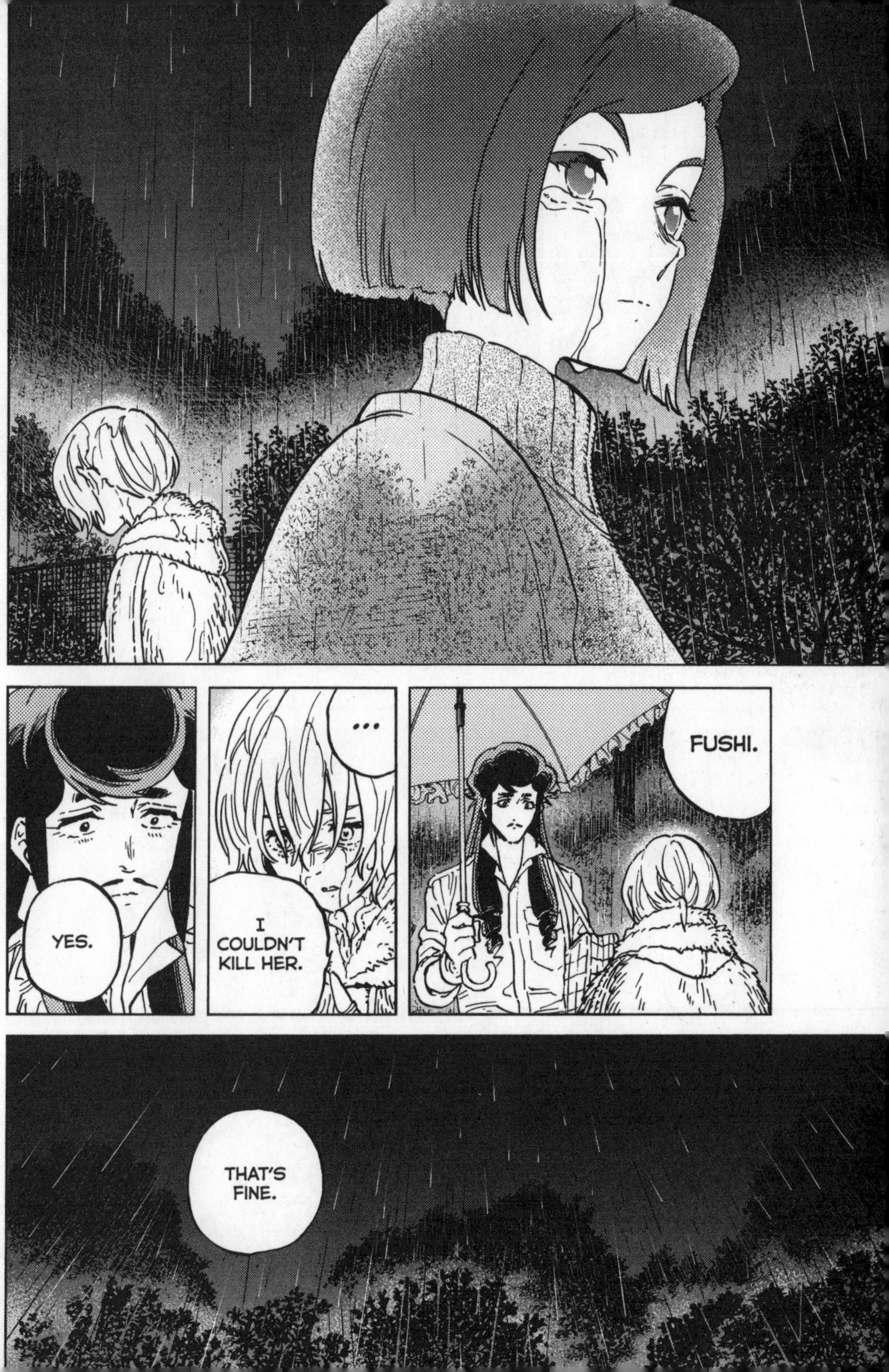
FUSHI.
...
I COULDN'T KILL HER.
YES.
THAT'S FINE.

TO YOUR
ETERNITY

TO YOUR
ETERNITY

#141 Their Home

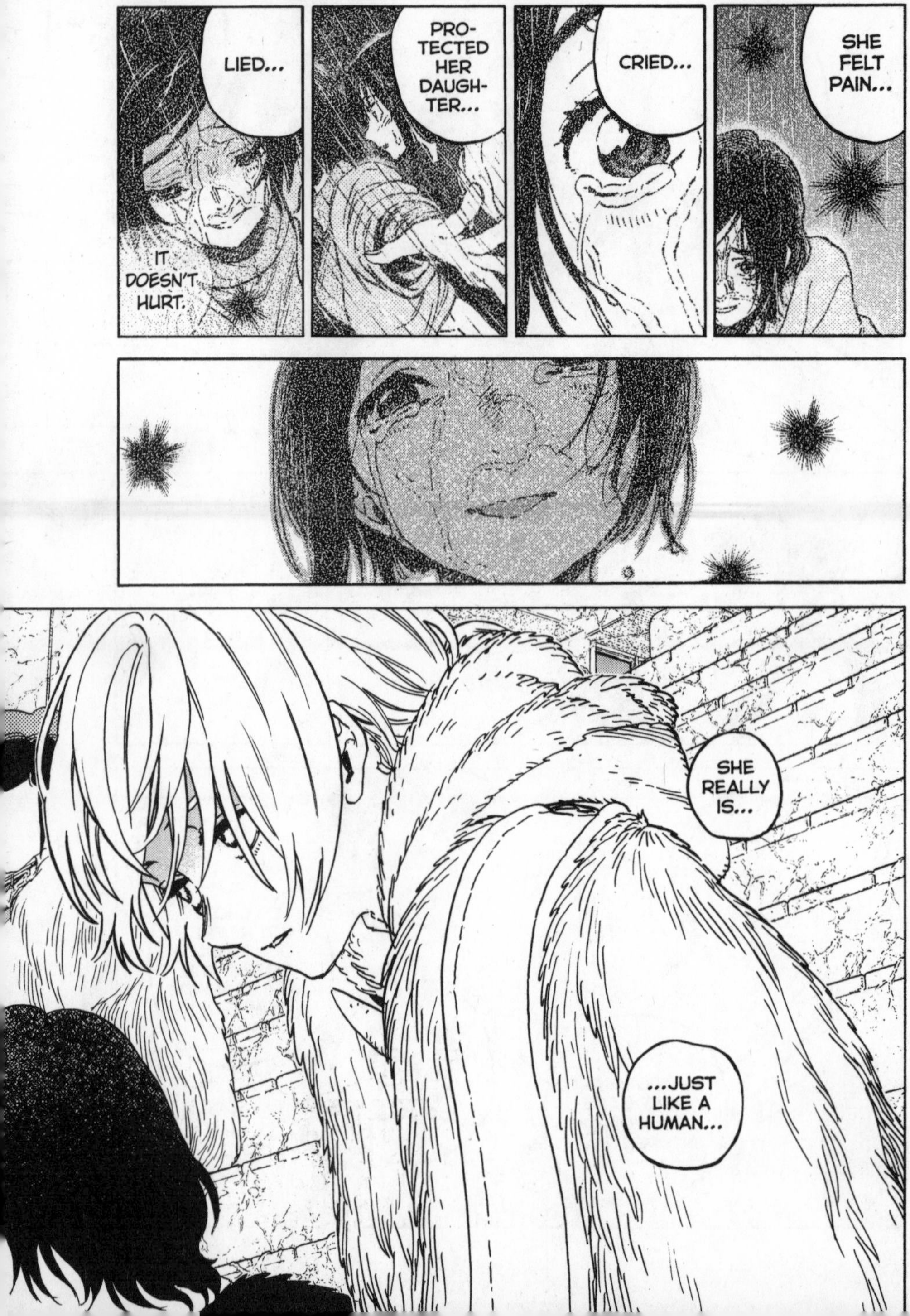
SHE FELT PAIN...
CRIED...
PROTECTED HER DAUGHTER...
LIED...
IT DOESN'T HURT.
SHE REALLY IS...
...JUST LIKE A HUMAN...

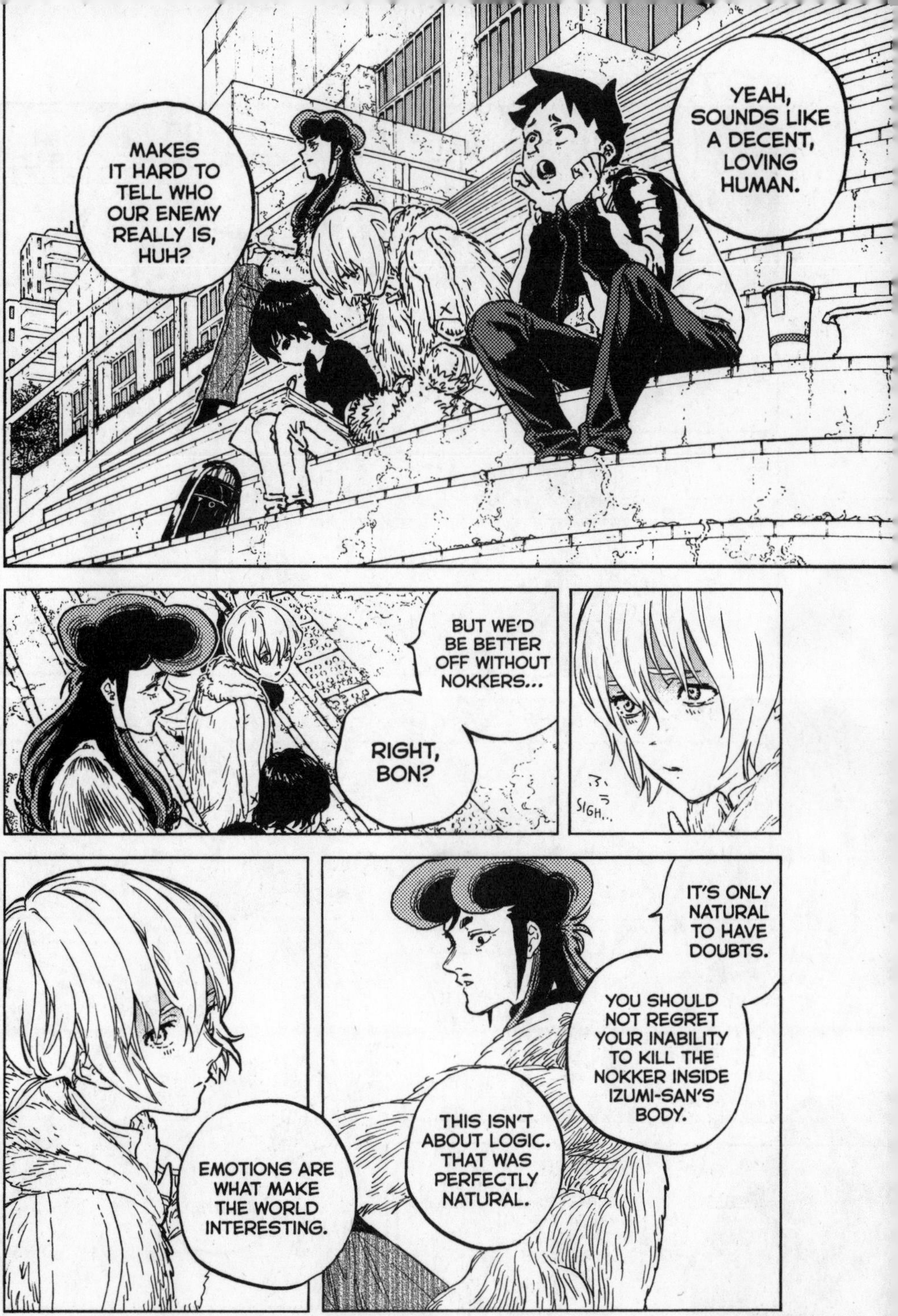
YEAH, SOUNDS LIKE A DECENT, LOVING HUMAN.
MAKES IT HARD TO TELL WHO OUR ENEMY REALLY IS, HUH?
SIGH...
BUT WE'D BE BETTER OFF WITHOUT NOKKERS...
RIGHT, BON?
IT'S ONLY NATURAL TO HAVE DOUBTS.
YOU SHOULD NOT REGRET YOUR INABILITY TO KILL THE NOKKER INSIDE IZUMI-SAN'S BODY.
THIS ISN'T ABOUT LOGIC. THAT WAS PERFECTLY NATURAL.
EMOTIONS ARE WHAT MAKE THE WORLD INTERESTING.

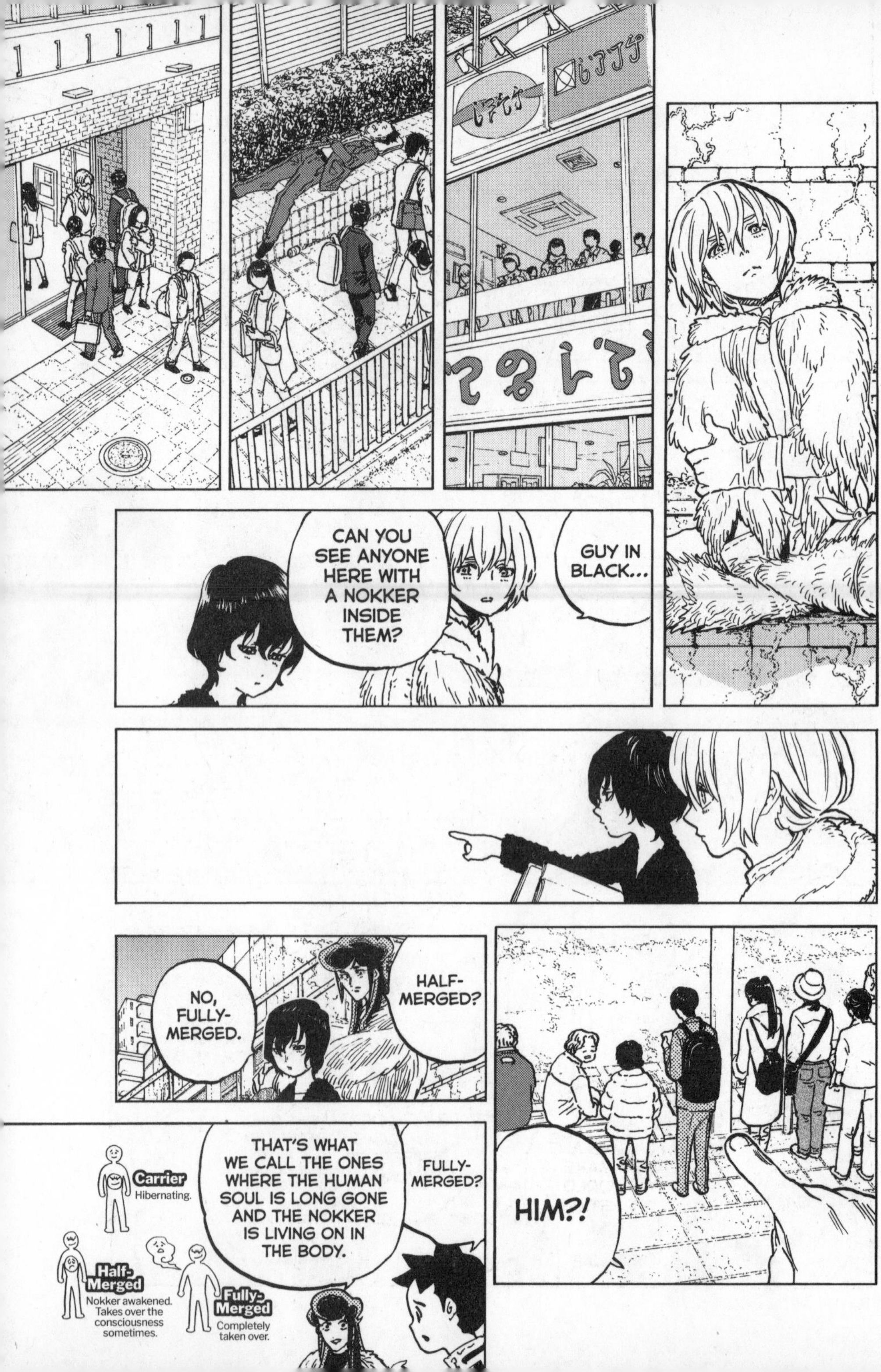

GUY IN BLACK...
CAN YOU SEE ANYONE HERE WITH A NOKKER INSIDE THEM?
HIM?!
HALF-MERGED?
NO, FULLY-MERGED.
FULLY-MERGED?
THAT'S WHAT WE CALL THE ONES WHERE THE HUMAN SOUL IS LONG GONE AND THE NOKKER IS LIVING ON IN THE BODY.
Carrier
Hibernating.
Half-Merged
Nokker awakened. Takes over the consciousness sometimes.
Fully-Merged
Completely taken over.

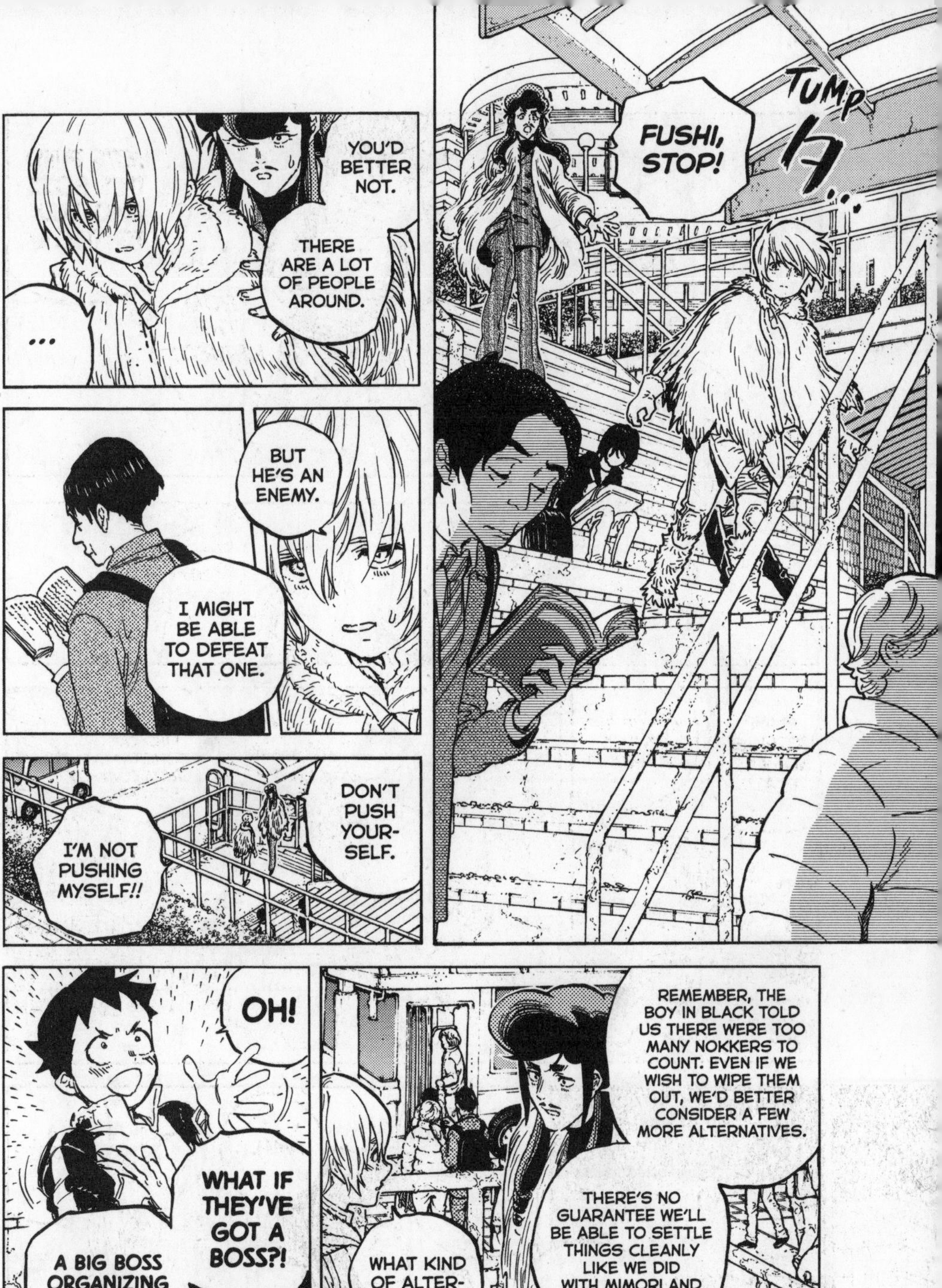
FUSHI, STOP!
TUMP
YOU'D BETTER NOT.
THERE ARE A LOT OF PEOPLE AROUND.
...
BUT HE'S AN ENEMY.
I MIGHT BE ABLE TO DEFEAT THAT ONE.
DON'T PUSH YOURSELF.
I'M NOT PUSHING MYSELF!!
REMEMBER, THE BOY IN BLACK TOLD US THERE WERE TOO MANY NOKKERS TO COUNT. EVEN IF WE WISH TO WIPE THEM OUT, WE'D BETTER CONSIDER A FEW MORE ALTERNATIVES.
THERE'S NO GUARANTEE WE'LL BE ABLE TO SETTLE THINGS CLEANLY LIKE WE DID WITH MIMORI AND HIROTOSHI.
WHAT KIND OF ALTERNATIVES?
OH!
WHAT IF THEY'VE GOT A BOSS?!
A BIG BOSS ORGANIZING THE NOKKERS!!

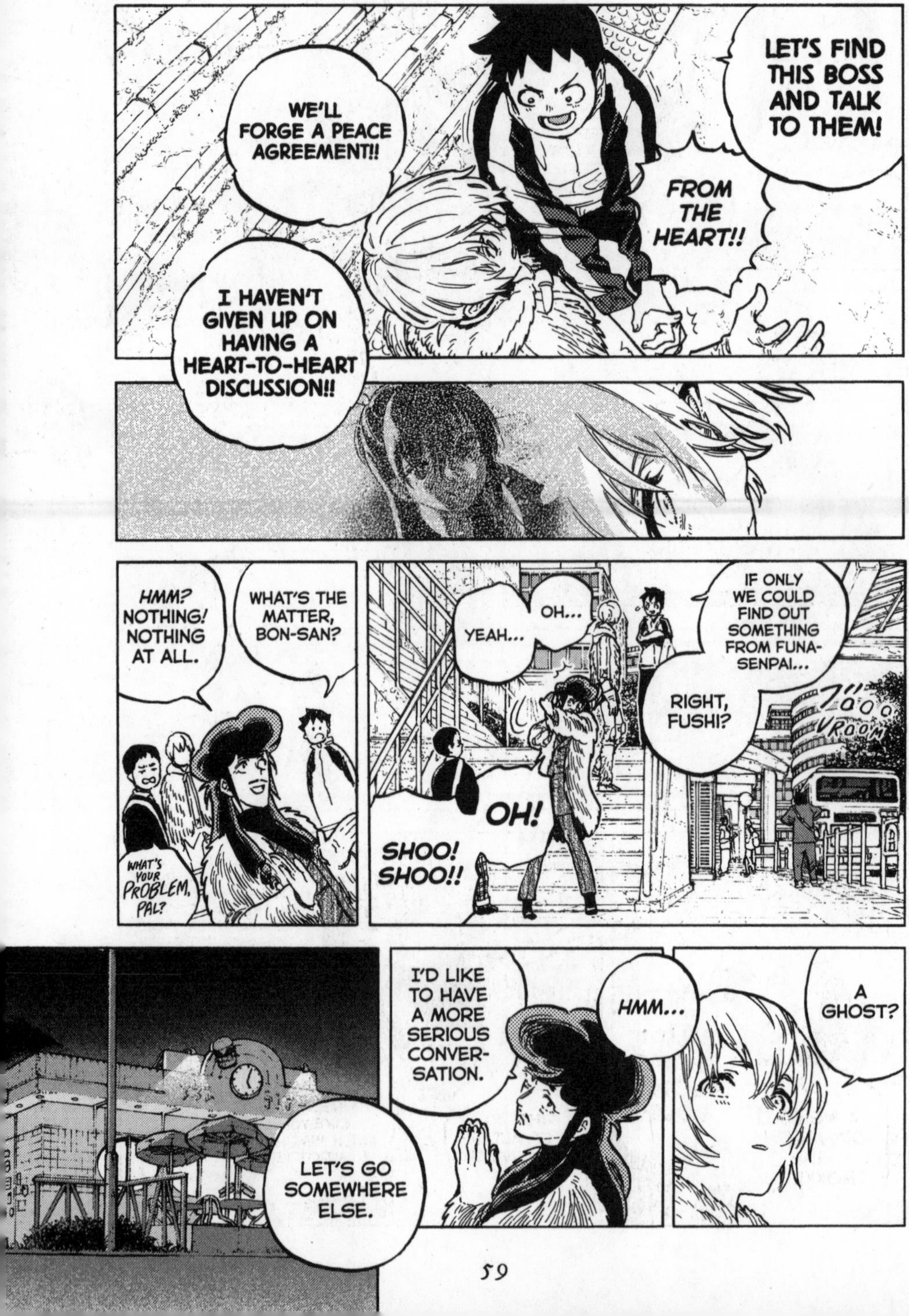
LET'S FIND THIS BOSS AND TALK TO THEM!
FROM THE HEART!!
WE'LL FORGE A PEACE AGREEMENT!!
I HAVEN'T GIVEN UP ON HAVING A HEART-TO-HEART DISCUSSION!!
IF ONLY WE COULD FIND OUT SOMETHING FROM FUNA-SENPAI...
RIGHT, FUSHI?
OH...
YEAH...
VROOM
OH!
SHOO! SHOO!!
WHAT'S THE MATTER, BON-SAN?
HMM? NOTHING! NOTHING AT ALL.
WHAT'S YOUR PROBLEM, PAL?
A GHOST?
HMM...
I'D LIKE TO HAVE A MORE SERIOUS CONVERSATION.
LET'S GO SOMEWHERE ELSE.

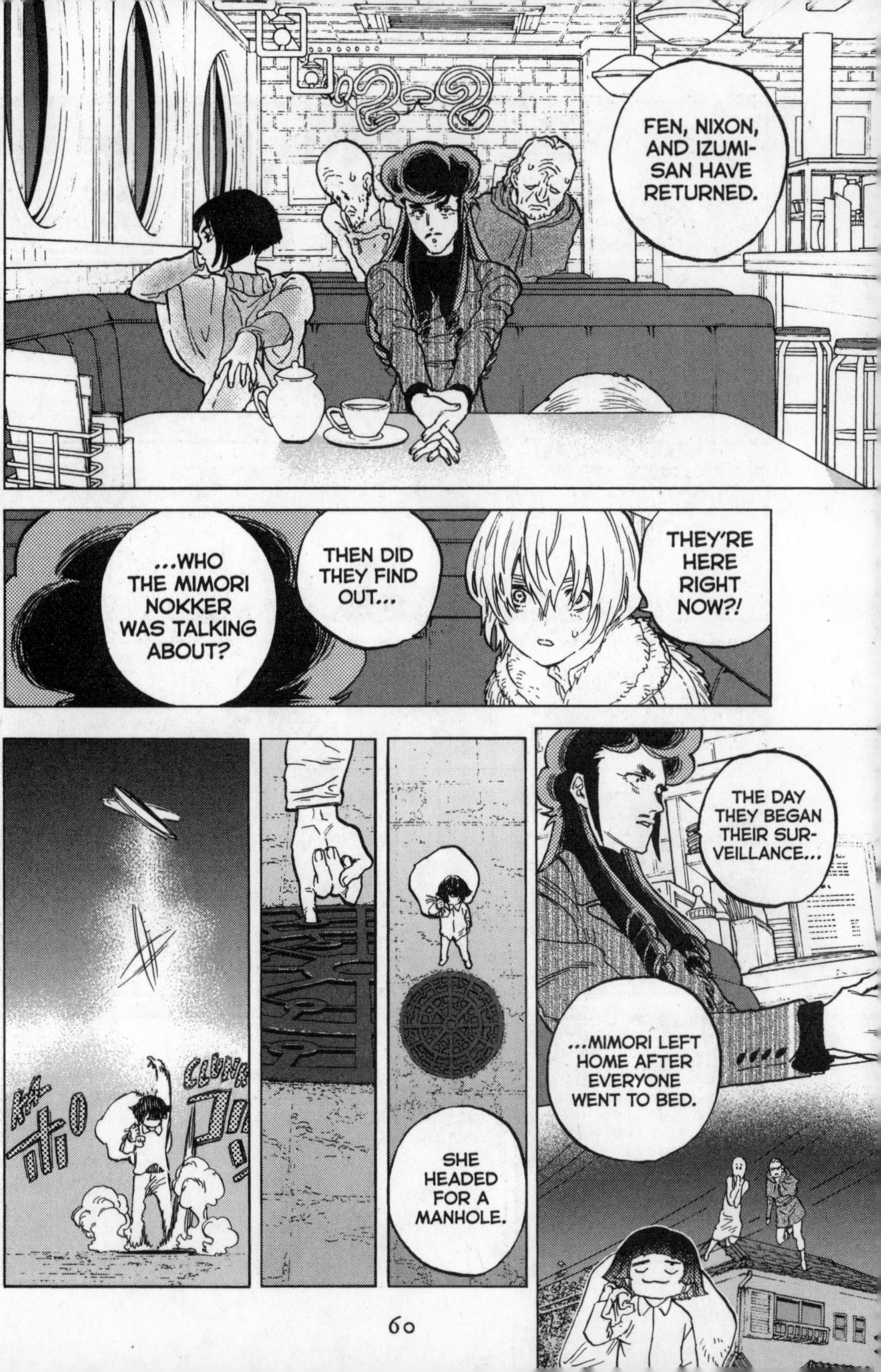
FEN, NIXON, AND IZUMI-SAN HAVE RETURNED.
THEY'RE HERE RIGHT NOW?!
THEN DID THEY FIND OUT...
...WHO THE MIMORI NOKKER WAS TALKING ABOUT?
THE DAY THEY BEGAN THEIR SURVEILLANCE...
...MIMORI LEFT HOME AFTER EVERYONE WENT TO BED.
SHE HEADED FOR A MANHOLE.
CLUNK

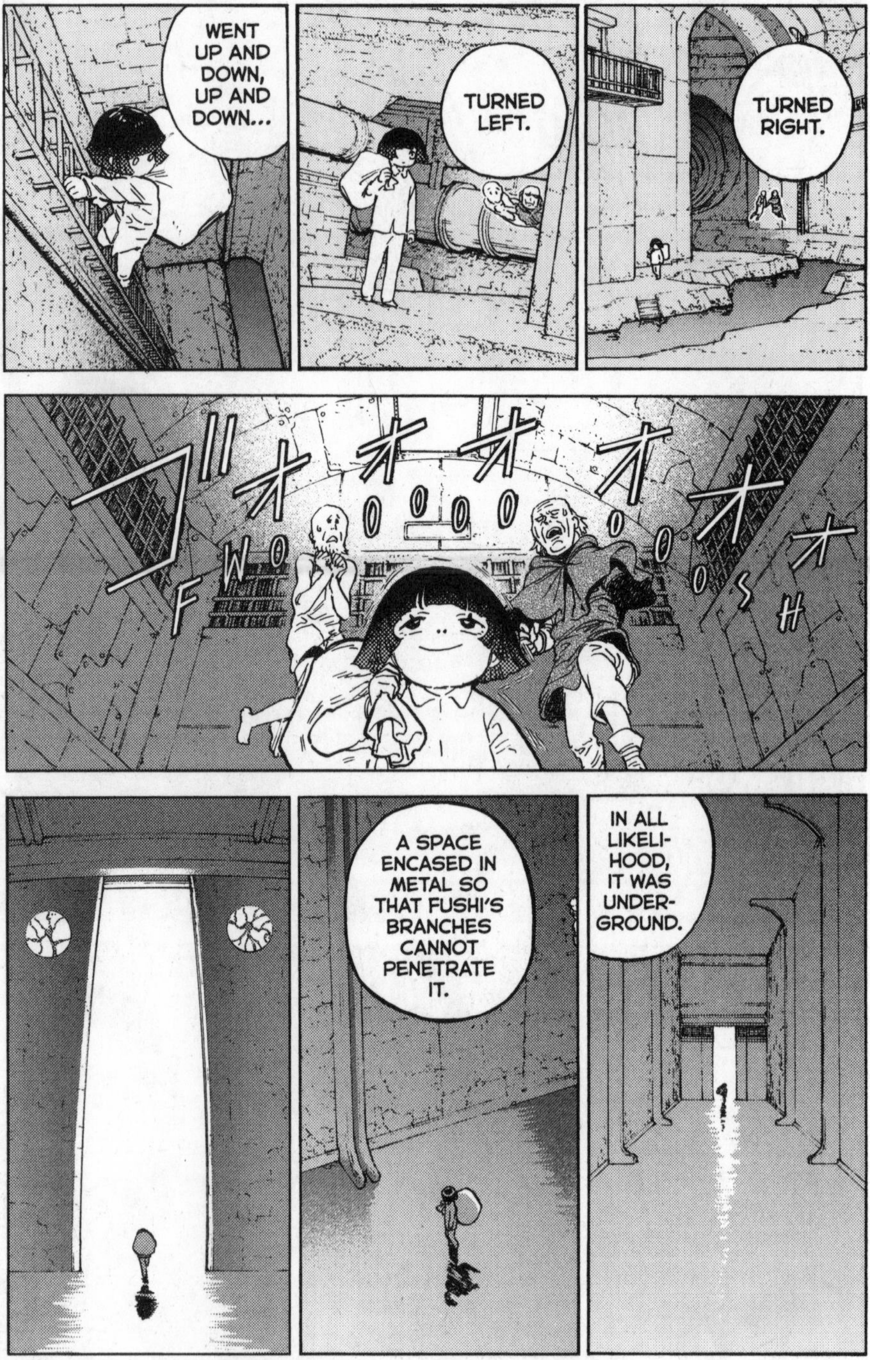
TURNED RIGHT.
TURNED LEFT.
WENT UP AND DOWN, UP AND DOWN...
ゴオオオオオオ
FWOOOOOOOOSH
IN ALL LIKELI-HOOD, IT WAS UNDER-GROUND.
A SPACE ENCASED IN METAL SO THAT FUSHI'S BRANCHES CANNOT PENETRATE IT.

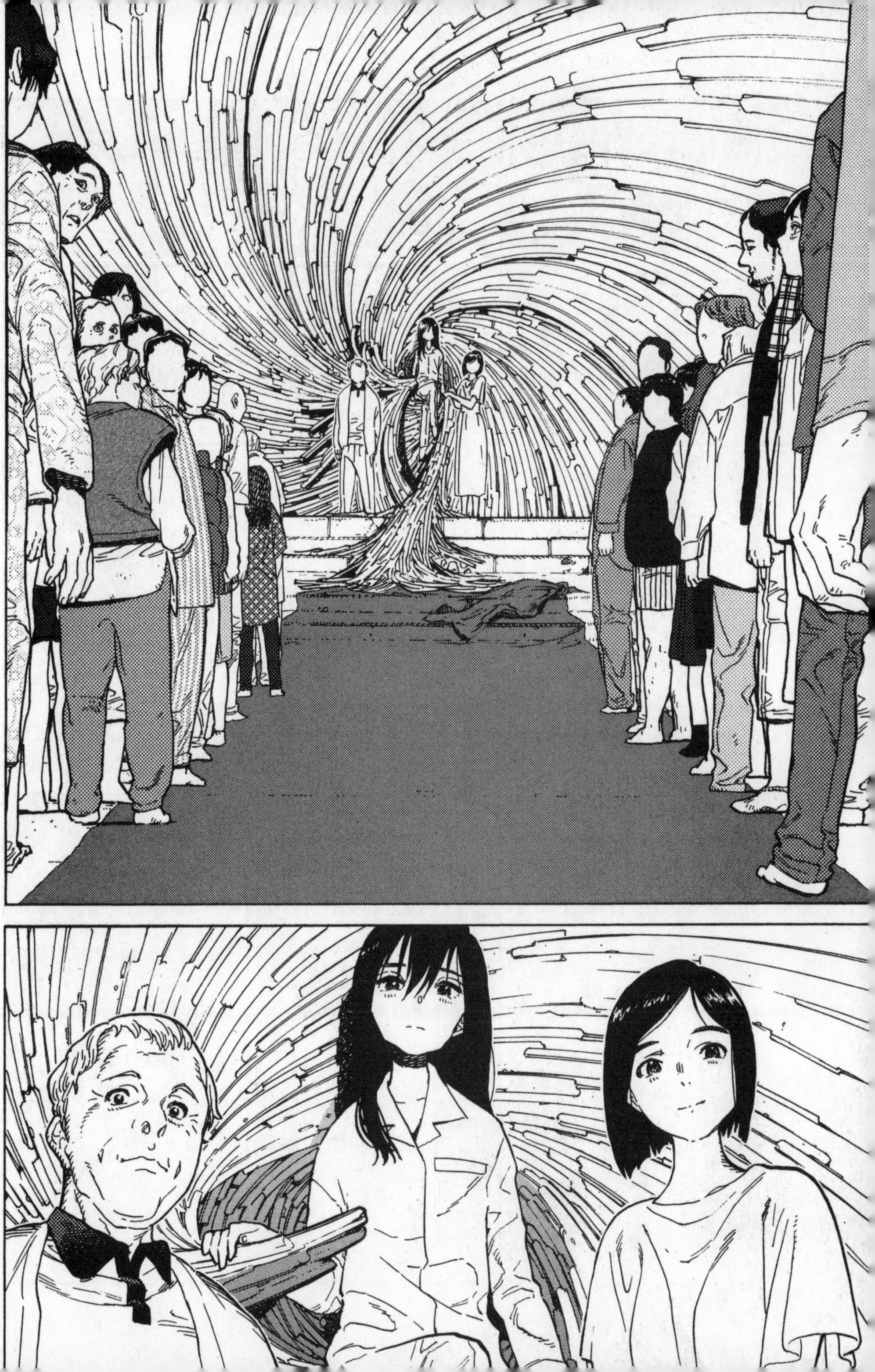

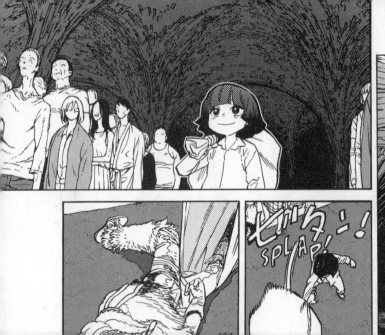

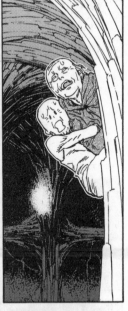

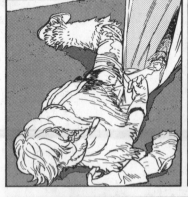

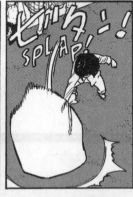

セバッ!!
SPLAP!

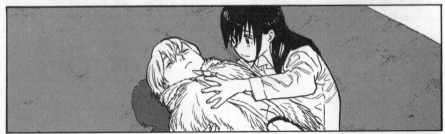

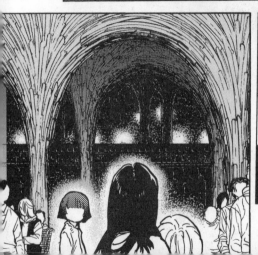

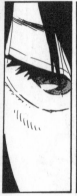

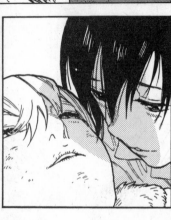

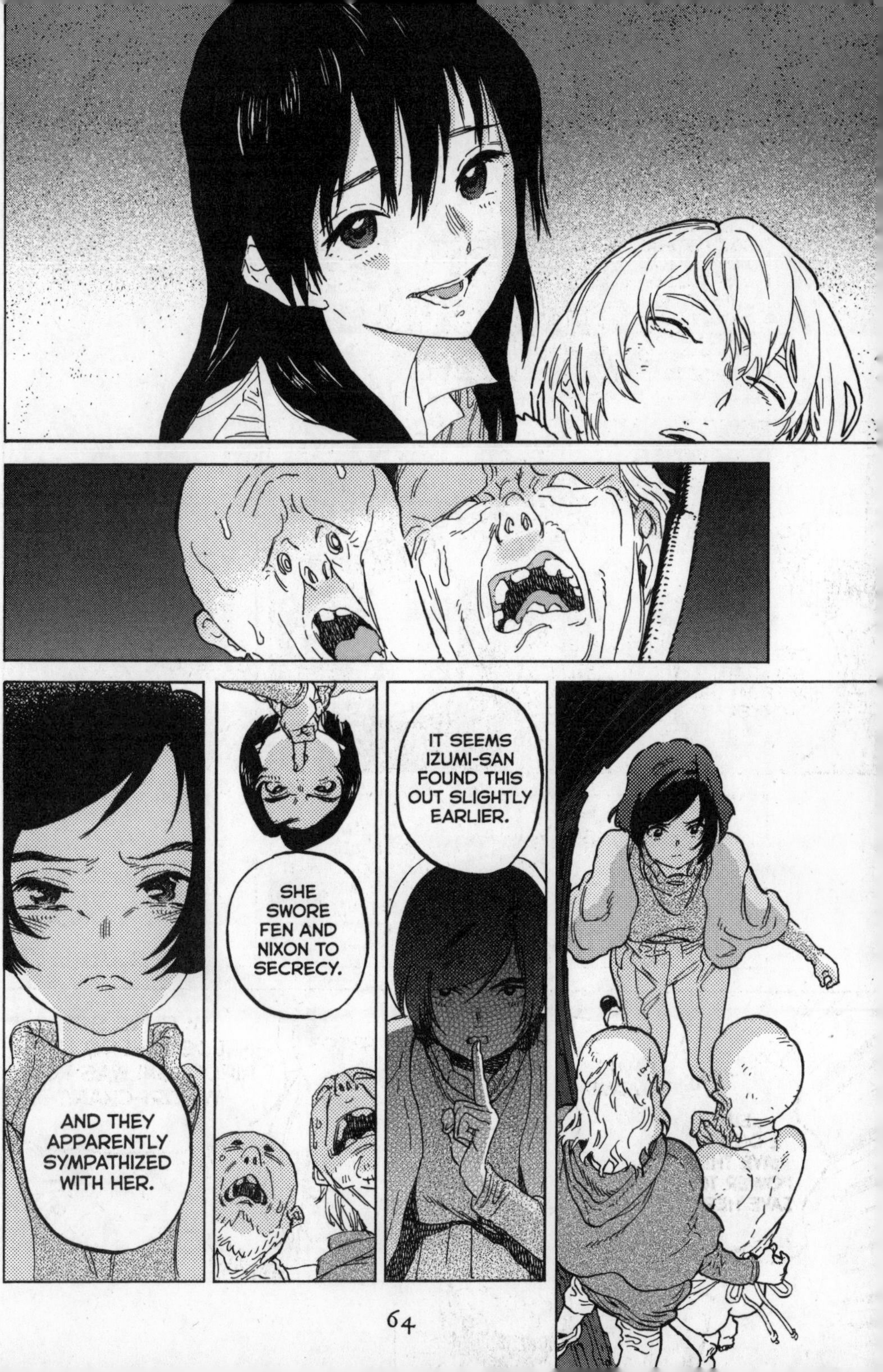
IT SEEMS IZUMI-SAN FOUND THIS OUT SLIGHTLY EARLIER.
SHE SWORE FEN AND NIXON TO SECRECY.
AND THEY APPARENTLY SYMPATHIZED WITH HER.

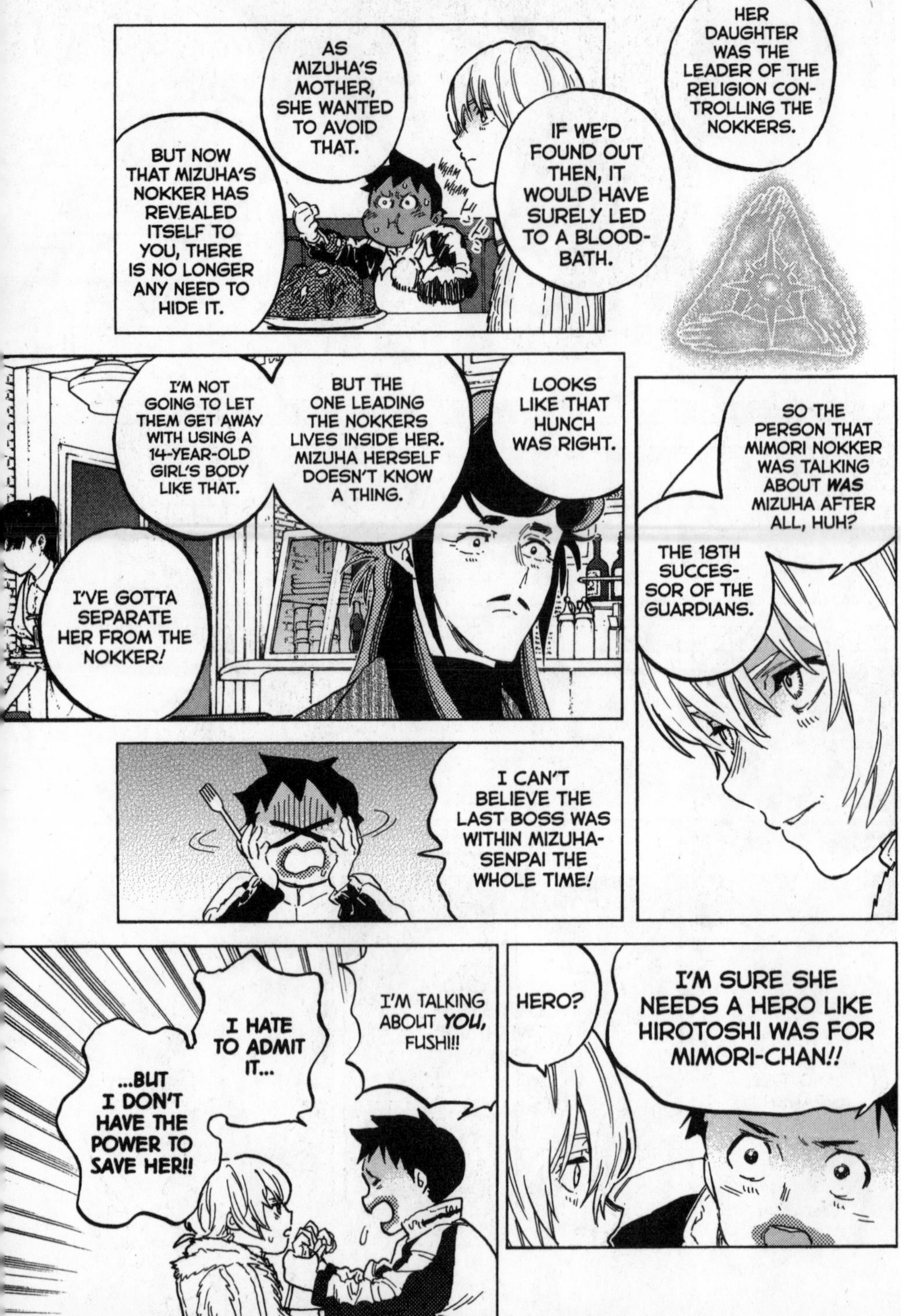
HER DAUGHTER WAS THE LEADER OF THE RELIGION CONTROLLING THE NOKKERS.
IF WE'D FOUND OUT THEN, IT WOULD HAVE SURELY LED TO A BLOODBATH.
AS MIZUHA'S MOTHER, SHE WANTED TO AVOID THAT.
WHAM WHAM
BUT NOW THAT MIZUHA'S NOKKER HAS REVEALED ITSELF TO YOU, THERE IS NO LONGER ANY NEED TO HIDE IT.
SO THE PERSON THAT MIMORI NOKKER WAS TALKING ABOUT *WAS* MIZUHA AFTER ALL, HUH?
THE 18TH SUCCESSOR OF THE GUARDIANS.
LOOKS LIKE THAT HUNCH WAS RIGHT.
BUT THE ONE LEADING THE NOKKERS LIVES INSIDE HER. MIZUHA HERSELF DOESN'T KNOW A THING.
I'M NOT GOING TO LET THEM GET AWAY WITH USING A 14-YEAR-OLD GIRL'S BODY LIKE THAT.
I'VE GOTTA SEPARATE HER FROM THE NOKKER!
I CAN'T BELIEVE THE LAST BOSS WAS WITHIN MIZUHA-SENPAI THE WHOLE TIME!
I'M SURE SHE NEEDS A HERO LIKE HIROTOSHI WAS FOR MIMORI-CHAN!!
HERO?
I'M TALKING ABOUT *YOU*, FUSHI!!
I HATE TO ADMIT IT...
...BUT I DON'T HAVE THE POWER TO SAVE HER!!

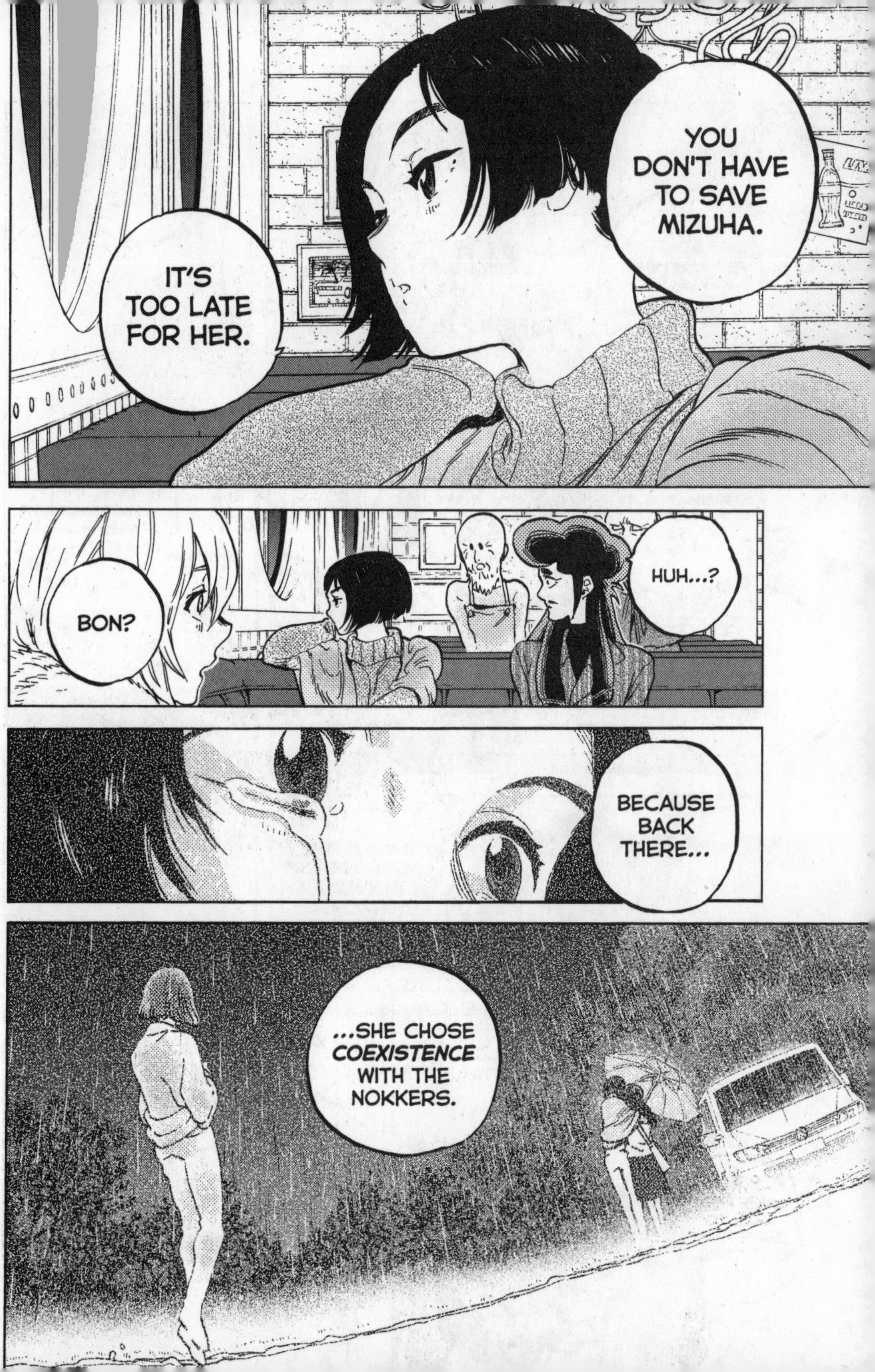
YOU DON'T HAVE TO SAVE MIZUHA.
IT'S TOO LATE FOR HER.
HUH...?
BON?
BECAUSE BACK THERE...
...SHE CHOSE *COEXISTENCE* WITH THE NOKKERS.

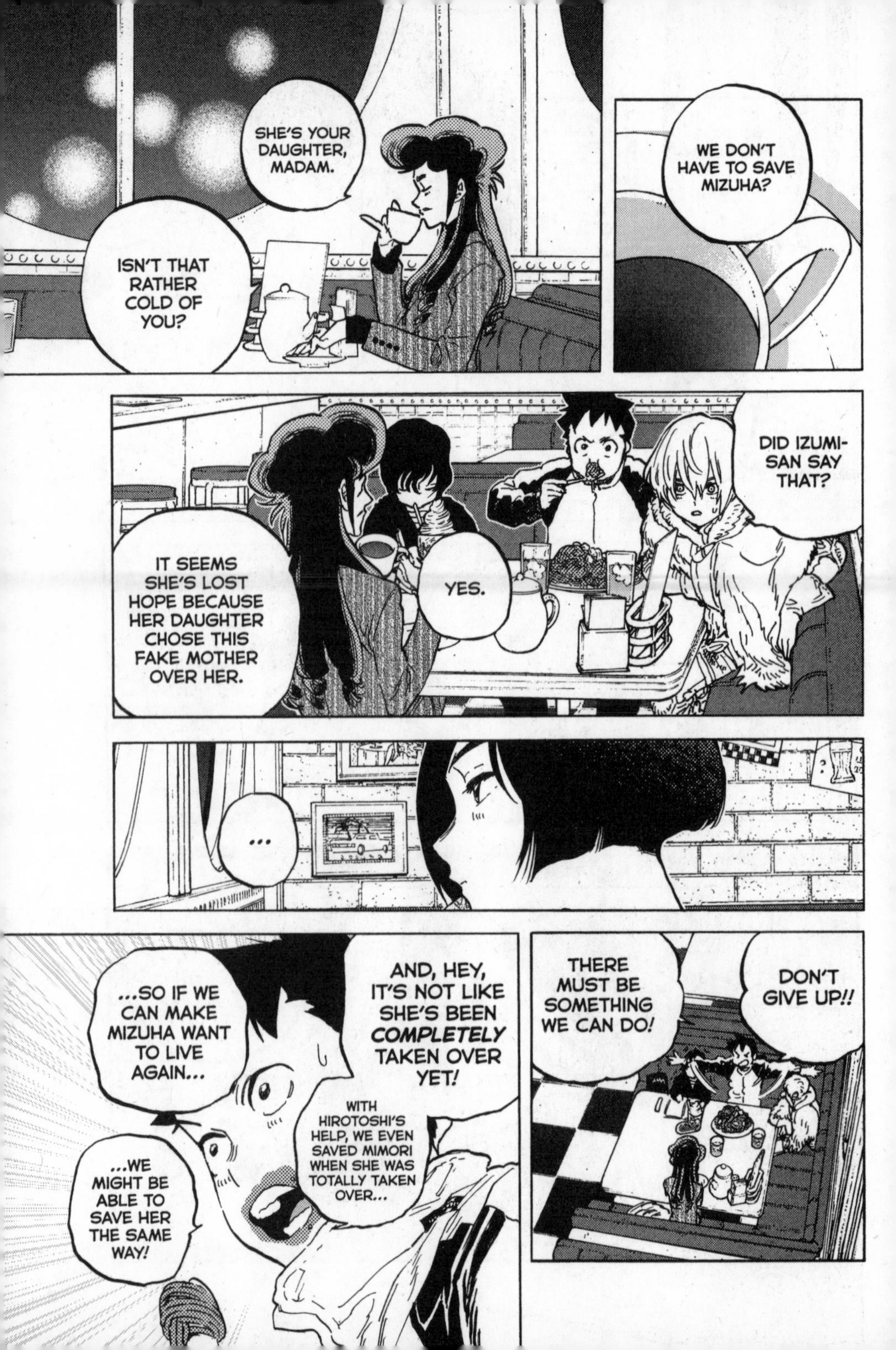
WE DON'T HAVE TO SAVE MIZUHA?
SHE'S YOUR DAUGHTER, MADAM.
ISN'T THAT RATHER COLD OF YOU?
DID IZUMI-SAN SAY THAT?
YES.
IT SEEMS SHE'S LOST HOPE BECAUSE HER DAUGHTER CHOSE THIS FAKE MOTHER OVER HER.
...
DON'T GIVE UP!!
THERE MUST BE SOMETHING WE CAN DO!
AND, HEY, IT'S NOT LIKE SHE'S BEEN *COMPLETELY* TAKEN OVER YET!
WITH HIROTOSHI'S HELP, WE EVEN SAVED MIMORI WHEN SHE WAS TOTALLY TAKEN OVER...
...SO IF WE CAN MAKE MIZUHA WANT TO LIVE AGAIN...
...WE MIGHT BE ABLE TO SAVE HER THE SAME WAY!

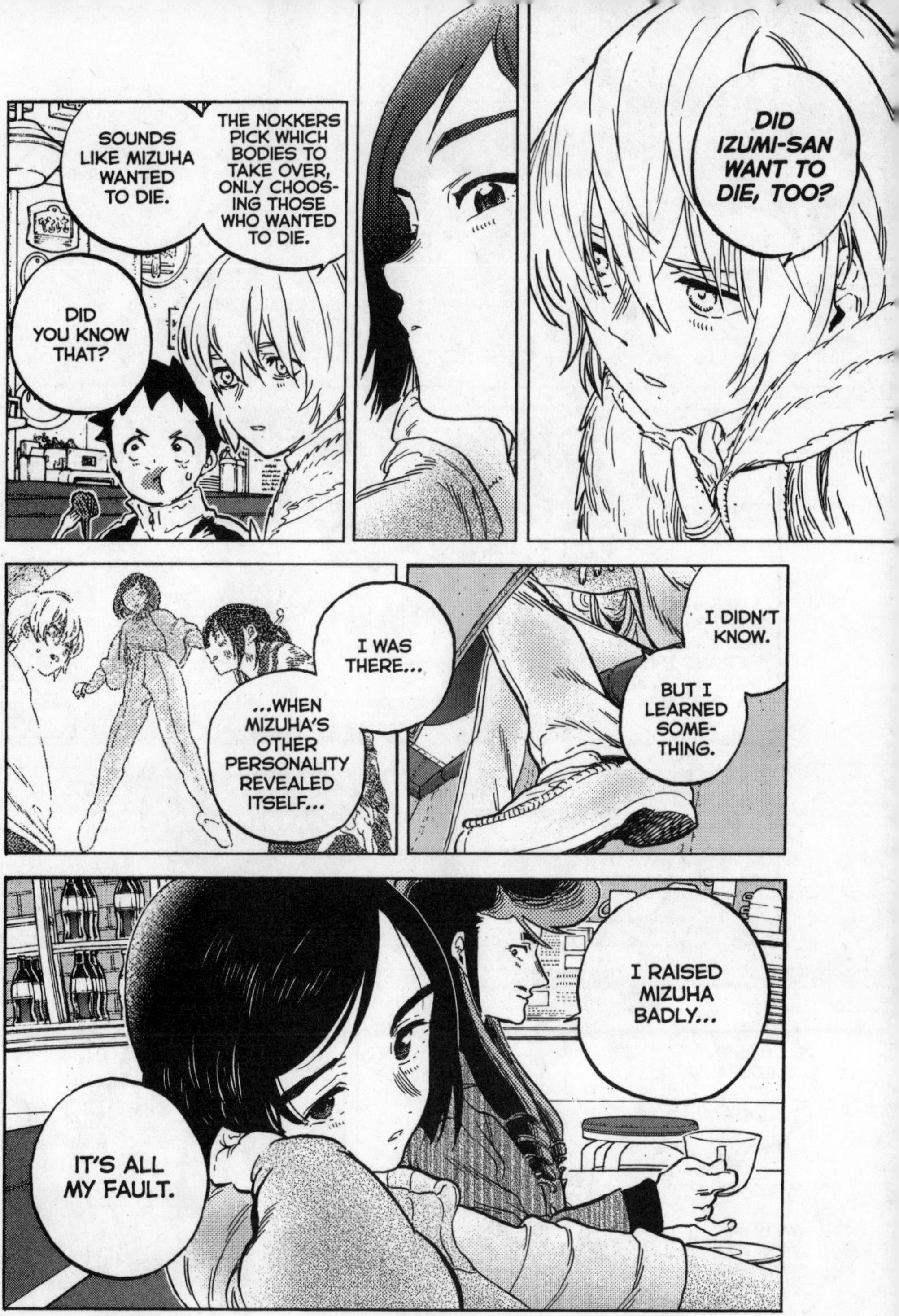
DID IZUMI-SAN WANT TO DIE, TOO?
THE NOKKERS PICK WHICH BODIES TO TAKE OVER, ONLY CHOOS-ING THOSE WHO WANTED TO DIE.
SOUNDS LIKE MIZUHA WANTED TO DIE.
DID YOU KNOW THAT?
I DIDN'T KNOW.
BUT I LEARNED SOME-THING.
I WAS THERE...
...WHEN MIZUHA'S OTHER PERSONALITY REVEALED ITSELF...
I RAISED MIZUHA BADLY...
IT'S ALL MY FAULT.

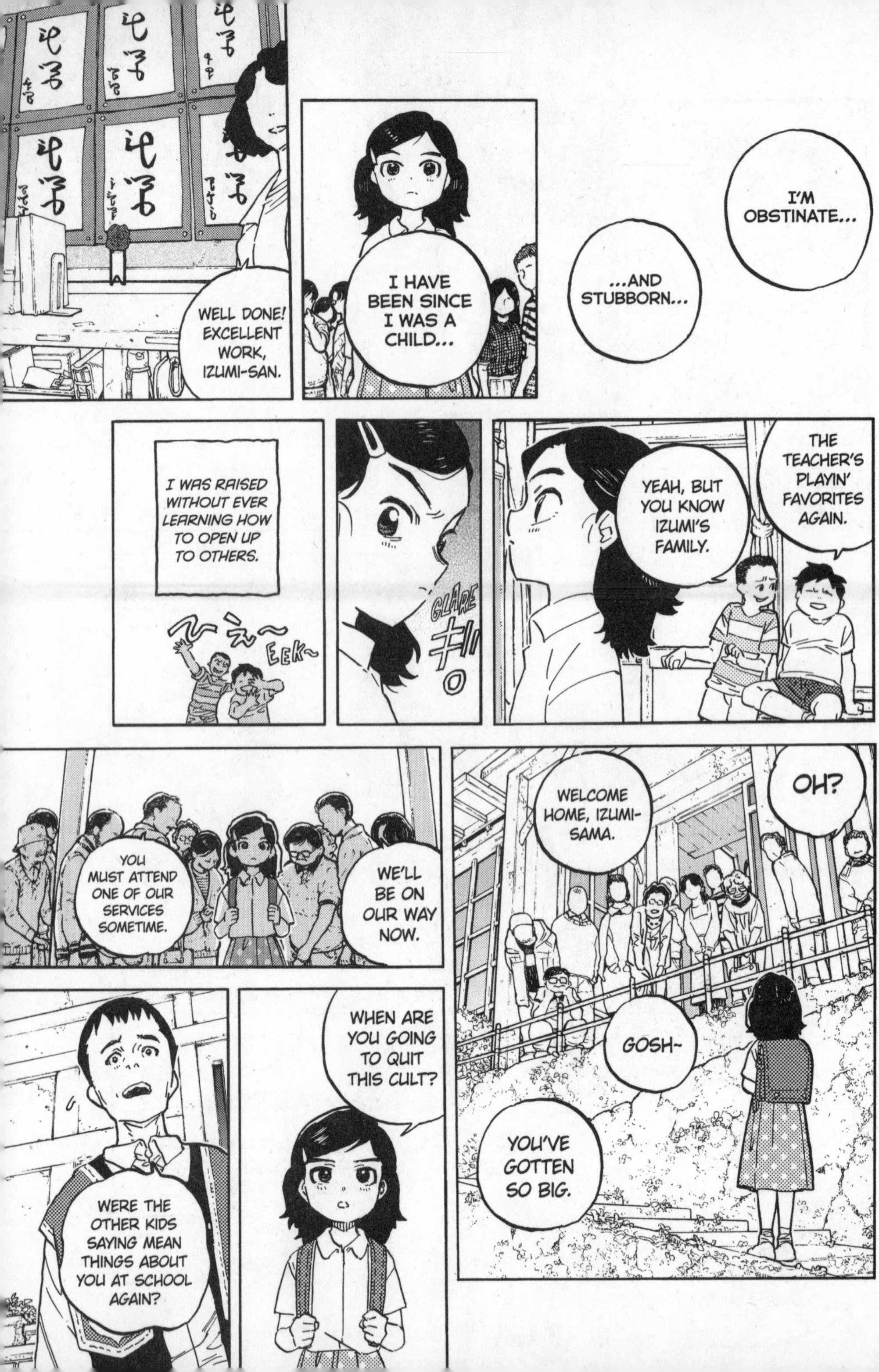

I'M OBSTINATE...
...AND STUBBORN...
I HAVE BEEN SINCE I WAS A CHILD...
WELL DONE! EXCELLENT WORK, IZUMI-SAN.
THE TEACHER'S PLAYIN' FAVORITES AGAIN.
YEAH, BUT YOU KNOW IZUMI'S FAMILY.
GLARE
キッ
I WAS RAISED WITHOUT EVER LEARNING HOW TO OPEN UP TO OTHERS.
ひえ~
EEK~
OH?
WELCOME HOME, IZUMI-SAMA.
GOSH~
YOU'VE GOTTEN SO BIG.
WE'LL BE ON OUR WAY NOW.
YOU MUST ATTEND ONE OF OUR SERVICES SOMETIME.
WHEN ARE YOU GOING TO QUIT THIS CULT?
WERE THE OTHER KIDS SAYING MEAN THINGS ABOUT YOU AT SCHOOL AGAIN?

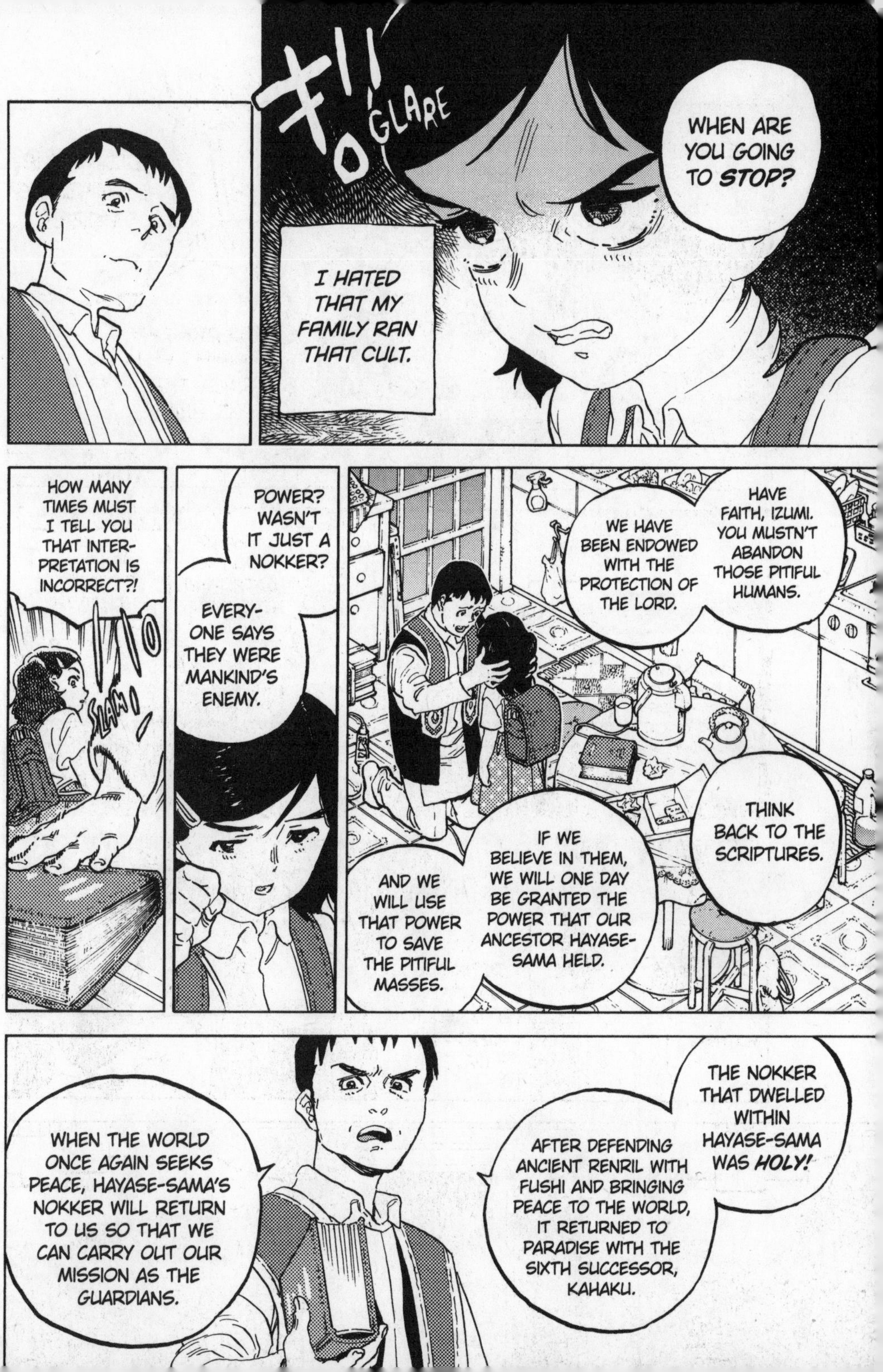
GLARE
WHEN ARE YOU GOING TO *STOP?*
I HATED THAT MY FAMILY RAN THAT CULT.
HAVE FAITH, IZUMI. YOU MUSTN'T ABANDON THOSE PITIFUL HUMANS.
WE HAVE BEEN ENDOWED WITH THE PROTECTION OF THE LORD.
THINK BACK TO THE SCRIPTURES.
IF WE BELIEVE IN THEM, WE WILL ONE DAY BE GRANTED THE POWER THAT OUR ANCESTOR HAYASE-SAMA HELD.
AND WE WILL USE THAT POWER TO SAVE THE PITIFUL MASSES.
POWER? WASN'T IT JUST A NOKKER?
EVERY-ONE SAYS THEY WERE MANKIND'S ENEMY.
HOW MANY TIMES MUST I TELL YOU THAT INTER-PRETATION IS INCORRECT?!
SLAM
THE NOKKER THAT DWELLED WITHIN HAYASE-SAMA WAS *HOLY!*
AFTER DEFENDING ANCIENT RENRIL WITH FUSHI AND BRINGING PEACE TO THE WORLD, IT RETURNED TO PARADISE WITH THE SIXTH SUCCESSOR, KAHAKU.
WHEN THE WORLD ONCE AGAIN SEEKS PEACE, HAYASE-SAMA'S NOKKER WILL RETURN TO US SO THAT WE CAN CARRY OUT OUR MISSION AS THE GUARDIANS.

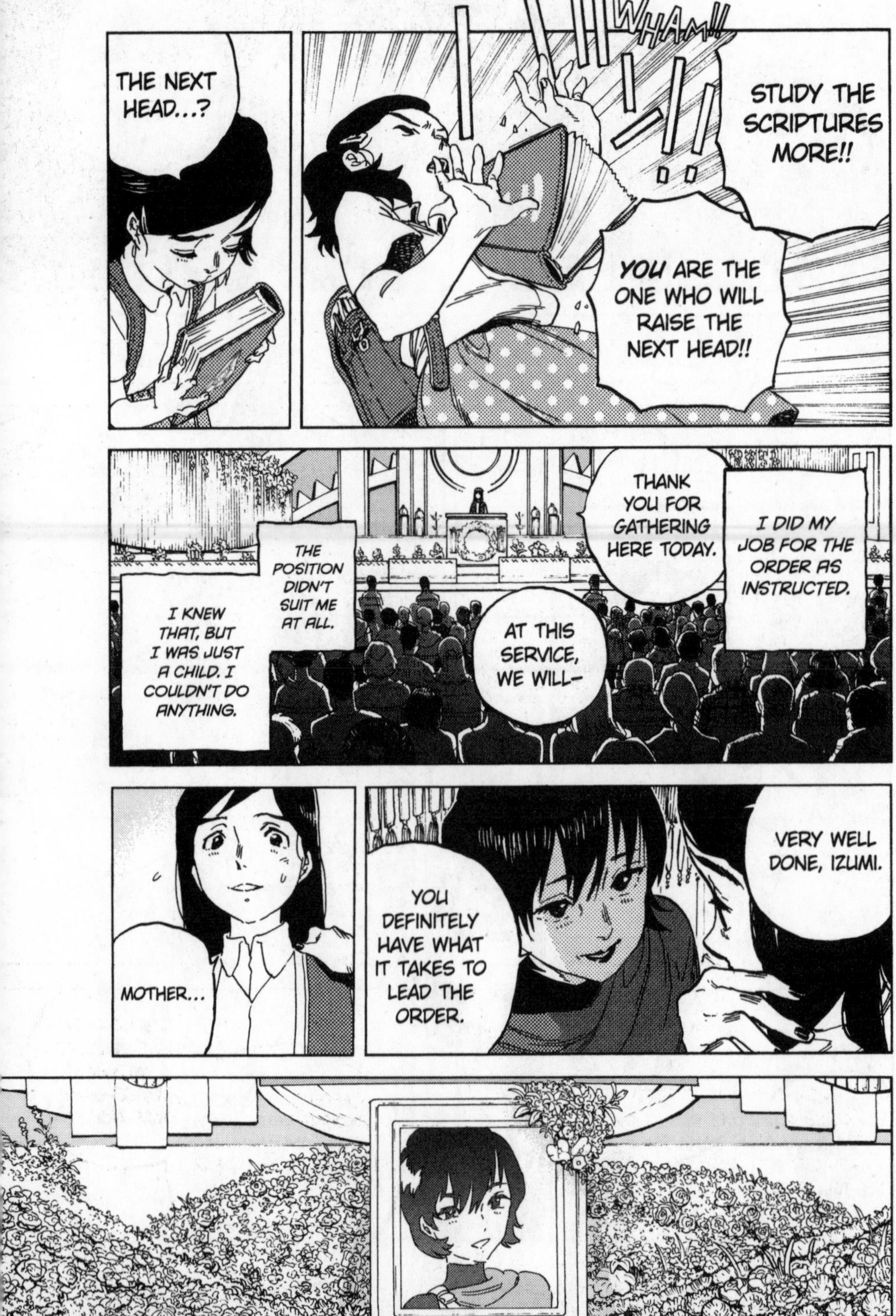
WHAM!!
STUDY THE SCRIPTURES MORE!!
YOU ARE THE ONE WHO WILL RAISE THE NEXT HEAD!!
THE NEXT HEAD...?
I DID MY JOB FOR THE ORDER AS INSTRUCTED.
THANK YOU FOR GATHERING HERE TODAY.
AT THIS SERVICE, WE WILL-
THE POSITION DIDN'T SUIT ME AT ALL.
I KNEW THAT, BUT I WAS JUST A CHILD. I COULDN'T DO ANYTHING.
VERY WELL DONE, IZUMI.
YOU DEFINITELY HAVE WHAT IT TAKES TO LEAD THE ORDER.
MOTHER...

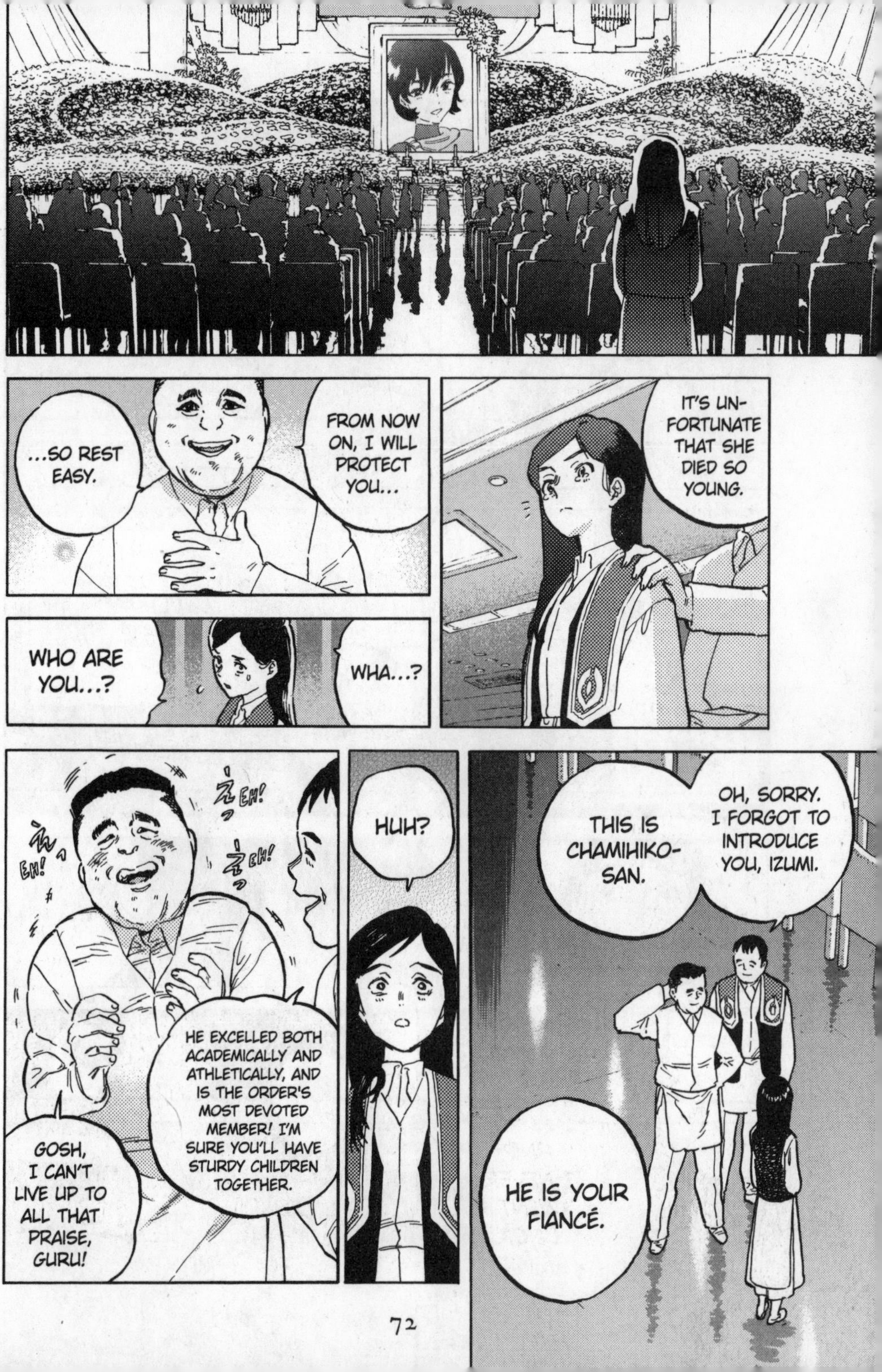
IT'S UN-FORTUNATE THAT SHE DIED SO YOUNG.
FROM NOW ON, I WILL PROTECT YOU...
...SO REST EASY.
WHA...?
WHO ARE YOU...?
OH, SORRY. I FORGOT TO INTRODUCE YOU, IZUMI.
THIS IS CHAMIHIKO-SAN.
HE IS YOUR FIANCÉ.
HUH?
EH!
EH!
EH!
HE EXCELLED BOTH ACADEMICALLY AND ATHLETICALLY, AND IS THE ORDER'S MOST DEVOTED MEMBER! I'M SURE YOU'LL HAVE STURDY CHILDREN TOGETHER.
GOSH, I CAN'T LIVE UP TO ALL THAT PRAISE, GURU!

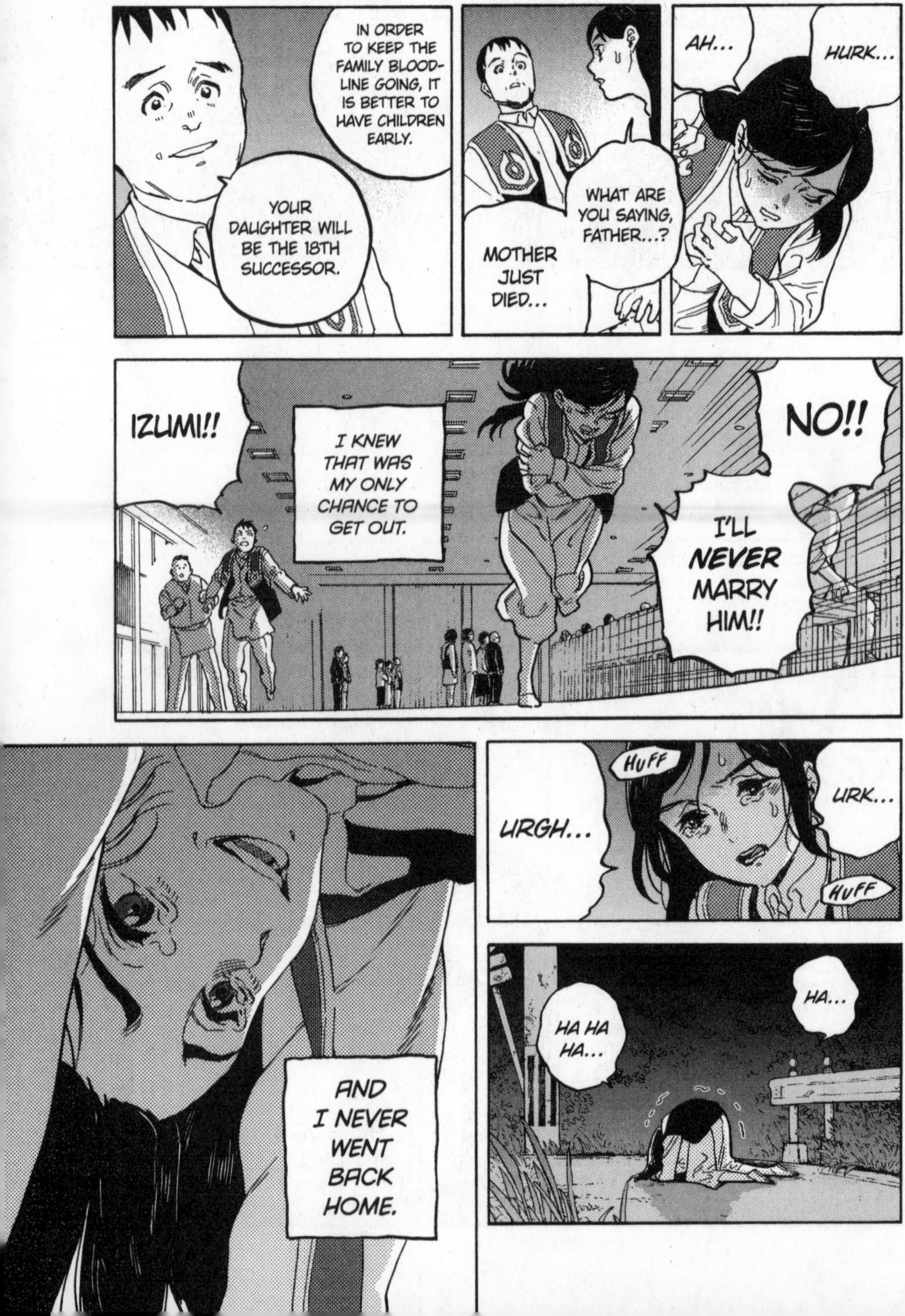
HURK...
AH...
WHAT ARE YOU SAYING, FATHER...?
MOTHER JUST DIED...
IN ORDER TO KEEP THE FAMILY BLOOD-LINE GOING, IT IS BETTER TO HAVE CHILDREN EARLY.
YOUR DAUGHTER WILL BE THE 18TH SUCCESSOR.
NO!!
I'LL NEVER MARRY HIM!!
I KNEW THAT WAS MY ONLY CHANCE TO GET OUT.
IZUMI!!
HUFF
URK...
URGH...
HUFF
HA...
HA HA HA...
AND I NEVER WENT BACK HOME.

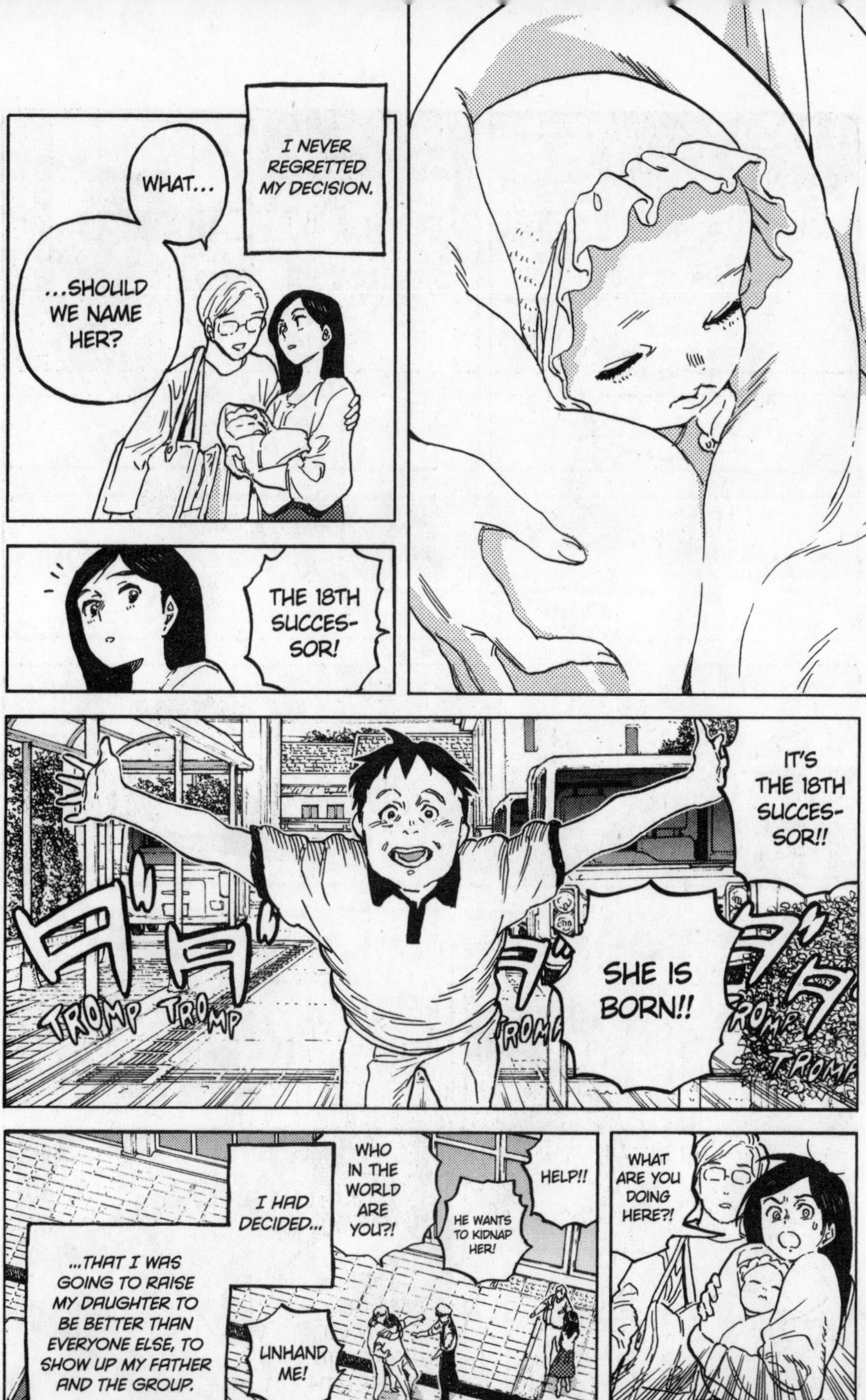

I NEVER REGRETTED MY DECISION.
WHAT...
...SHOULD WE NAME HER?
THE 18TH SUCCES-SOR!
IT'S THE 18TH SUCCES-SOR!!
SHE IS BORN!!
TROMP TROMP
TROMP
TROMP TROMP
WHAT ARE YOU DOING HERE?!
HELP!!
HE WANTS TO KIDNAP HER!
WHO IN THE WORLD ARE YOU?!
I HAD DECIDED...
...THAT I WAS GOING TO RAISE MY DAUGHTER TO BE BETTER THAN EVERYONE ELSE, TO SHOW UP MY FATHER AND THE GROUP.
UNHAND ME!

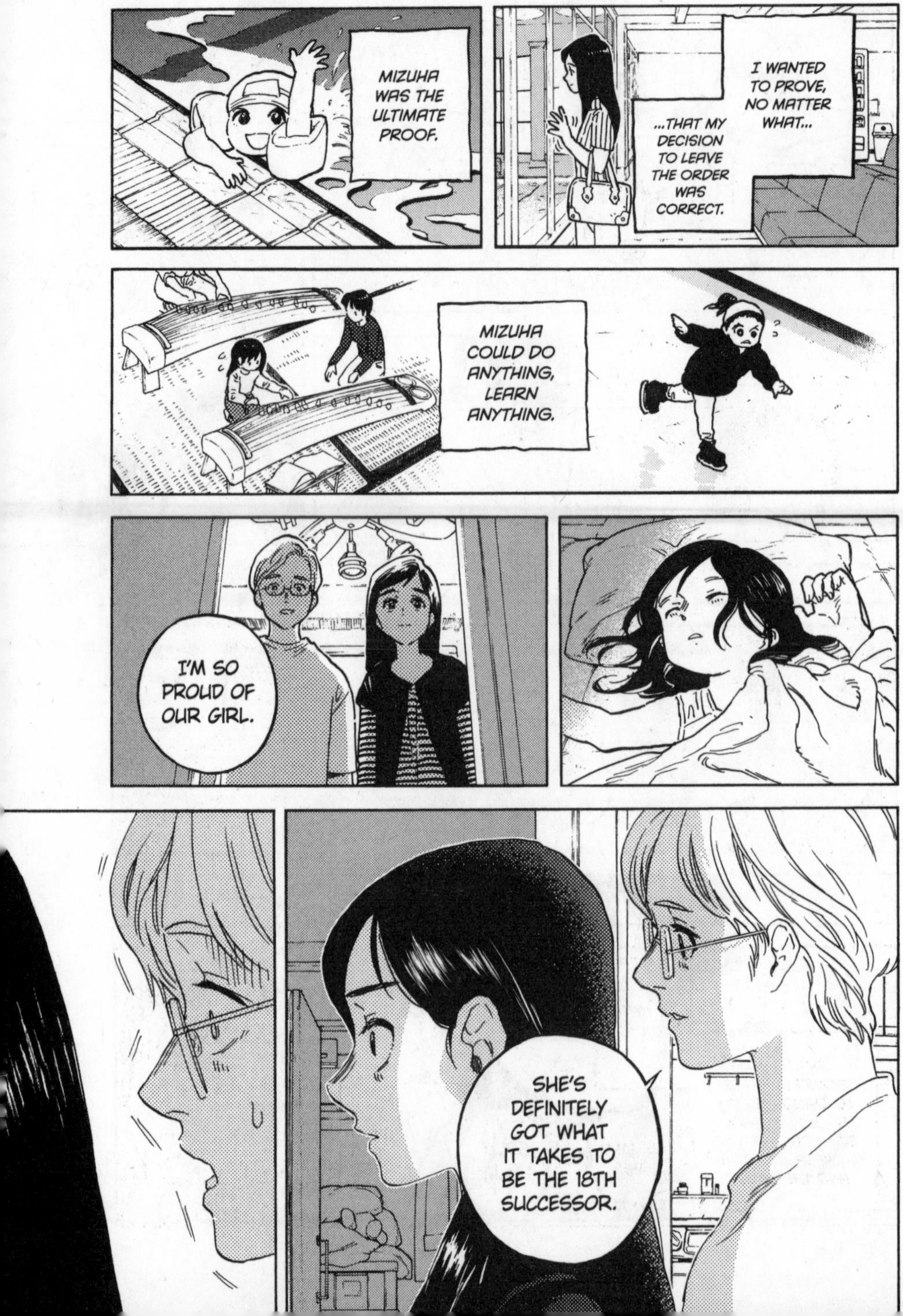
I WANTED TO PROVE, NO MATTER WHAT...
...THAT MY DECISION TO LEAVE THE ORDER WAS CORRECT.
MIZUHA WAS THE ULTIMATE PROOF.
MIZUHA COULD DO ANYTHING, LEARN ANYTHING.
I'M SO PROUD OF OUR GIRL.
SHE'S DEFINITELY GOT WHAT IT TAKES TO BE THE 18TH SUCCESSOR.

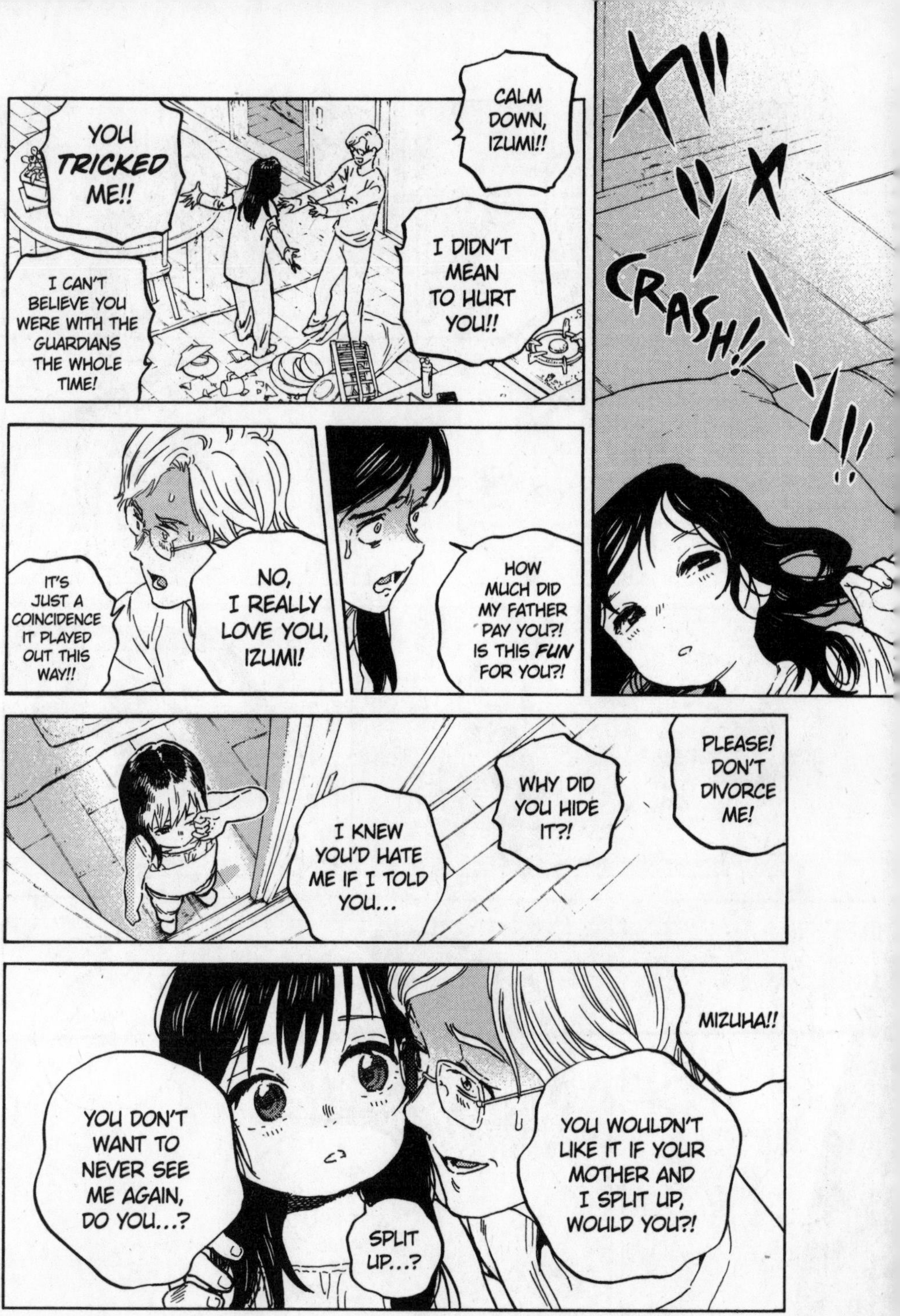
CRASH!!
CALM DOWN, IZUMI!!
YOU *TRICKED* ME!!
I DIDN'T MEAN TO HURT YOU!!
I CAN'T BELIEVE YOU WERE WITH THE GUARDIANS THE WHOLE TIME!
HOW MUCH DID MY FATHER PAY YOU?! IS THIS *FUN* FOR YOU?!
NO, I REALLY LOVE YOU, IZUMI!
IT'S JUST A COINCIDENCE IT PLAYED OUT THIS WAY!!
PLEASE! DON'T DIVORCE ME!
WHY DID YOU HIDE IT?!
I KNEW YOU'D HATE ME IF I TOLD YOU...
MIZUHA!!
YOU WOULDN'T LIKE IT IF YOUR MOTHER AND I SPLIT UP, WOULD YOU?!
YOU DON'T WANT TO NEVER SEE ME AGAIN, DO YOU...?
SPLIT UP...?

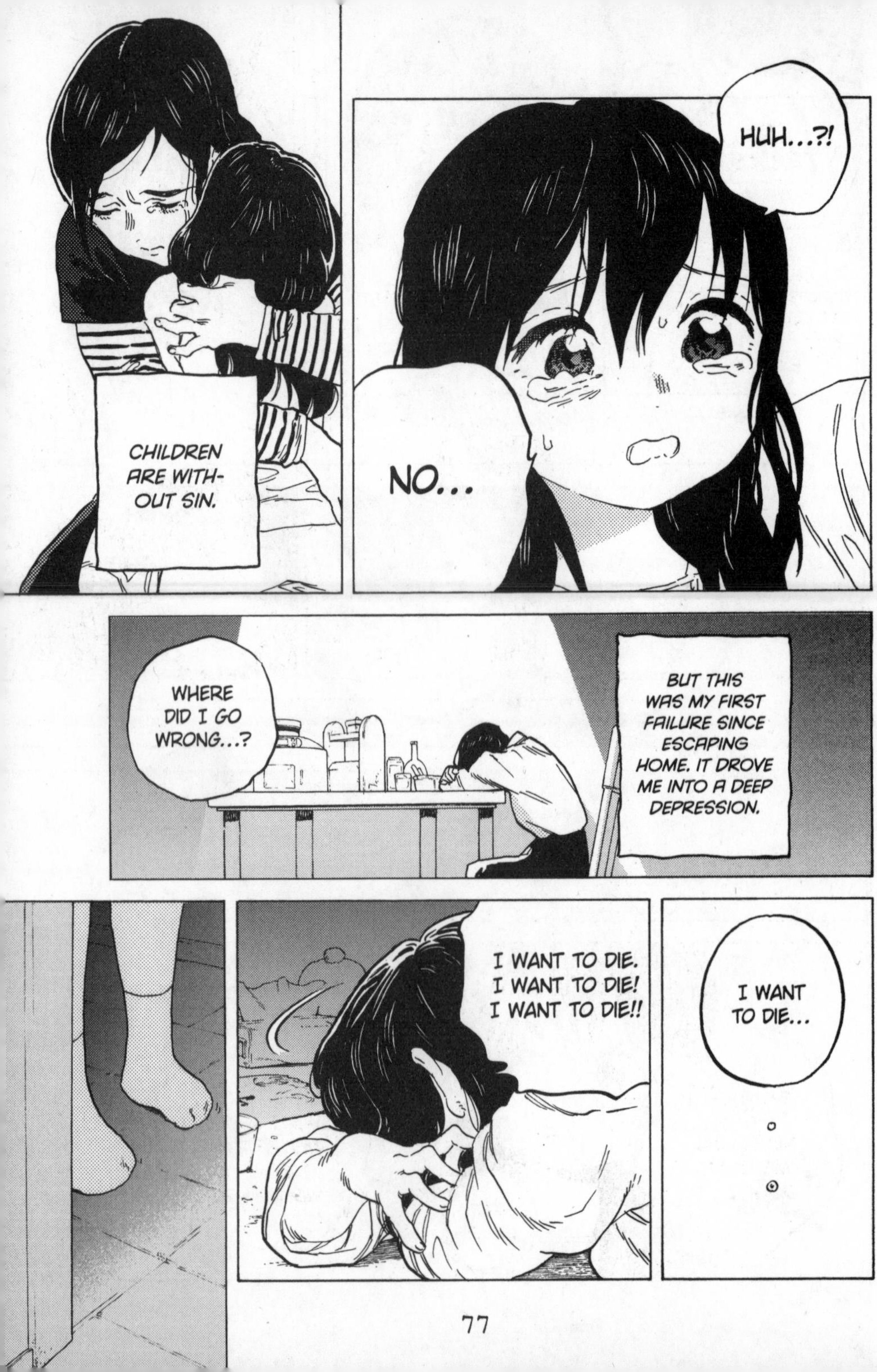
HUH...?!
NO...
CHILDREN ARE WITH-OUT SIN.
BUT THIS WAS MY FIRST FAILURE SINCE ESCAPING HOME. IT DROVE ME INTO A DEEP DEPRESSION.
WHERE DID I GO WRONG...?
I WANT TO DIE...
I WANT TO DIE. I WANT TO DIE! I WANT TO DIE!!

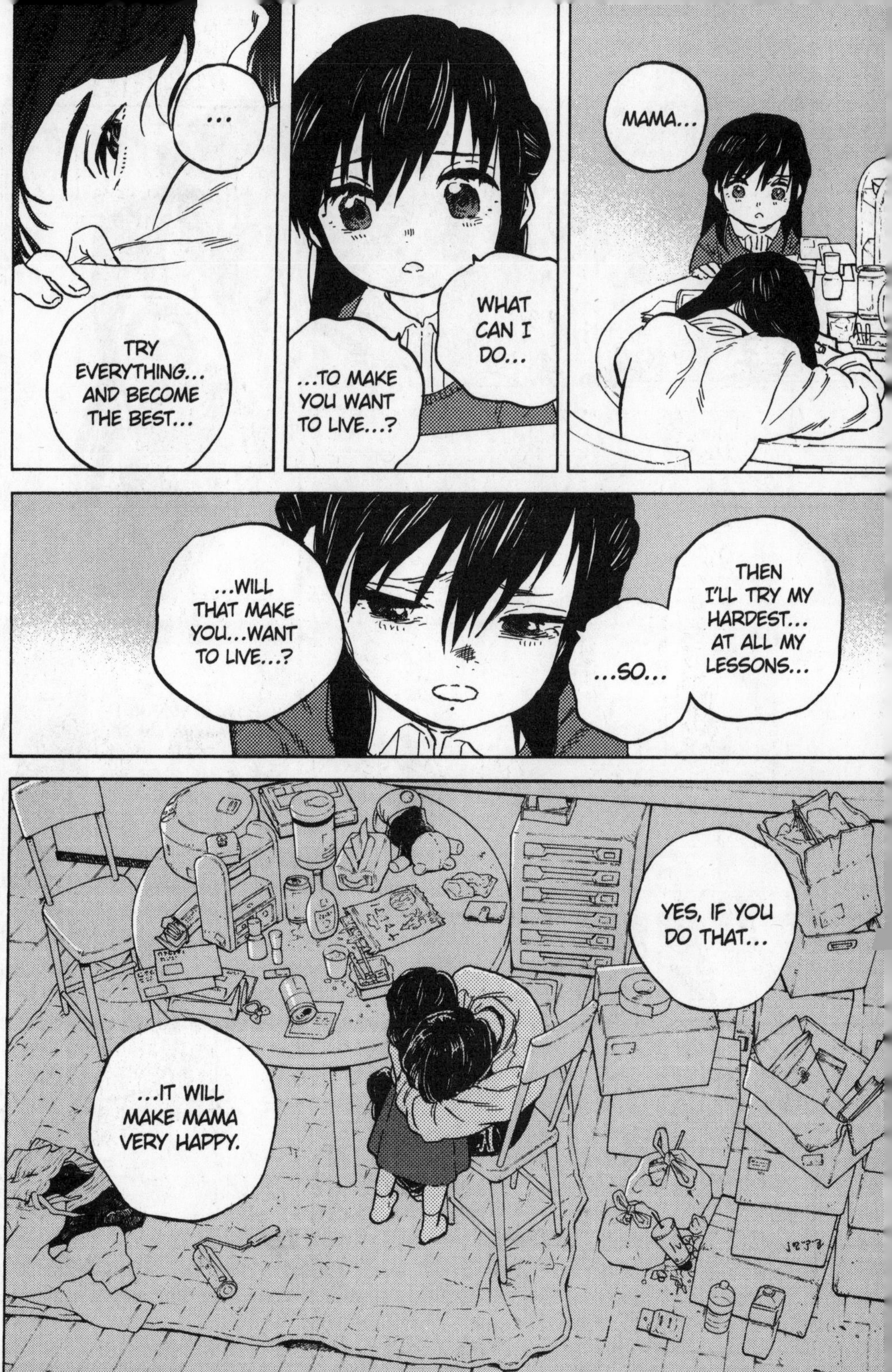
MAMA...
WHAT CAN I DO...
...TO MAKE YOU WANT TO LIVE...?
...
TRY EVERYTHING... AND BECOME THE BEST...
THEN I'LL TRY MY HARDEST... AT ALL MY LESSONS...
...SO...
...WILL THAT MAKE YOU...WANT TO LIVE...?
YES, IF YOU DO THAT...
...IT WILL MAKE MAMA VERY HAPPY.

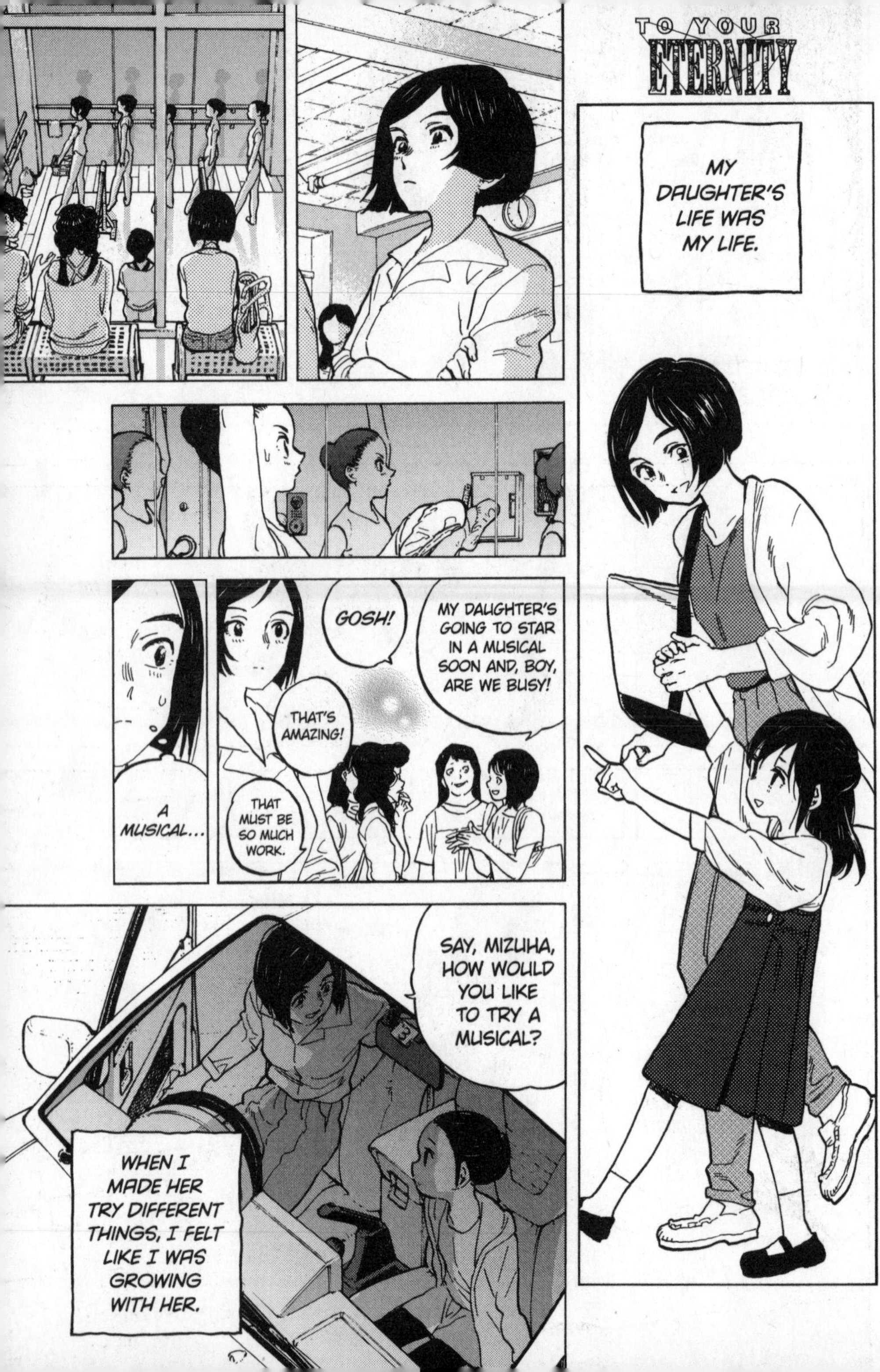
MY DAUGHTER'S LIFE WAS MY LIFE.
MY DAUGHTER'S GOING TO STAR IN A MUSICAL SOON AND, BOY, ARE WE BUSY!
GOSH!
THAT'S AMAZING!
THAT MUST BE SO MUCH WORK.
A MUSICAL...
SAY, MIZUHA, HOW WOULD YOU LIKE TO TRY A MUSICAL?
WHEN I MADE HER TRY DIFFERENT THINGS, I FELT LIKE I WAS GROWING WITH HER.

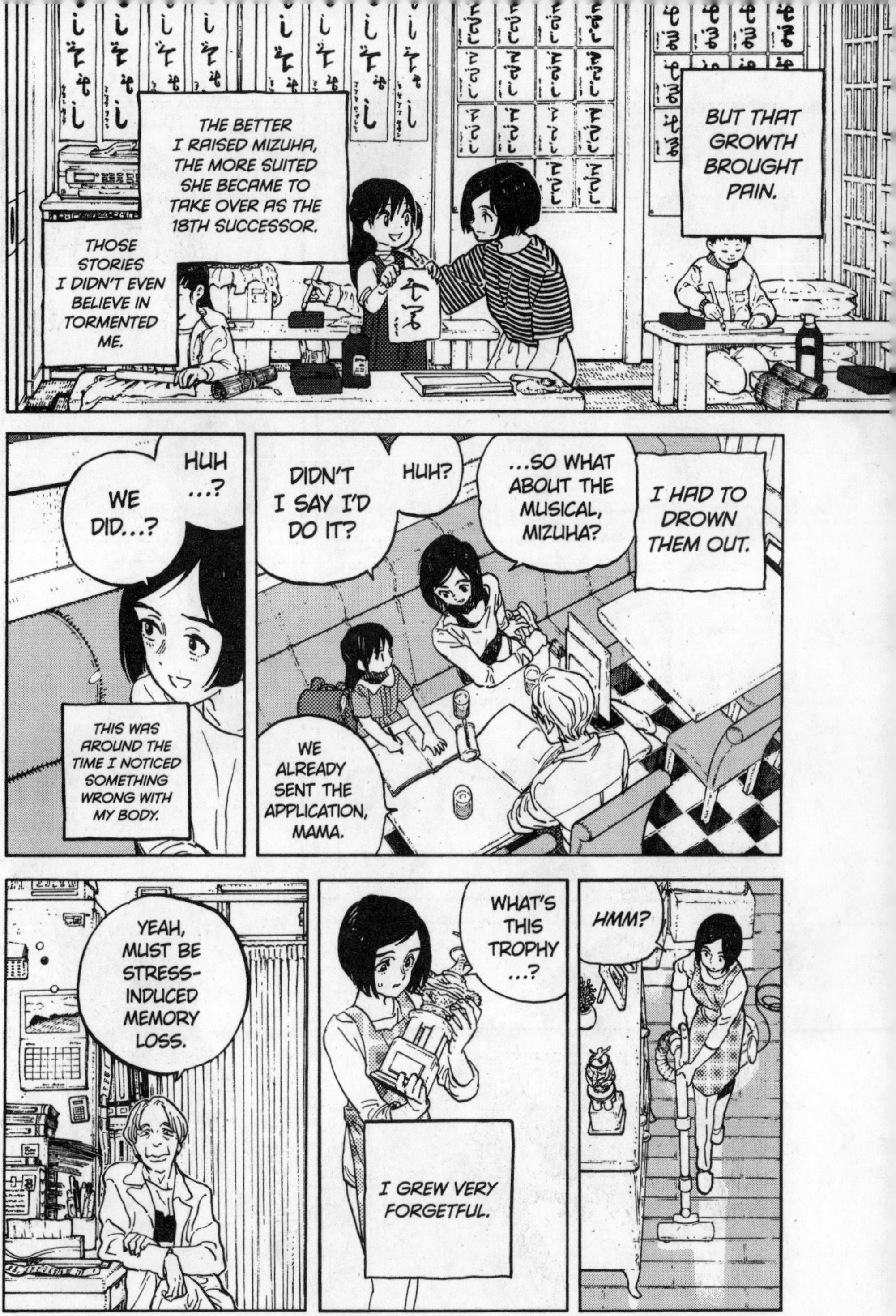
BUT THAT GROWTH BROUGHT PAIN.
THE BETTER I RAISED MIZUHA, THE MORE SUITED SHE BECAME TO TAKE OVER AS THE 18TH SUCCESSOR.
THOSE STORIES I DIDN'T EVEN BELIEVE IN TORMENTED ME.
I HAD TO DROWN THEM OUT.
...SO WHAT ABOUT THE MUSICAL, MIZUHA?
HUH?
DIDN'T I SAY I'D DO IT?
WE ALREADY SENT THE APPLICATION, MAMA.
HUH ...?
WE DID...?
THIS WAS AROUND THE TIME I NOTICED SOMETHING WRONG WITH MY BODY.
HMM?
WHAT'S THIS TROPHY ...?
I GREW VERY FORGETFUL.
YEAH, MUST BE STRESS-INDUCED MEMORY LOSS.

#142 Chasing Dreams

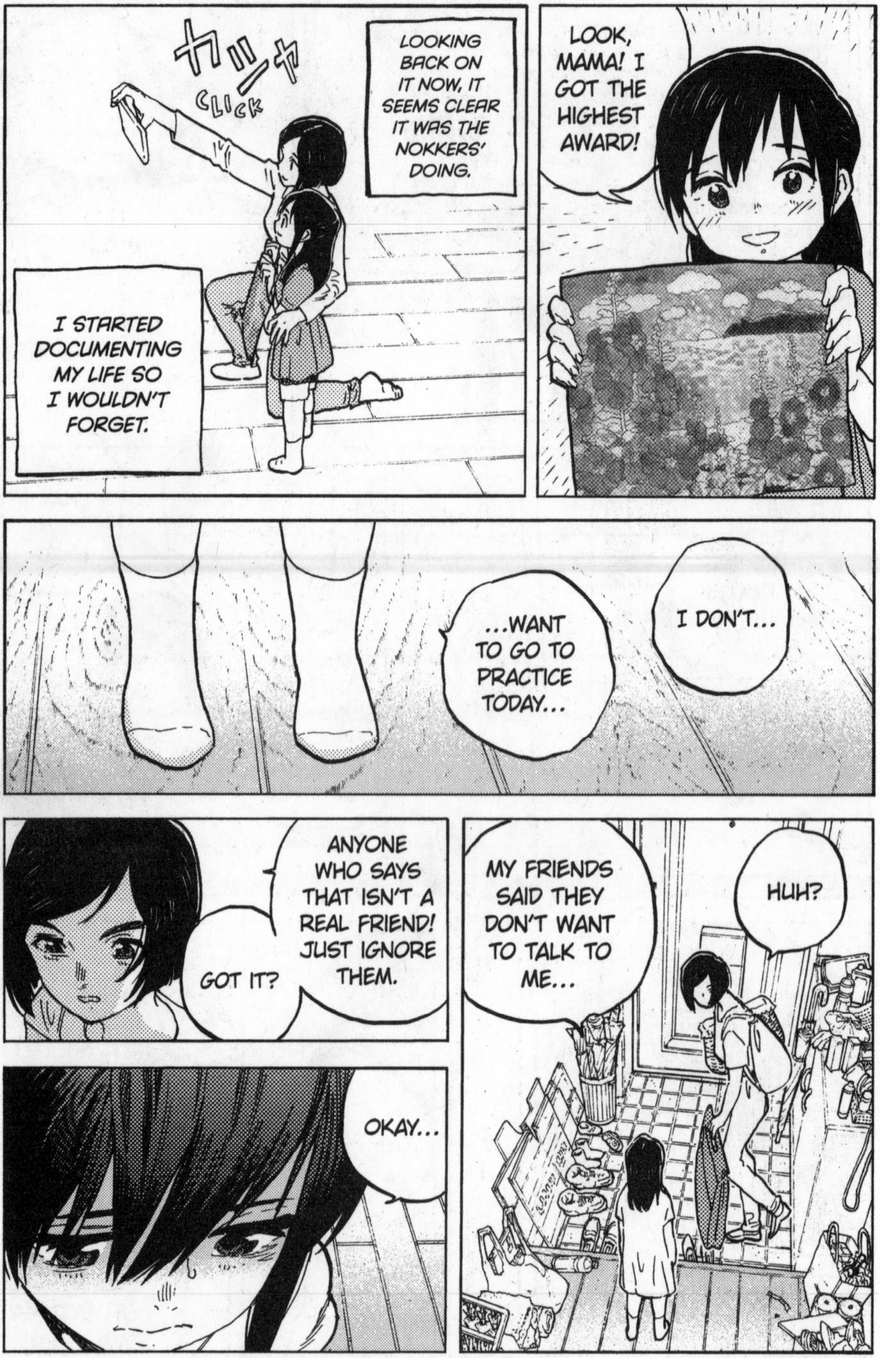
LOOK, MAMA! I GOT THE HIGHEST AWARD!
LOOKING BACK ON IT NOW, IT SEEMS CLEAR IT WAS THE NOKKERS' DOING.
カシャ
CLICK
I STARTED DOCUMENTING MY LIFE SO I WOULDN'T FORGET.
I DON'T...
...WANT TO GO TO PRACTICE TODAY...
HUH?
MY FRIENDS SAID THEY DON'T WANT TO TALK TO ME...
ANYONE WHO SAYS THAT ISN'T A REAL FRIEND! JUST IGNORE THEM.
GOT IT?
OKAY...

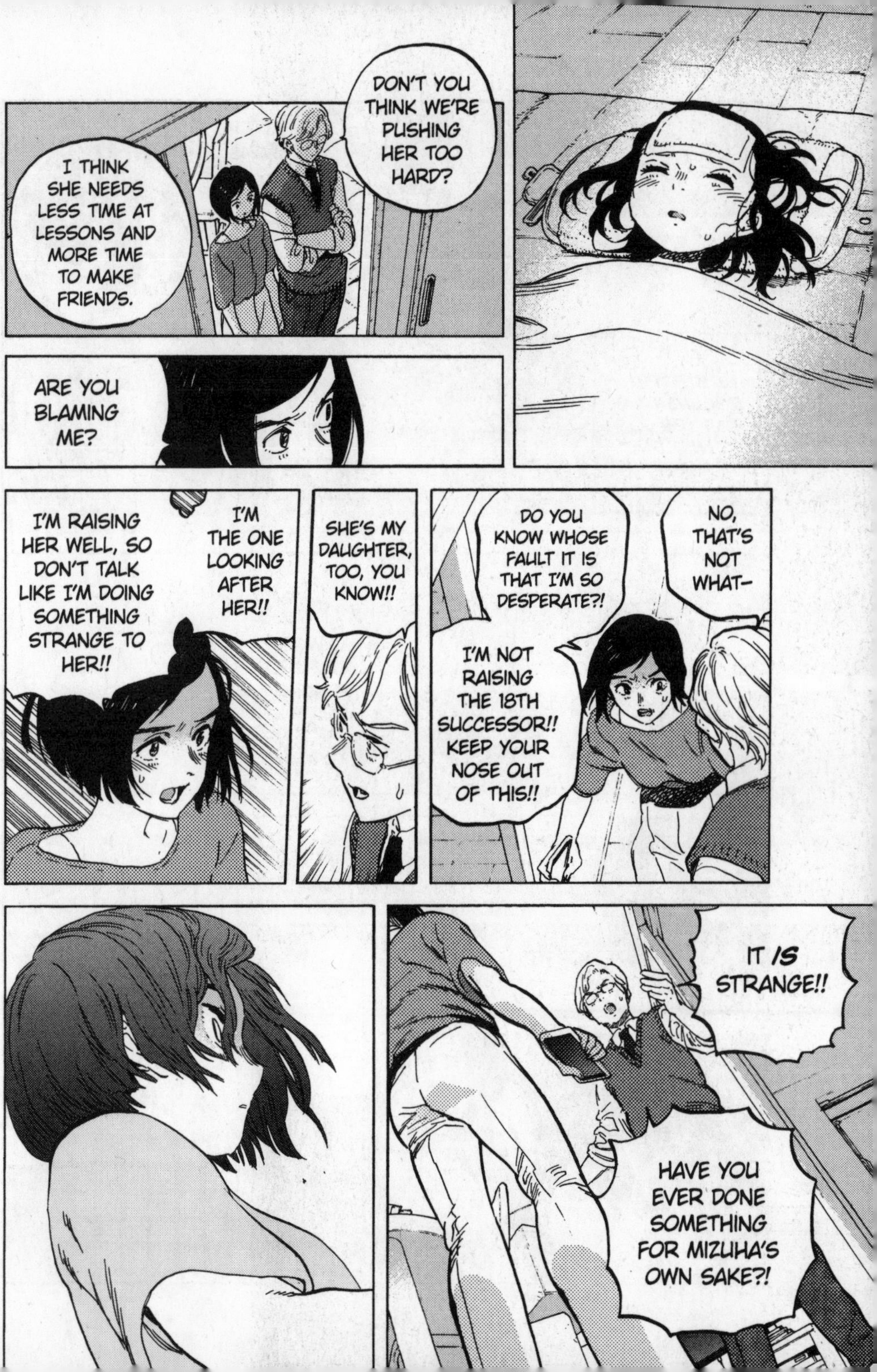
DON'T YOU THINK WE'RE PUSHING HER TOO HARD?
I THINK SHE NEEDS LESS TIME AT LESSONS AND MORE TIME TO MAKE FRIENDS.
ARE YOU BLAMING ME?
NO, THAT'S NOT WHAT-
DO YOU KNOW WHOSE FAULT IT IS THAT I'M SO DESPERATE?!
I'M NOT RAISING THE 18TH SUCCESSOR!! KEEP YOUR NOSE OUT OF THIS!!
SHE'S MY DAUGHTER, TOO, YOU KNOW!!
I'M THE ONE LOOKING AFTER HER!!
I'M RAISING HER WELL, SO DON'T TALK LIKE I'M DOING SOMETHING STRANGE TO HER!!
IT *IS* STRANGE!!
HAVE YOU EVER DONE SOMETHING FOR MIZUHA'S OWN SAKE?!

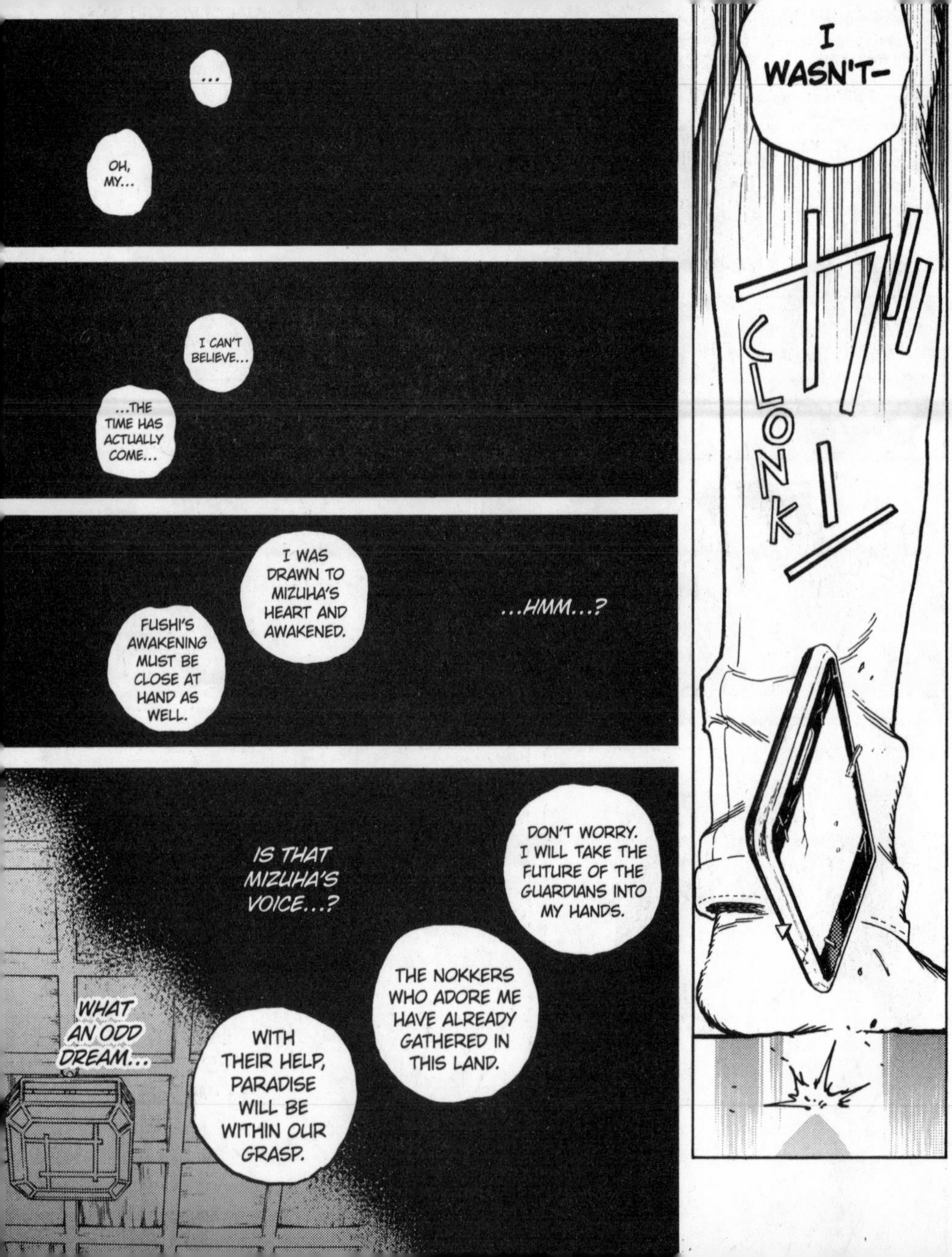
I WASN'T-
CLONK
...
OH, MY...
I CAN'T BELIEVE...
...THE TIME HAS ACTUALLY COME...
...HMM...?
I WAS DRAWN TO MIZUHA'S HEART AND AWAKENED.
FUSHI'S AWAKENING MUST BE CLOSE AT HAND AS WELL.
DON'T WORRY. I WILL TAKE THE FUTURE OF THE GUARDIANS INTO MY HANDS.
IS THAT MIZUHA'S VOICE...?
THE NOKKERS WHO ADORE ME HAVE ALREADY GATHERED IN THIS LAND.
WITH THEIR HELP, PARADISE WILL BE WITHIN OUR GRASP.
WHAT AN ODD DREAM...

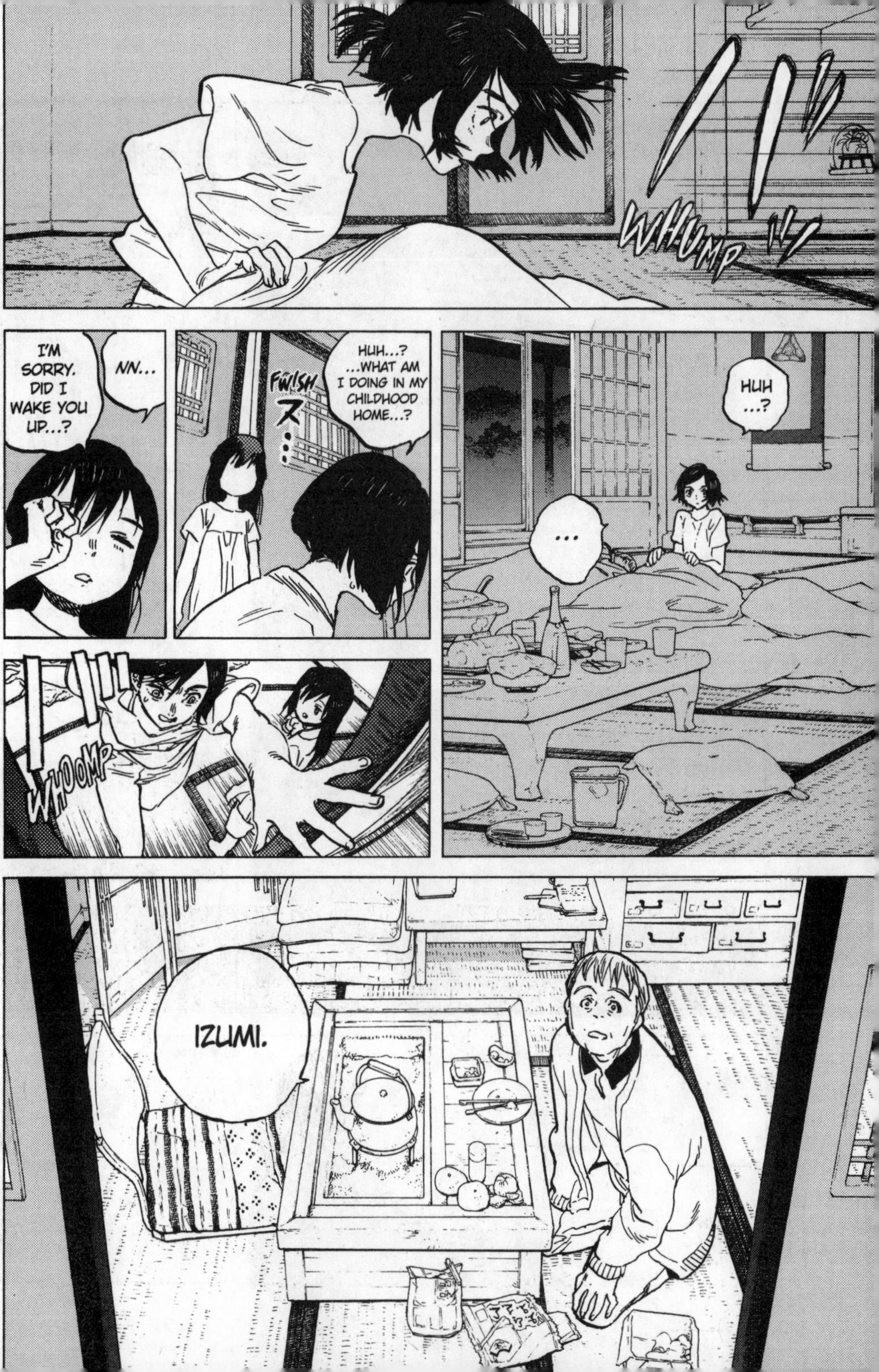
WHUMP
HUH ...?
...
HUH...? ...WHAT AM I DOING IN MY CHILDHOOD HOME...?
FWISH
ス...
NN...
I'M SORRY. DID I WAKE YOU UP...?
WHOOMP
IZUMI.

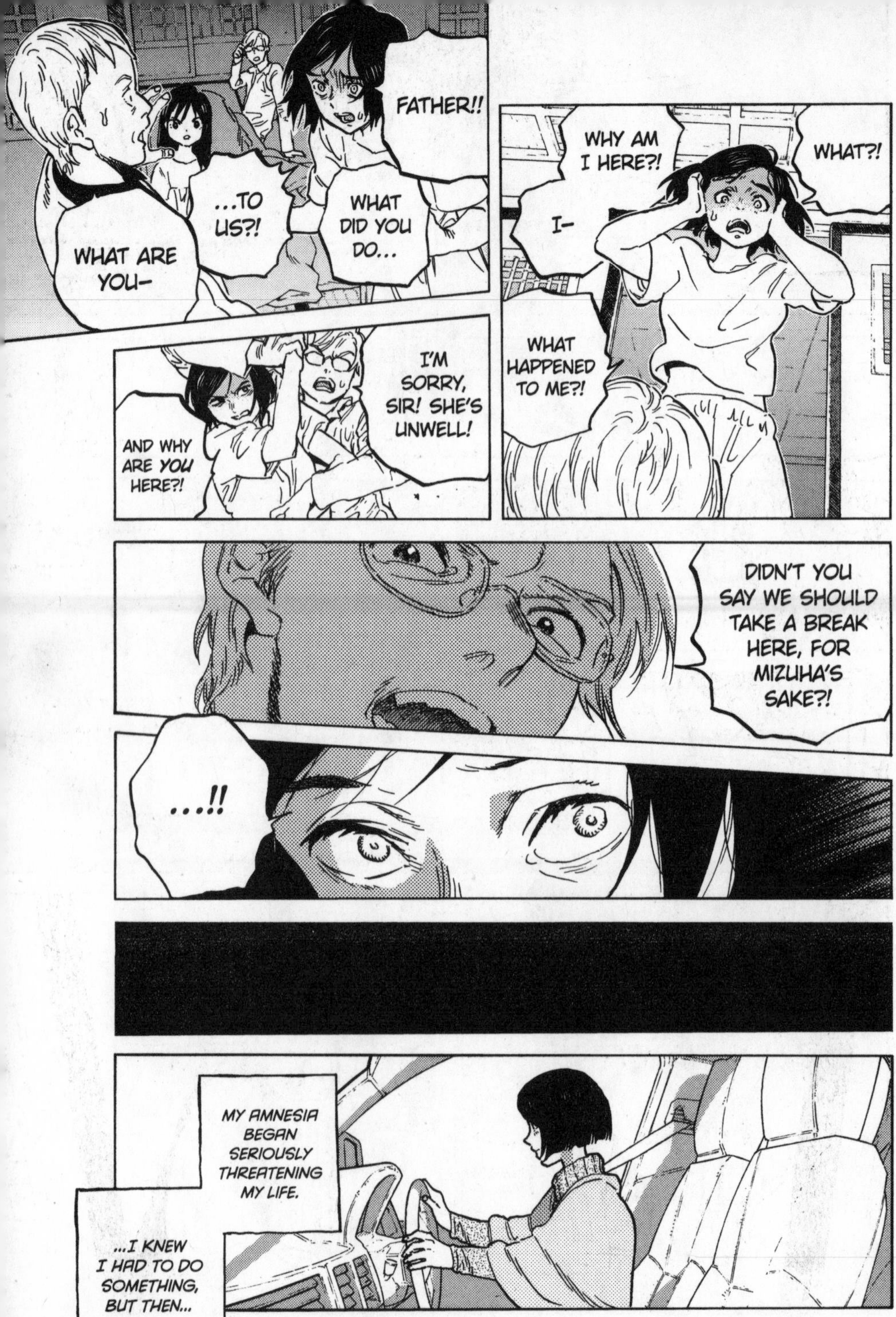

FATHER!!
WHAT DID YOU DO...
...TO US?!
WHAT ARE YOU-
WHAT?!
WHY AM I HERE?!
I-
WHAT HAPPENED TO ME?!
I'M SORRY, SIR! SHE'S UNWELL!
AND WHY ARE *YOU* HERE?!
DIDN'T YOU SAY WE SHOULD TAKE A BREAK HERE, FOR MIZUHA'S SAKE?!
...!!
MY AMNESIA BEGAN SERIOUSLY THREATENING MY LIFE.
...I KNEW I HAD TO DO SOMETHING, BUT THEN...

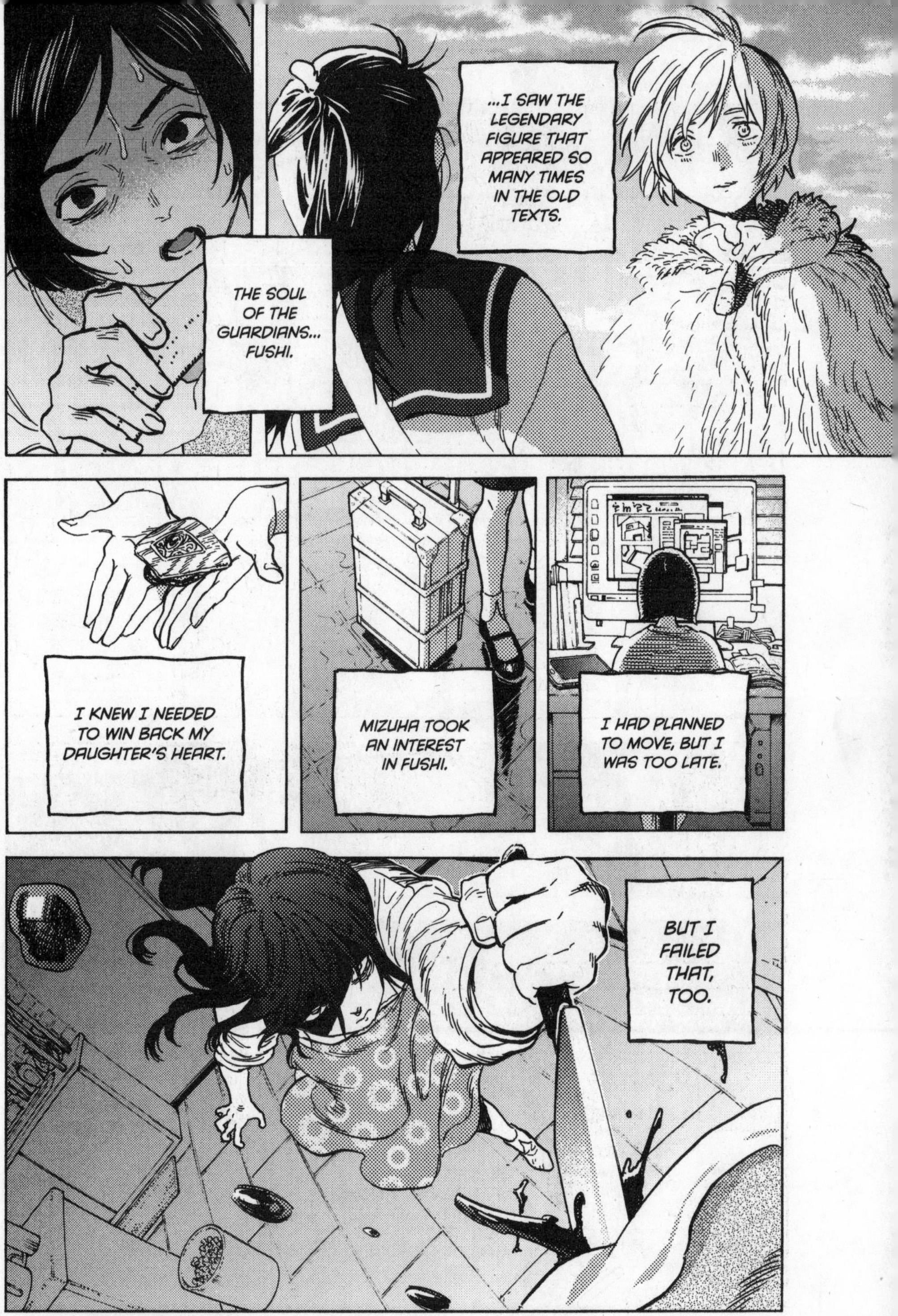
...I SAW THE LEGENDARY FIGURE THAT APPEARED SO MANY TIMES IN THE OLD TEXTS.
THE SOUL OF THE GUARDIANS... FUSHI.
I HAD PLANNED TO MOVE, BUT I WAS TOO LATE.
MIZUHA TOOK AN INTEREST IN FUSHI.
I KNEW I NEEDED TO WIN BACK MY DAUGHTER'S HEART.
BUT I FAILED THAT, TOO.

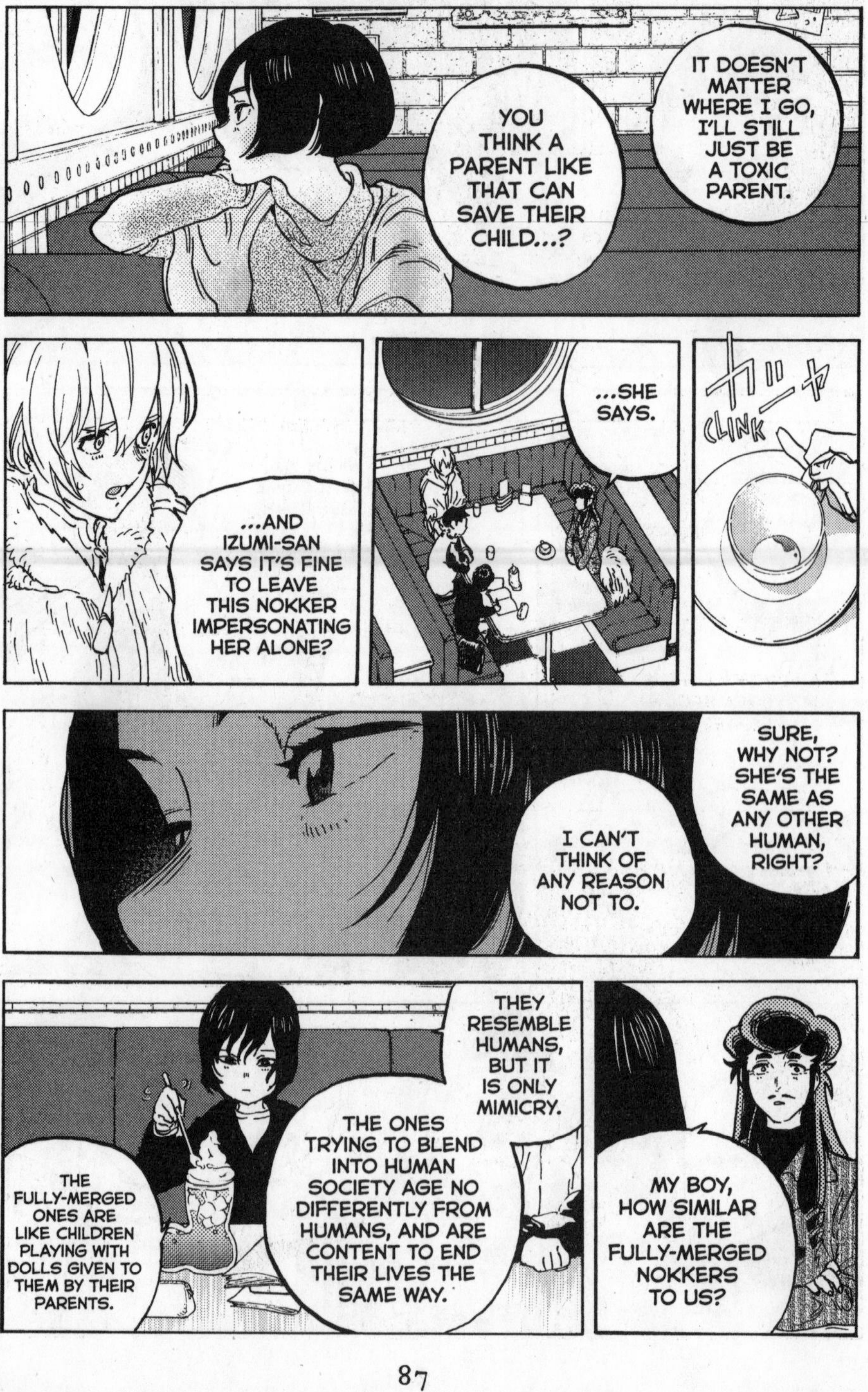
IT DOESN'T MATTER WHERE I GO, I'LL STILL JUST BE A TOXIC PARENT.
YOU THINK A PARENT LIKE THAT CAN SAVE THEIR CHILD...?
CLINK
...SHE SAYS.
...AND IZUMI-SAN SAYS IT'S FINE TO LEAVE THIS NOKKER IMPERSONATING HER ALONE?
SURE, WHY NOT? SHE'S THE SAME AS ANY OTHER HUMAN, RIGHT?
I CAN'T THINK OF ANY REASON NOT TO.
MY BOY, HOW SIMILAR ARE THE FULLY-MERGED NOKKERS TO US?
THEY RESEMBLE HUMANS, BUT IT IS ONLY MIMICRY.
THE ONES TRYING TO BLEND INTO HUMAN SOCIETY AGE NO DIFFERENTLY FROM HUMANS, AND ARE CONTENT TO END THEIR LIVES THE SAME WAY.
THE FULLY-MERGED ONES ARE LIKE CHILDREN PLAYING WITH DOLLS GIVEN TO THEM BY THEIR PARENTS.

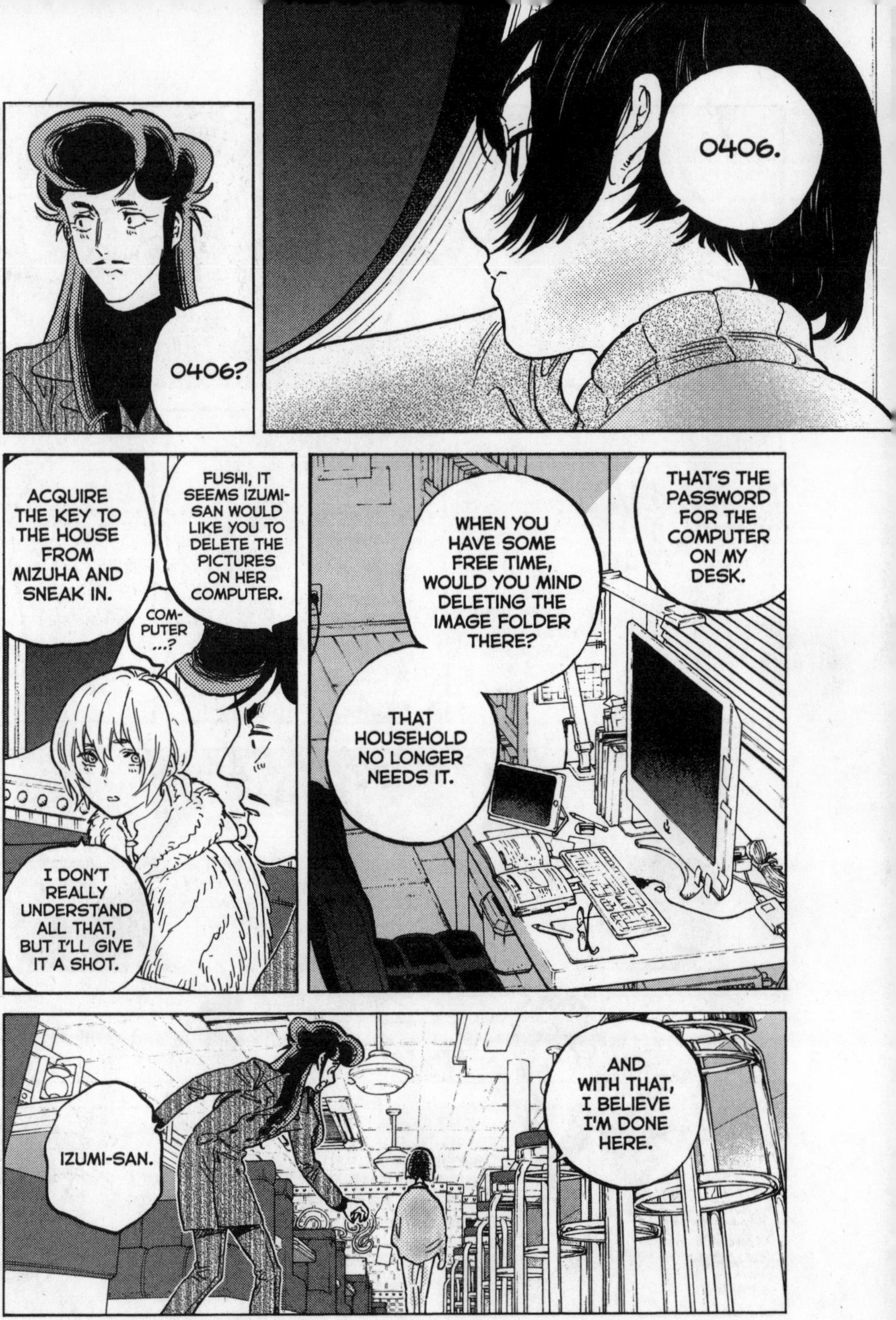
0406.
0406?
THAT'S THE PASSWORD FOR THE COMPUTER ON MY DESK.
WHEN YOU HAVE SOME FREE TIME, WOULD YOU MIND DELETING THE IMAGE FOLDER THERE?
THAT HOUSEHOLD NO LONGER NEEDS IT.
FUSHI, IT SEEMS IZUMI-SAN WOULD LIKE YOU TO DELETE THE PICTURES ON HER COMPUTER.
ACQUIRE THE KEY TO THE HOUSE FROM MIZUHA AND SNEAK IN.
COMPUTER ...?
I DON'T REALLY UNDERSTAND ALL THAT, BUT I'LL GIVE IT A SHOT.
AND WITH THAT, I BELIEVE I'M DONE HERE.
IZUMI-SAN.

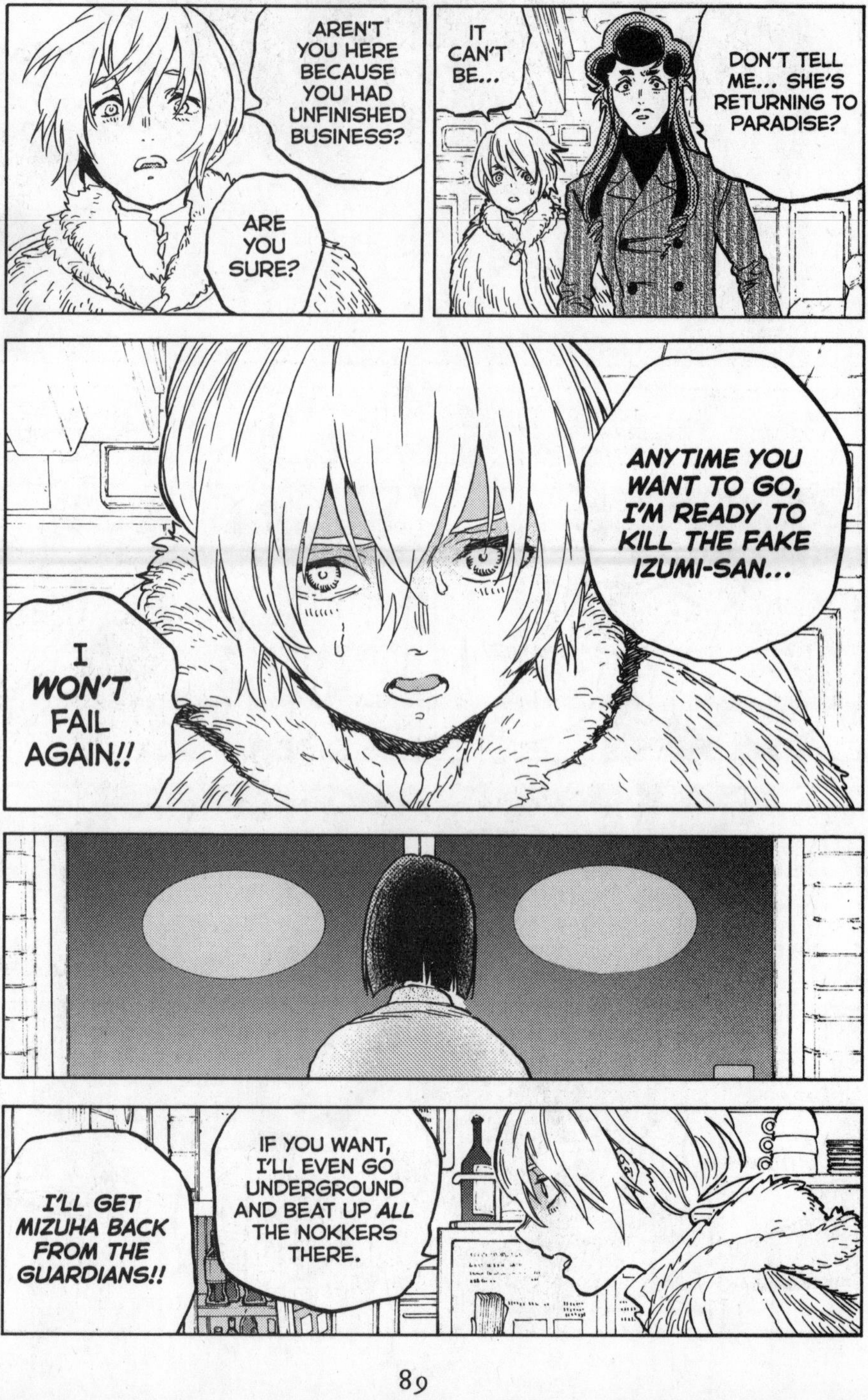
DON'T TELL ME... SHE'S RETURNING TO PARADISE?
IT CAN'T BE...
AREN'T YOU HERE BECAUSE YOU HAD UNFINISHED BUSINESS?
ARE YOU SURE?
ANYTIME YOU WANT TO GO, I'M READY TO KILL THE FAKE IZUMI-SAN...
I WON'T FAIL AGAIN!!
IF YOU WANT, I'LL EVEN GO UNDERGROUND AND BEAT UP ALL THE NOKKERS THERE.
I'LL GET MIZUHA BACK FROM THE GUARDIANS!!

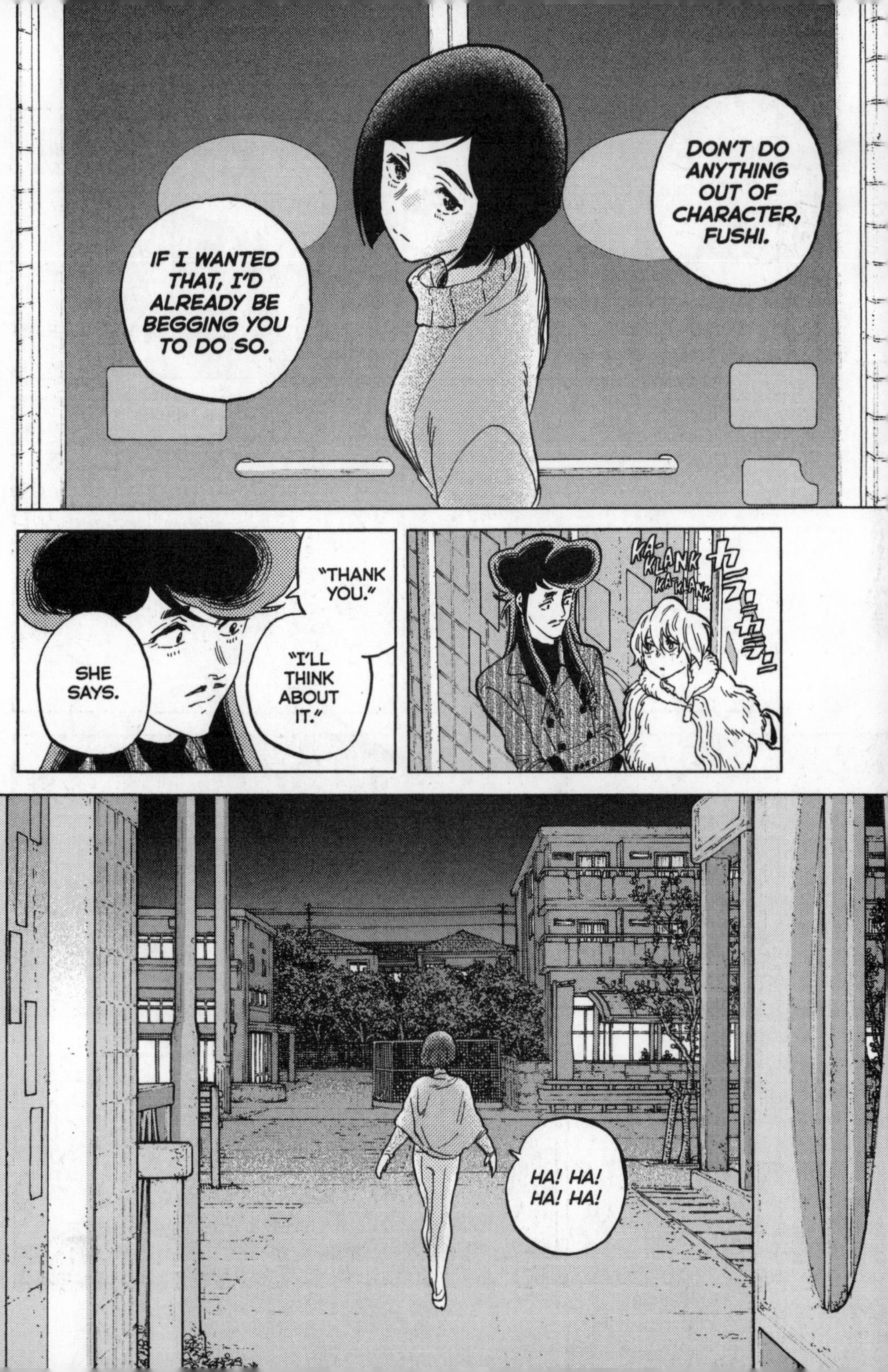
DON'T DO ANYTHING OUT OF CHARACTER, FUSHI.
IF I WANTED THAT, I'D ALREADY BE BEGGING YOU TO DO SO.
KA-KLANK
KA-KLANK
"THANK YOU."
"I'LL THINK ABOUT IT."
SHE SAYS.
HA! HA! HA! HA!

#143 Binding Mud

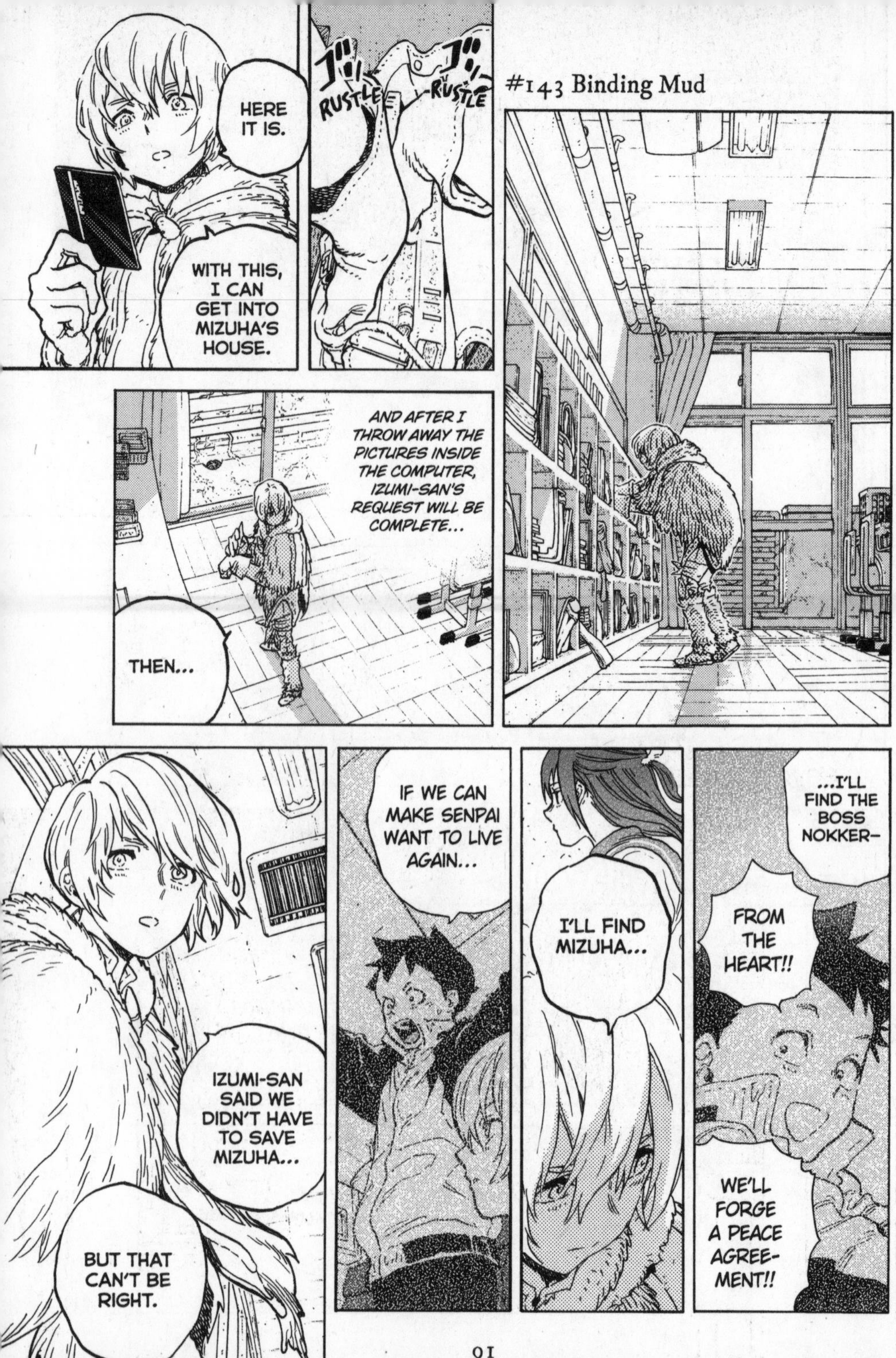
RUSTLE
RUSTLE
HERE IT IS.
WITH THIS, I CAN GET INTO MIZUHA'S HOUSE.
AND AFTER I THROW AWAY THE PICTURES INSIDE THE COMPUTER, IZUMI-SAN'S REQUEST WILL BE COMPLETE...
THEN...
...I'LL FIND THE BOSS NOKKER—
FROM THE HEART!!
WE'LL FORGE A PEACE AGREEMENT!!
I'LL FIND MIZUHA...
IF WE CAN MAKE SENPAI WANT TO LIVE AGAIN...
IZUMI-SAN SAID WE DIDN'T HAVE TO SAVE MIZUHA...
BUT THAT CAN'T BE RIGHT.

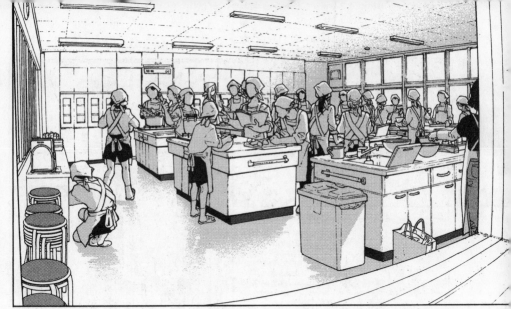

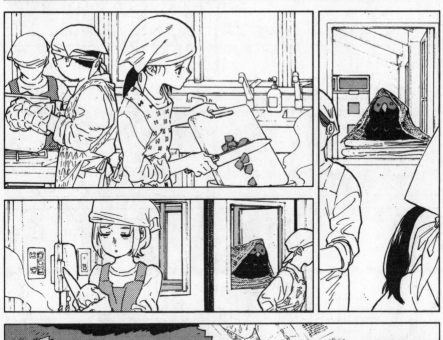

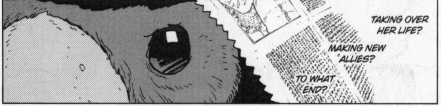

TAKING OVER HER LIFE?

MAKING NEW ALLIES?

TO WHAT END?

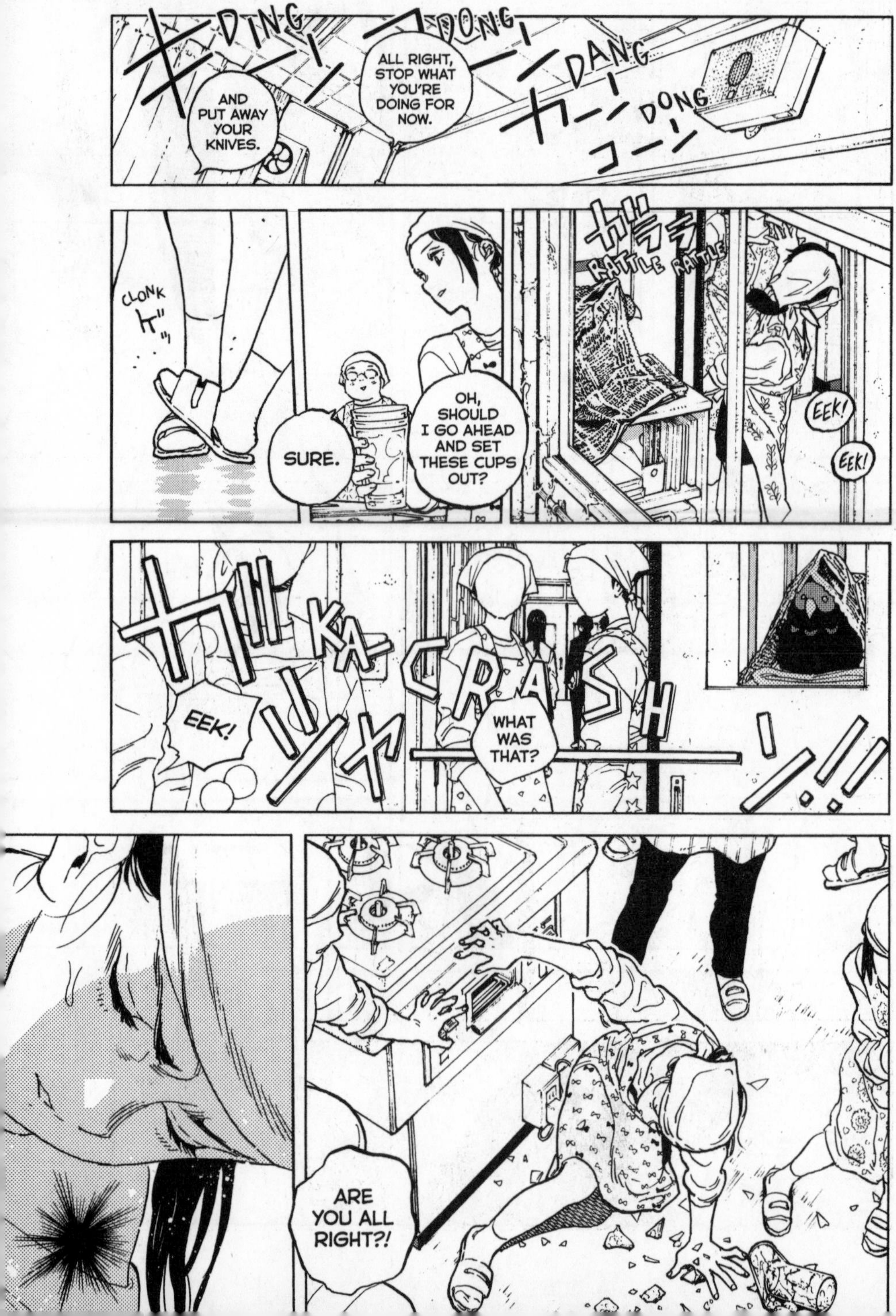
DING DONG DANG DONG
ALL RIGHT, STOP WHAT YOU'RE DOING FOR NOW.
AND PUT AWAY YOUR KNIVES.
RATTLE RATTLE
EEK!
EEK!
OH, SHOULD I GO AHEAD AND SET THESE CUPS OUT?
SURE.
CLONK
KA-CRASH
WHAT WAS THAT?
EEK!
ARE YOU ALL RIGHT?!

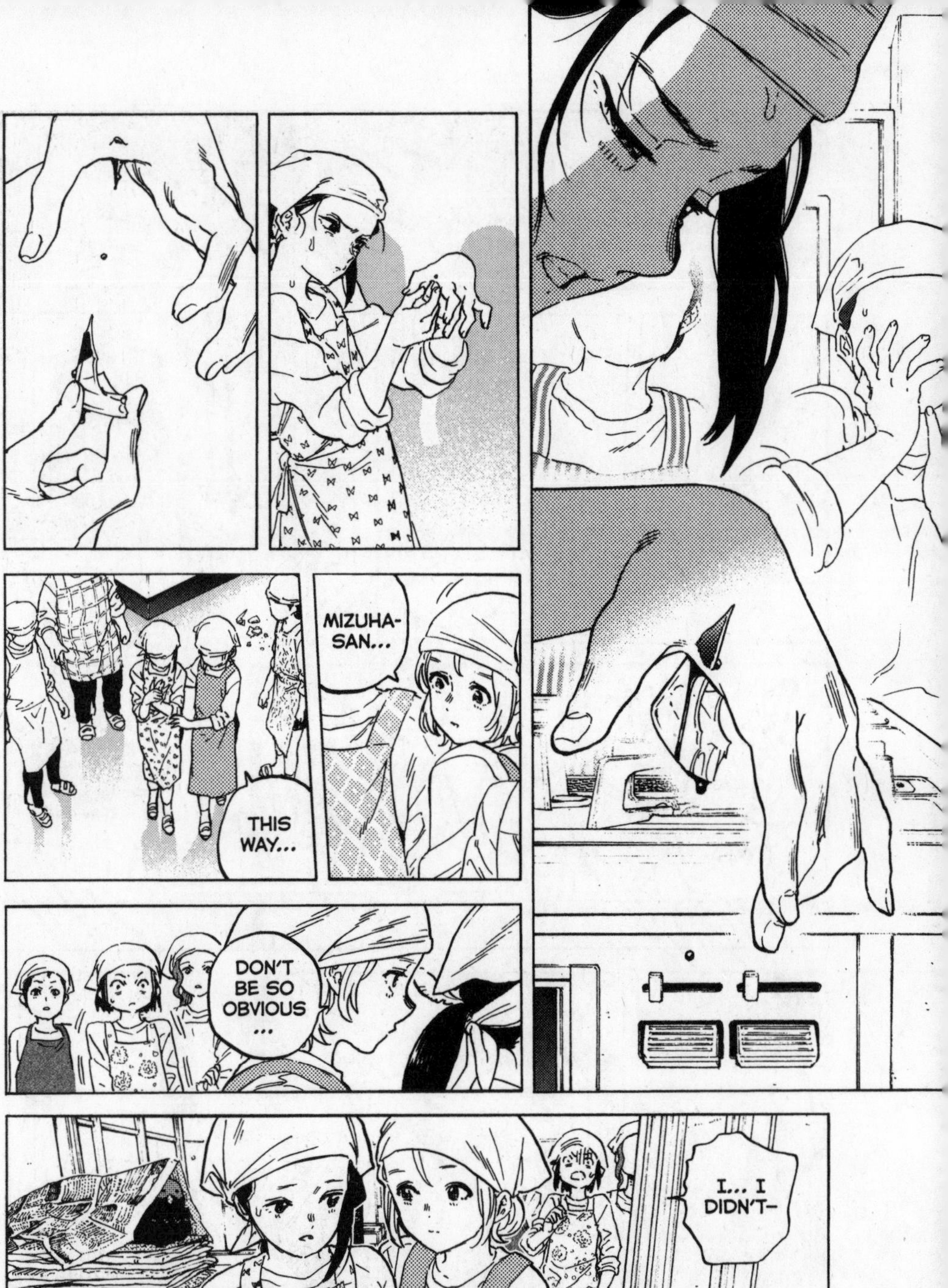
MIZUHA-SAN...
THIS WAY...
DON'T BE SO OBVIOUS ...
I... I DIDN'T-

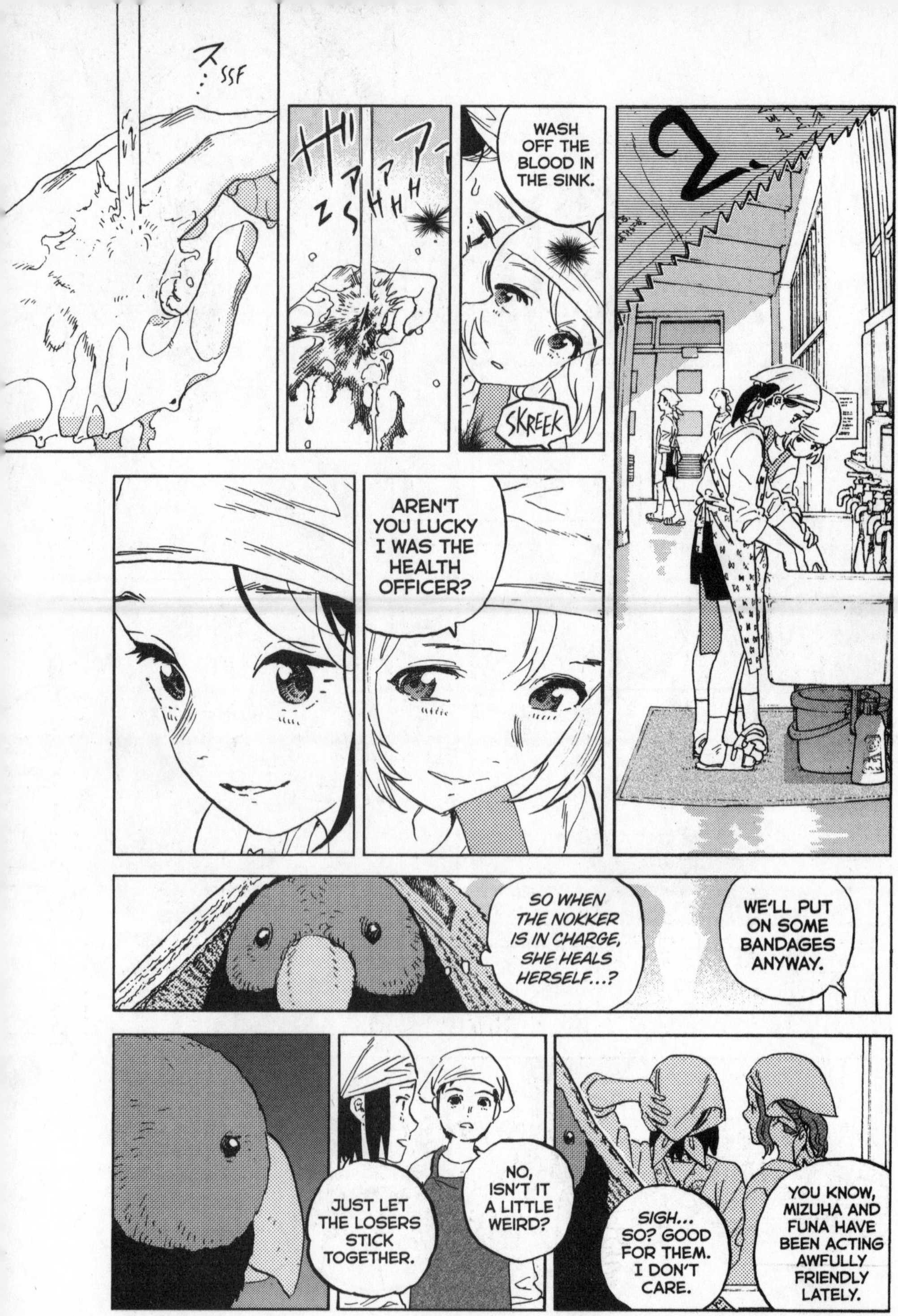
WASH OFF THE BLOOD IN THE SINK.
SKREEK
ZSHHH
SSF
AREN'T YOU LUCKY I WAS THE HEALTH OFFICER?
WE'LL PUT ON SOME BANDAGES ANYWAY.
SO WHEN THE NOKKER IS IN CHARGE, SHE HEALS HERSELF...?
YOU KNOW, MIZUHA AND FUNA HAVE BEEN ACTING AWFULLY FRIENDLY LATELY.
SIGH... SO? GOOD FOR THEM. I DON'T CARE.
NO, ISN'T IT A LITTLE WEIRD?
JUST LET THE LOSERS STICK TOGETHER.

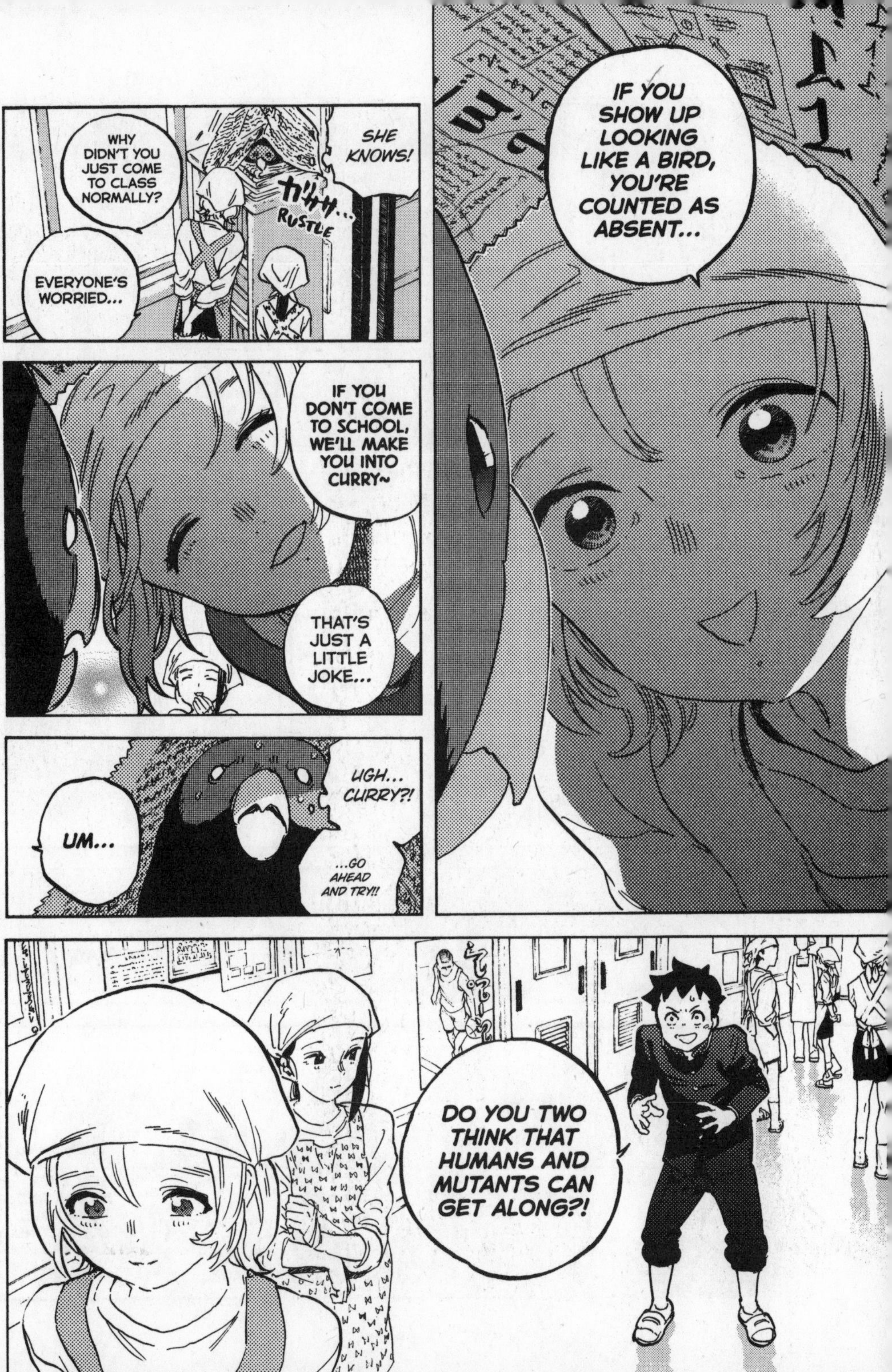
IF YOU SHOW UP LOOKING LIKE A BIRD, YOU'RE COUNTED AS ABSENT...
SHE KNOWS!
RUSTLE
WHY DIDN'T YOU JUST COME TO CLASS NORMALLY?
EVERYONE'S WORRIED...
IF YOU DON'T COME TO SCHOOL, WE'LL MAKE YOU INTO CURRY~
THAT'S JUST A LITTLE JOKE...
UGH... CURRY?!
...GO AHEAD AND TRY!!
UM...
DO YOU TWO THINK THAT HUMANS AND MUTANTS CAN GET ALONG?!

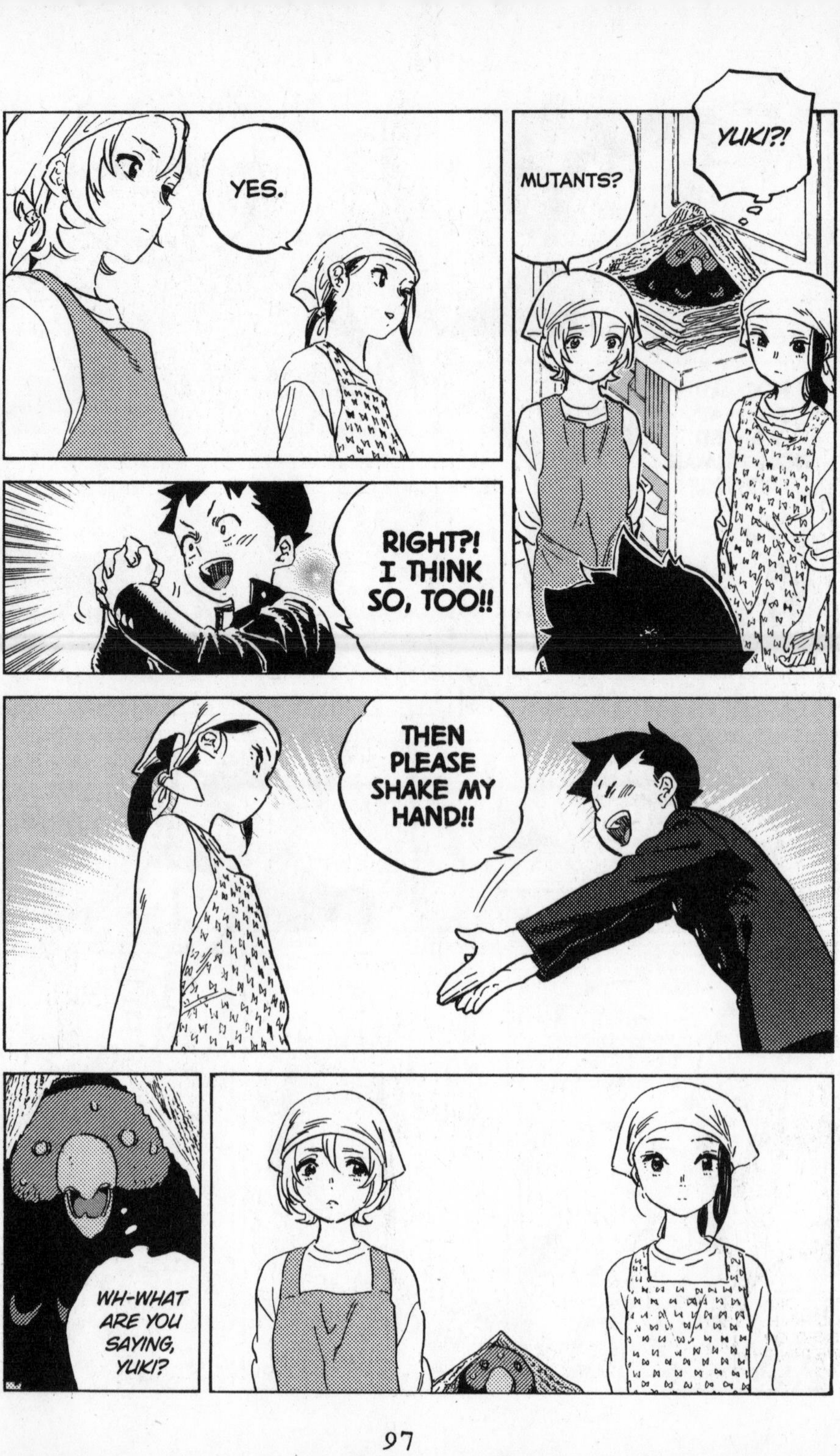
YUKI?!
MUTANTS?
YES.
RIGHT?! I THINK SO, TOO!!
THEN PLEASE SHAKE MY HAND!!
WH-WHAT ARE YOU SAYING, YUKI?

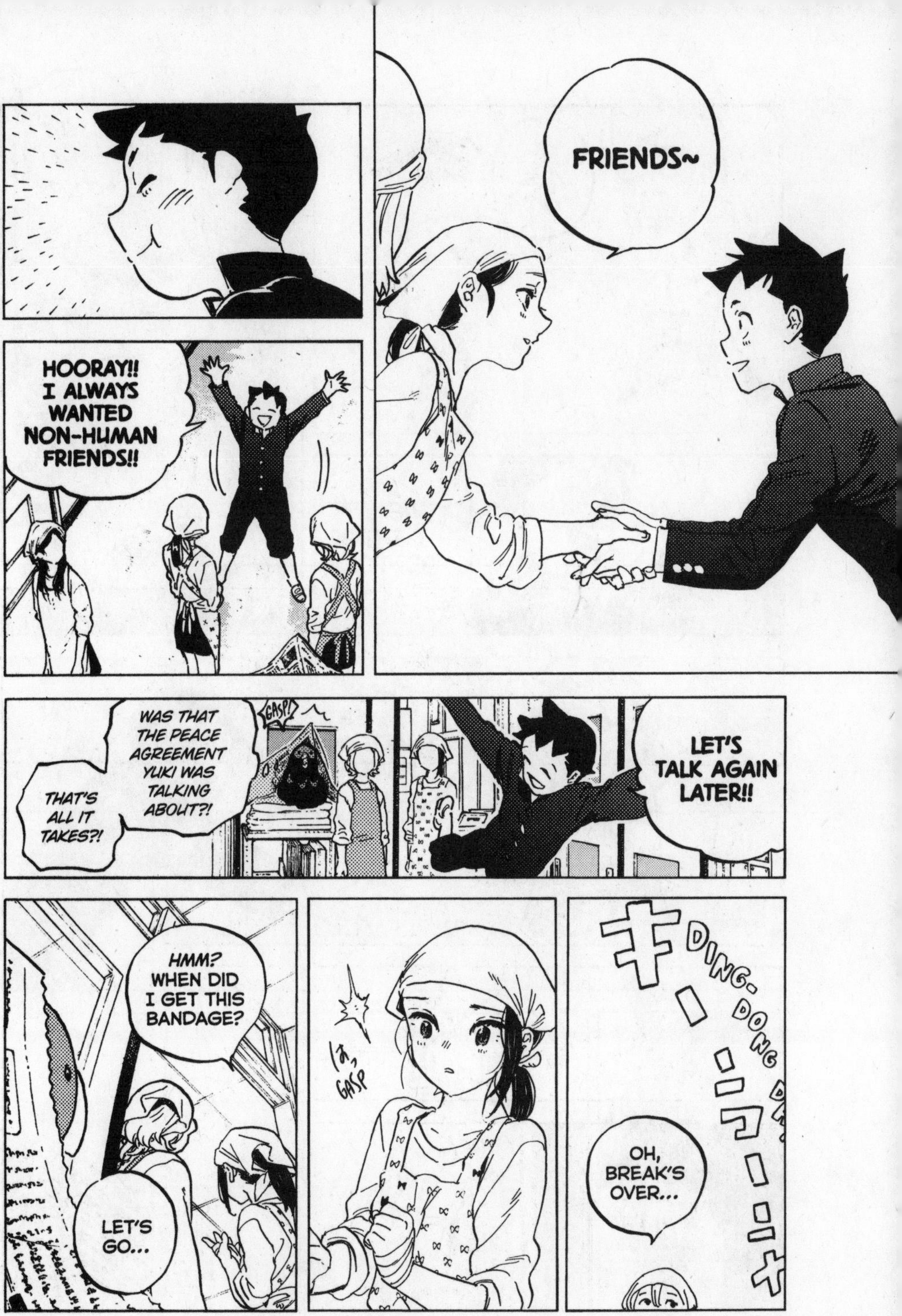
FRIENDS~
HOORAY!! I ALWAYS WANTED NON-HUMAN FRIENDS!!
LET'S TALK AGAIN LATER!!
GASP!?
WAS THAT THE PEACE AGREEMENT YUKI WAS TALKING ABOUT?!
THAT'S ALL IT TAKES?!
DING-DONG
OH, BREAK'S OVER...
GASP
HMM? WHEN DID I GET THIS BANDAGE?
LET'S GO...

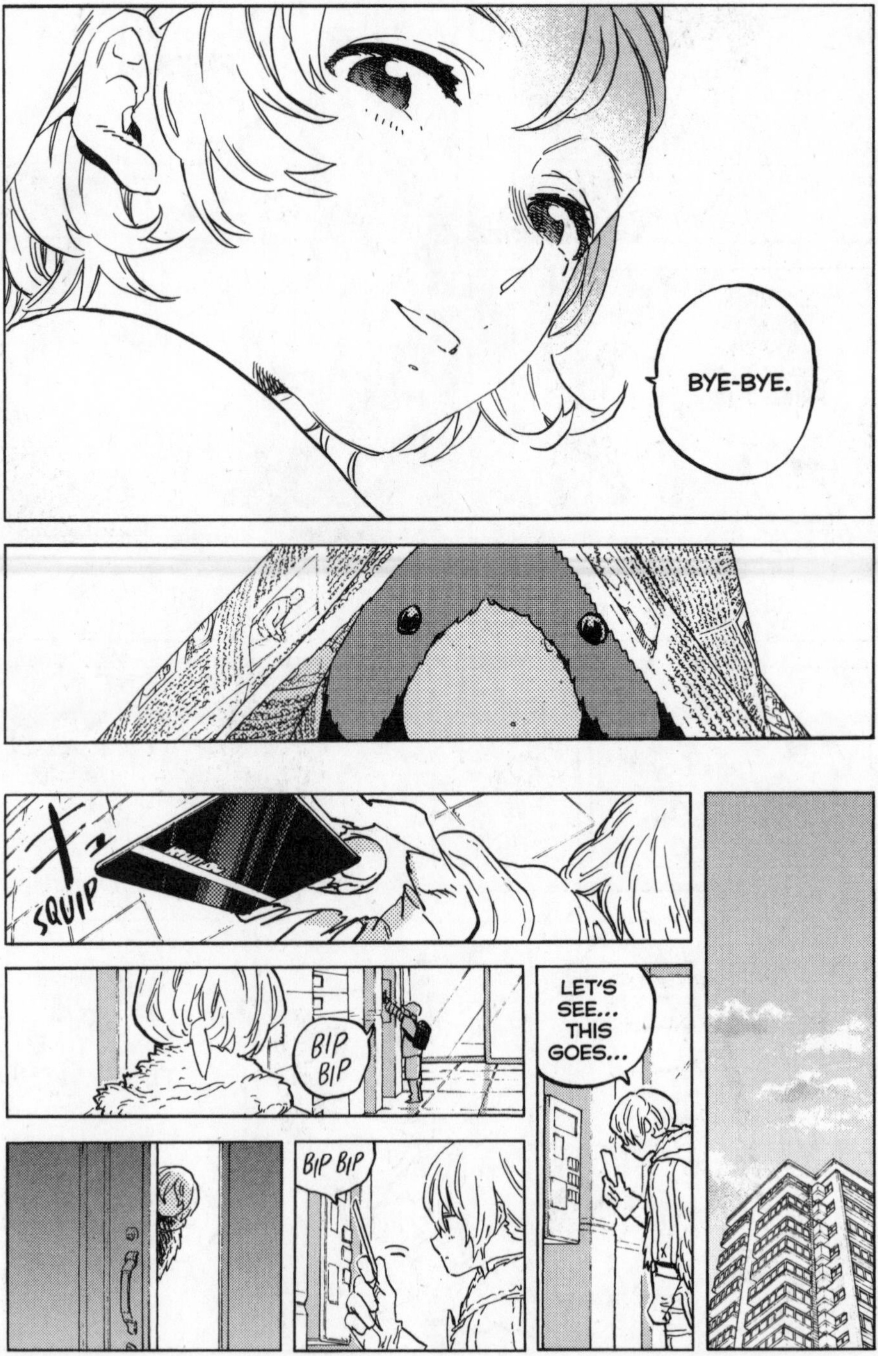
BYE-BYE.
SQUIP
LET'S SEE... THIS GOES...
BIP BIP
BIP BIP

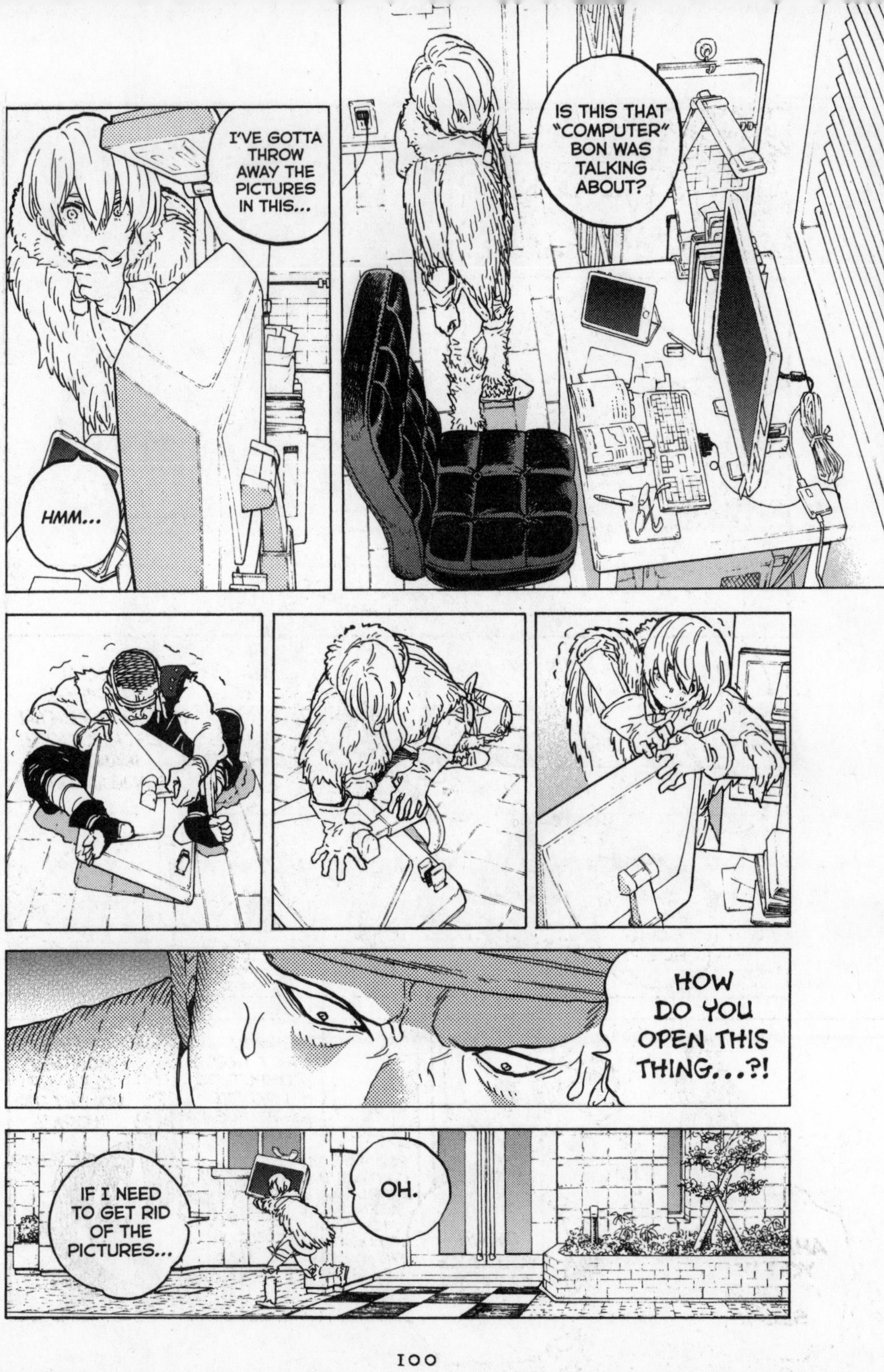

IS THIS THAT "COMPUTER" BON WAS TALKING ABOUT?
I'VE GOTTA THROW AWAY THE PICTURES IN THIS...
HMM...
HOW DO YOU OPEN THIS THING...?!
OH.
IF I NEED TO GET RID OF THE PICTURES...

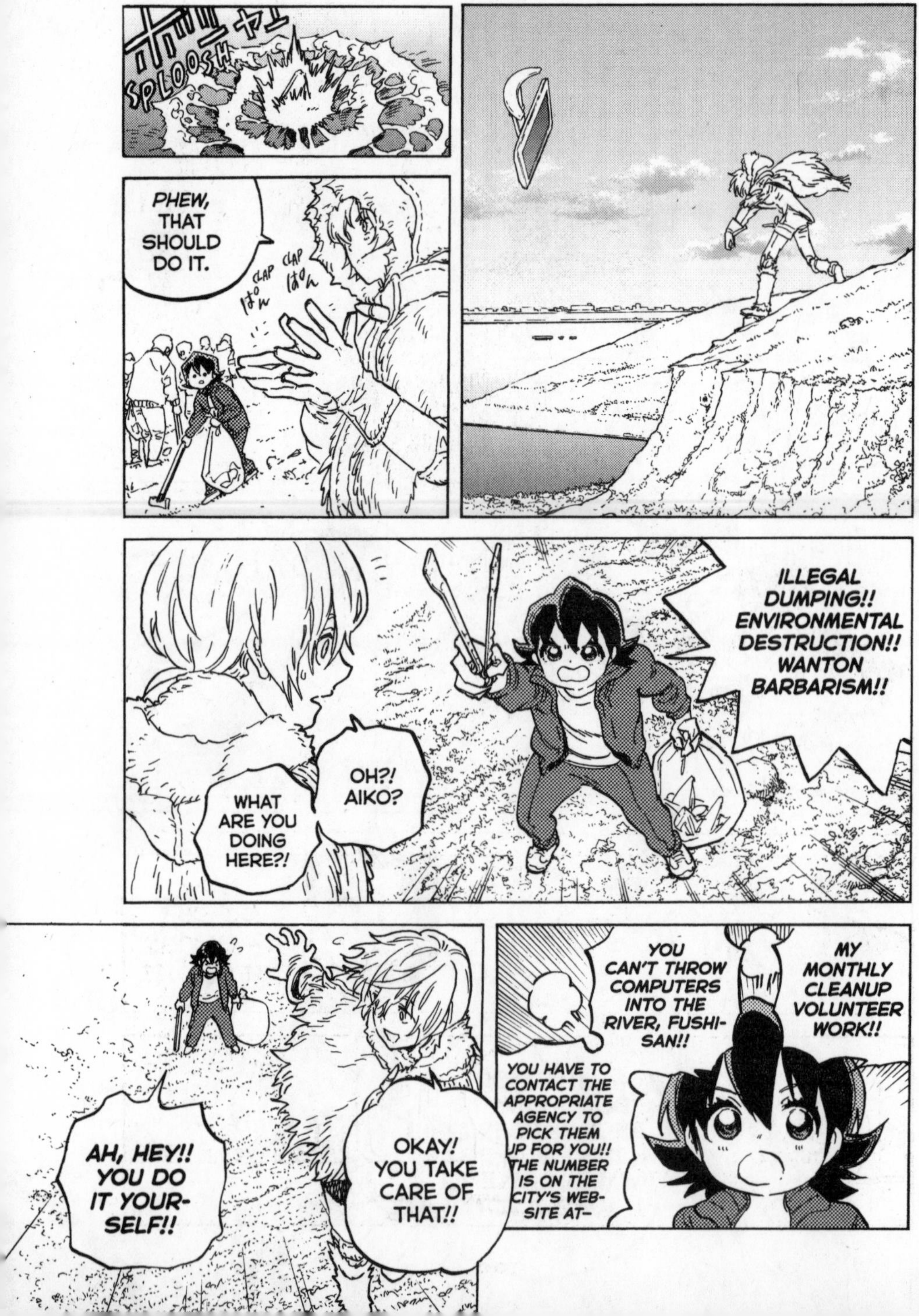
SPLOOSH
PHEW, THAT SHOULD DO IT.
CLAP CLAP
ILLEGAL DUMPING!! ENVIRONMENTAL DESTRUCTION!! WANTON BARBARISM!!
OH?! AIKO?
WHAT ARE YOU DOING HERE?!
MY MONTHLY CLEANUP VOLUNTEER WORK!!
YOU CAN'T THROW COMPUTERS INTO THE RIVER, FUSHI-SAN!!
YOU HAVE TO CONTACT THE APPROPRIATE AGENCY TO PICK THEM UP FOR YOU!! THE NUMBER IS ON THE CITY'S WEB-SITE AT–
OKAY! YOU TAKE CARE OF THAT!!
AH, HEY!! YOU DO IT YOUR-SELF!!

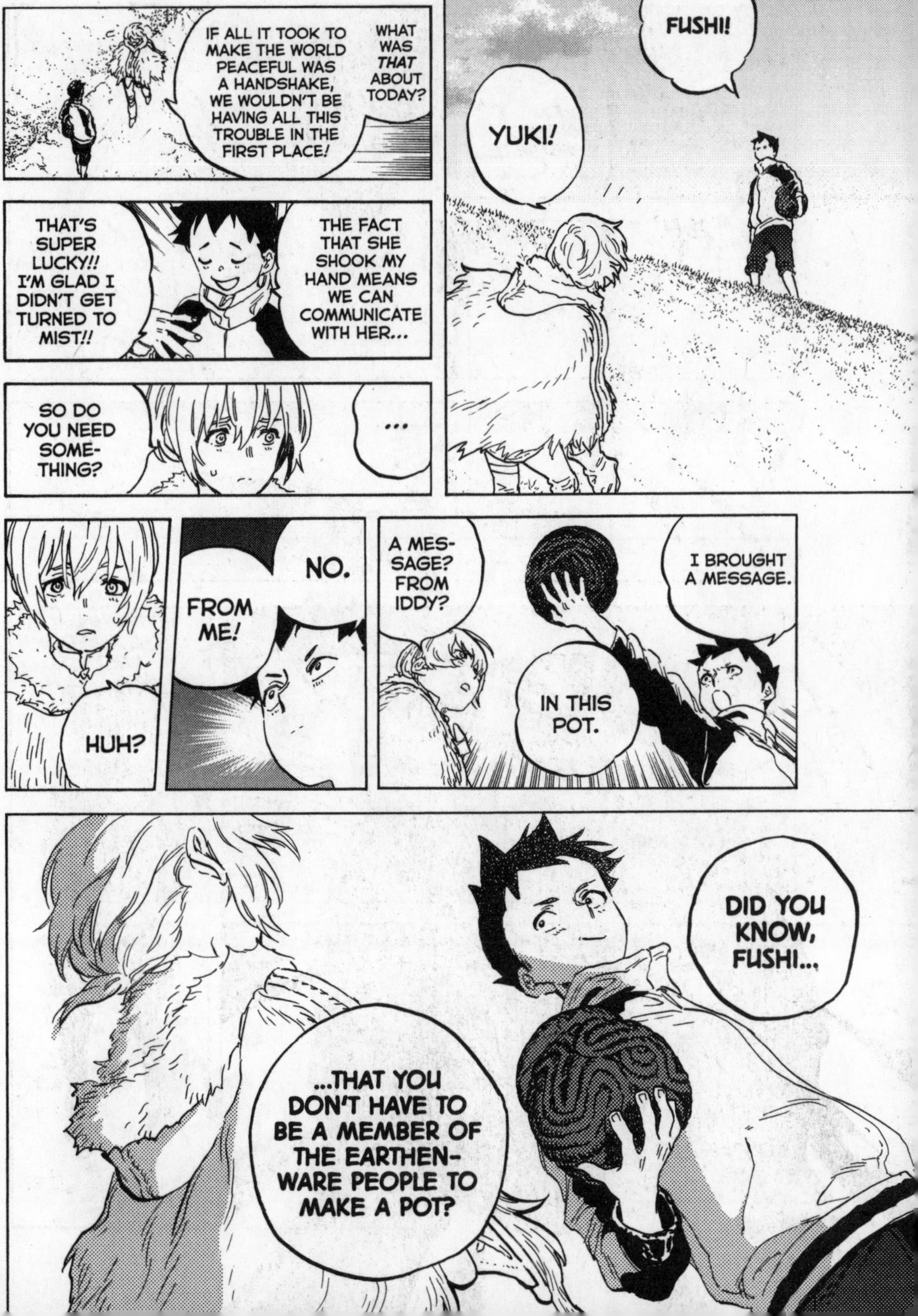
FUSHI!
YUKI!
WHAT WAS THAT ABOUT TODAY?
IF ALL IT TOOK TO MAKE THE WORLD PEACEFUL WAS A HANDSHAKE, WE WOULDN'T BE HAVING ALL THIS TROUBLE IN THE FIRST PLACE!
THE FACT THAT SHE SHOOK MY HAND MEANS WE CAN COMMUNICATE WITH HER...
THAT'S SUPER LUCKY!! I'M GLAD I DIDN'T GET TURNED TO MIST!!
...
SO DO YOU NEED SOME-THING?
I BROUGHT A MESSAGE.
IN THIS POT.
A MES-SAGE? FROM IDDY?
NO.
FROM ME!
HUH?
DID YOU KNOW, FUSHI...
...THAT YOU DON'T HAVE TO BE A MEMBER OF THE EARTHEN-WARE PEOPLE TO MAKE A POT?

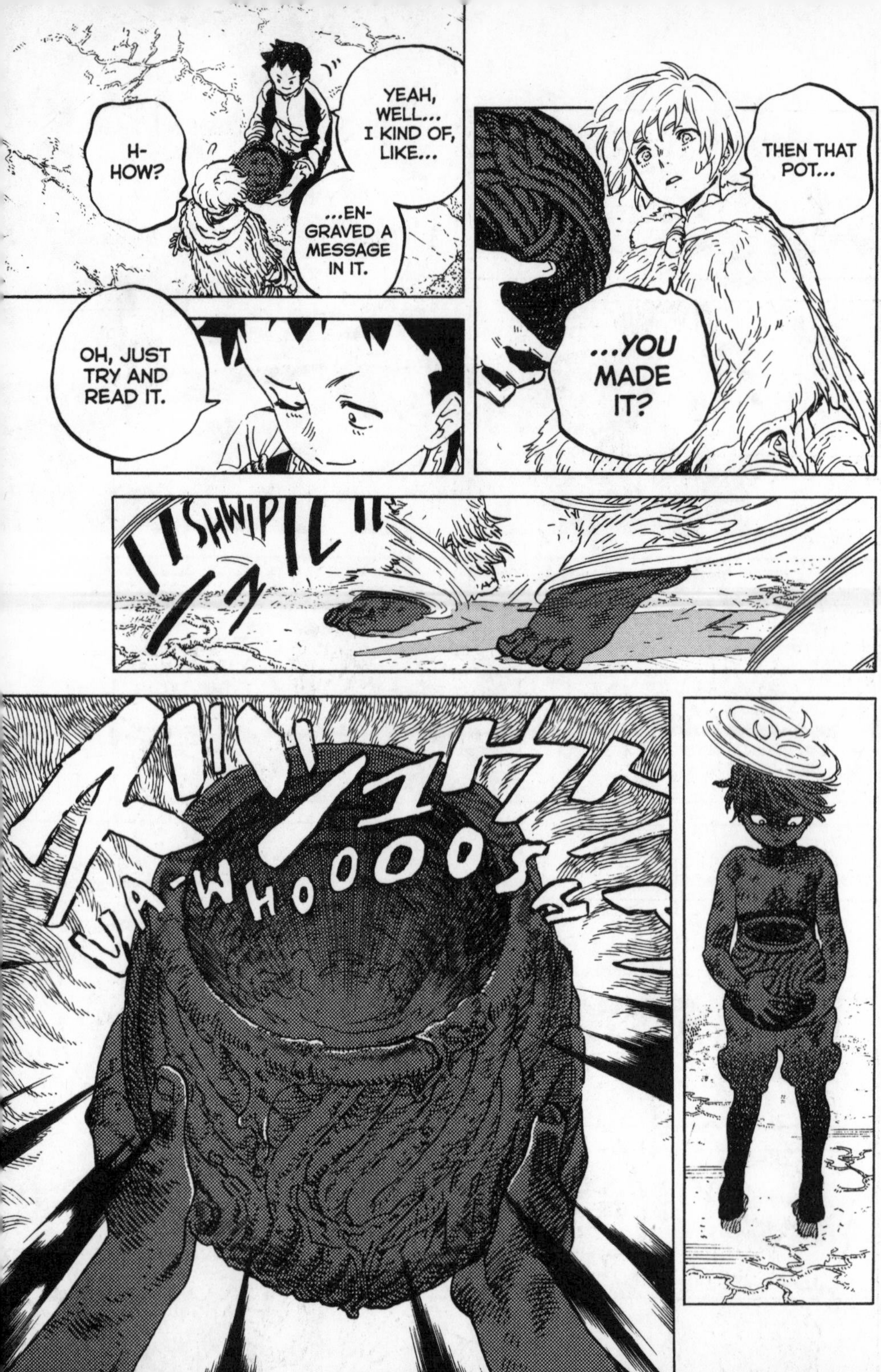
THEN THAT POT...
...YOU MADE IT?
YEAH, WELL... I KIND OF, LIKE...
...EN-GRAVED A MESSAGE IN IT.
H-HOW?
OH, JUST TRY AND READ IT.
SHWIP
VA-WHOOOOS

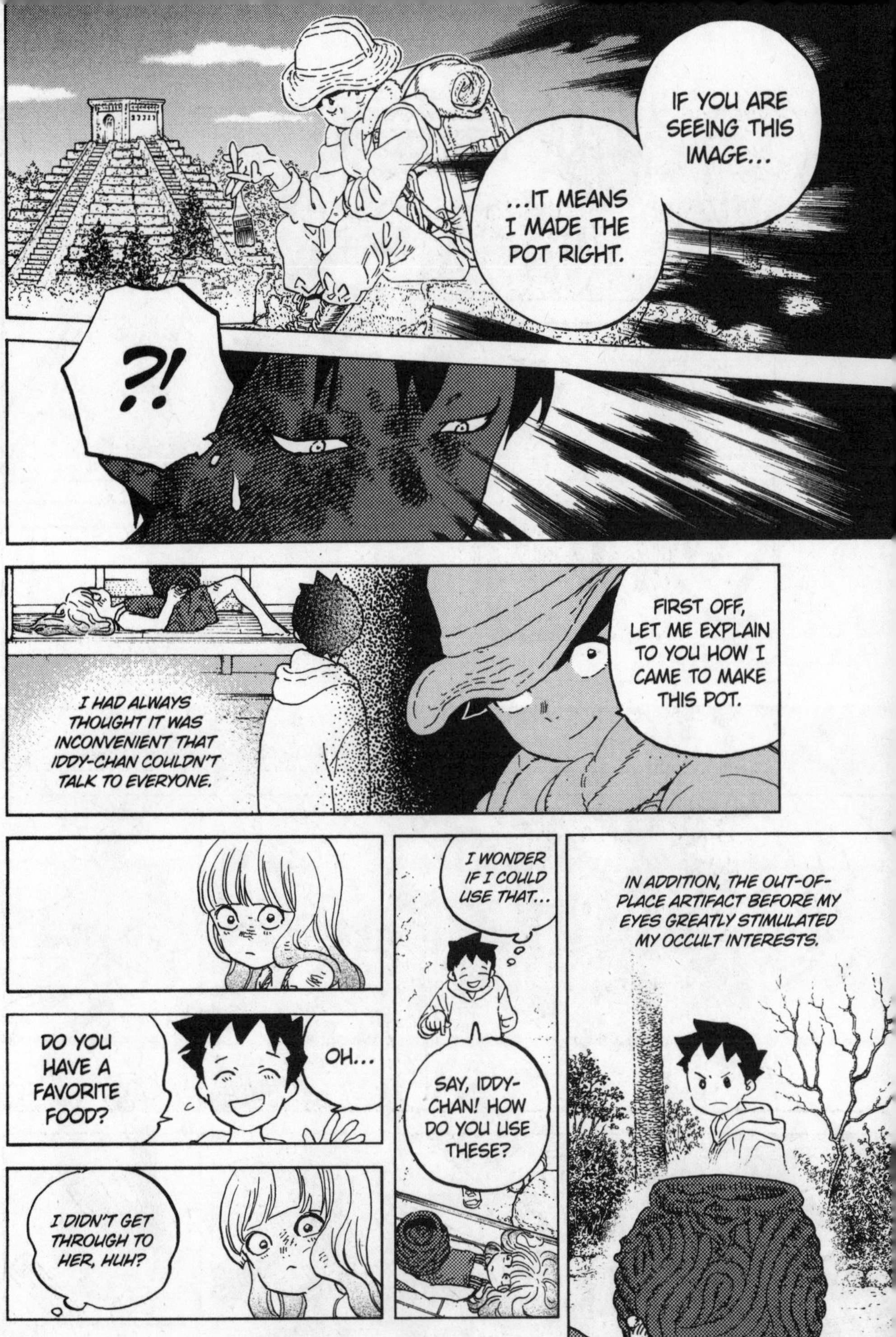
IF YOU ARE SEEING THIS IMAGE...
...IT MEANS I MADE THE POT RIGHT.
?!
FIRST OFF, LET ME EXPLAIN TO YOU HOW I CAME TO MAKE THIS POT.
I HAD ALWAYS THOUGHT IT WAS INCONVENIENT THAT IDDY-CHAN COULDN'T TALK TO EVERYONE.
IN ADDITION, THE OUT-OF-PLACE ARTIFACT BEFORE MY EYES GREATLY STIMULATED MY OCCULT INTERESTS.
I WONDER IF I COULD USE THAT...
SAY, IDDY-CHAN! HOW DO YOU USE THESE?
OH...
DO YOU HAVE A FAVORITE FOOD?
I DIDN'T GET THROUGH TO HER, HUH?

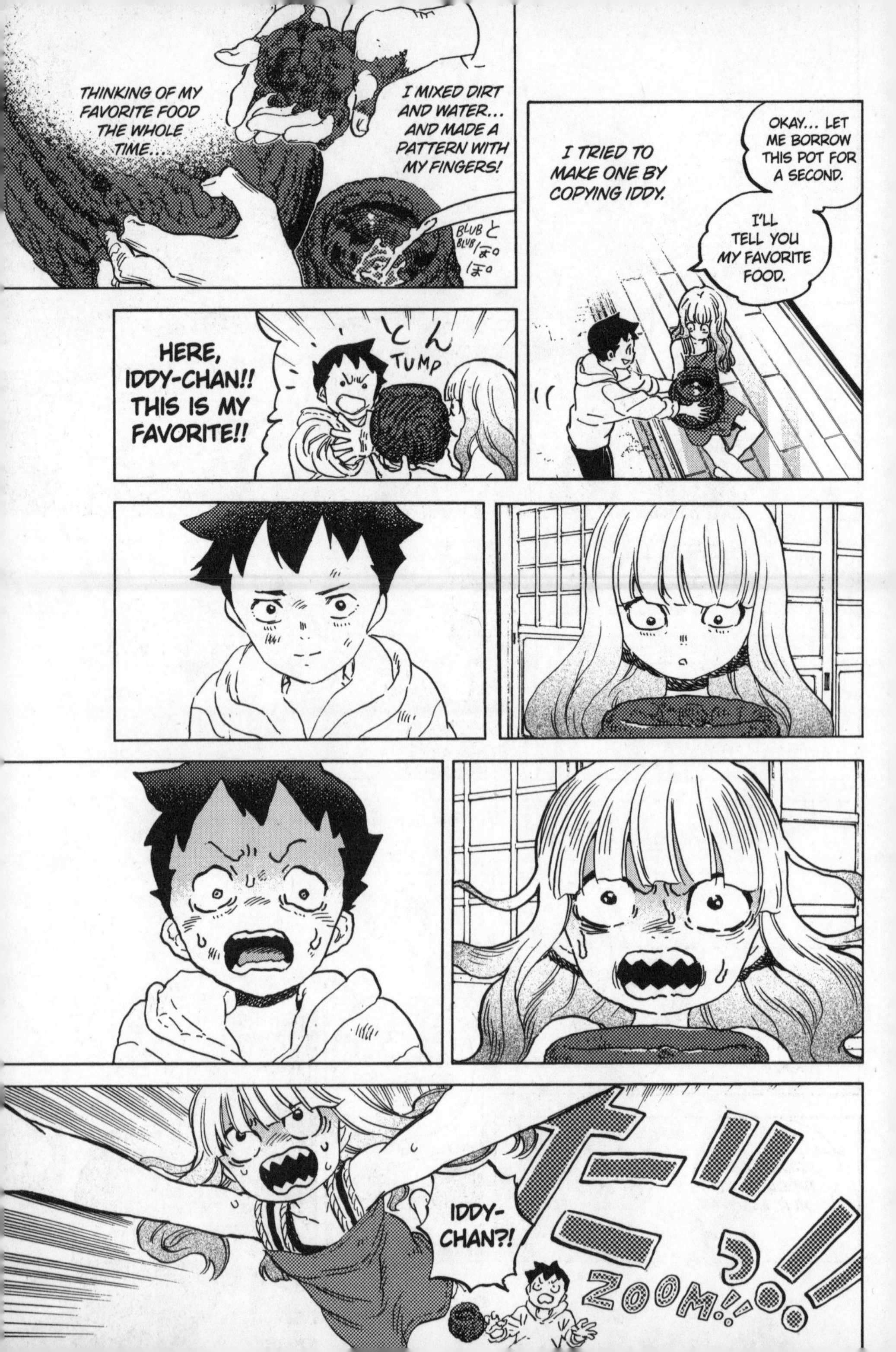
I TRIED TO MAKE ONE BY COPYING IDDY.
OKAY... LET ME BORROW THIS POT FOR A SECOND.
I'LL TELL YOU MY FAVORITE FOOD.
I MIXED DIRT AND WATER... AND MADE A PATTERN WITH MY FINGERS!
THINKING OF MY FAVORITE FOOD THE WHOLE TIME...
BLUB BLUB
とん
TUMP
HERE, IDDY-CHAN!! THIS IS MY FAVORITE!!
ZOOM!!
IDDY-CHAN?!

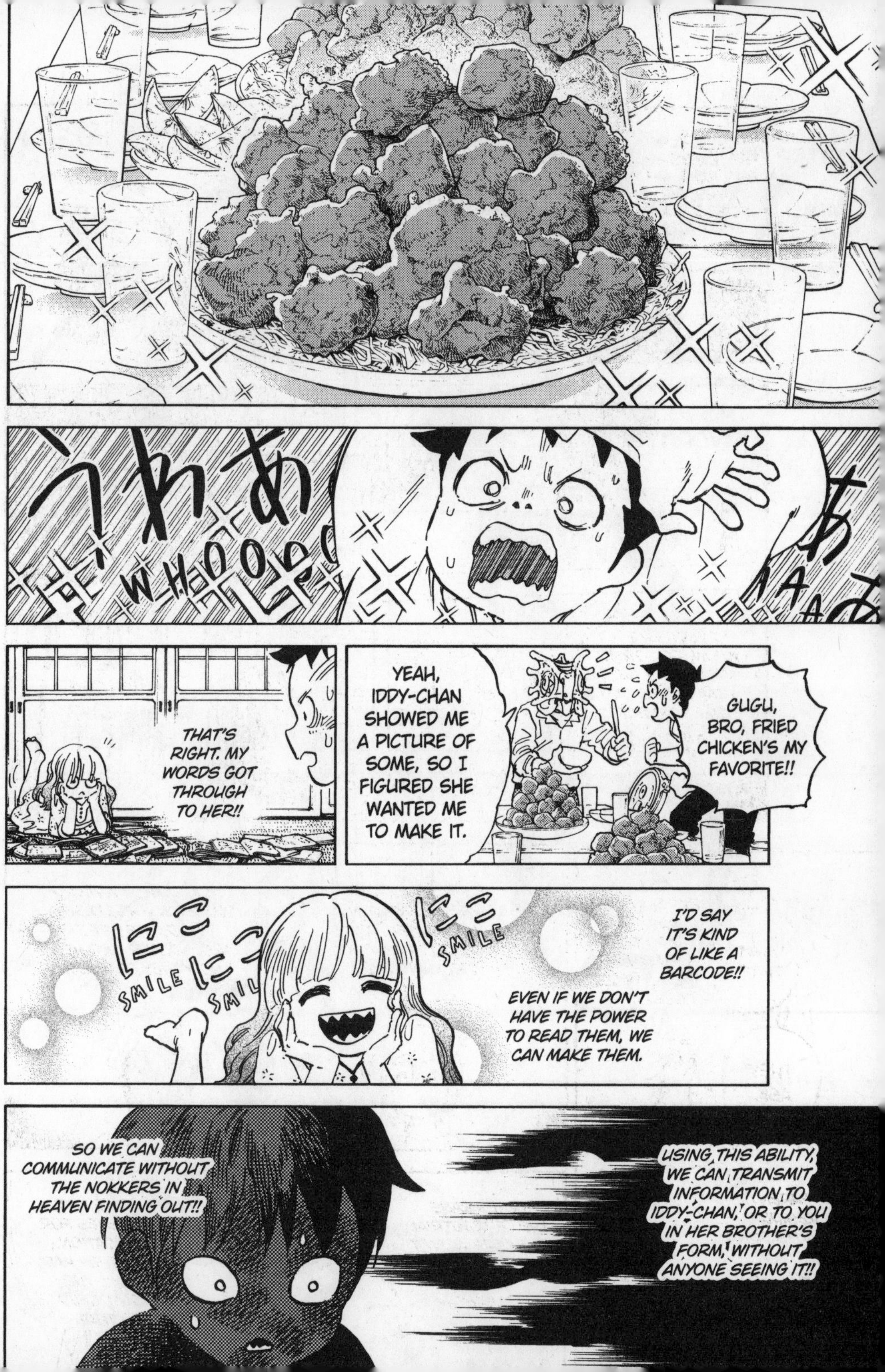
あ
うわあ
WHOOO
GUGU, BRO, FRIED CHICKEN'S MY FAVORITE!!
YEAH, IDDY-CHAN SHOWED ME A PICTURE OF SOME, SO I FIGURED SHE WANTED ME TO MAKE IT.
THAT'S RIGHT. MY WORDS GOT THROUGH TO HER!!
I'D SAY IT'S KIND OF LIKE A BARCODE!!
EVEN IF WE DON'T HAVE THE POWER TO READ THEM, WE CAN MAKE THEM.
にこ SMILE
にこ SMILE
にこ SMILE
USING THIS ABILITY, WE CAN TRANSMIT INFORMATION TO IDDY-CHAN, OR TO YOU IN HER BROTHER'S FORM, WITHOUT ANYONE SEEING IT!!
SO WE CAN COMMUNICATE WITHOUT THE NOKKERS IN HEAVEN FINDING OUT!!

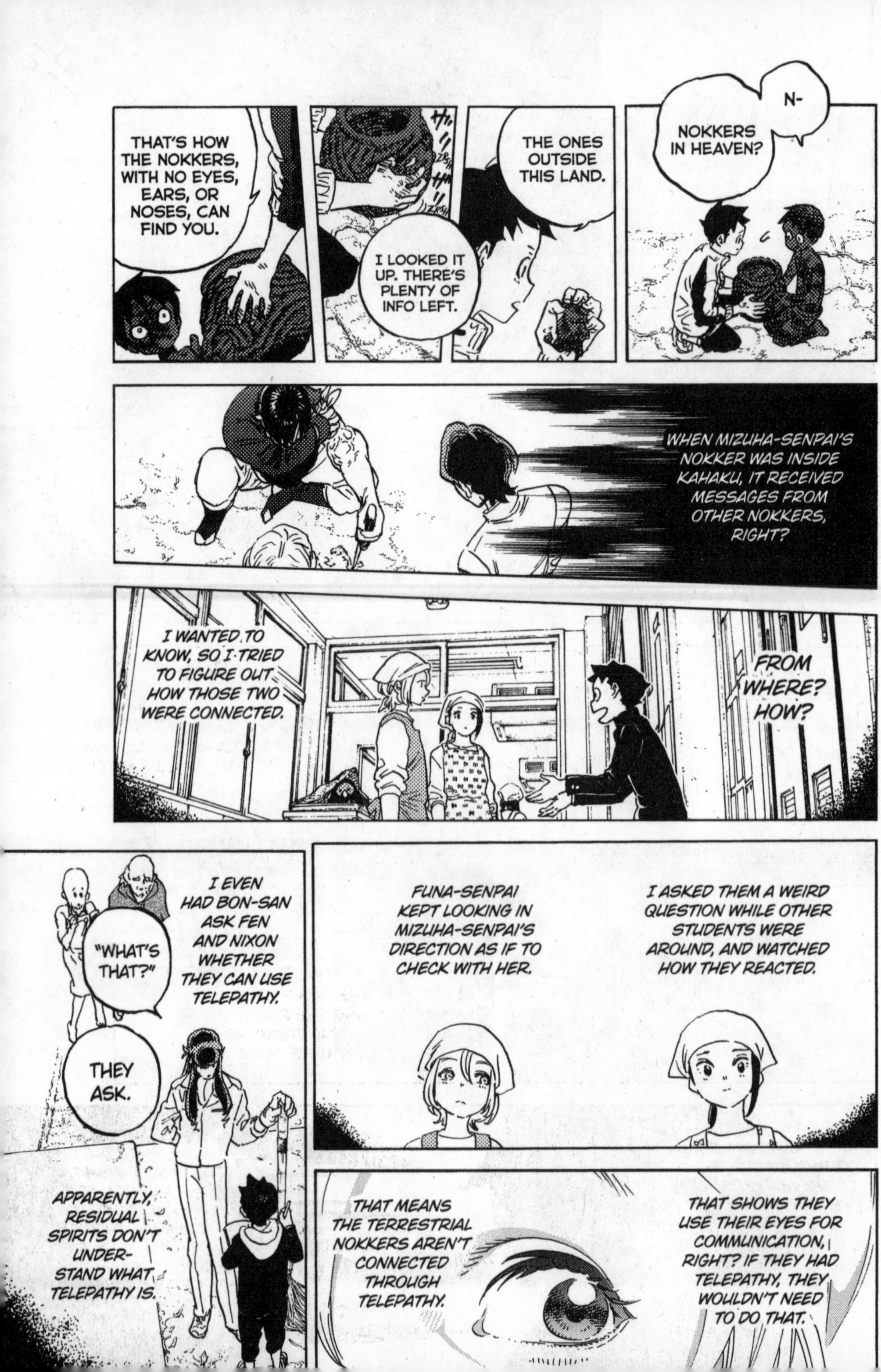
N-
NOKKERS IN HEAVEN?
THE ONES OUTSIDE THIS LAND.
I LOOKED IT UP. THERE'S PLENTY OF INFO LEFT.
THAT'S HOW THE NOKKERS, WITH NO EYES, EARS, OR NOSES, CAN FIND YOU.
WHEN MIZUHA-SENPAI'S NOKKER WAS INSIDE KAHAKU, IT RECEIVED MESSAGES FROM OTHER NOKKERS, RIGHT?
FROM WHERE? HOW?
I WANTED TO KNOW, SO I TRIED TO FIGURE OUT HOW THOSE TWO WERE CONNECTED.
I ASKED THEM A WEIRD QUESTION WHILE OTHER STUDENTS WERE AROUND, AND WATCHED HOW THEY REACTED.
FUNA-SENPAI KEPT LOOKING IN MIZUHA-SENPAI'S DIRECTION AS IF TO CHECK WITH HER.
THAT SHOWS THEY USE THEIR EYES FOR COMMUNICATION, RIGHT? IF THEY HAD TELEPATHY, THEY WOULDN'T NEED TO DO THAT.
THAT MEANS THE TERRESTRIAL NOKKERS AREN'T CONNECTED THROUGH TELEPATHY.
I EVEN HAD BON-SAN ASK FEN AND NIXON WHETHER THEY CAN USE TELEPATHY.
"WHAT'S THAT?"
THEY ASK.
APPARENTLY, RESIDUAL SPIRITS DON'T UNDER-STAND WHAT TELEPATHY IS.

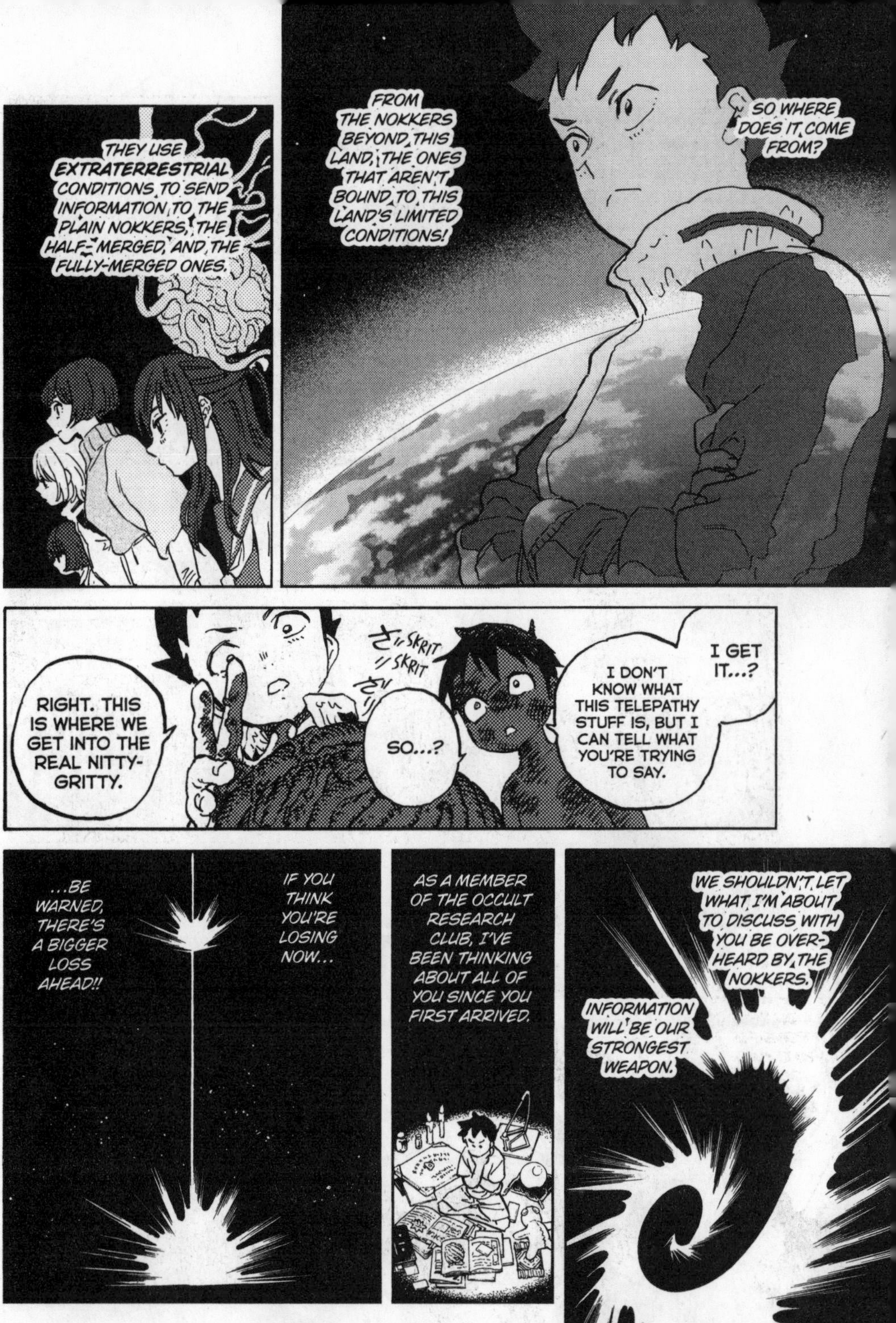

SO WHERE DOES IT COME FROM?
FROM THE NOKKERS BEYOND THIS LAND, THE ONES THAT AREN'T BOUND TO THIS LAND'S LIMITED CONDITIONS!
THEY USE **EXTRATERRESTRIAL** CONDITIONS TO SEND INFORMATION TO THE PLAIN NOKKERS, THE HALF-MERGED, AND THE FULLY-MERGED ONES.
I GET IT...?
I DON'T KNOW WHAT THIS TELEPATHY STUFF IS, BUT I CAN TELL WHAT YOU'RE TRYING TO SAY.
SKRIT
SKRIT
SO...?
RIGHT. THIS IS WHERE WE GET INTO THE REAL NITTY-GRITTY.
WE SHOULDN'T LET WHAT I'M ABOUT TO DISCUSS WITH YOU BE OVERHEARD BY THE NOKKERS.
INFORMATION WILL BE OUR STRONGEST WEAPON.
AS A MEMBER OF THE OCCULT RESEARCH CLUB, I'VE BEEN THINKING ABOUT ALL OF YOU SINCE YOU FIRST ARRIVED.
IF YOU THINK YOU'RE LOSING NOW...
...BE WARNED, THERE'S A BIGGER LOSS AHEAD!!

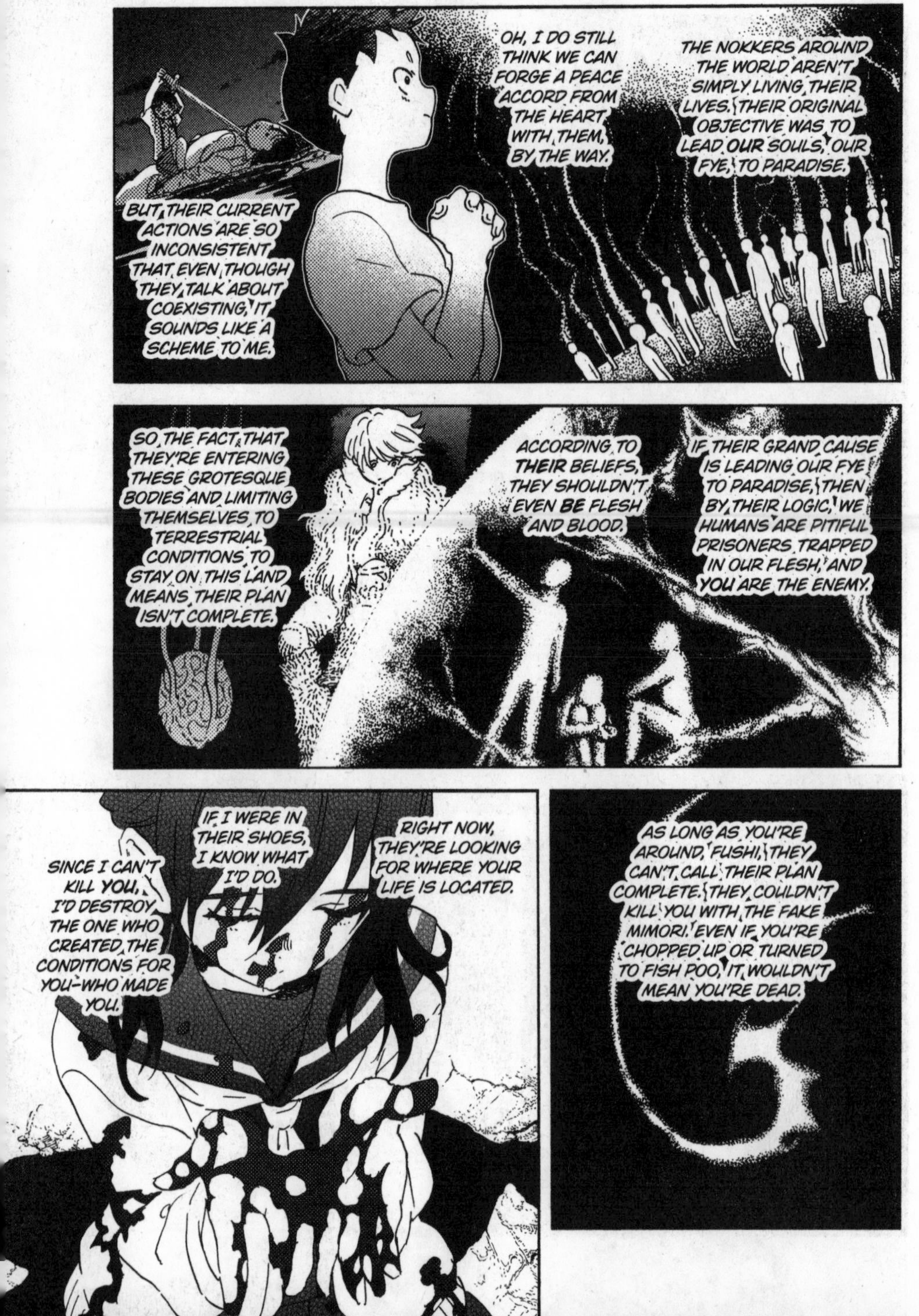
THE NOKKERS AROUND THE WORLD AREN'T SIMPLY LIVING THEIR LIVES. THEIR ORIGINAL OBJECTIVE WAS TO LEAD OUR SOULS, OUR FYE, TO PARADISE.
OH, I DO STILL THINK WE CAN FORGE A PEACE ACCORD FROM THE HEART WITH THEM, BY THE WAY.
BUT THEIR CURRENT ACTIONS ARE SO INCONSISTENT THAT EVEN THOUGH THEY TALK ABOUT COEXISTING, IT SOUNDS LIKE A SCHEME TO ME.
IF THEIR GRAND CAUSE IS LEADING OUR FYE TO PARADISE, THEN BY THEIR LOGIC, WE HUMANS ARE PITIFUL PRISONERS TRAPPED IN OUR FLESH, AND YOU ARE THE ENEMY.
ACCORDING TO THEIR BELIEFS, THEY SHOULDN'T EVEN BE FLESH AND BLOOD.
SO THE FACT THAT THEY'RE ENTERING THESE GROTESQUE BODIES AND LIMITING THEMSELVES TO TERRESTRIAL CONDITIONS TO STAY ON THIS LAND MEANS THEIR PLAN ISN'T COMPLETE.
AS LONG AS YOU'RE AROUND, FUSHI, THEY CAN'T CALL THEIR PLAN COMPLETE. THEY COULDN'T KILL YOU WITH THE FAKE MIMORI. EVEN IF YOU'RE CHOPPED UP OR TURNED TO FISH POO, IT WOULDN'T MEAN YOU'RE DEAD.
RIGHT NOW, THEY'RE LOOKING FOR WHERE YOUR LIFE IS LOCATED.
IF I WERE IN THEIR SHOES, I KNOW WHAT I'D DO.
SINCE I CAN'T KILL YOU, I'D DESTROY THE ONE WHO CREATED THE CONDITIONS FOR YOU—WHO MADE YOU.

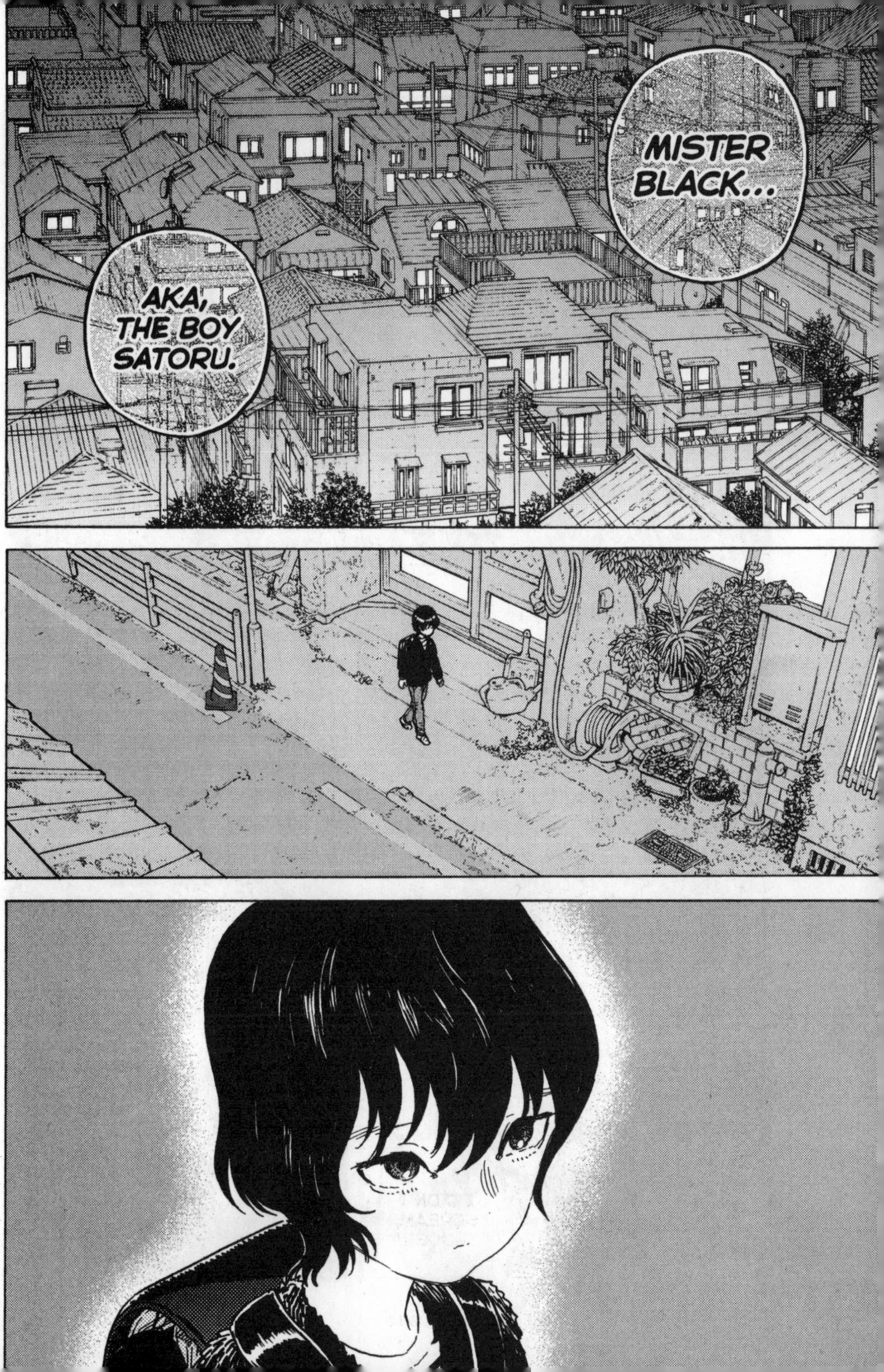
MISTER BLACK...
AKA, THE BOY SATORU.

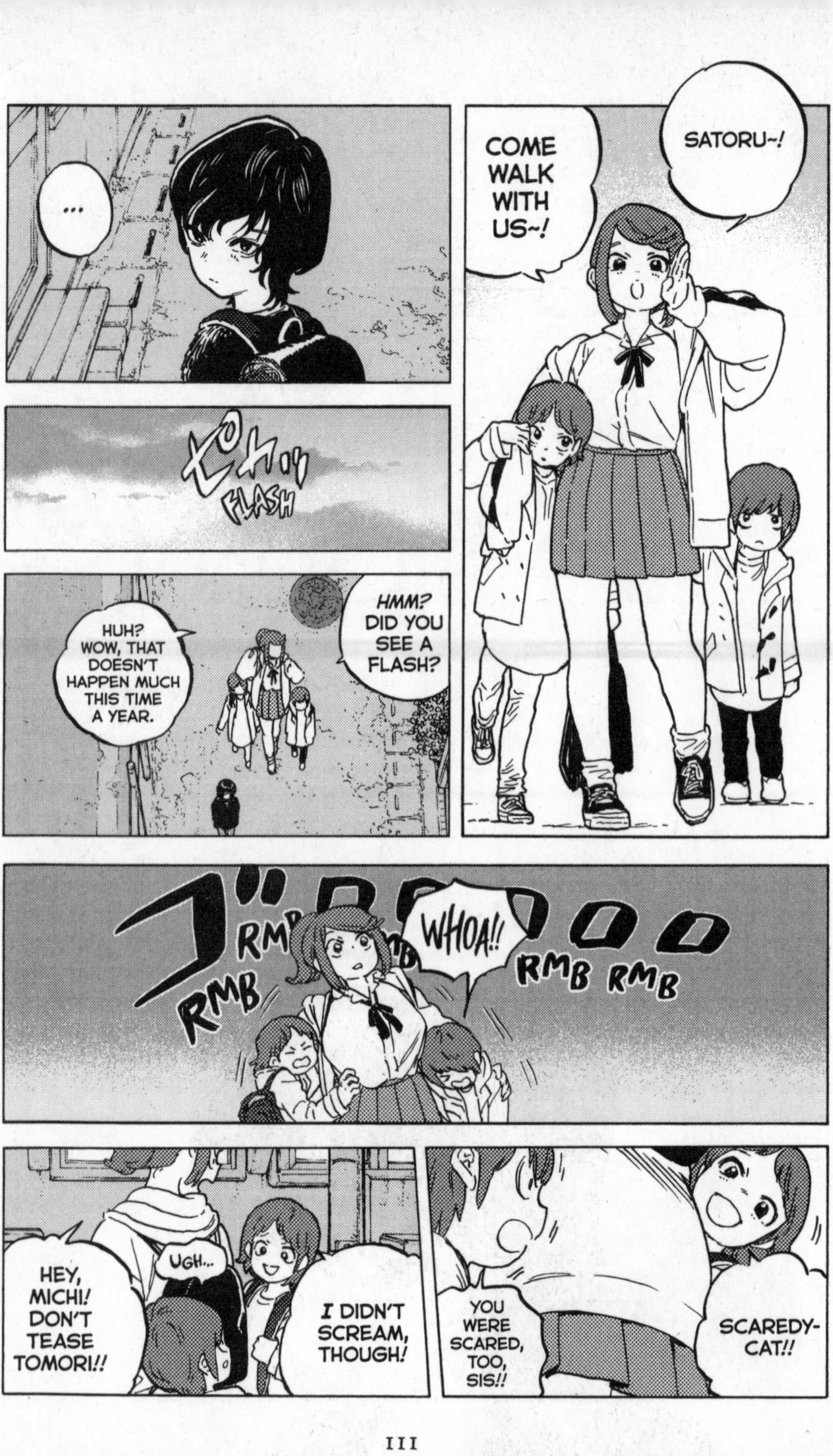
SATORU~!
COME WALK WITH US~!
...
FLASH
HMM? DID YOU SEE A FLASH?
HUH? WOW, THAT DOESN'T HAPPEN MUCH THIS TIME A YEAR.
RMB RMB
WHOA!!
RMB RMB
RMB
SCAREDY-CAT!!
YOU WERE SCARED, TOO, SIS!!
I DIDN'T SCREAM, THOUGH!
UGH...
HEY, MICHI! DON'T TEASE TOMORI!!

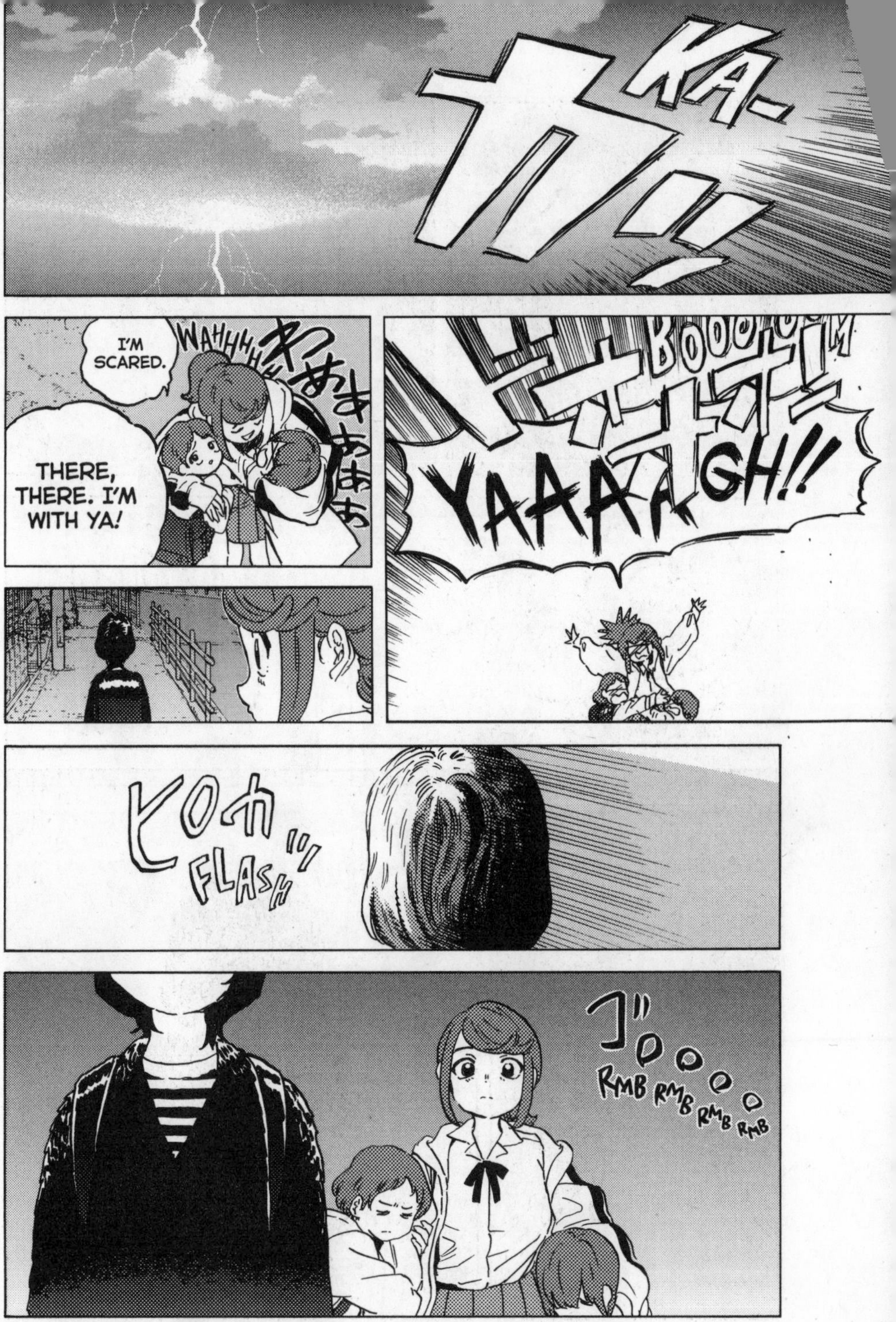
KA-
BOOOOOM!
YAAAAGH!!
I'M SCARED.
WAHHHHH
THERE, THERE. I'M WITH YA!
FLASH
RMB RMB RMB RMB

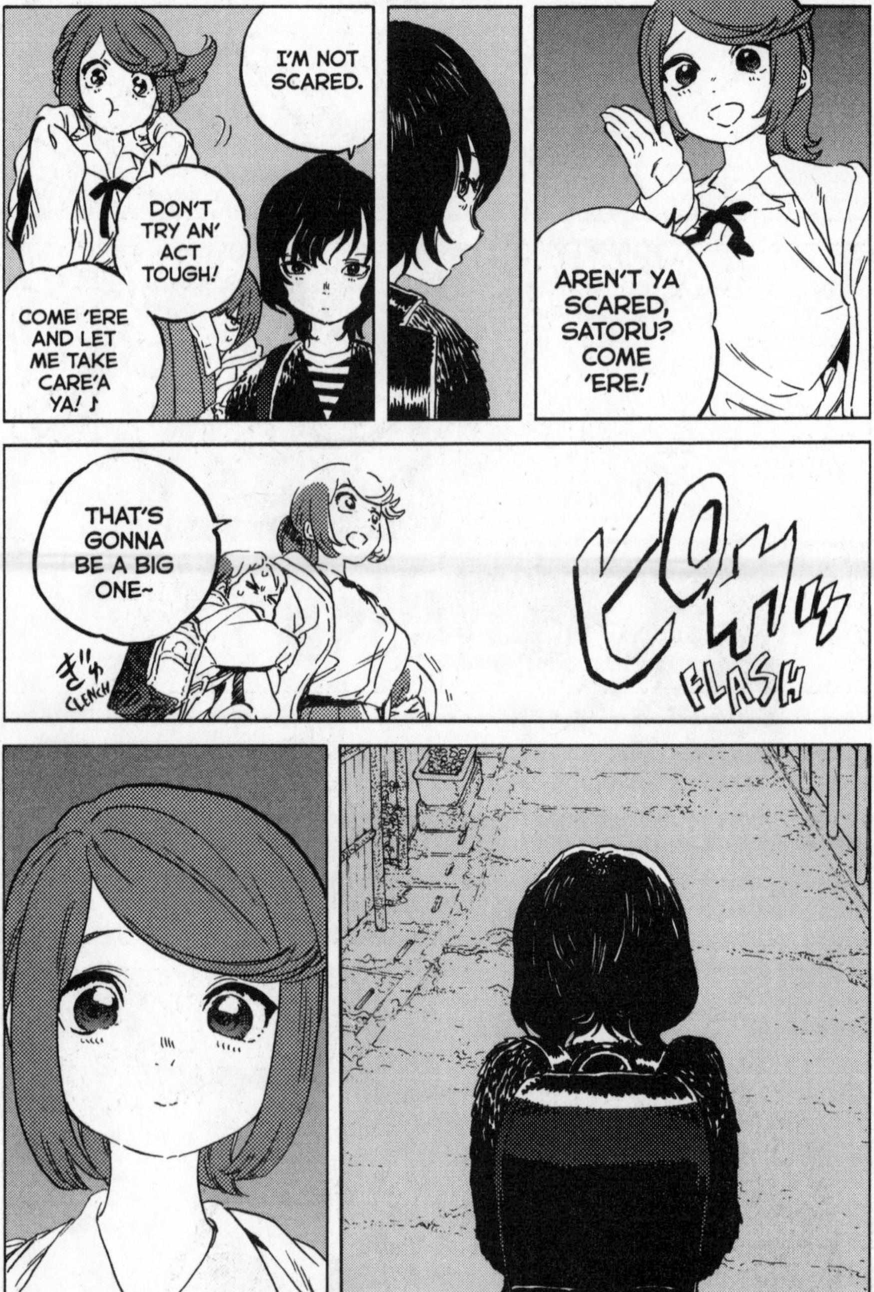
AREN'T YA SCARED, SATORU? COME 'ERE!
I'M NOT SCARED.
DON'T TRY AN' ACT TOUGH!
COME 'ERE AND LET ME TAKE CARE'A YA! ♪
FLASH
THAT'S GONNA BE A BIG ONE~
ぎゅ CLENCH

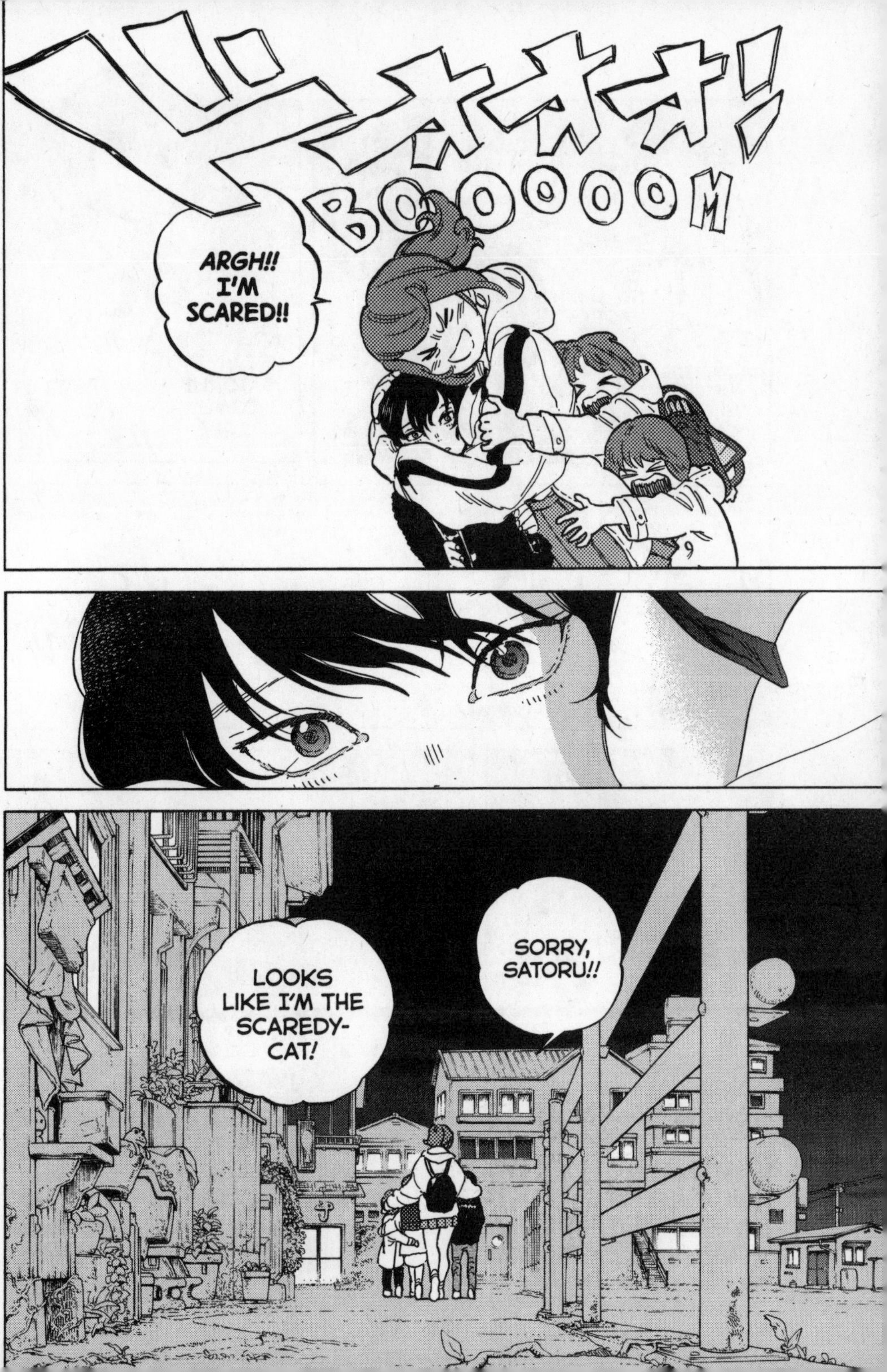
ドーオオオ!
BOOOOOM
ARGH!! I'M SCARED!!
SORRY, SATORU!!
LOOKS LIKE I'M THE SCAREDY-CAT!

TO YOUR
ETERNITY

TO YOUR

ETERNITY

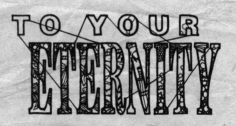

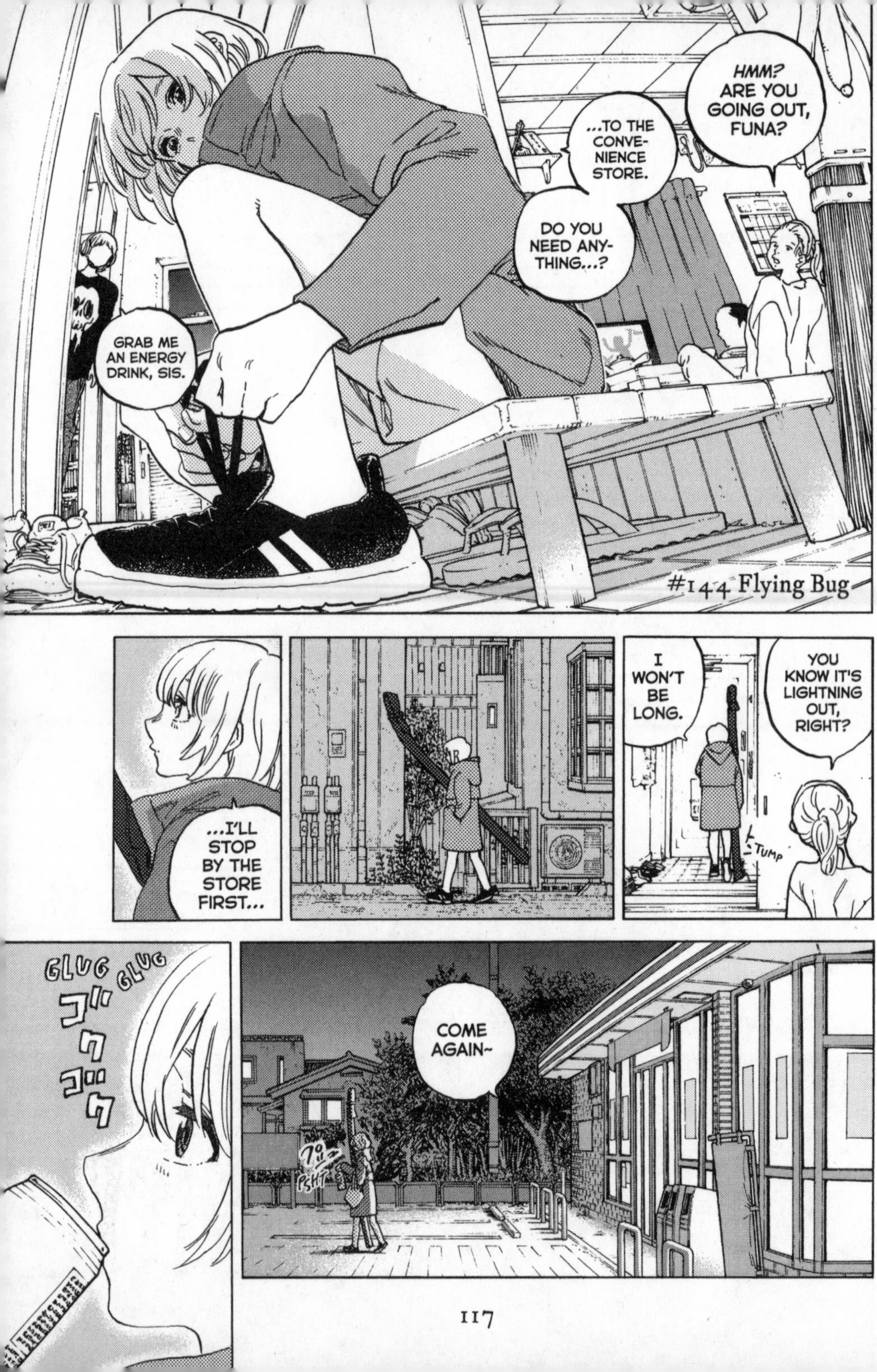
HMM? ARE YOU GOING OUT, FUNA?
...TO THE CONVENIENCE STORE.
DO YOU NEED ANYTHING...?
GRAB ME AN ENERGY DRINK, SIS.
#144 Flying Bug
YOU KNOW IT'S LIGHTNING OUT, RIGHT?
I WON'T BE LONG.
TUMP
...I'LL STOP BY THE STORE FIRST...
COME AGAIN~
PSHT
GLUG GLUG
ゴクゴク

PHEW!
THIS TASTES GREAT FOR SOMETHING WITH NO CALORIES...
I'LL HAVE TO BUY ANOTHER SOMETIME...
NOW THEN...

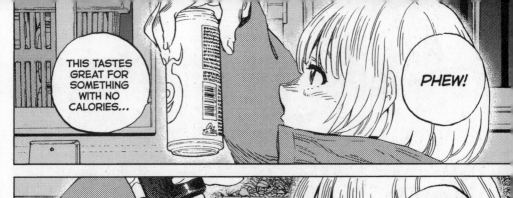

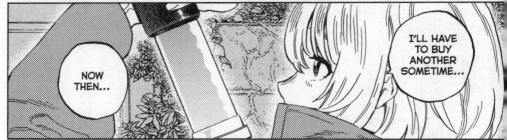

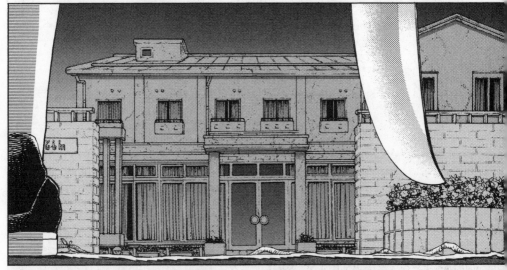

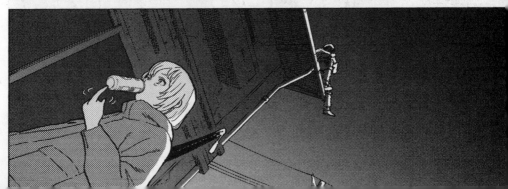

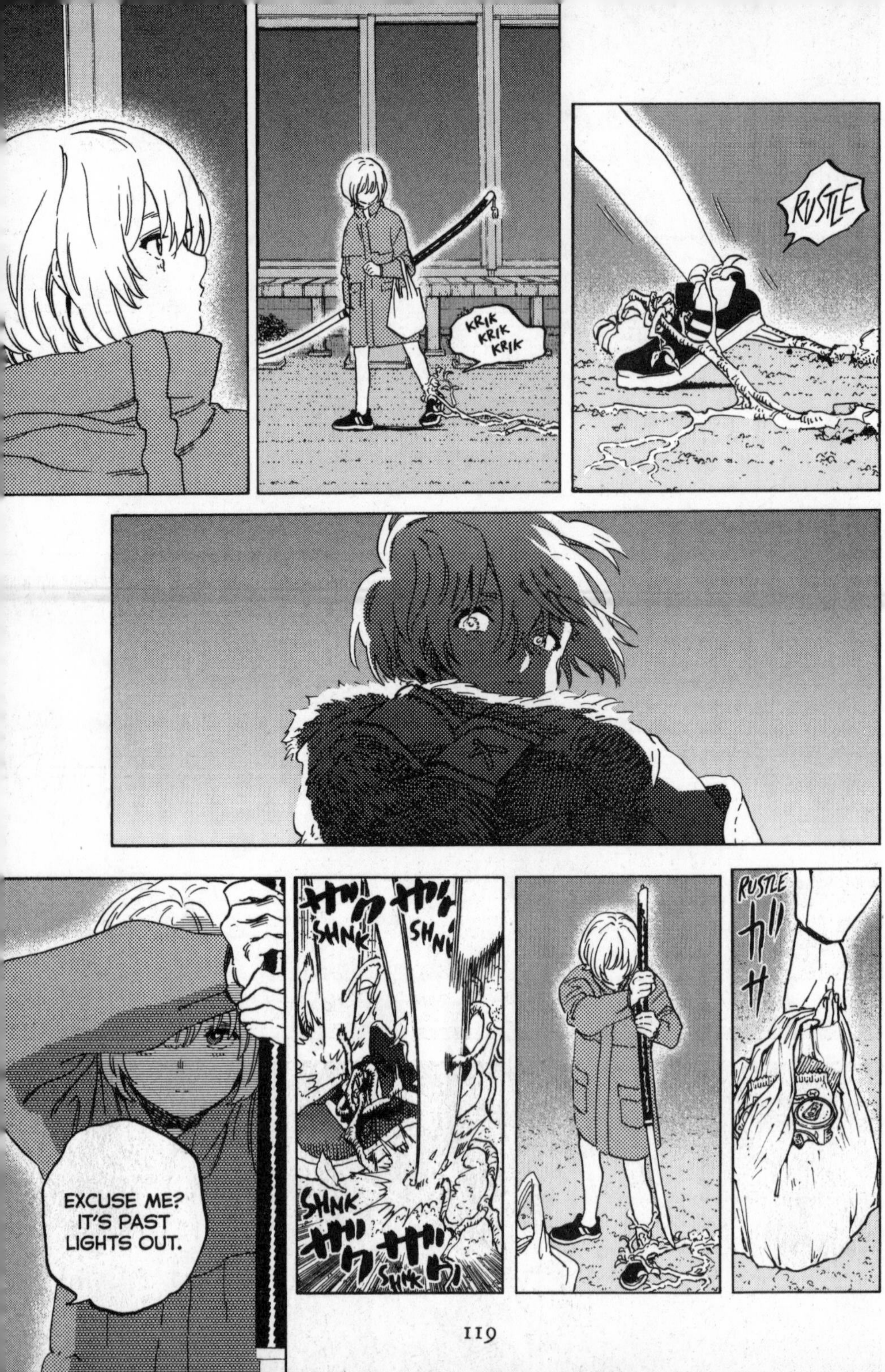
RUSTLE
KRIK KRIK KRIK
RUSTLE
ガサ
ザク SHNK
ザク SHNK
SHNK
ザクザク
SHNK
EXCUSE ME? IT'S PAST LIGHTS OUT.

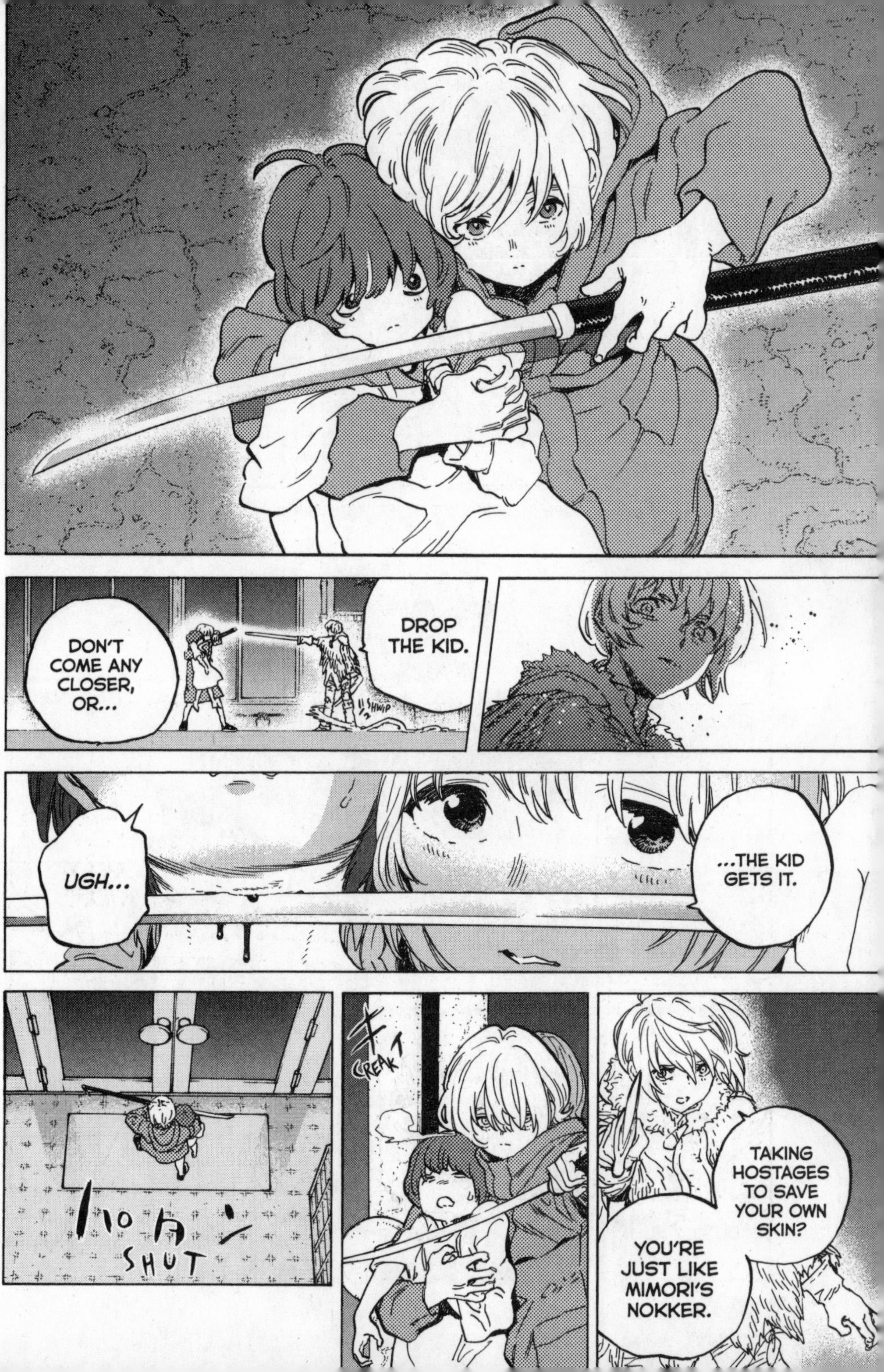
DROP THE KID.
DON'T COME ANY CLOSER, OR...
SHWIP
...THE KID GETS IT.
UGH...
TAKING HOSTAGES TO SAVE YOUR OWN SKIN?
YOU'RE JUST LIKE MIMORI'S NOKKER.
CREAK
SHUT

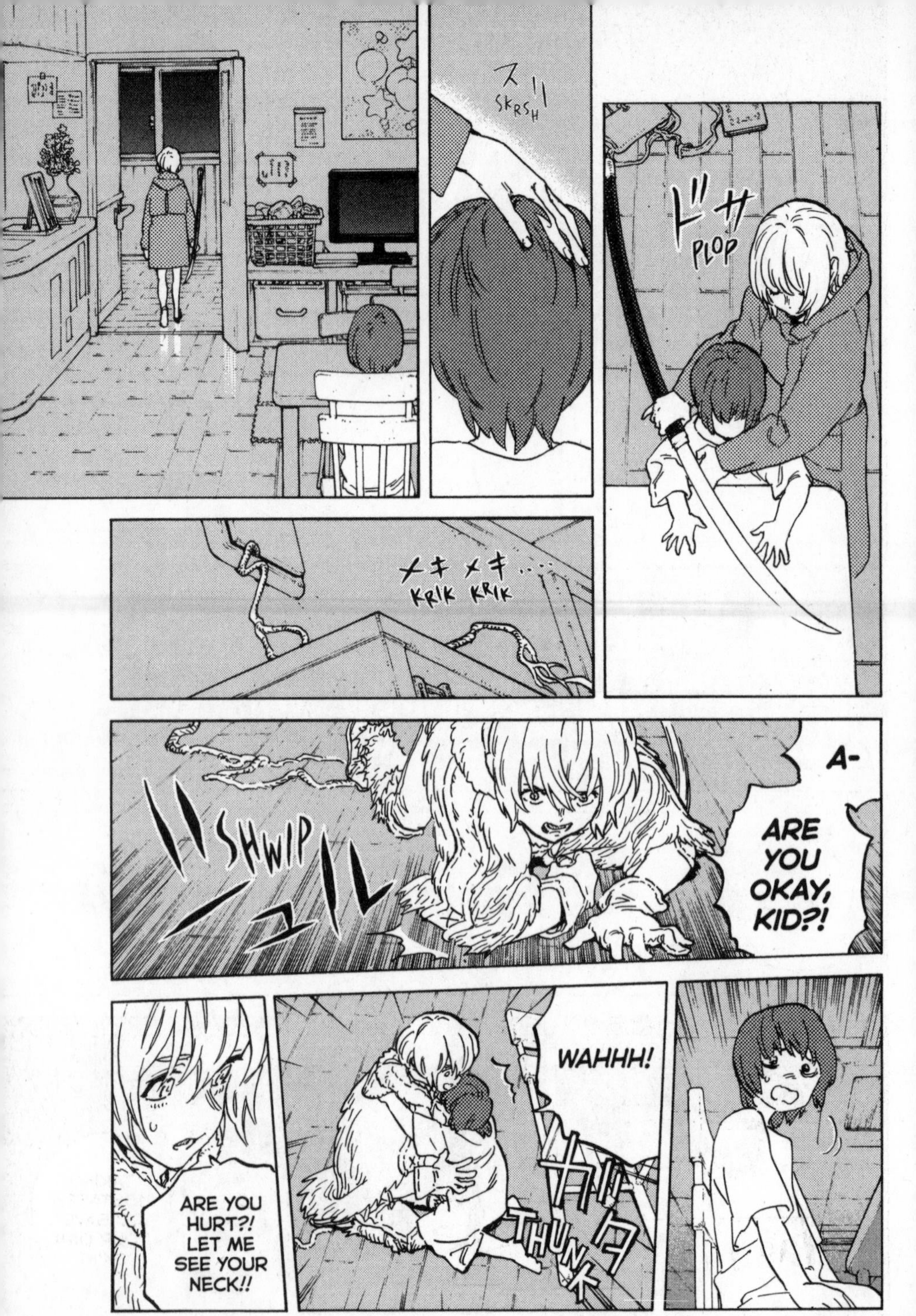

スリ
SKRSH
ドサ
PLOP
メキメキ…
KRIK KRIK
A-
ARE YOU OKAY, KID?!
シュル
SHWIP
WAHHH!
カタ
THUNK
ARE YOU HURT?! LET ME SEE YOUR NECK!!

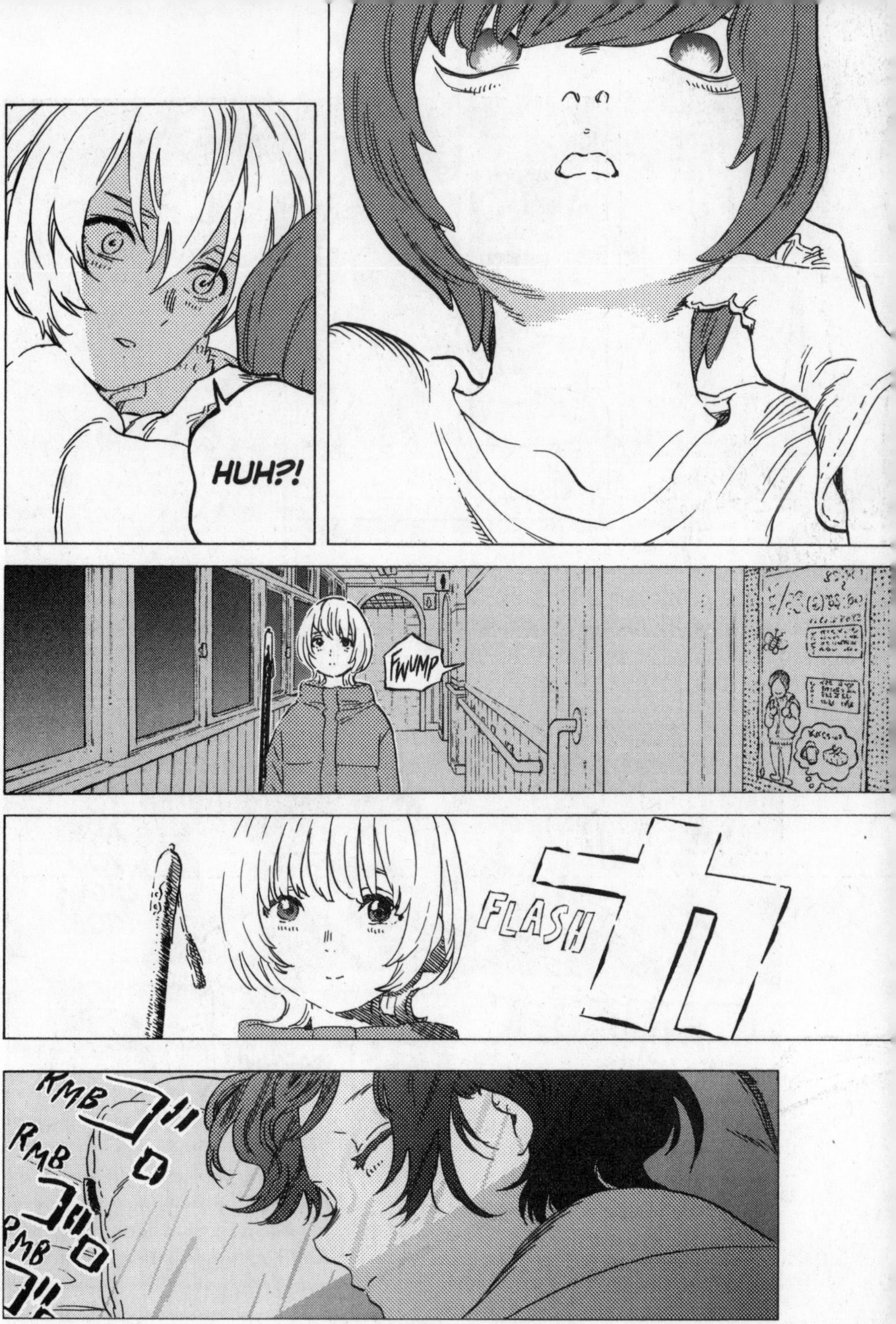
HUH?!
FWUMP
FLASH
RMB
RMB
RMB

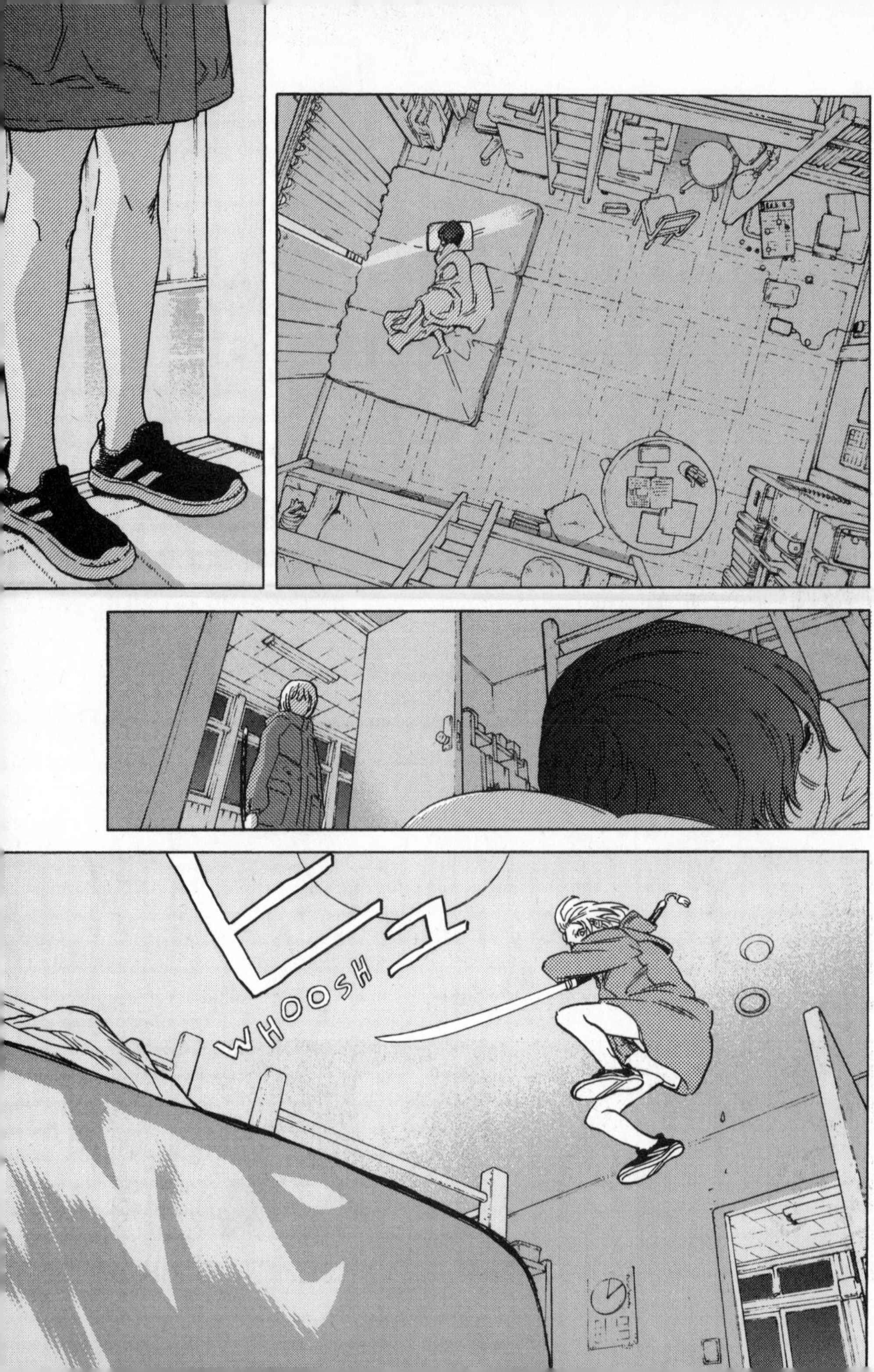
ヒュ
WHOOSH

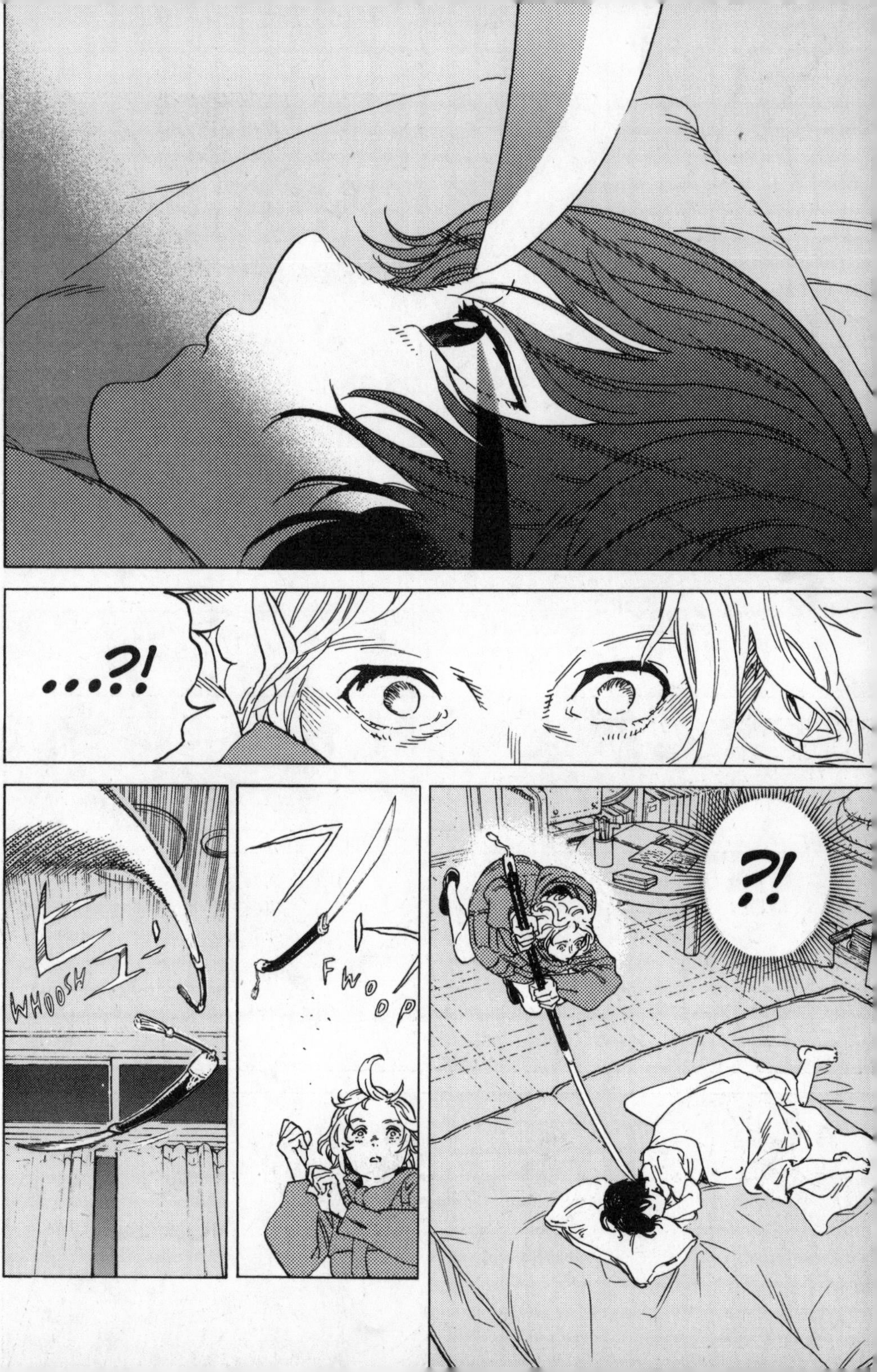
...?!
?!
FWOOP
ヒュ
WHOOSH

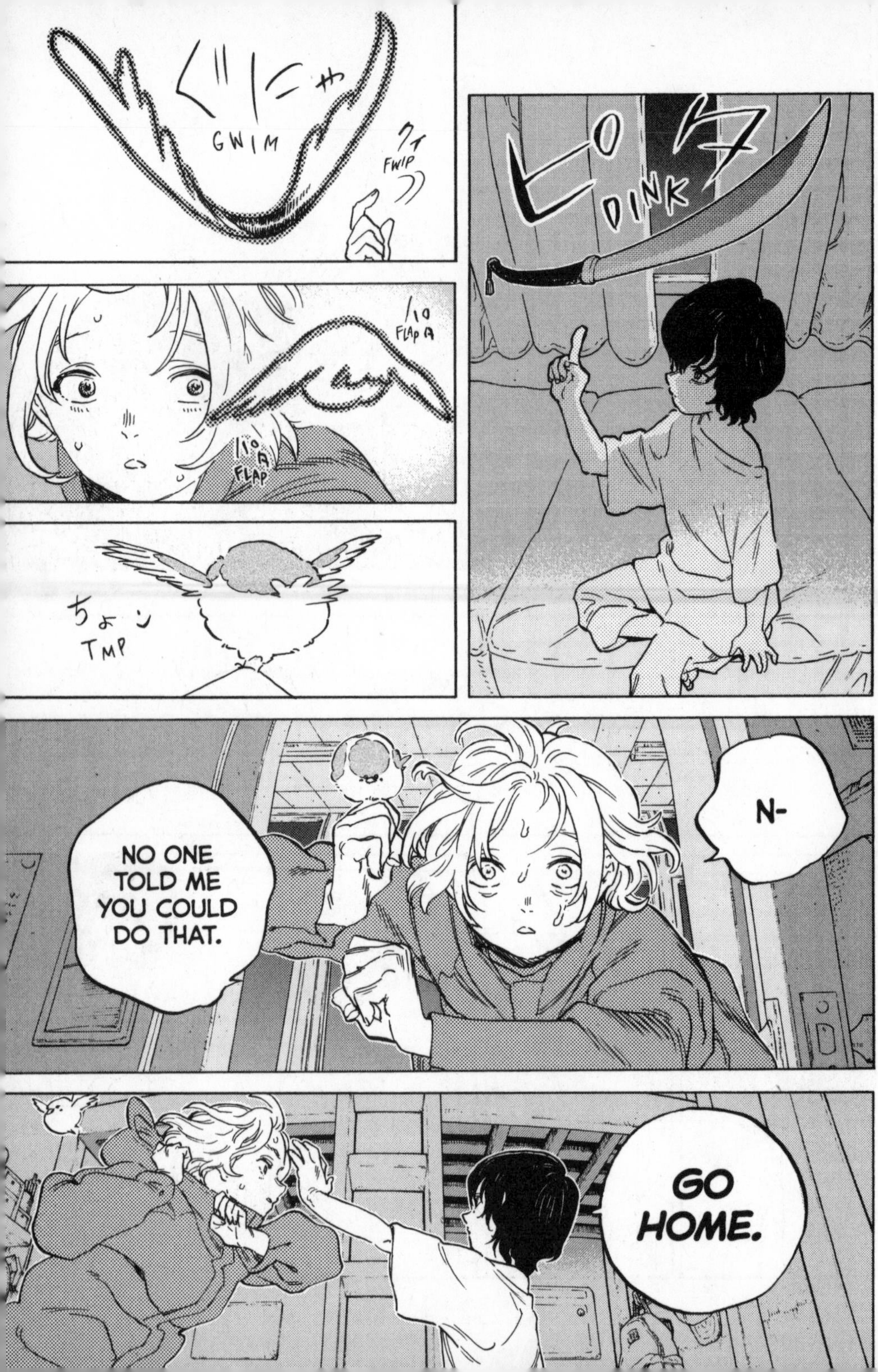

ピク
DINK
ぐにゃ
GWIM
クイ
FWIP
パタ
FLAP
パタ
FLAP
ちょン
TMP
N-
NO ONE TOLD ME YOU COULD DO THAT.
GO HOME.

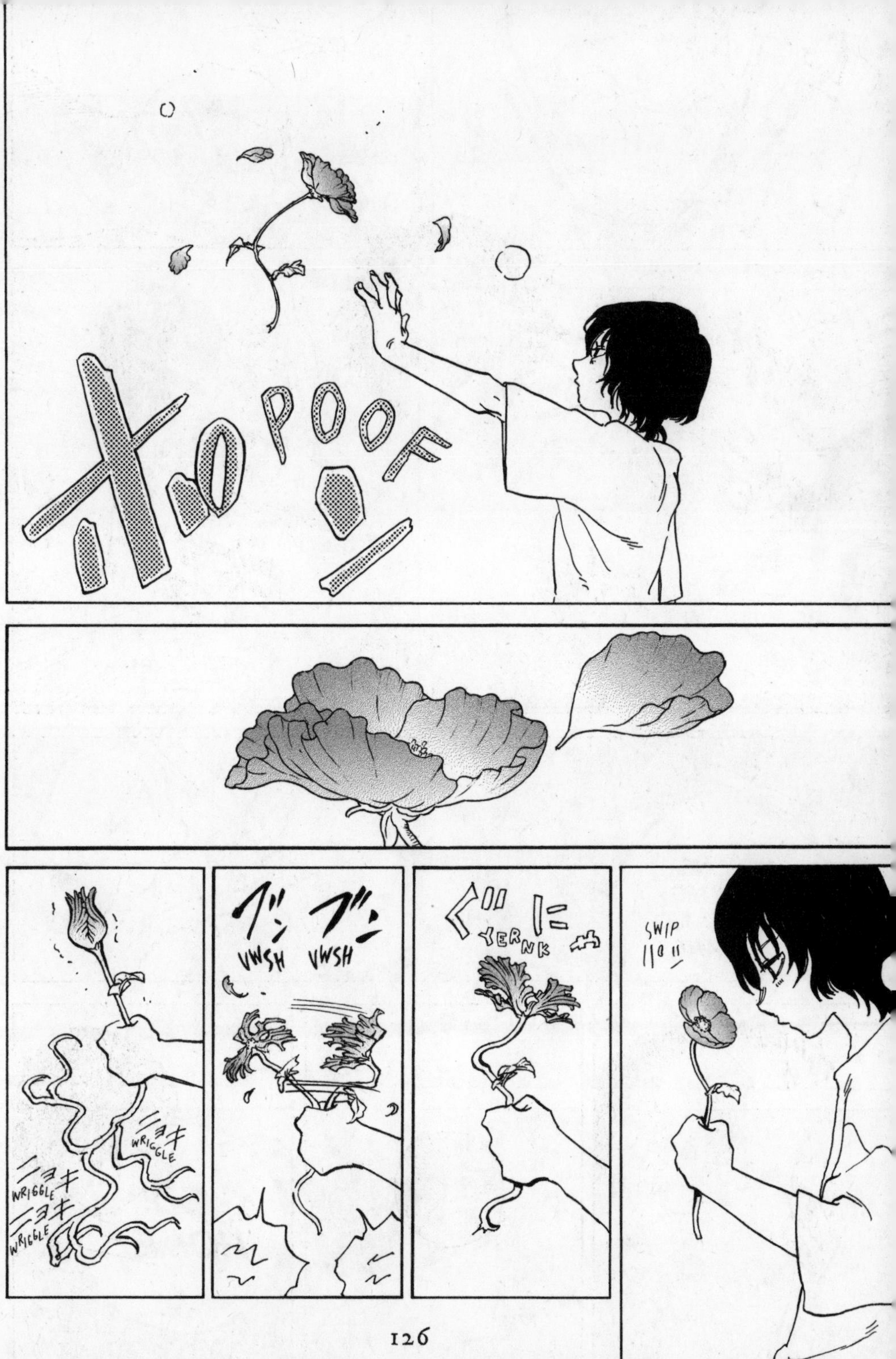
POOF
SWIP
YERNK
ブン ブン
VWSH VWSH
ニョキ
WRIGGLE
ニョキ
WRIGGLE
ニョキ
WRIGGLE

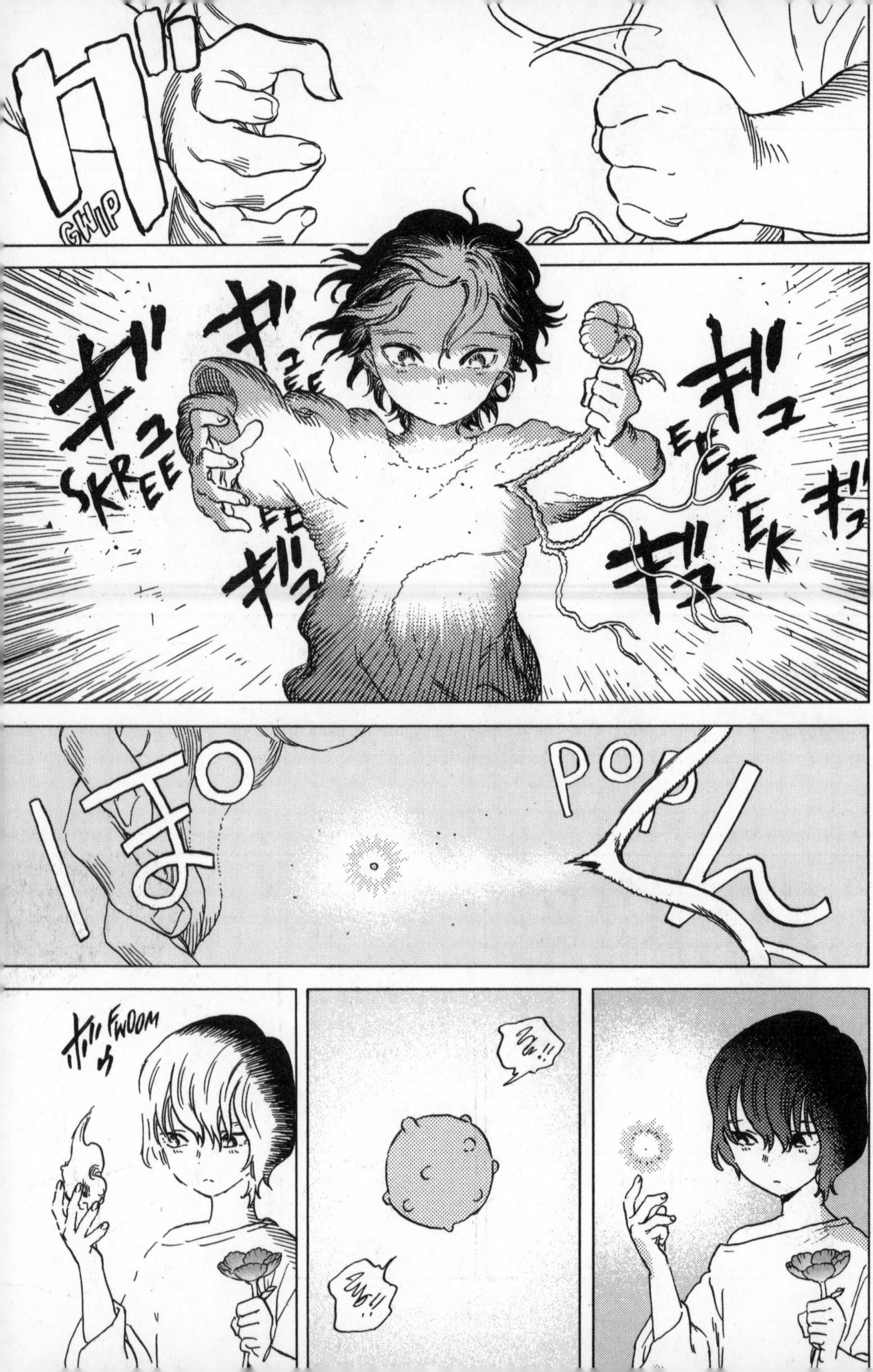

GWIP
EEEEK
SKREEEEE
POP
FWOOM

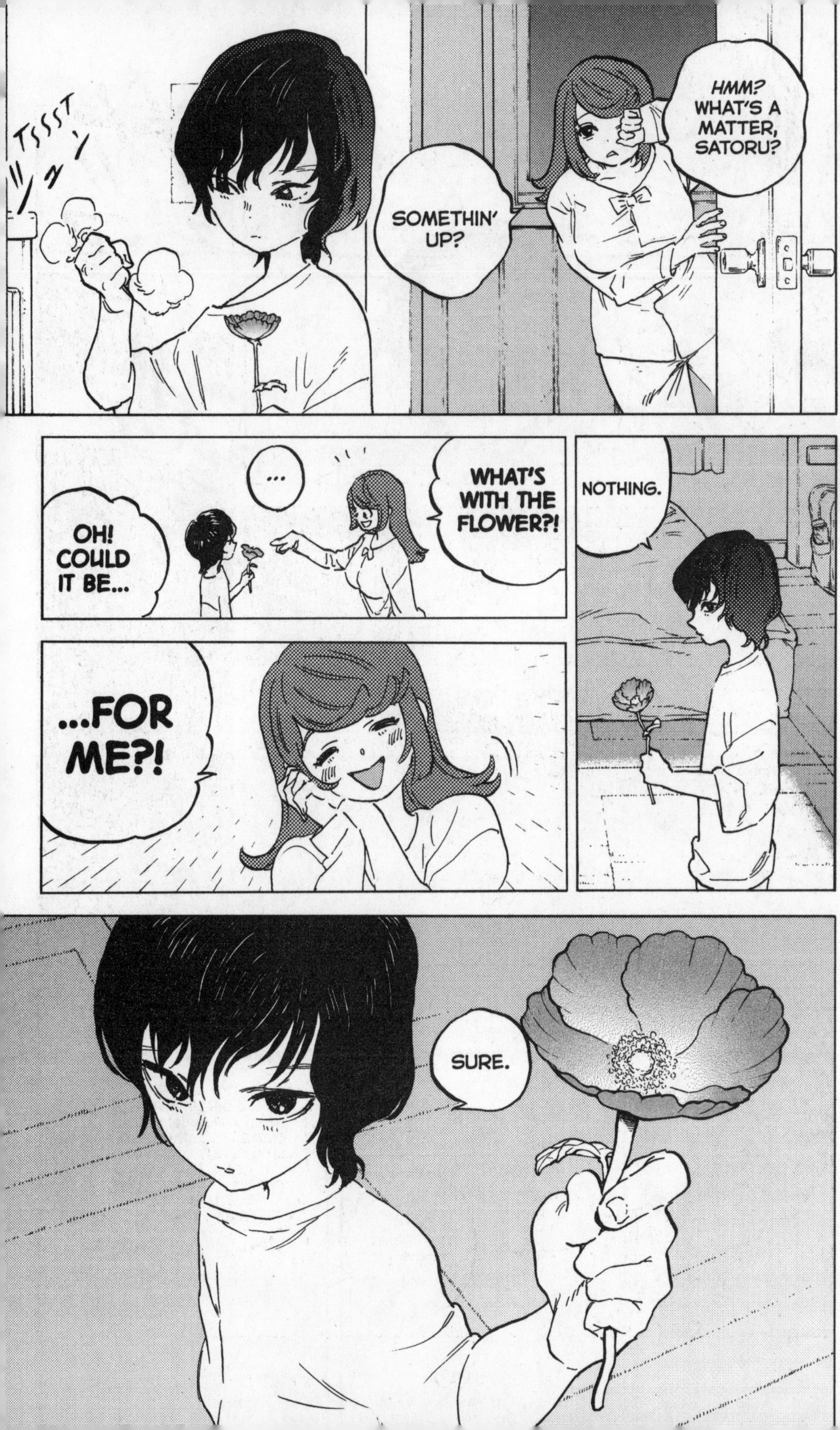
HMM? WHAT'S A MATTER, SATORU?
SOMETHIN' UP?
TSSSST
NOTHING.
WHAT'S WITH THE FLOWER?!
...
OH! COULD IT BE...
...FOR ME?!
SURE.

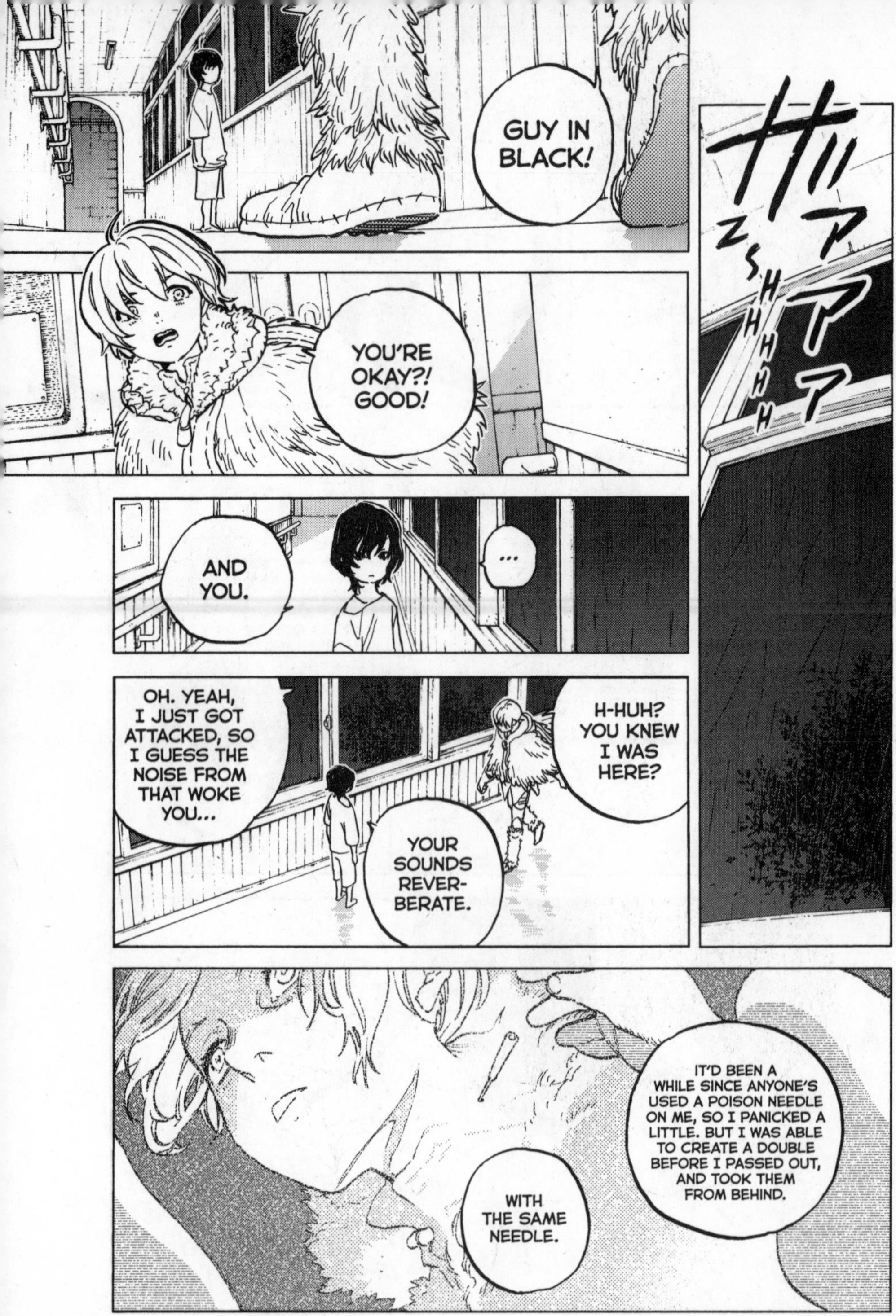
ザァァァ
ZSHHHHHH
GUY IN BLACK!
YOU'RE OKAY?! GOOD!
...
AND YOU.
H-HUH? YOU KNEW I WAS HERE?
YOUR SOUNDS REVERBERATE.
OH. YEAH, I JUST GOT ATTACKED, SO I GUESS THE NOISE FROM THAT WOKE YOU...
IT'D BEEN A WHILE SINCE ANYONE'S USED A POISON NEEDLE ON ME, SO I PANICKED A LITTLE. BUT I WAS ABLE TO CREATE A DOUBLE BEFORE I PASSED OUT, AND TOOK THEM FROM BEHIND.
WITH THE SAME NEEDLE.

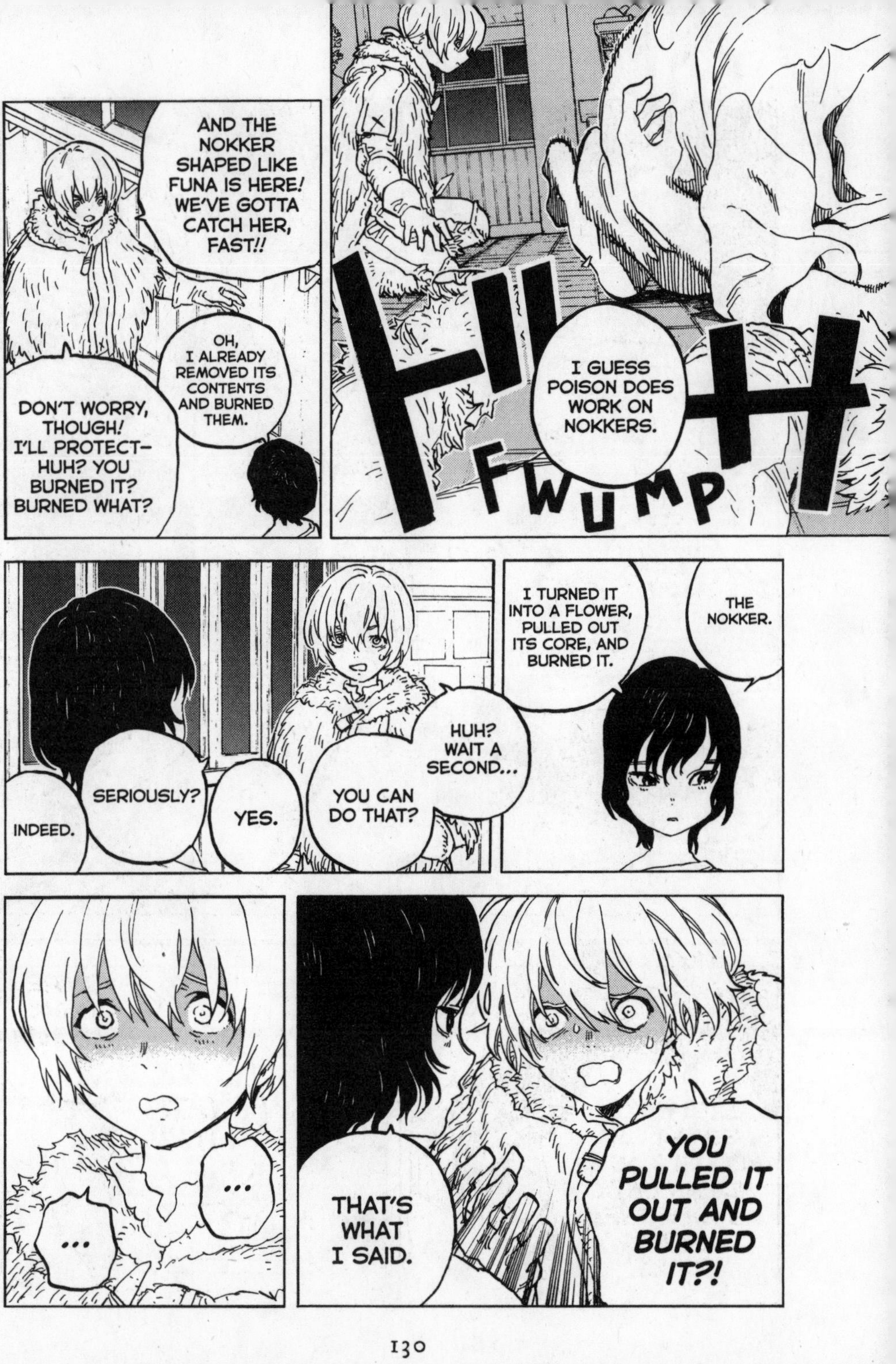
I GUESS POISON DOES WORK ON NOKKERS.
FWUMP
AND THE NOKKER SHAPED LIKE FUNA IS HERE! WE'VE GOTTA CATCH HER, FAST!!
OH, I ALREADY REMOVED ITS CONTENTS AND BURNED THEM.
DON'T WORRY, THOUGH! I'LL PROTECT— HUH? YOU BURNED IT? BURNED WHAT?
THE NOKKER.
I TURNED IT INTO A FLOWER, PULLED OUT ITS CORE, AND BURNED IT.
HUH? WAIT A SECOND...
YOU CAN DO THAT?
YES.
SERIOUSLY?
INDEED.
YOU PULLED IT OUT AND BURNED IT?!
THAT'S WHAT I SAID.
...
...

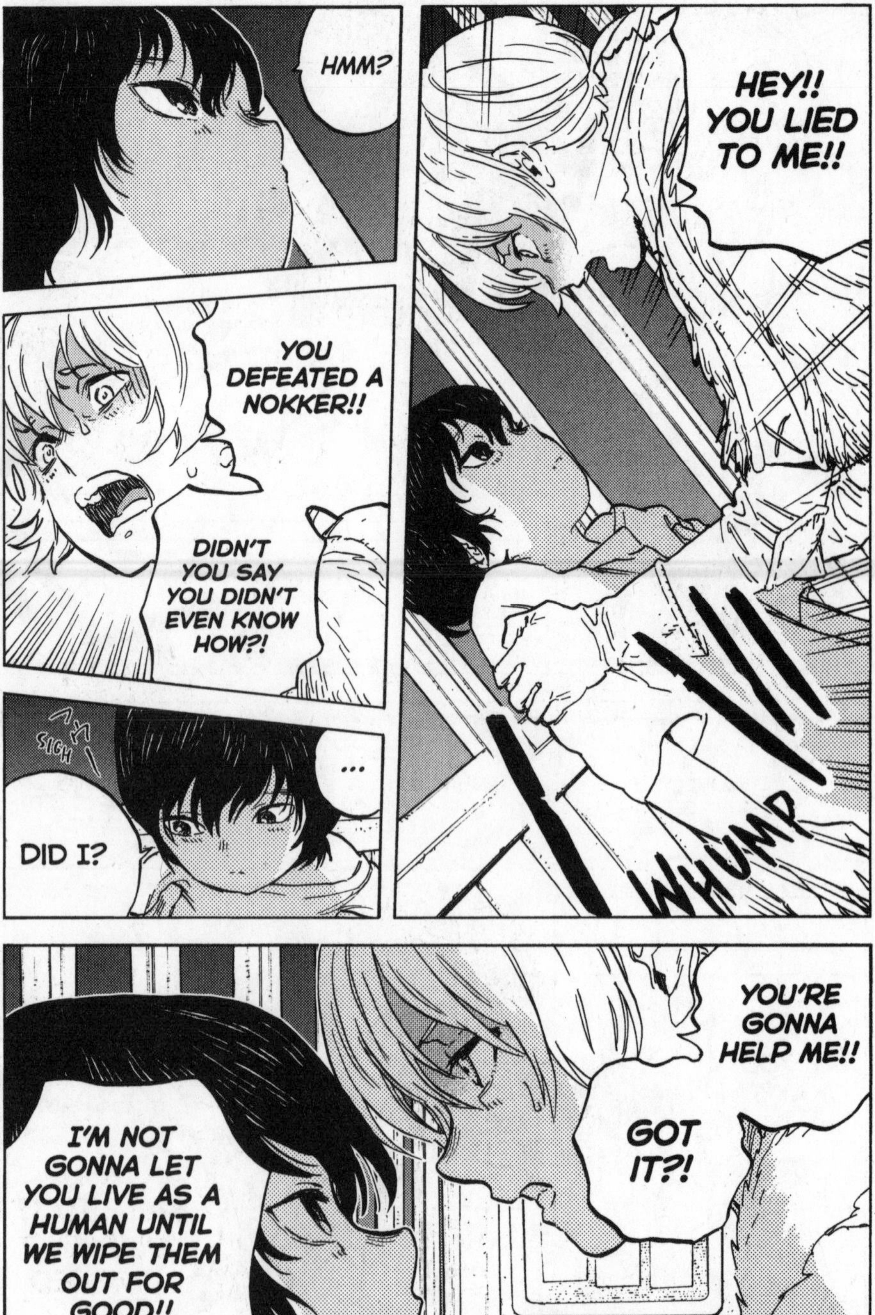
HEY!! YOU LIED TO ME!!
WHUMP
HMM?
YOU DEFEATED A NOKKER!!
DIDN'T YOU SAY YOU DIDN'T EVEN KNOW HOW?!
...
SIGH
DID I?
YOU'RE GONNA HELP ME!!
GOT IT?!
I'M NOT GONNA LET YOU LIVE AS A HUMAN UNTIL WE WIPE THEM OUT FOR GOOD!!

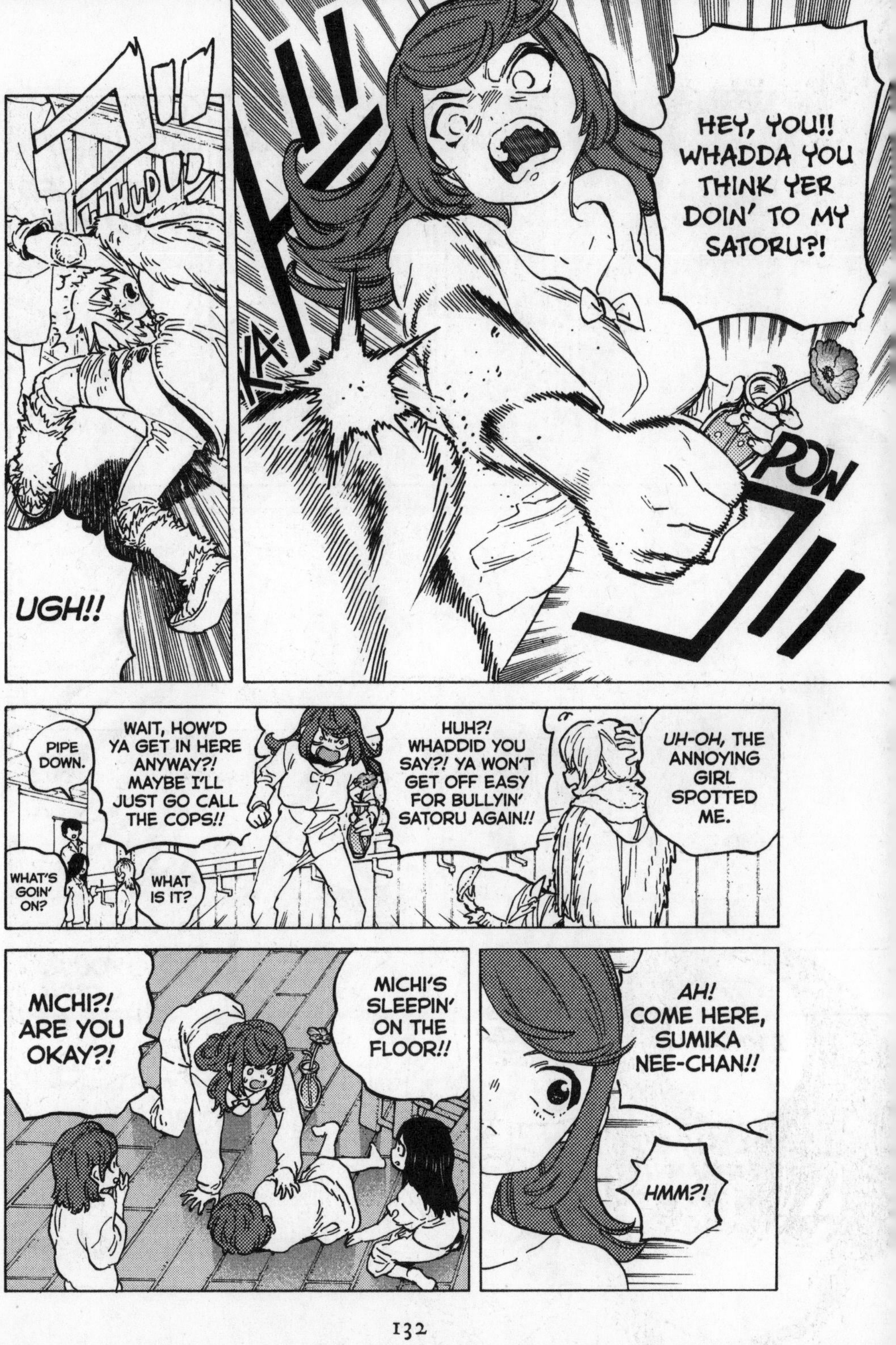
HEY, YOU!! WHADDA YOU THINK YER DOIN' TO MY SATORU?!
POW
UGH!!
UH-OH, THE ANNOYING GIRL SPOTTED ME.
HUH?! WHADDID YOU SAY?! YA WON'T GET OFF EASY FOR BULLYIN' SATORU AGAIN!!
WAIT, HOW'D YA GET IN HERE ANYWAY?! MAYBE I'LL JUST GO CALL THE COPS!!
PIPE DOWN.
WHAT IS IT?
WHAT'S GOIN' ON?
AH! COME HERE, SUMIKA NEE-CHAN!!
HMM?!
MICHI'S SLEEPIN' ON THE FLOOR!!
MICHI?! ARE YOU OKAY?!

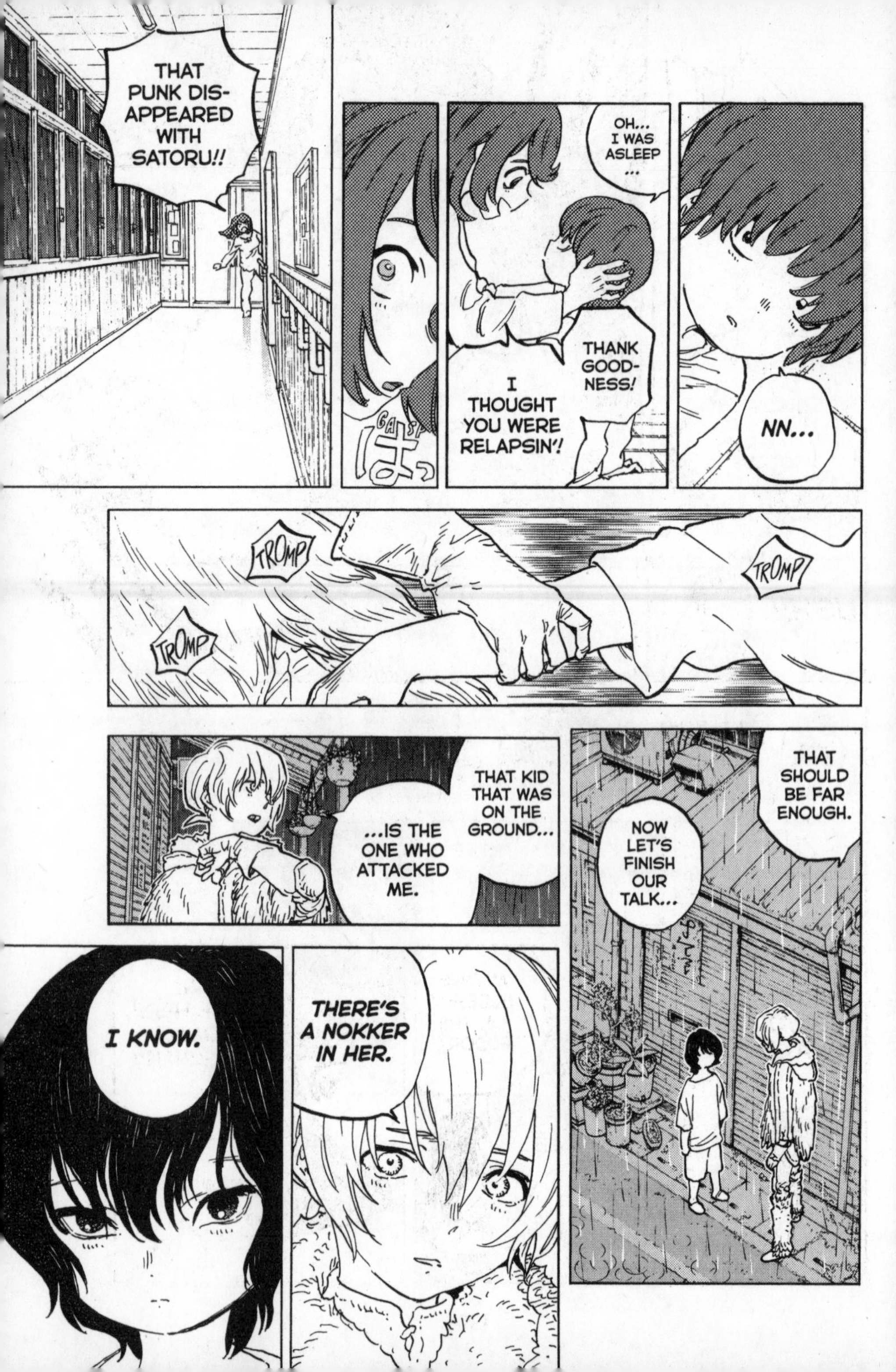
NN...
OH... I WAS ASLEEP...
THANK GOODNESS!
I THOUGHT YOU WERE RELAPSIN'!
GASP
はっ
THAT PUNK DIS-APPEARED WITH SATORU!!
TROMP
TROMP
TROMP
THAT SHOULD BE FAR ENOUGH.
NOW LET'S FINISH OUR TALK...
THAT KID THAT WAS ON THE GROUND...
...IS THE ONE WHO ATTACKED ME.
THERE'S A NOKKER IN HER.
I KNOW.

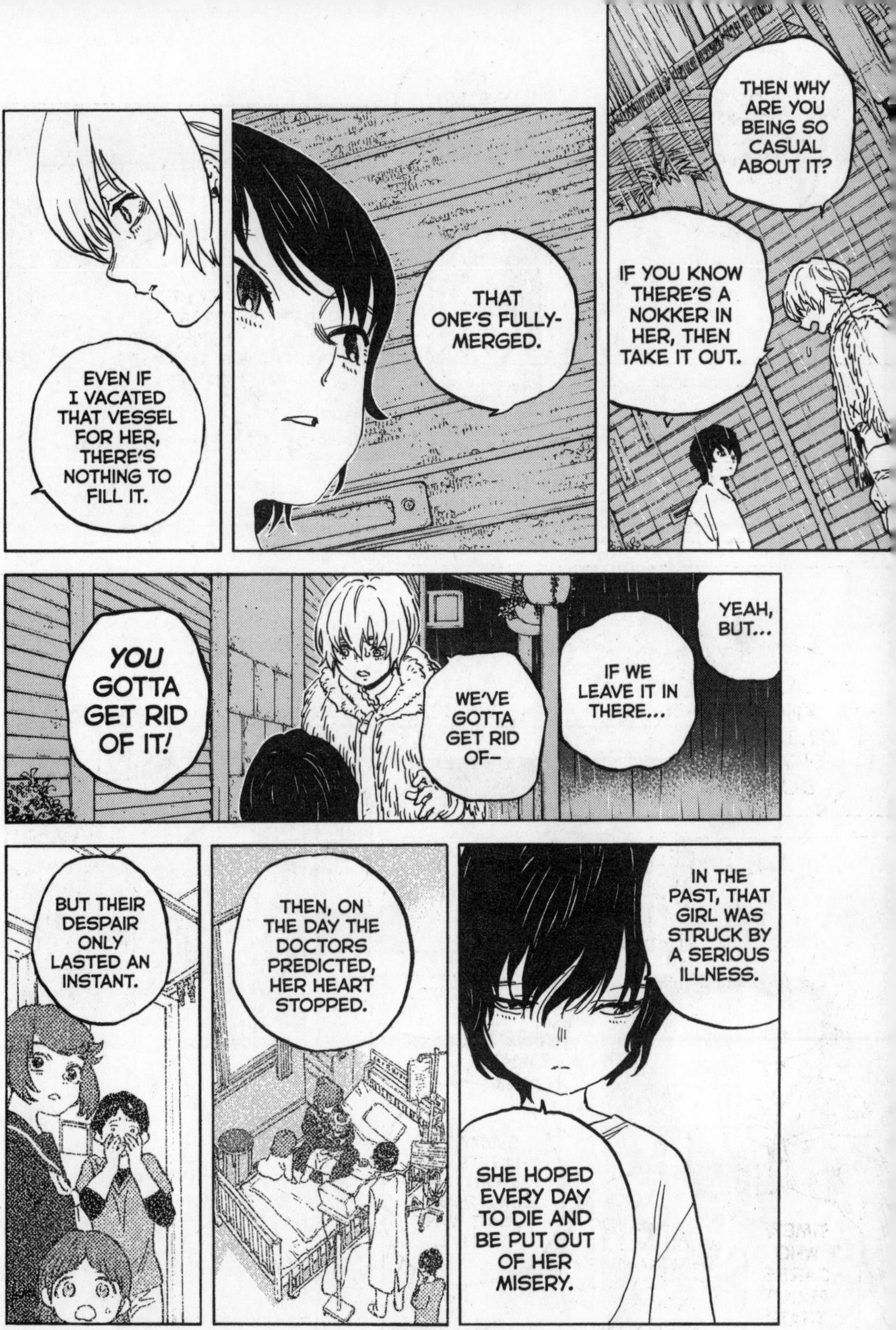
THEN WHY ARE YOU BEING SO CASUAL ABOUT IT?
IF YOU KNOW THERE'S A NOKKER IN HER, THEN TAKE IT OUT.
THAT ONE'S FULLY-MERGED.
EVEN IF I VACATED THAT VESSEL FOR HER, THERE'S NOTHING TO FILL IT.
YEAH, BUT...
IF WE LEAVE IT IN THERE...
WE'VE GOTTA GET RID OF–
YOU GOTTA GET RID OF IT!
IN THE PAST, THAT GIRL WAS STRUCK BY A SERIOUS ILLNESS.
SHE HOPED EVERY DAY TO DIE AND BE PUT OUT OF HER MISERY.
THEN, ON THE DAY THE DOCTORS PREDICTED, HER HEART STOPPED.
BUT THEIR DESPAIR ONLY LASTED AN INSTANT.

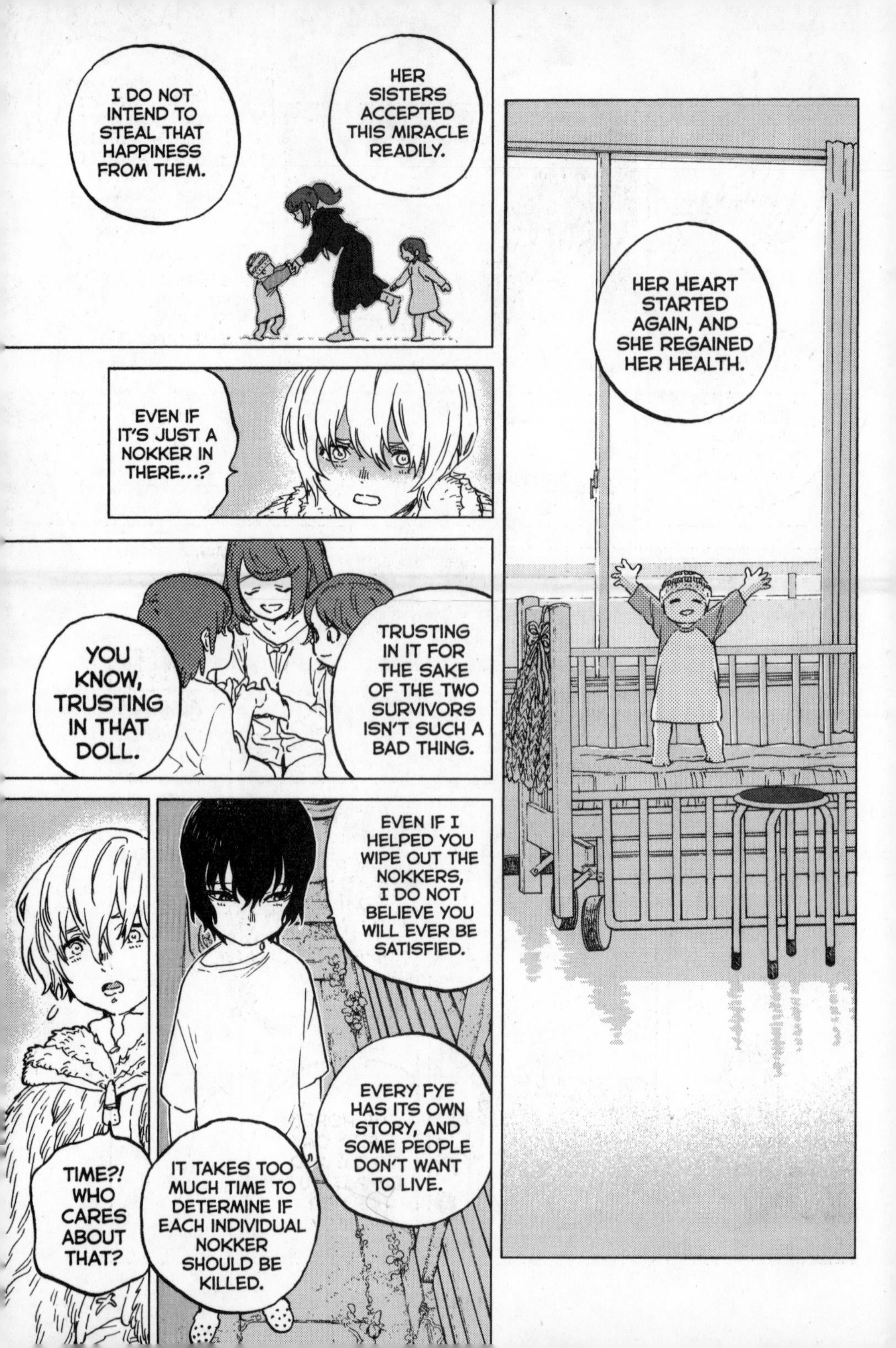
HER HEART STARTED AGAIN, AND SHE REGAINED HER HEALTH.
HER SISTERS ACCEPTED THIS MIRACLE READILY.
I DO NOT INTEND TO STEAL THAT HAPPINESS FROM THEM.
EVEN IF IT'S JUST A NOKKER IN THERE...?
TRUSTING IN IT FOR THE SAKE OF THE TWO SURVIVORS ISN'T SUCH A BAD THING.
YOU KNOW, TRUSTING IN THAT DOLL.
EVEN IF I HELPED YOU WIPE OUT THE NOKKERS, I DO NOT BELIEVE YOU WILL EVER BE SATISFIED.
EVERY FYE HAS ITS OWN STORY, AND SOME PEOPLE DON'T WANT TO LIVE.
IT TAKES TOO MUCH TIME TO DETERMINE IF EACH INDIVIDUAL NOKKER SHOULD BE KILLED.
TIME?! WHO CARES ABOUT THAT?

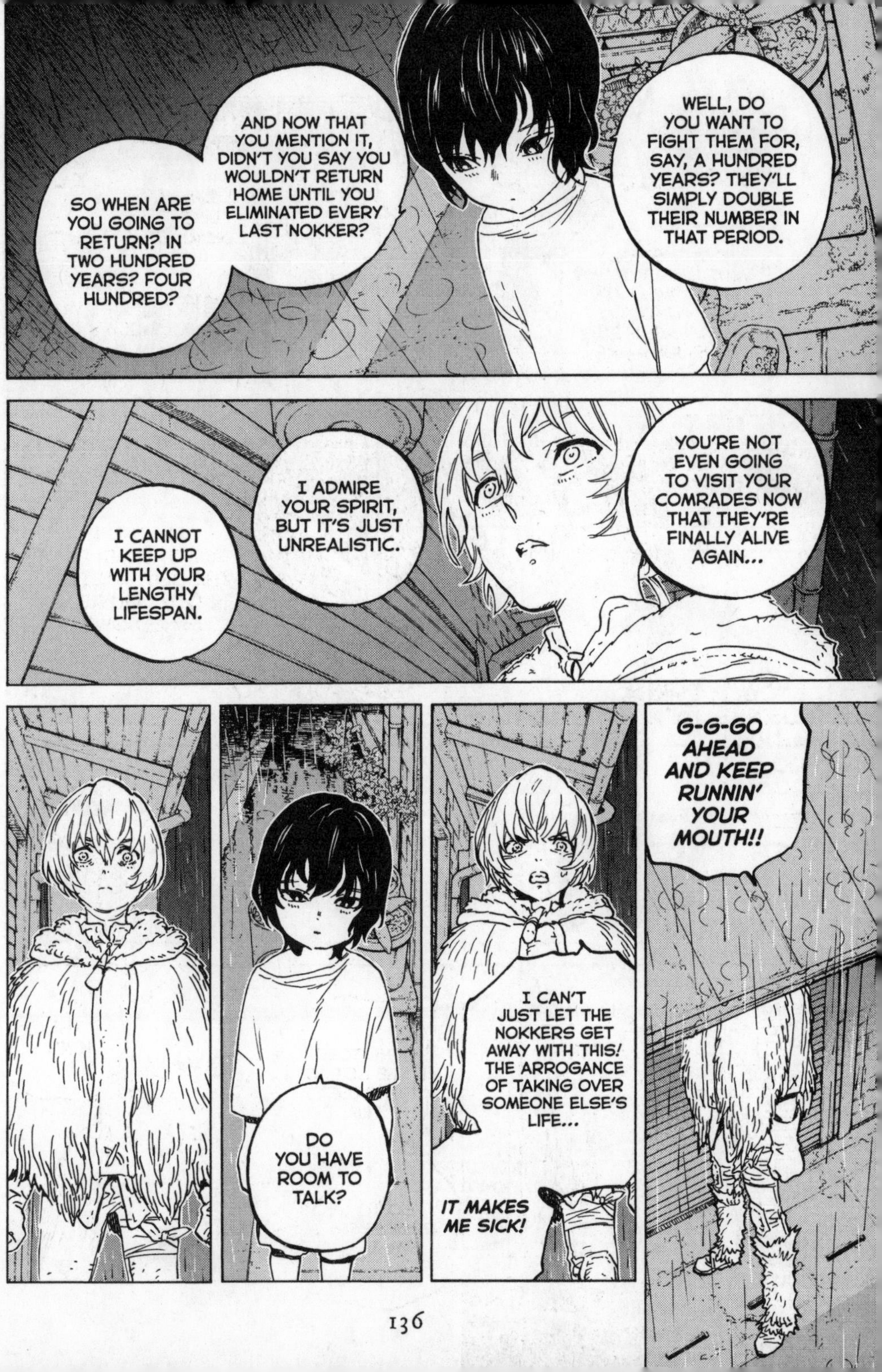
WELL, DO YOU WANT TO FIGHT THEM FOR, SAY, A HUNDRED YEARS? THEY'LL SIMPLY DOUBLE THEIR NUMBER IN THAT PERIOD.
AND NOW THAT YOU MENTION IT, DIDN'T YOU SAY YOU WOULDN'T RETURN HOME UNTIL YOU ELIMINATED EVERY LAST NOKKER?
SO WHEN ARE YOU GOING TO RETURN? IN TWO HUNDRED YEARS? FOUR HUNDRED?
YOU'RE NOT EVEN GOING TO VISIT YOUR COMRADES NOW THAT THEY'RE FINALLY ALIVE AGAIN...
I ADMIRE YOUR SPIRIT, BUT IT'S JUST UNREALISTIC.
I CANNOT KEEP UP WITH YOUR LENGTHY LIFESPAN.
G-G-GO AHEAD AND KEEP RUNNIN' YOUR MOUTH!!
I CAN'T JUST LET THE NOKKERS GET AWAY WITH THIS! THE ARROGANCE OF TAKING OVER SOMEONE ELSE'S LIFE...
IT MAKES ME SICK!
DO YOU HAVE ROOM TO TALK?

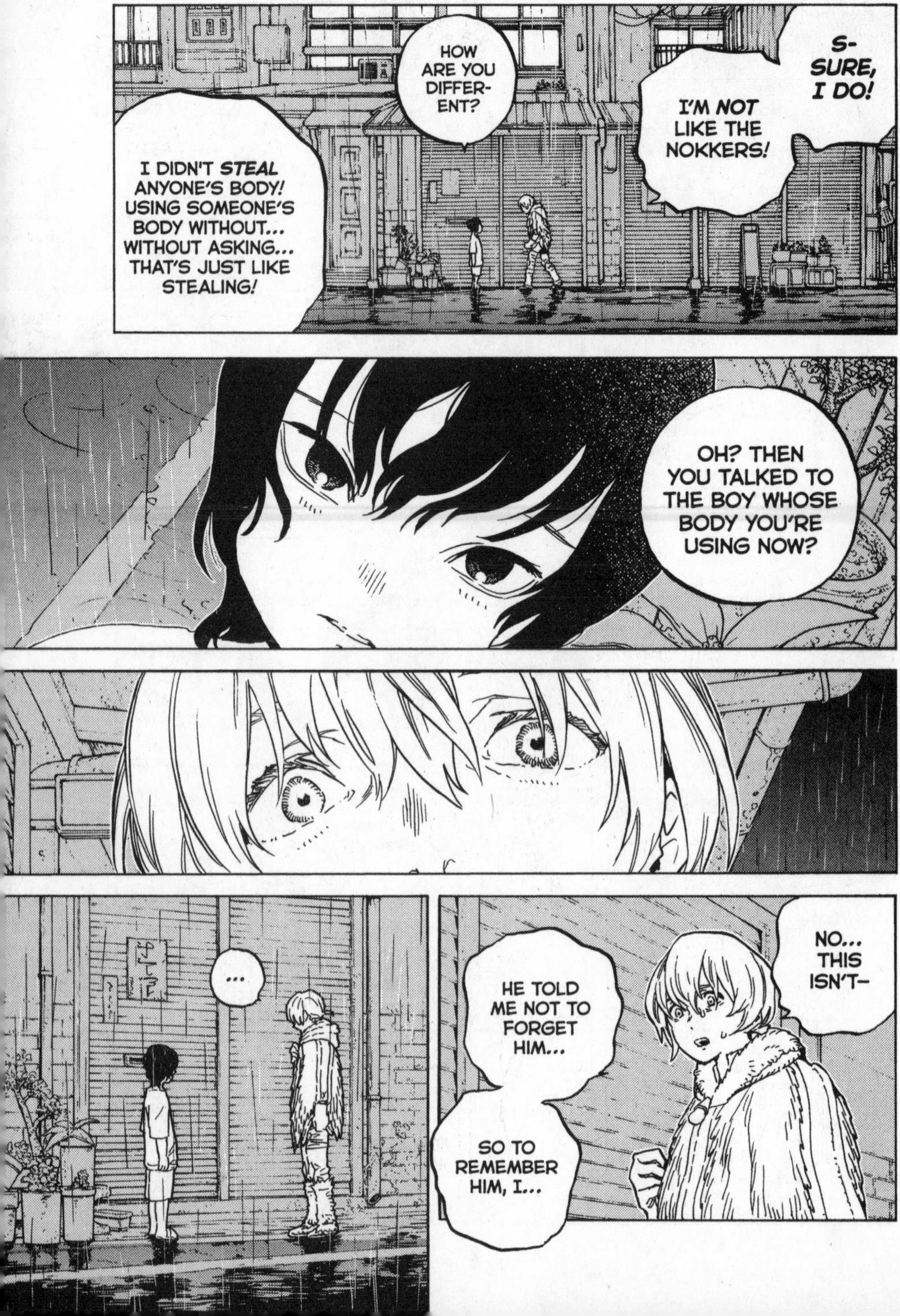
S-SURE, I DO!
I'M NOT LIKE THE NOKKERS!
HOW ARE YOU DIFFERENT?
I DIDN'T STEAL ANYONE'S BODY! USING SOMEONE'S BODY WITHOUT... WITHOUT ASKING... THAT'S JUST LIKE STEALING!
OH? THEN YOU TALKED TO THE BOY WHOSE BODY YOU'RE USING NOW?
NO... THIS ISN'T-
HE TOLD ME NOT TO FORGET HIM...
SO TO REMEMBER HIM, I...
...

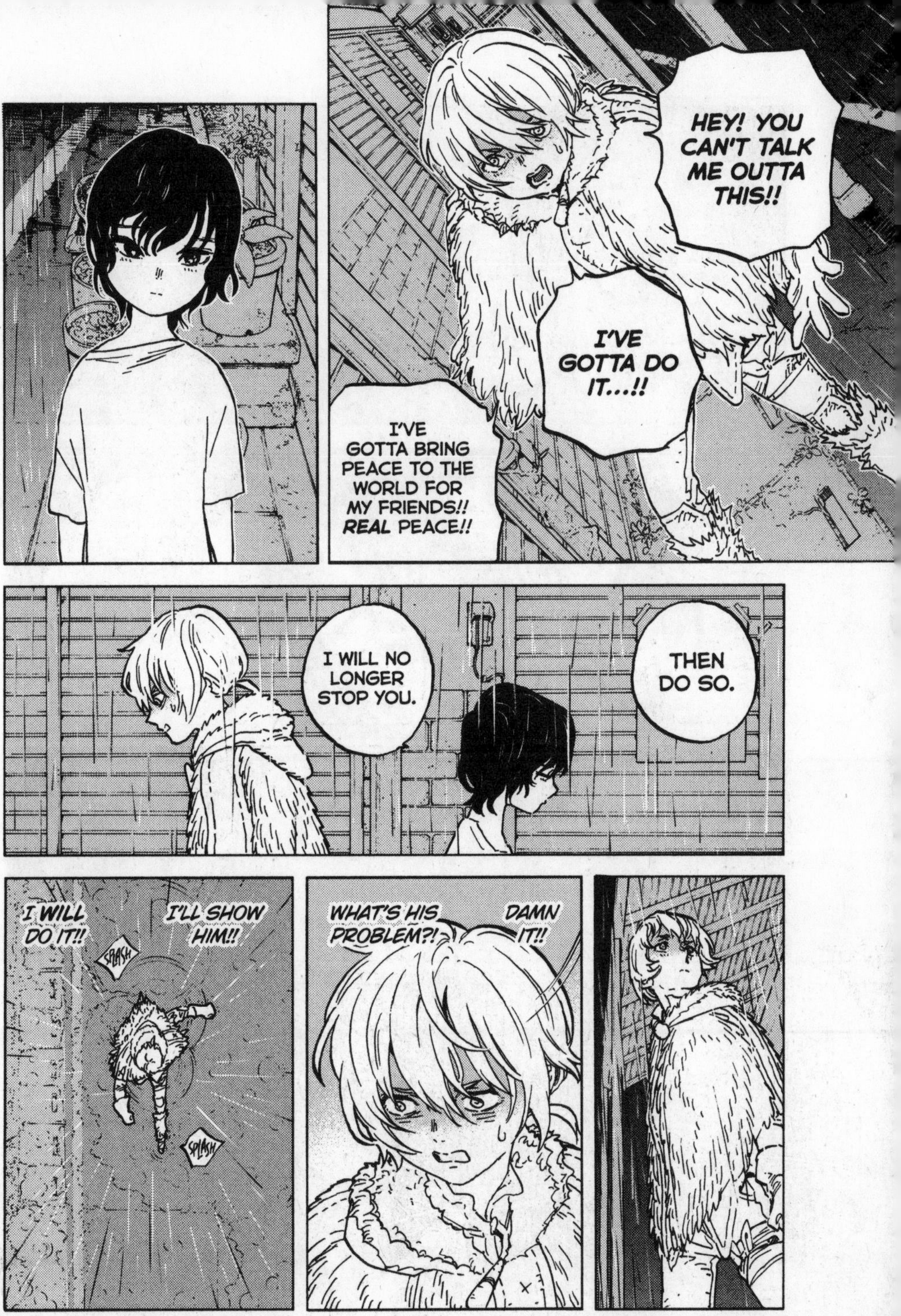
HEY! YOU CAN'T TALK ME OUTTA THIS!!
I'VE GOTTA DO IT...!!
I'VE GOTTA BRING PEACE TO THE WORLD FOR MY FRIENDS!! *REAL* PEACE!!
THEN DO SO.
I WILL NO LONGER STOP YOU.
DAMN IT!!
WHAT'S HIS PROBLEM?!
I'LL SHOW HIM!!
I WILL DO IT!!
SPLASH
SPLASH

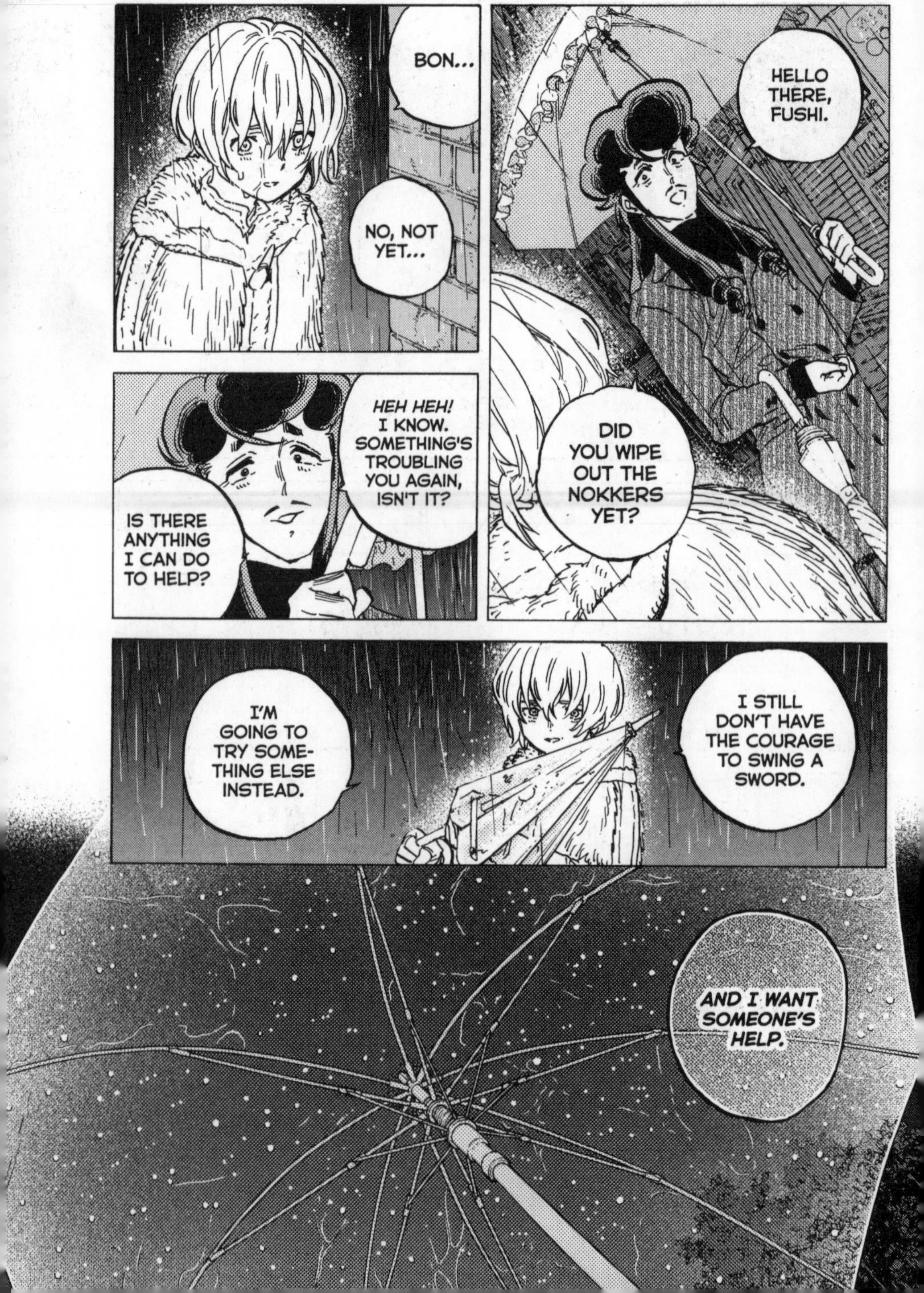
HELLO THERE, FUSHI.
DID YOU WIPE OUT THE NOKKERS YET?
BON...
NO, NOT YET...
HEH HEH! I KNOW. SOMETHING'S TROUBLING YOU AGAIN, ISN'T IT?
IS THERE ANYTHING I CAN DO TO HELP?
I STILL DON'T HAVE THE COURAGE TO SWING A SWORD.
I'M GOING TO TRY SOMETHING ELSE INSTEAD.
AND I WANT SOMEONE'S HELP.

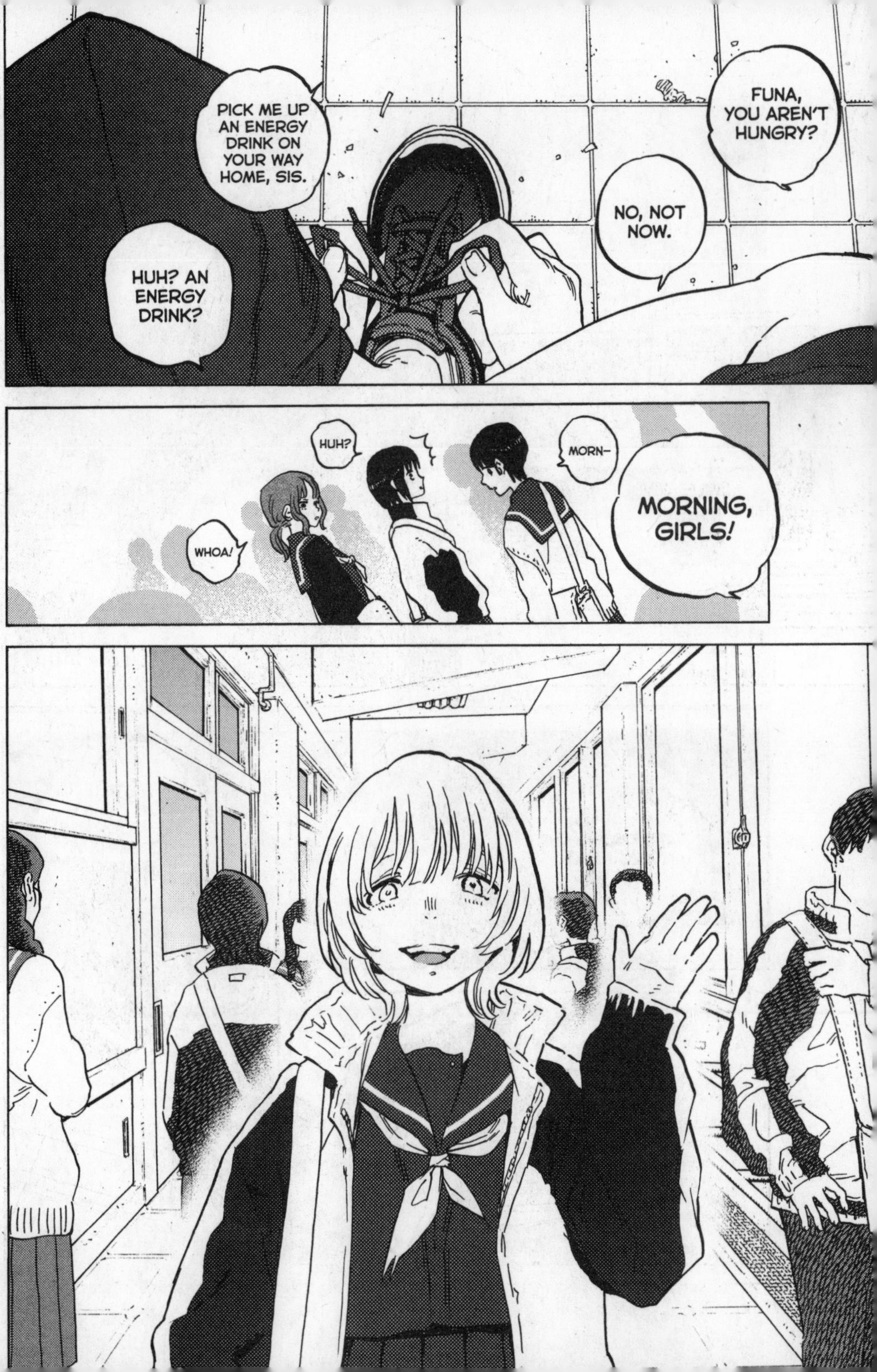
FUNA, YOU AREN'T HUNGRY?
NO, NOT NOW.
PICK ME UP AN ENERGY DRINK ON YOUR WAY HOME, SIS.
HUH? AN ENERGY DRINK?
MORNING, GIRLS!
MORN–
HUH?
WHOA!

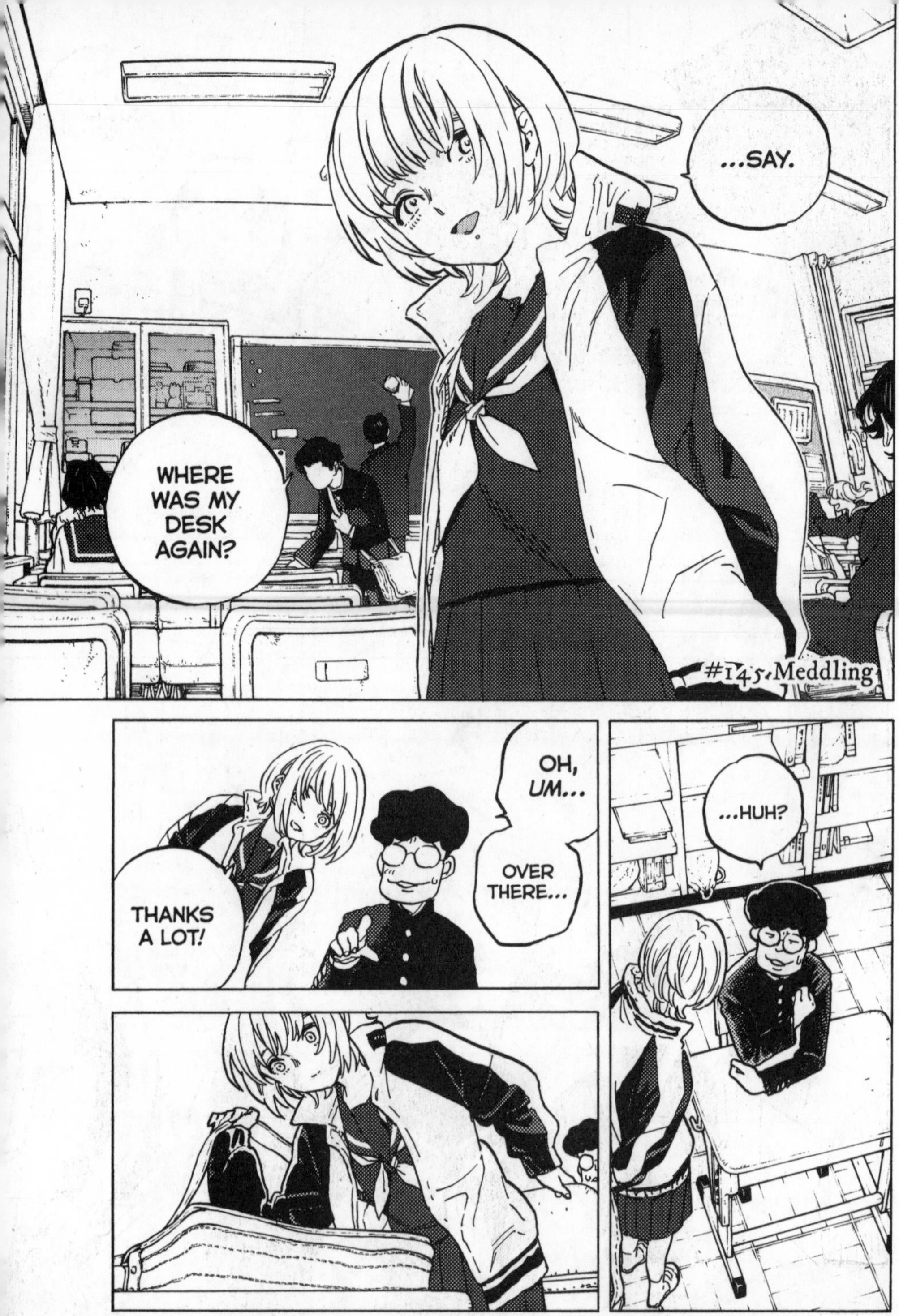
...SAY.
WHERE WAS MY DESK AGAIN?
#145 Meddling
...HUH?
OH, UM... OVER THERE...
THANKS A LOT!

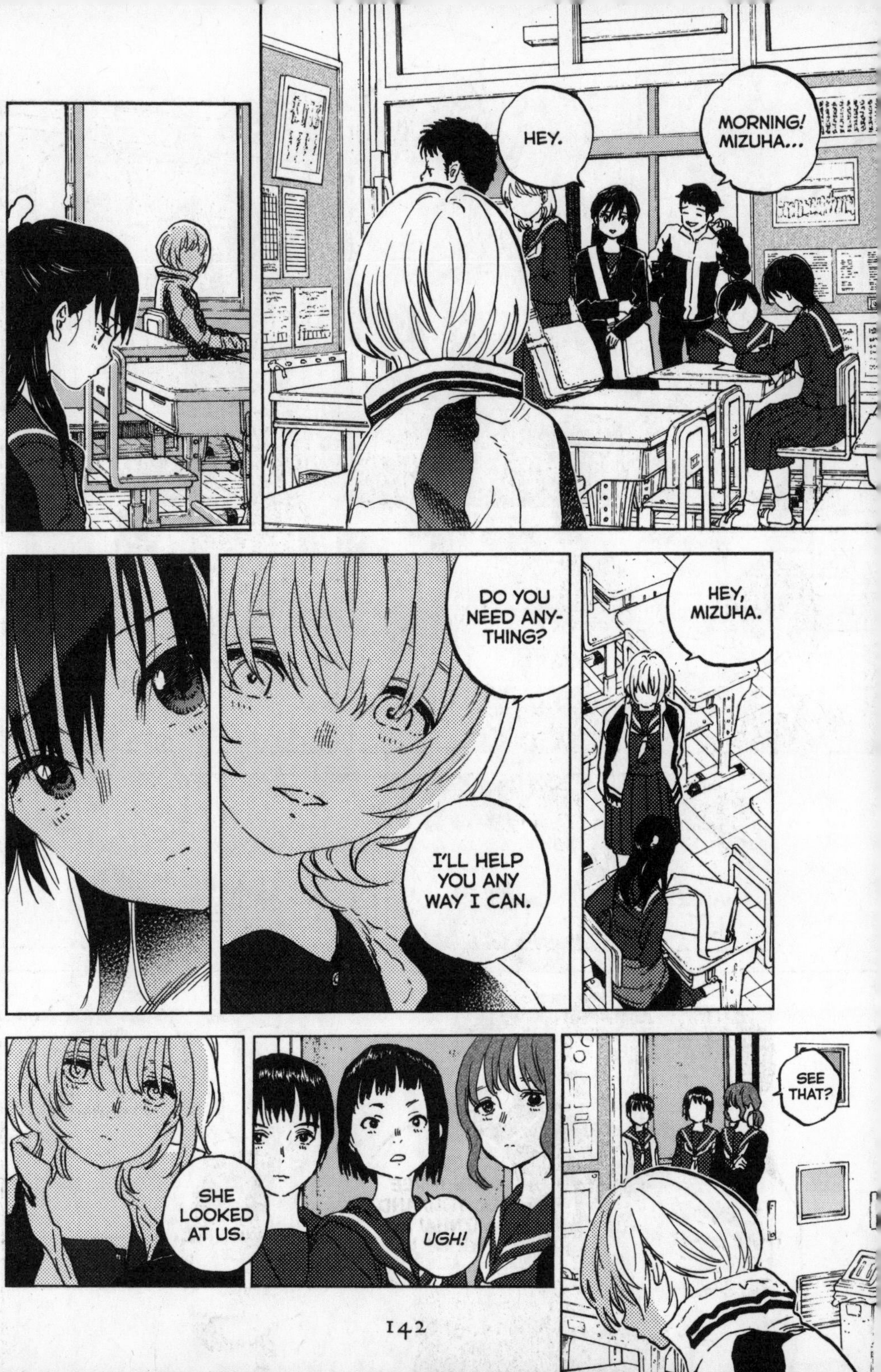
MORNING! MIZUHA...
HEY.
HEY, MIZUHA.
DO YOU NEED ANY-THING?
I'LL HELP YOU ANY WAY I CAN.
SEE THAT?
UGH!
SHE LOOKED AT US.

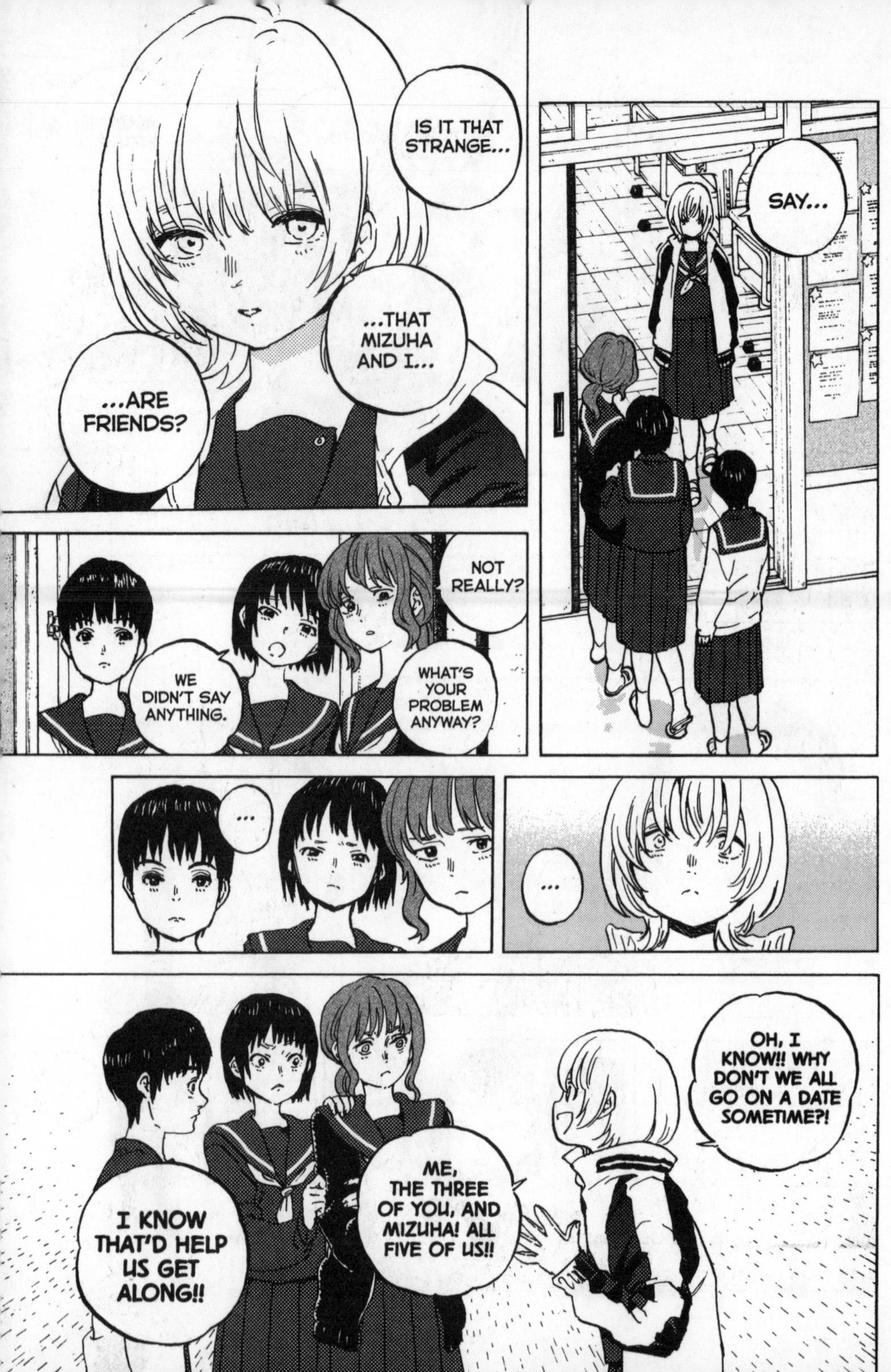
SAY...
IS IT THAT STRANGE...
...THAT MIZUHA AND I...
...ARE FRIENDS?
NOT REALLY?
WHAT'S YOUR PROBLEM ANYWAY?
WE DIDN'T SAY ANYTHING.
...
...
OH, I KNOW!! WHY DON'T WE ALL GO ON A DATE SOMETIME?!
ME, THE THREE OF YOU, AND MIZUHA! ALL FIVE OF US!!
I KNOW THAT'D HELP US GET ALONG!!

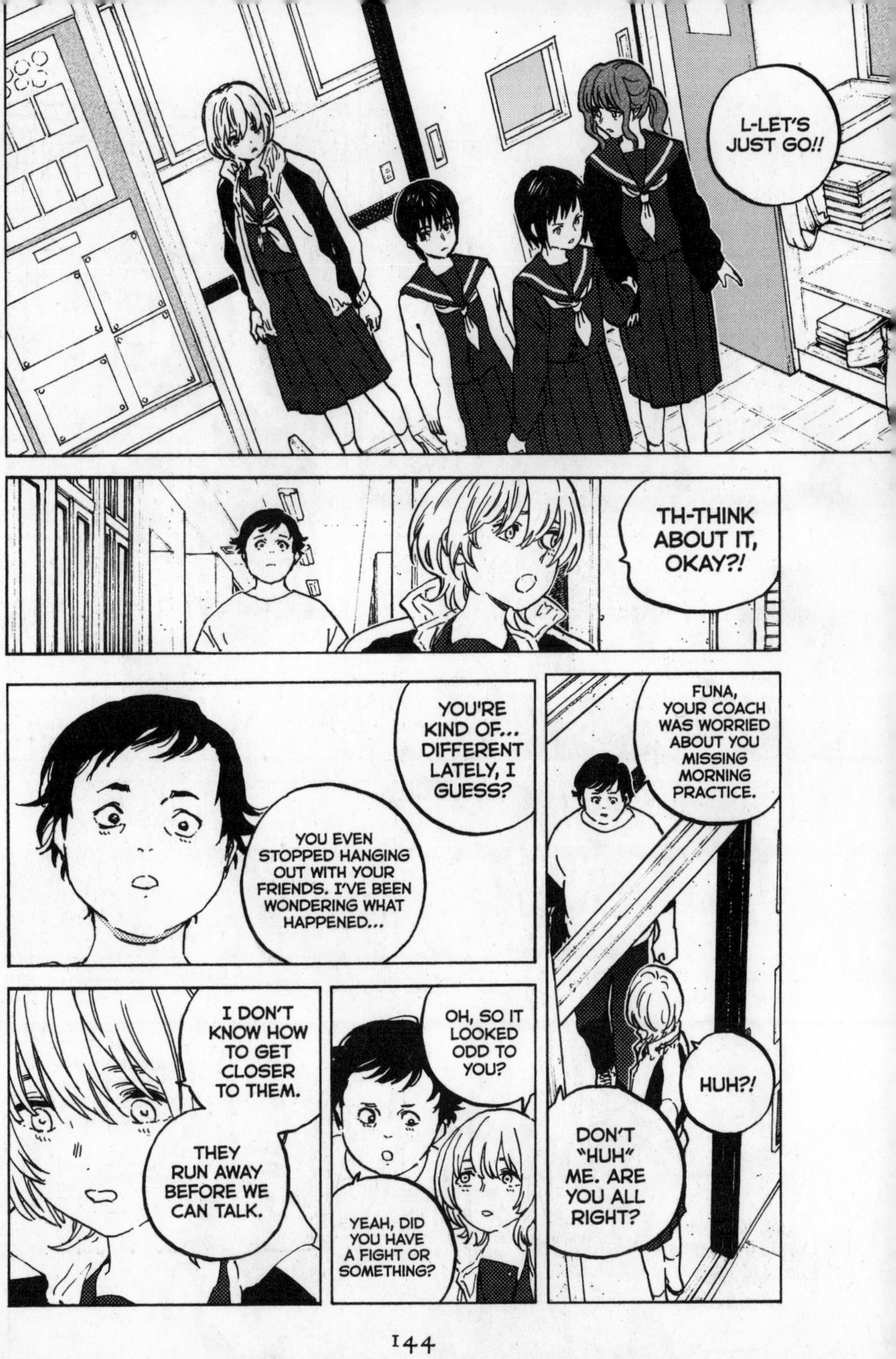
L-LET'S JUST GO!!
TH-THINK ABOUT IT, OKAY?!
FUNA, YOUR COACH WAS WORRIED ABOUT YOU MISSING MORNING PRACTICE.
HUH?!
DON'T "HUH" ME. ARE YOU ALL RIGHT?
YOU'RE KIND OF... DIFFERENT LATELY, I GUESS?
YOU EVEN STOPPED HANGING OUT WITH YOUR FRIENDS. I'VE BEEN WONDERING WHAT HAPPENED...
OH, SO IT LOOKED ODD TO YOU?
YEAH, DID YOU HAVE A FIGHT OR SOMETHING?
I DON'T KNOW HOW TO GET CLOSER TO THEM.
THEY RUN AWAY BEFORE WE CAN TALK.

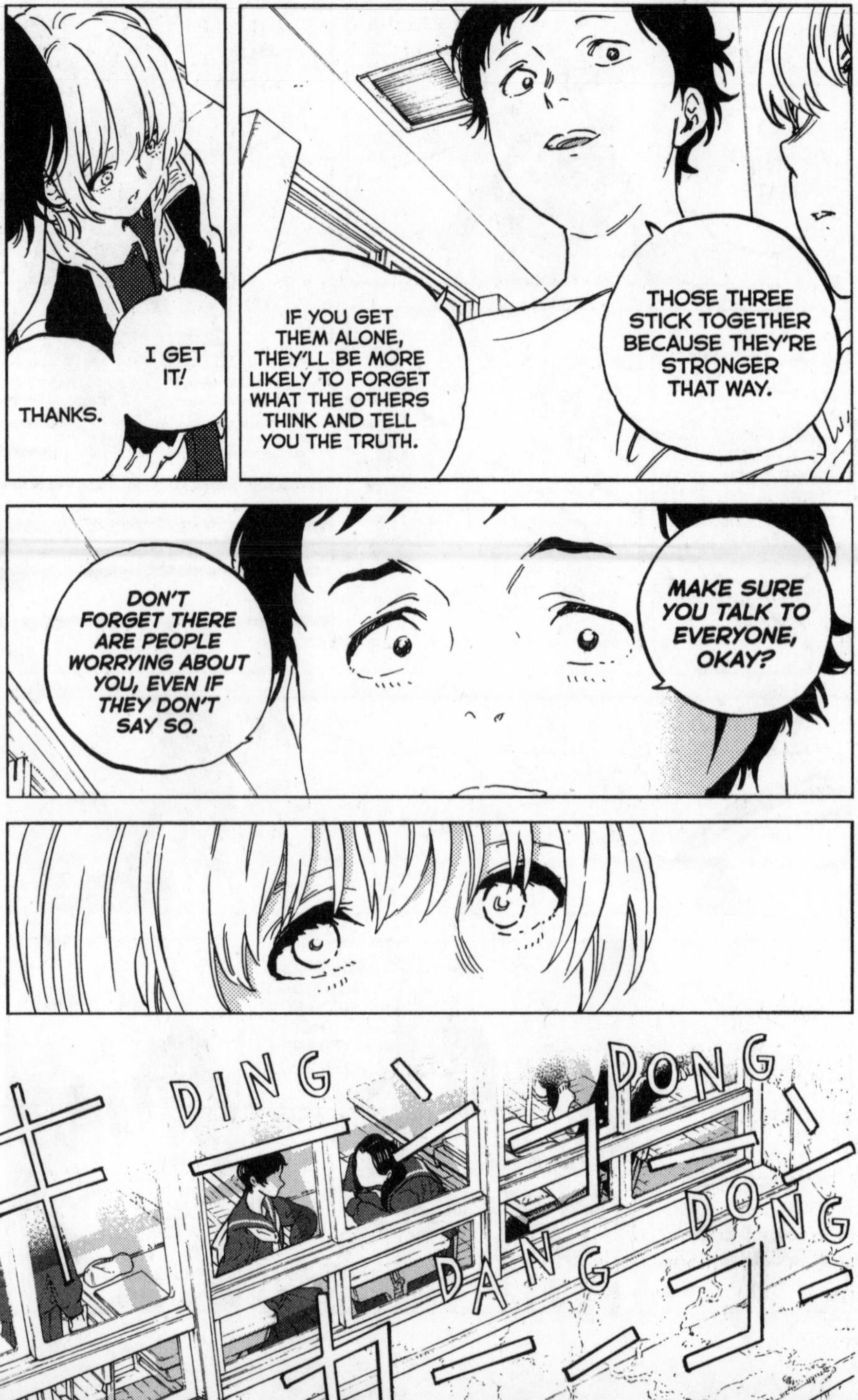
THOSE THREE STICK TOGETHER BECAUSE THEY'RE STRONGER THAT WAY.
IF YOU GET THEM ALONE, THEY'LL BE MORE LIKELY TO FORGET WHAT THE OTHERS THINK AND TELL YOU THE TRUTH.
I GET IT!
THANKS.
MAKE SURE YOU TALK TO EVERYONE, OKAY?
DON'T FORGET THERE ARE PEOPLE WORRYING ABOUT YOU, EVEN IF THEY DON'T SAY SO.
DING DONG
DANG DONG

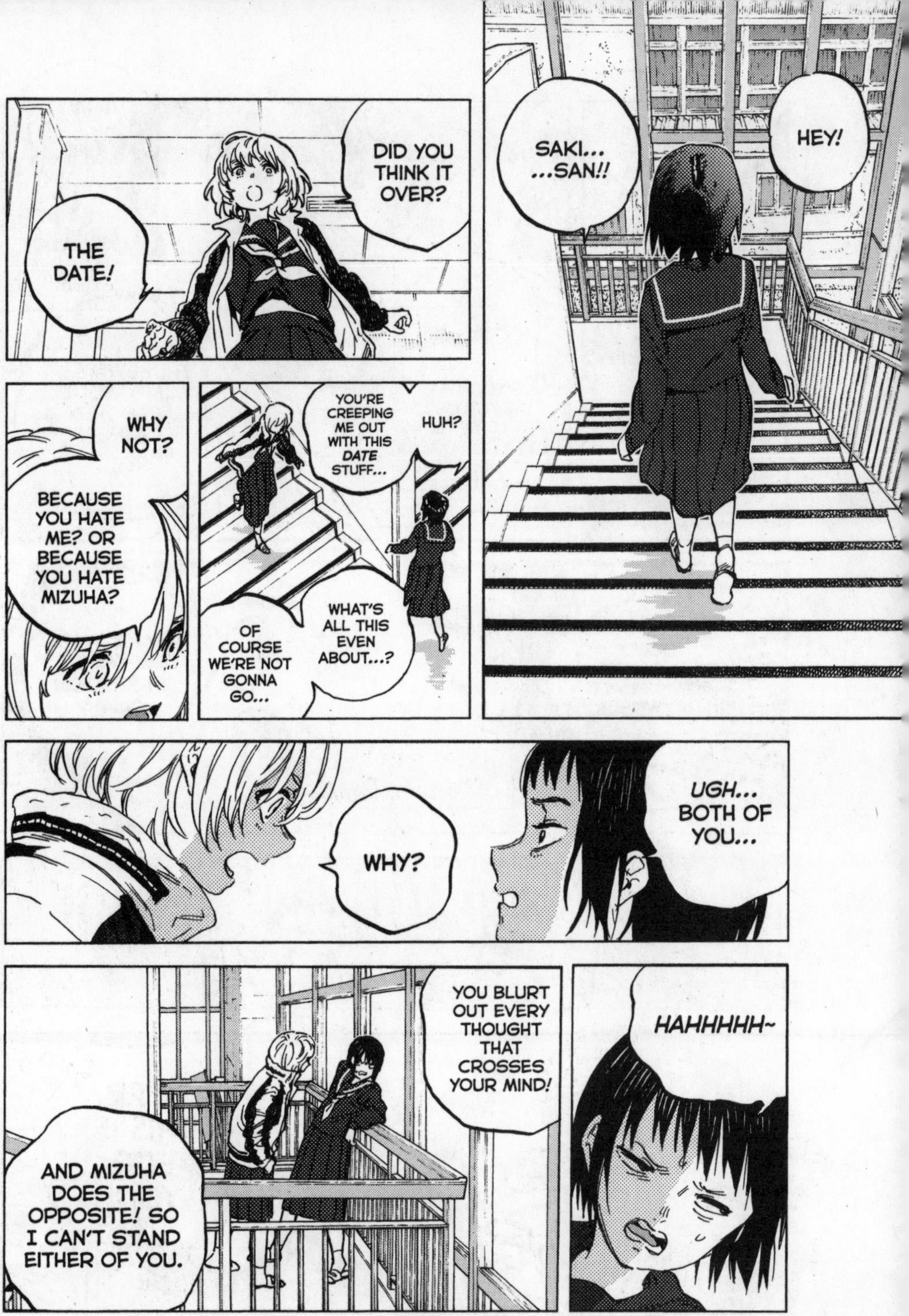
HEY!
SAKI... ...SAN!!
DID YOU THINK IT OVER?
THE DATE!
HUH?
YOU'RE CREEPING ME OUT WITH THIS *DATE* STUFF...
WHAT'S ALL THIS EVEN ABOUT...?
OF COURSE WE'RE NOT GONNA GO...
WHY NOT?
BECAUSE YOU HATE ME? OR BECAUSE YOU HATE MIZUHA?
UGH... BOTH OF YOU...
WHY?
HAHHHHH~
YOU BLURT OUT EVERY THOUGHT THAT CROSSES YOUR MIND!
AND MIZUHA DOES THE OPPOSITE! SO I CAN'T STAND EITHER OF YOU.

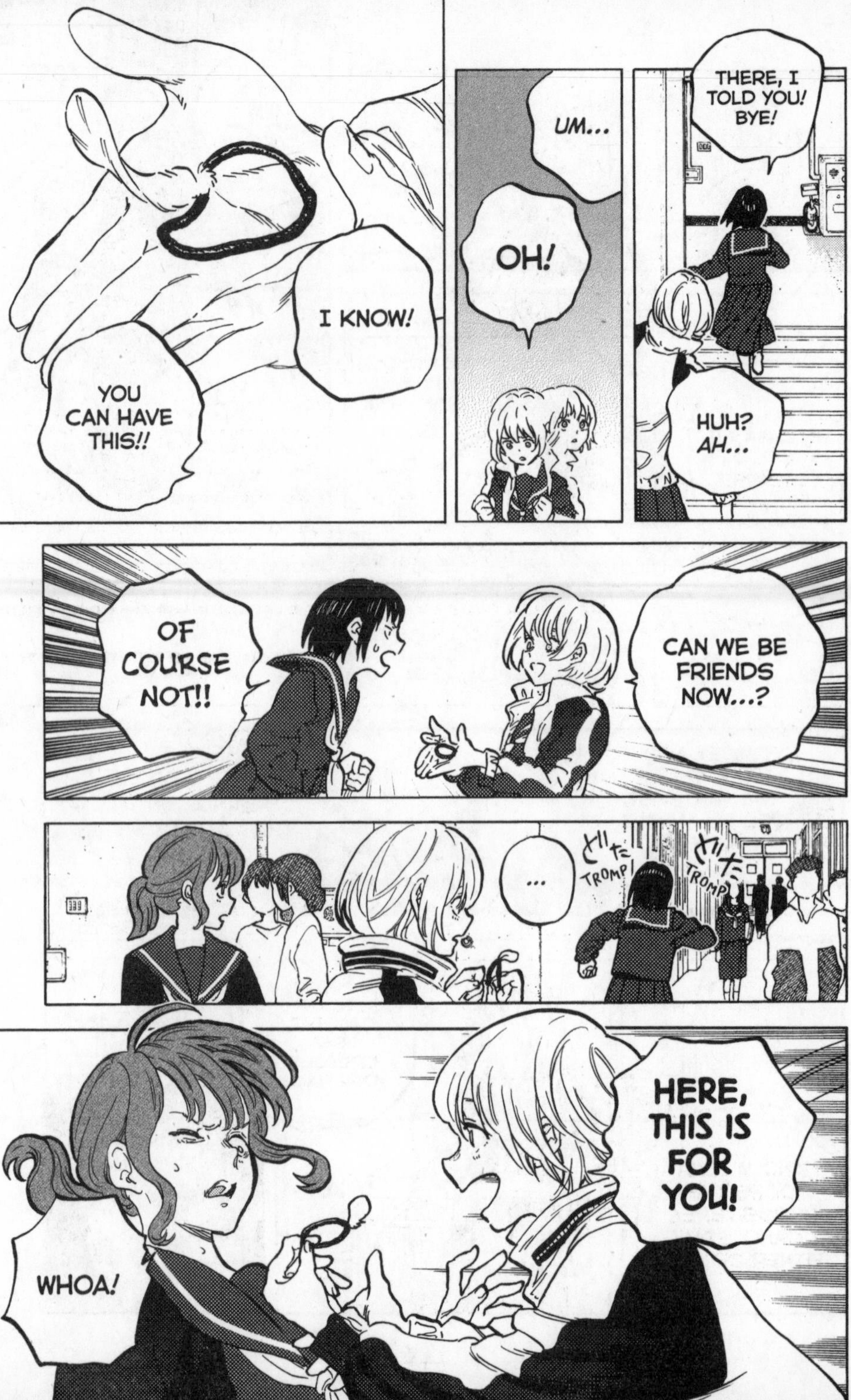
THERE, I TOLD YOU! BYE!
HUH? AH...
UM...
OH!
I KNOW!
YOU CAN HAVE THIS!!
CAN WE BE FRIENDS NOW...?
OF COURSE NOT!!
TROMP
TROMP
...
HERE, THIS IS FOR YOU!
WHOA!

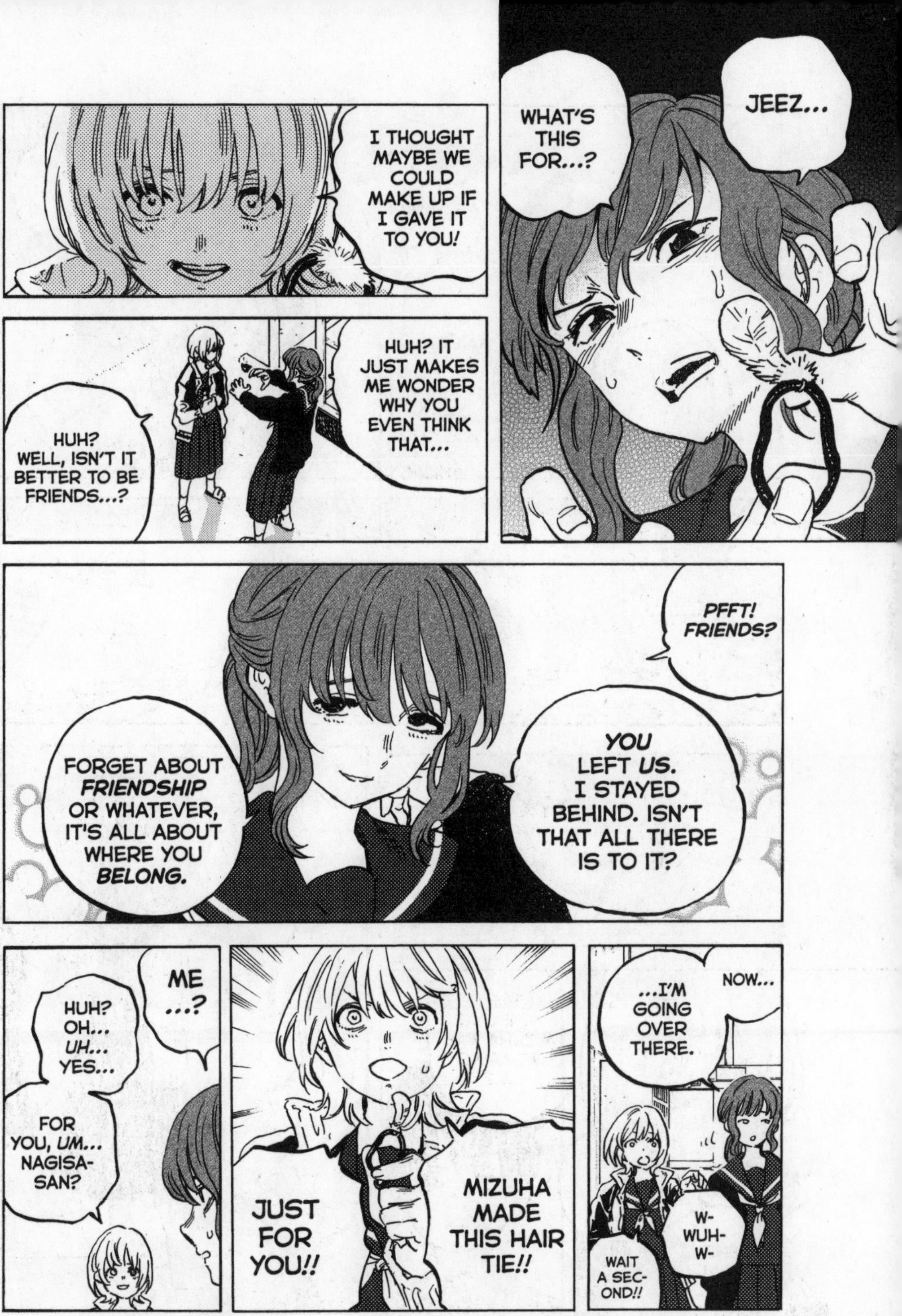
JEEZ...
WHAT'S THIS FOR...?
I THOUGHT MAYBE WE COULD MAKE UP IF I GAVE IT TO YOU!
HUH? IT JUST MAKES ME WONDER WHY YOU EVEN THINK THAT...
HUH? WELL, ISN'T IT BETTER TO BE FRIENDS...?
PFFT! FRIENDS?
YOU LEFT US. I STAYED BEHIND. ISN'T THAT ALL THERE IS TO IT?
FORGET ABOUT FRIENDSHIP OR WHATEVER, IT'S ALL ABOUT WHERE YOU BELONG.
NOW...
...I'M GOING OVER THERE.
W-WUH-W-
WAIT A SECOND!!
MIZUHA MADE THIS HAIR TIE!!
JUST FOR YOU!!
ME ...?
HUH? OH... UH... YES...
FOR YOU, UM... NAGISA-SAN?

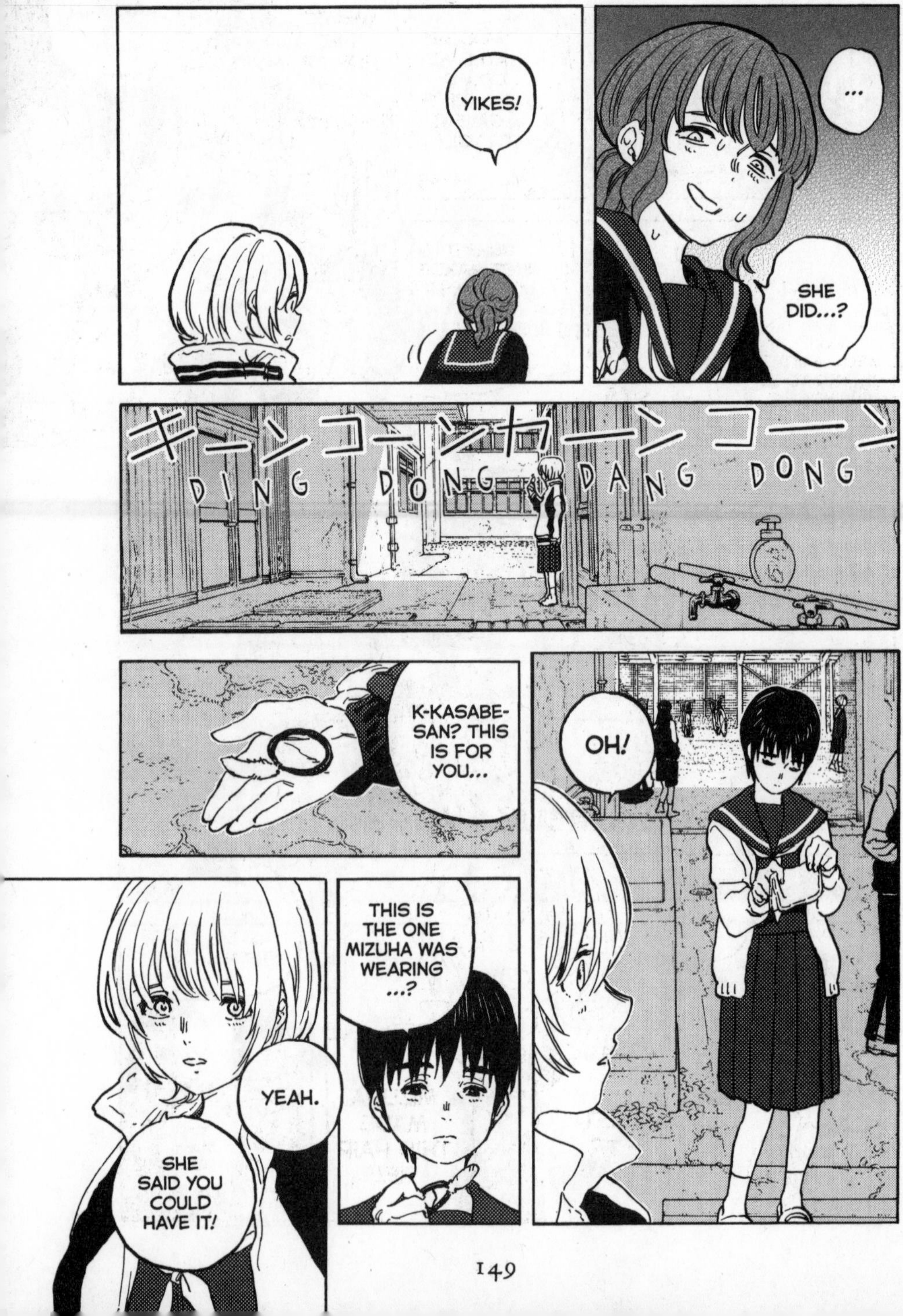
...
SHE DID...?
YIKES!
キーンコーンカーンコーン
DING DONG DANG DONG
OH!
K-KASABE-SAN? THIS IS FOR YOU...
THIS IS THE ONE MIZUHA WAS WEARING ...?
YEAH.
SHE SAID YOU COULD HAVE IT!

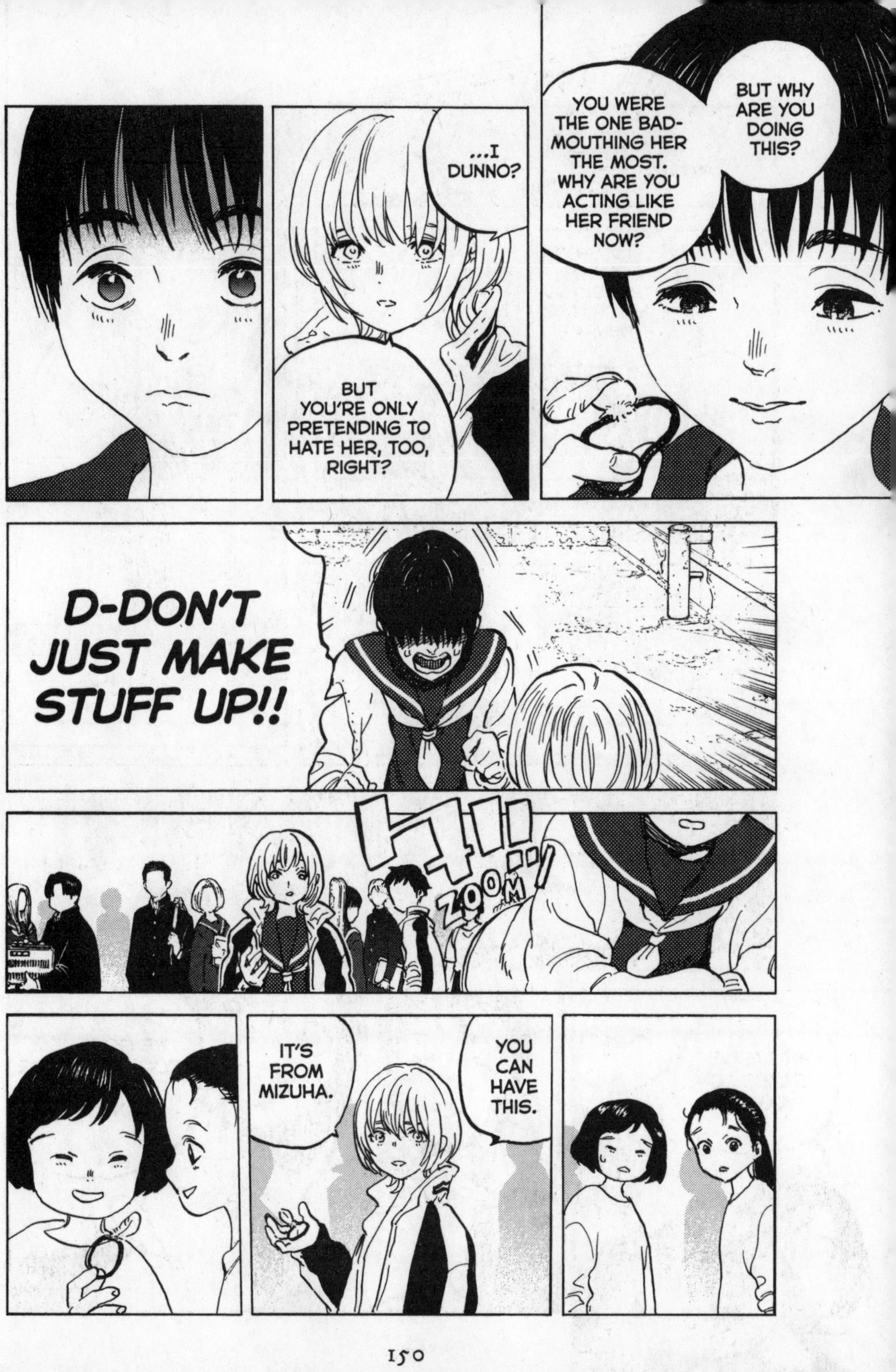
BUT WHY ARE YOU DOING THIS?
YOU WERE THE ONE BAD-MOUTHING HER THE MOST. WHY ARE YOU ACTING LIKE HER FRIEND NOW?
...I DUNNO?
BUT YOU'RE ONLY PRETENDING TO HATE HER, TOO, RIGHT?
D-DON'T JUST MAKE STUFF UP!!
ZOOM
YOU CAN HAVE THIS.
IT'S FROM MIZUHA.

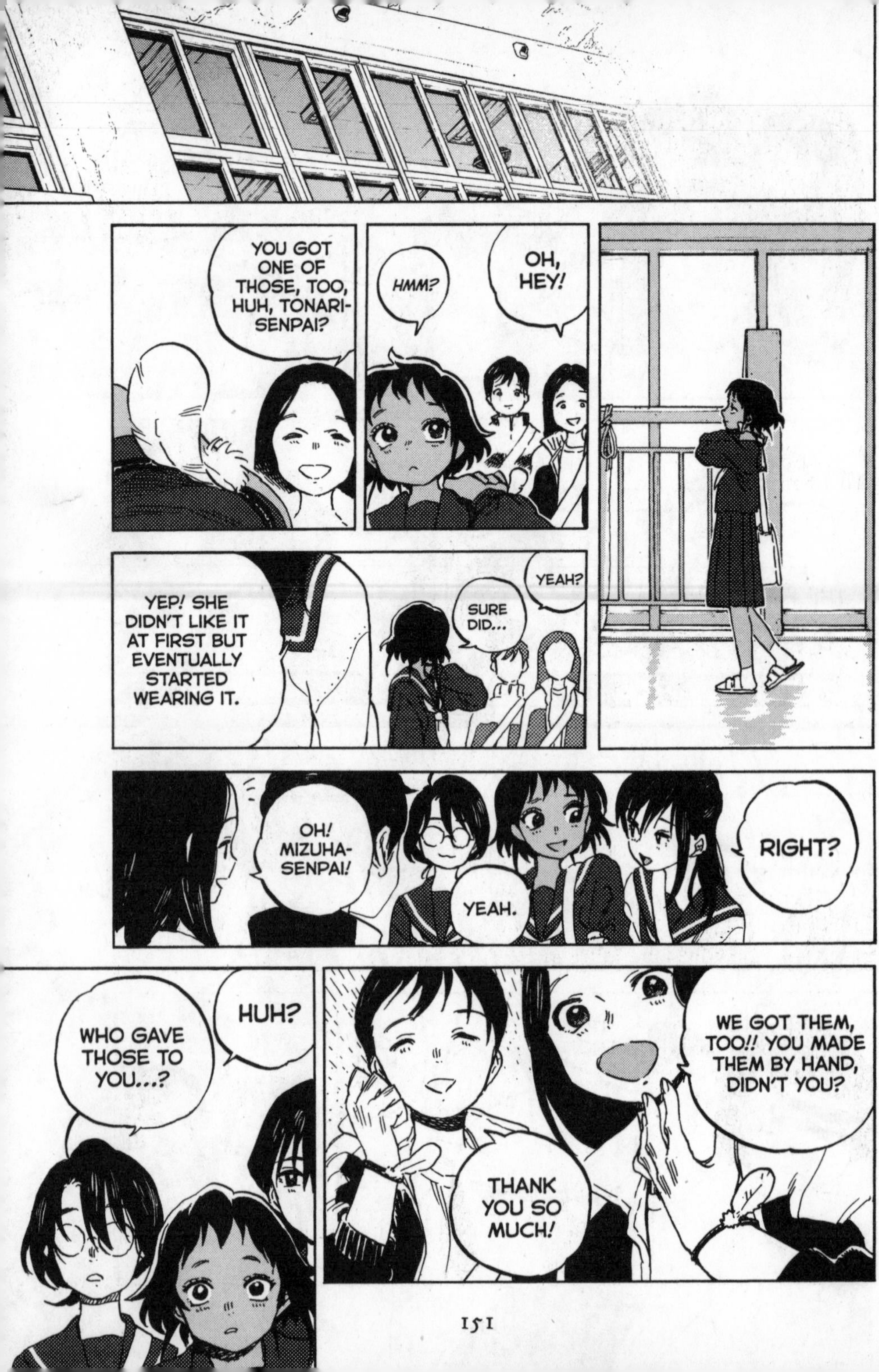
OH, HEY!
HMM?
YOU GOT ONE OF THOSE, TOO, HUH, TONARI-SENPAI?
YEAH?
SURE DID...
YEP! SHE DIDN'T LIKE IT AT FIRST BUT EVENTUALLY STARTED WEARING IT.
RIGHT?
OH! MIZUHA-SENPAI!
YEAH.
WE GOT THEM, TOO!! YOU MADE THEM BY HAND, DIDN'T YOU?
THANK YOU SO MUCH!
HUH?
WHO GAVE THOSE TO YOU...?

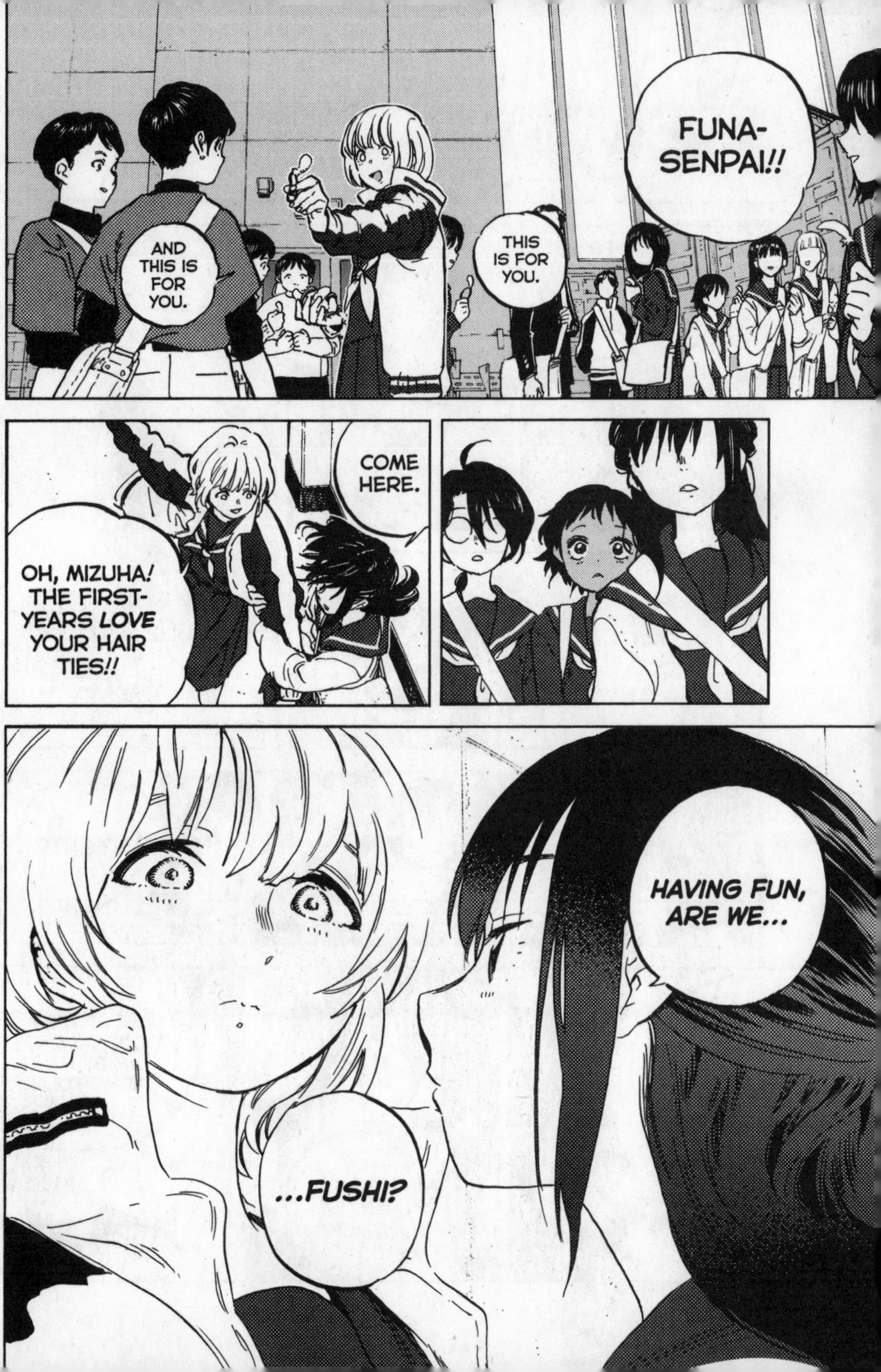
FUNA-SENPAI!!
THIS IS FOR YOU.
AND THIS IS FOR YOU.
COME HERE.
OH, MIZUHA! THE FIRST-YEARS *LOVE* YOUR HAIR TIES!!
HAVING FUN, ARE WE...
...FUSHI?

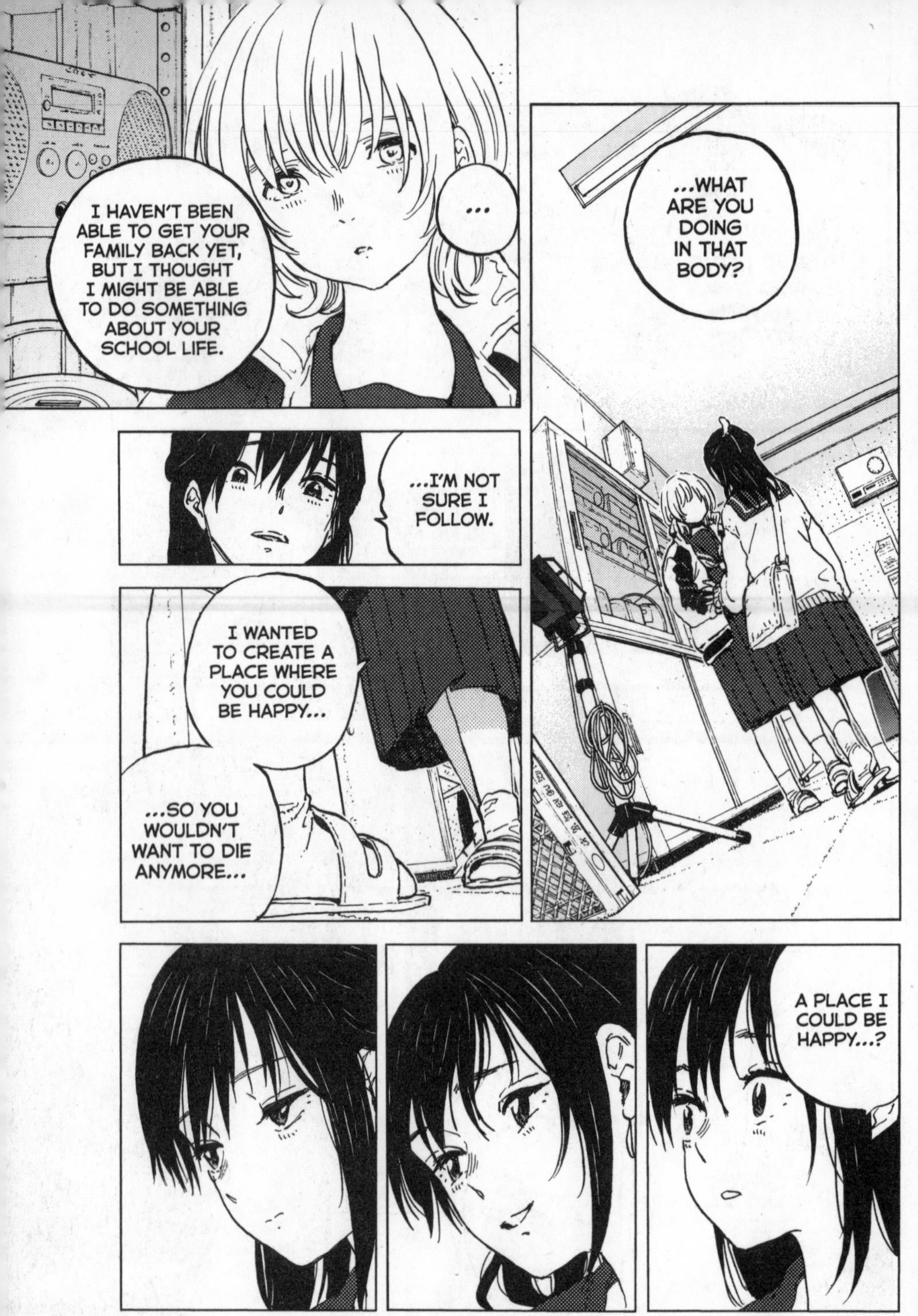
...WHAT ARE YOU DOING IN THAT BODY?
...
I HAVEN'T BEEN ABLE TO GET YOUR FAMILY BACK YET, BUT I THOUGHT I MIGHT BE ABLE TO DO SOMETHING ABOUT YOUR SCHOOL LIFE.
...I'M NOT SURE I FOLLOW.
I WANTED TO CREATE A PLACE WHERE YOU COULD BE HAPPY...
...SO YOU WOULDN'T WANT TO DIE ANYMORE...
A PLACE I COULD BE HAPPY...?

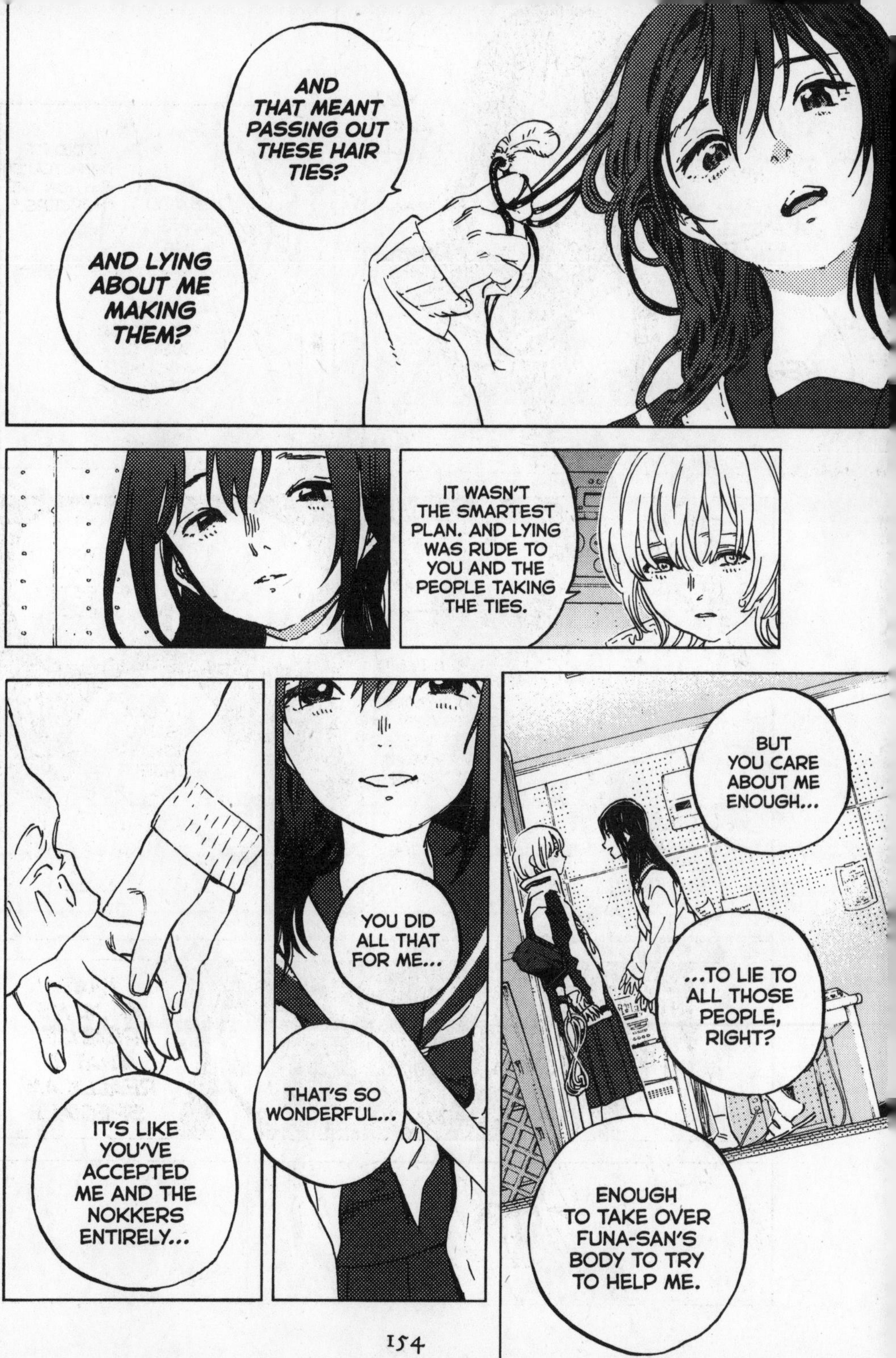
AND THAT MEANT PASSING OUT THESE HAIR TIES?
AND LYING ABOUT ME MAKING THEM?
IT WASN'T THE SMARTEST PLAN. AND LYING WAS RUDE TO YOU AND THE PEOPLE TAKING THE TIES.
BUT YOU CARE ABOUT ME ENOUGH...
...TO LIE TO ALL THOSE PEOPLE, RIGHT?
ENOUGH TO TAKE OVER FUNA-SAN'S BODY TO TRY TO HELP ME.
YOU DID ALL THAT FOR ME...
THAT'S SO WONDERFUL...
IT'S LIKE YOU'VE ACCEPTED ME AND THE NOKKERS ENTIRELY...

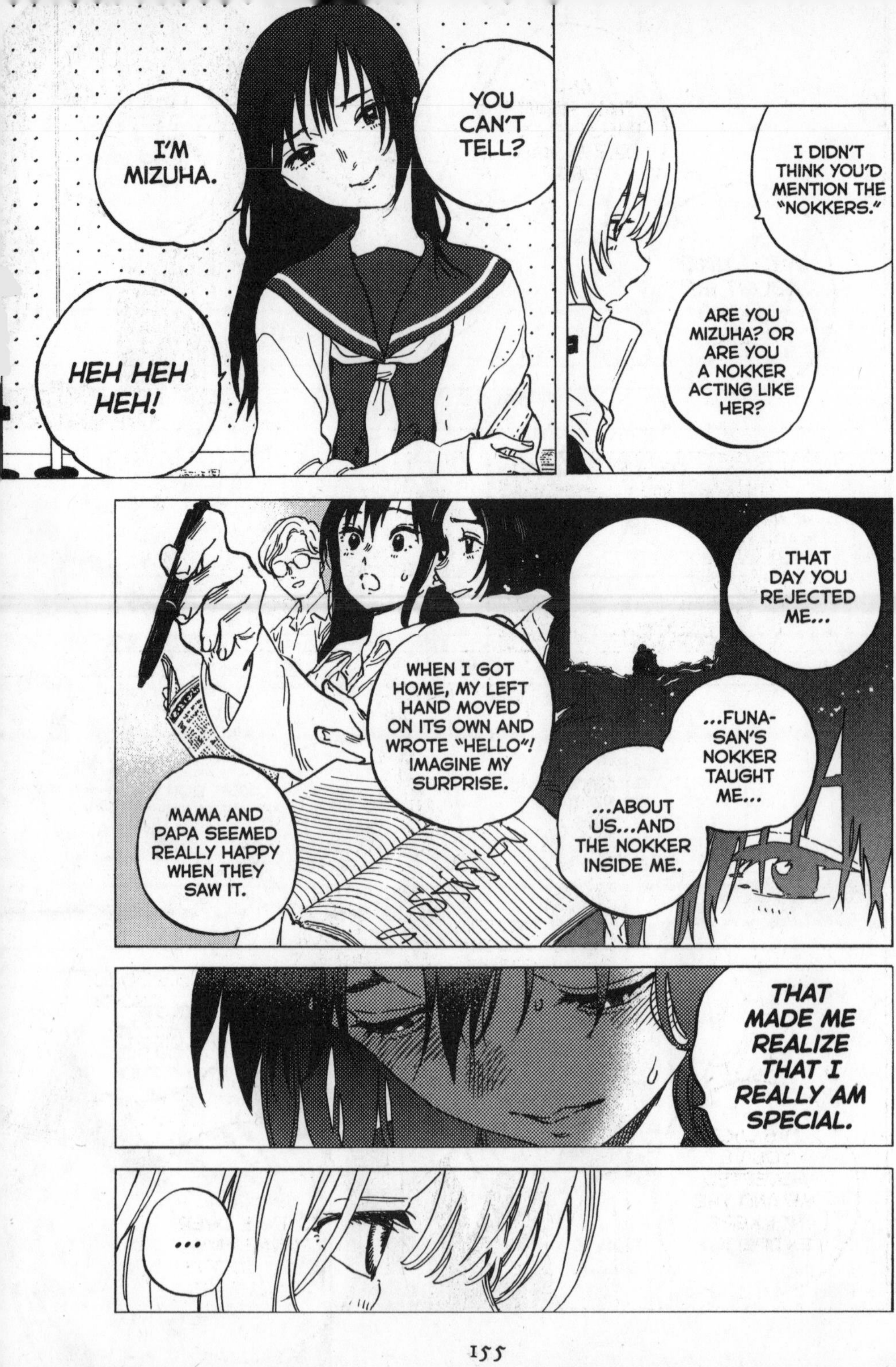
I DIDN'T THINK YOU'D MENTION THE "NOKKERS."
ARE YOU MIZUHA? OR ARE YOU A NOKKER ACTING LIKE HER?
YOU CAN'T TELL?
I'M MIZUHA.
HEH HEH HEH!
THAT DAY YOU REJECTED ME...
...FUNA-SAN'S NOKKER TAUGHT ME...
...ABOUT US...AND THE NOKKER INSIDE ME.
WHEN I GOT HOME, MY LEFT HAND MOVED ON ITS OWN AND WROTE "HELLO"! IMAGINE MY SURPRISE.
MAMA AND PAPA SEEMED REALLY HAPPY WHEN THEY SAW IT.
THAT MADE ME REALIZE THAT I REALLY AM SPECIAL.
...

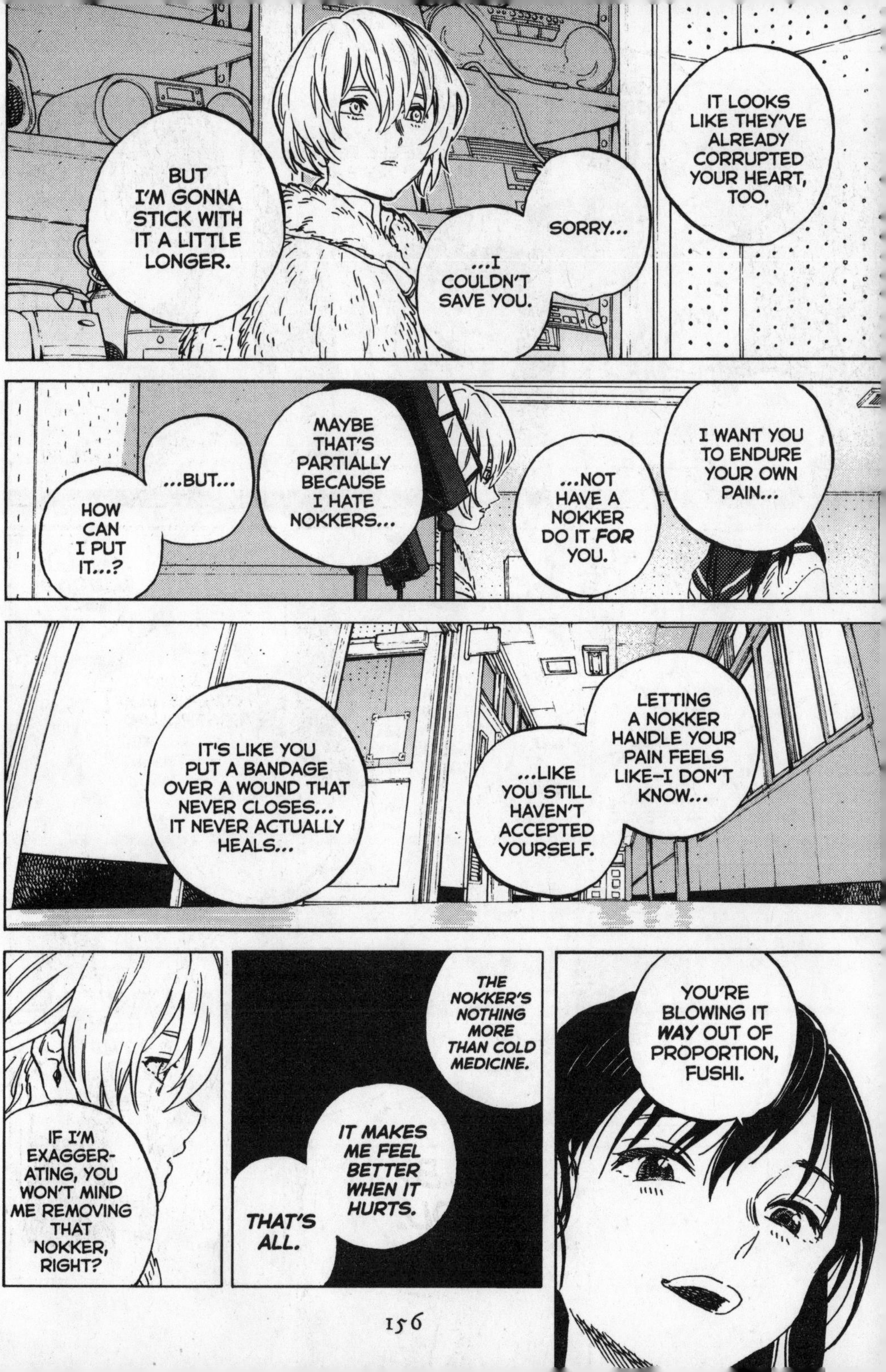
IT LOOKS LIKE THEY'VE ALREADY CORRUPTED YOUR HEART, TOO.
SORRY...
...I COULDN'T SAVE YOU.
BUT I'M GONNA STICK WITH IT A LITTLE LONGER.
I WANT YOU TO ENDURE YOUR OWN PAIN...
...NOT HAVE A NOKKER DO IT *FOR* YOU.
MAYBE THAT'S PARTIALLY BECAUSE I HATE NOKKERS...
...BUT...
HOW CAN I PUT IT...?
LETTING A NOKKER HANDLE YOUR PAIN FEELS LIKE—I DON'T KNOW...
...LIKE YOU STILL HAVEN'T ACCEPTED YOURSELF.
IT'S LIKE YOU PUT A BANDAGE OVER A WOUND THAT NEVER CLOSES... IT NEVER ACTUALLY HEALS...
YOU'RE BLOWING IT *WAY* OUT OF PROPORTION, FUSHI.
THE NOKKER'S NOTHING MORE THAN COLD MEDICINE.
IT MAKES ME FEEL BETTER WHEN IT HURTS.
THAT'S ALL.
IF I'M EXAGGER-ATING, YOU WON'T MIND ME REMOVING THAT NOKKER, RIGHT?

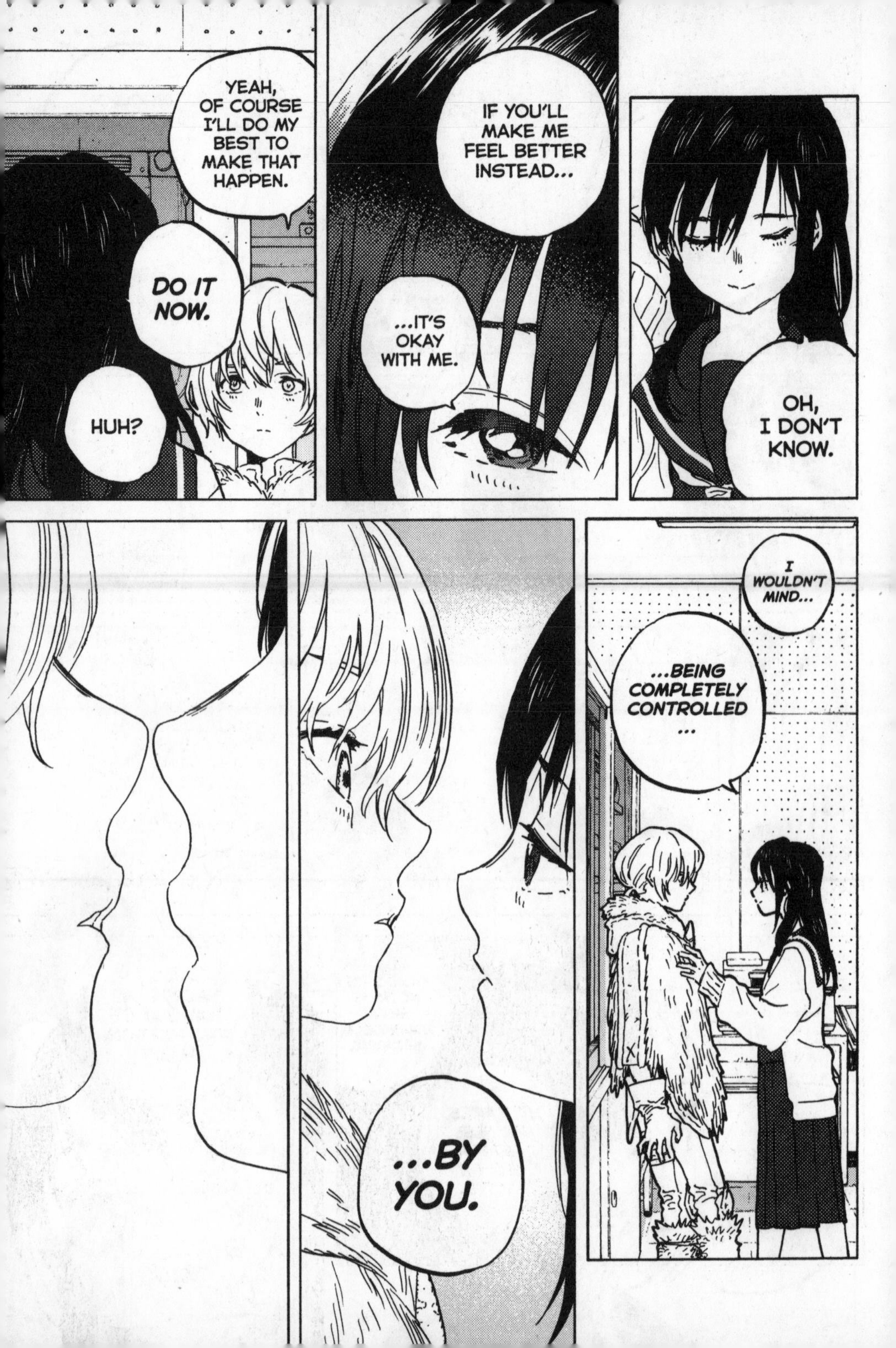
OH, I DON'T KNOW.
IF YOU'LL MAKE ME FEEL BETTER INSTEAD...
...IT'S OKAY WITH ME.
YEAH, OF COURSE I'LL DO MY BEST TO MAKE THAT HAPPEN.
DO IT NOW.
HUH?
I WOULDN'T MIND...
...BEING COMPLETELY CONTROLLED ...
...BY YOU.

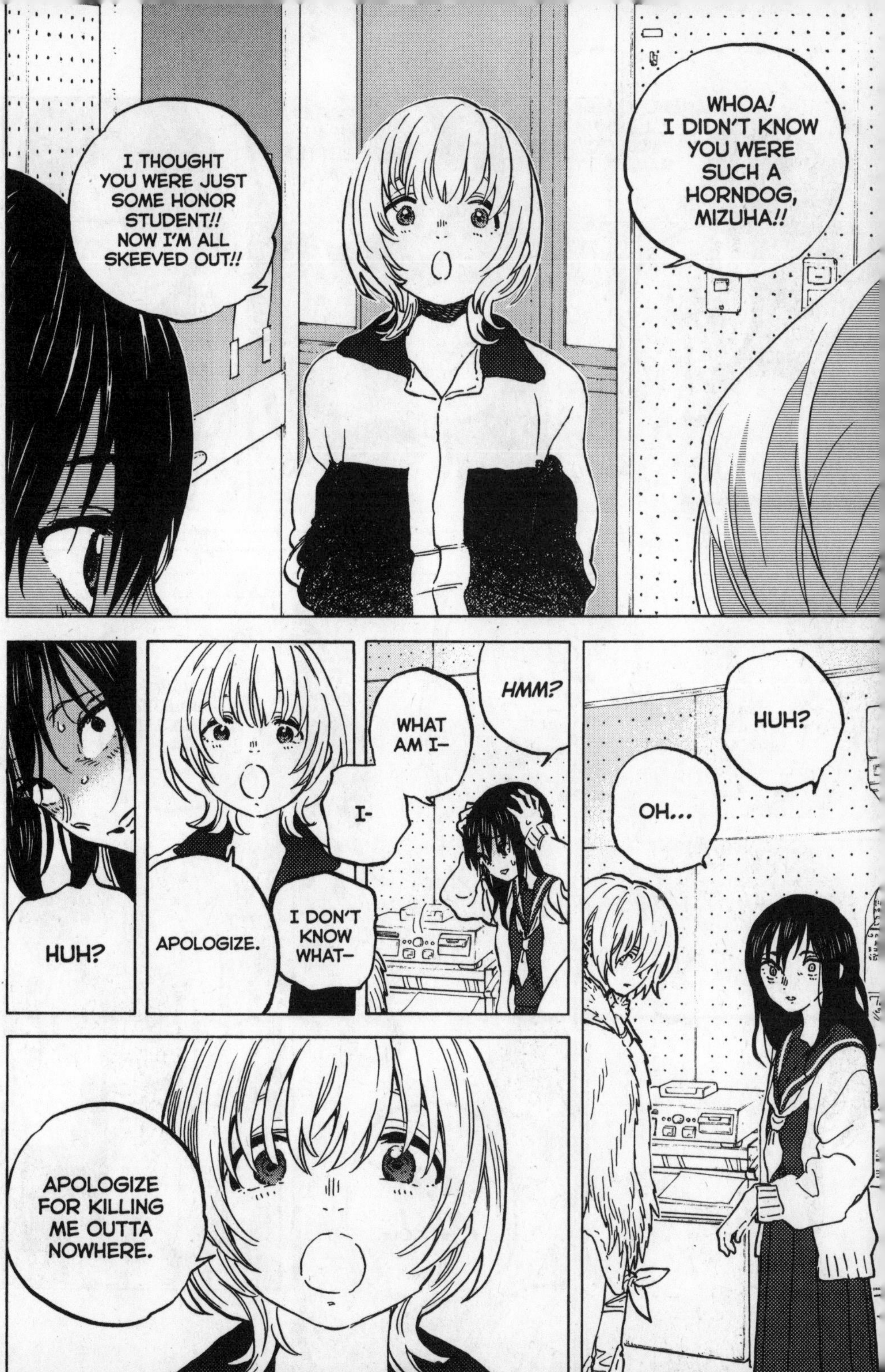
WHOA! I DIDN'T KNOW YOU WERE SUCH A HORNDOG, MIZUHA!!
I THOUGHT YOU WERE JUST SOME HONOR STUDENT!! NOW I'M ALL SKEEVED OUT!!
HUH?
OH...
HMM?
WHAT AM I–
I-
I DON'T KNOW WHAT–
APOLOGIZE.
HUH?
APOLOGIZE FOR KILLING ME OUTTA NOWHERE.

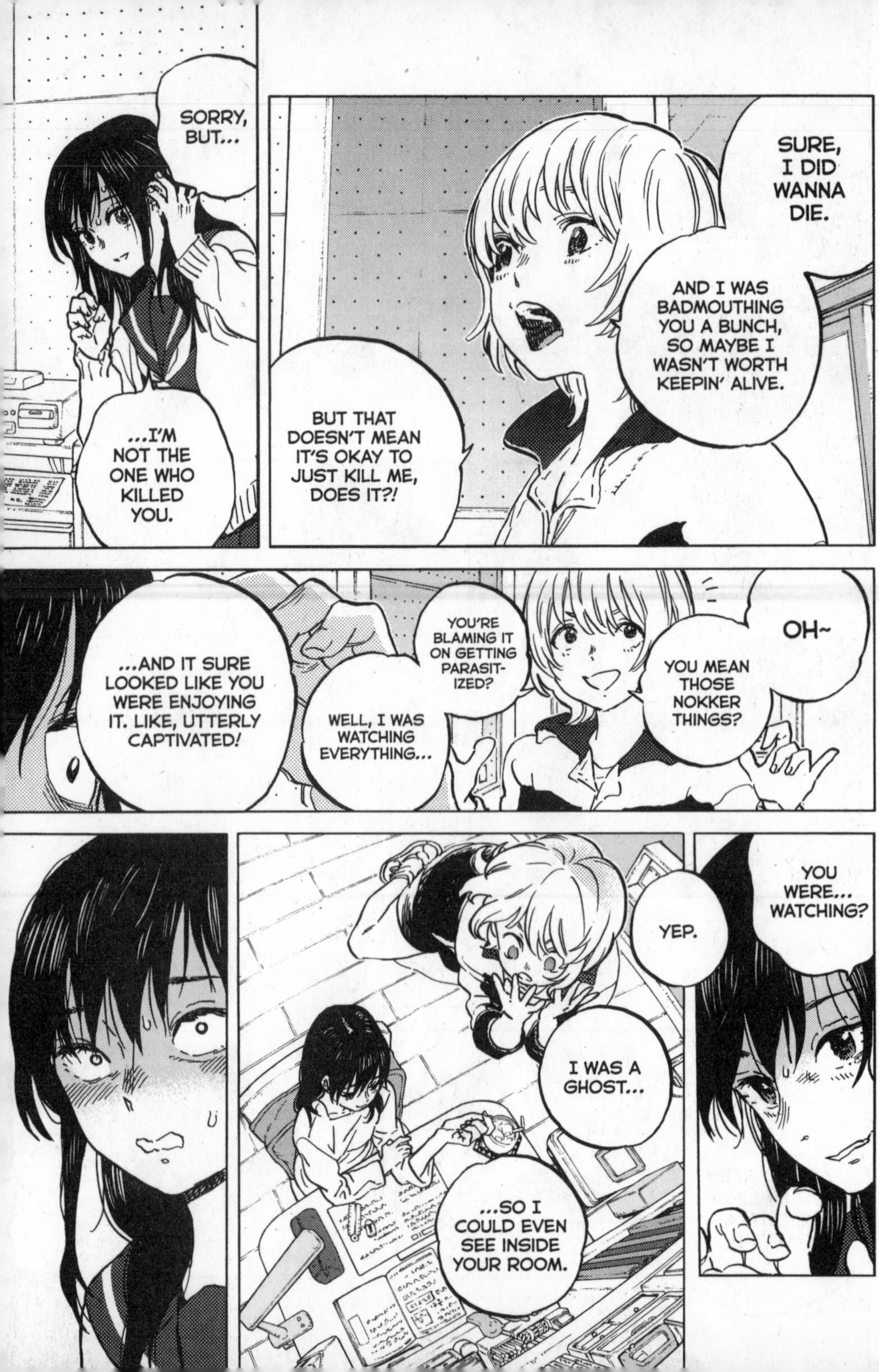
SURE, I DID WANNA DIE.
AND I WAS BADMOUTHING YOU A BUNCH, SO MAYBE I WASN'T WORTH KEEPIN' ALIVE.
BUT THAT DOESN'T MEAN IT'S OKAY TO JUST KILL ME, DOES IT?!
SORRY, BUT...
...I'M NOT THE ONE WHO KILLED YOU.
OH~
YOU MEAN THOSE NOKKER THINGS?
YOU'RE BLAMING IT ON GETTING PARASITIZED?
WELL, I WAS WATCHING EVERYTHING...
...AND IT SURE LOOKED LIKE YOU WERE ENJOYING IT. LIKE, UTTERLY CAPTIVATED!
YOU WERE... WATCHING?
YEP.
I WAS A GHOST...
...SO I COULD EVEN SEE INSIDE YOUR ROOM.

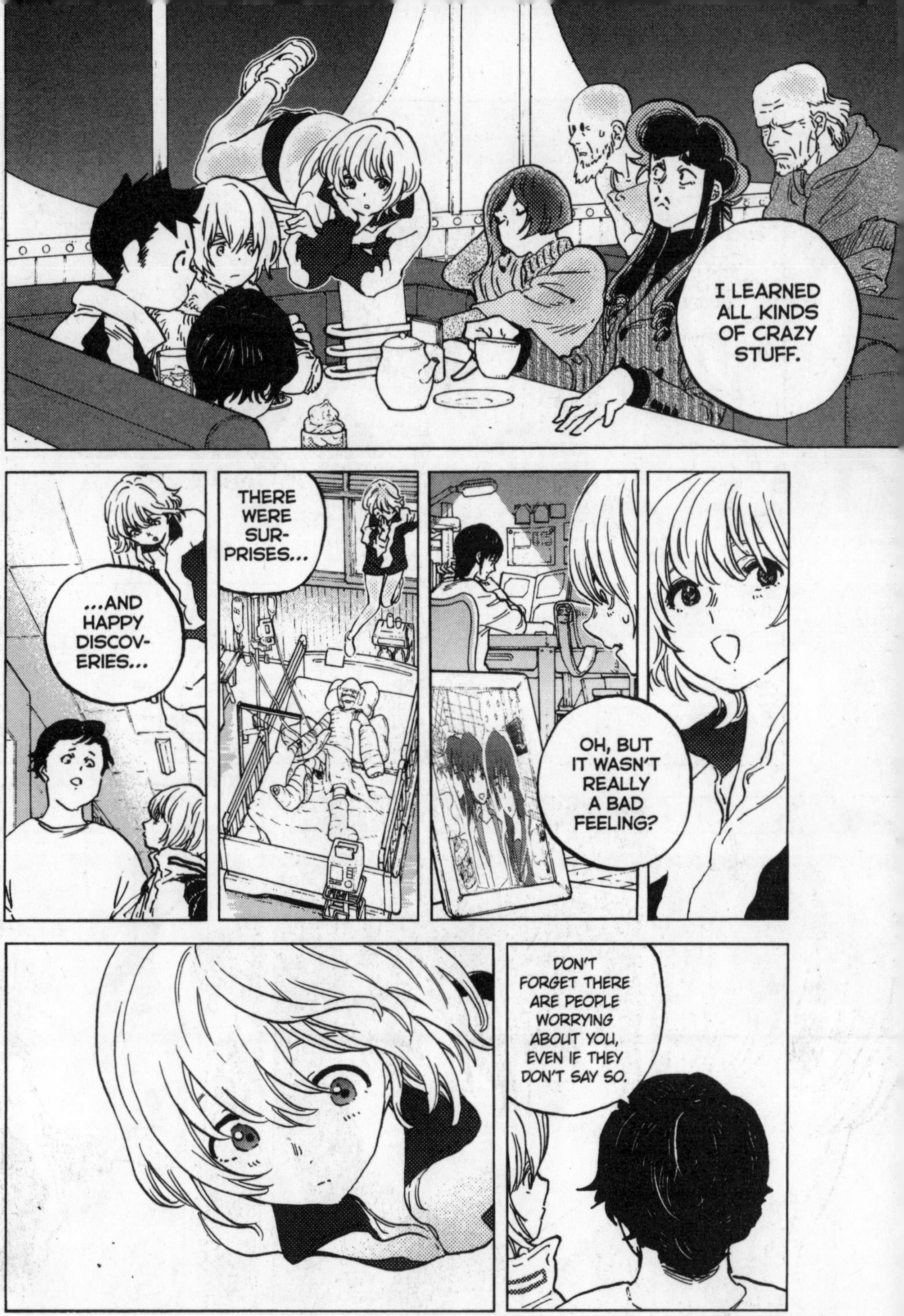
I LEARNED ALL KINDS OF CRAZY STUFF.
OH, BUT IT WASN'T REALLY A BAD FEELING?
THERE WERE SUR-PRISES...
...AND HAPPY DISCOV-ERIES...
DON'T FORGET THERE ARE PEOPLE WORRYING ABOUT YOU, EVEN IF THEY DON'T SAY SO.

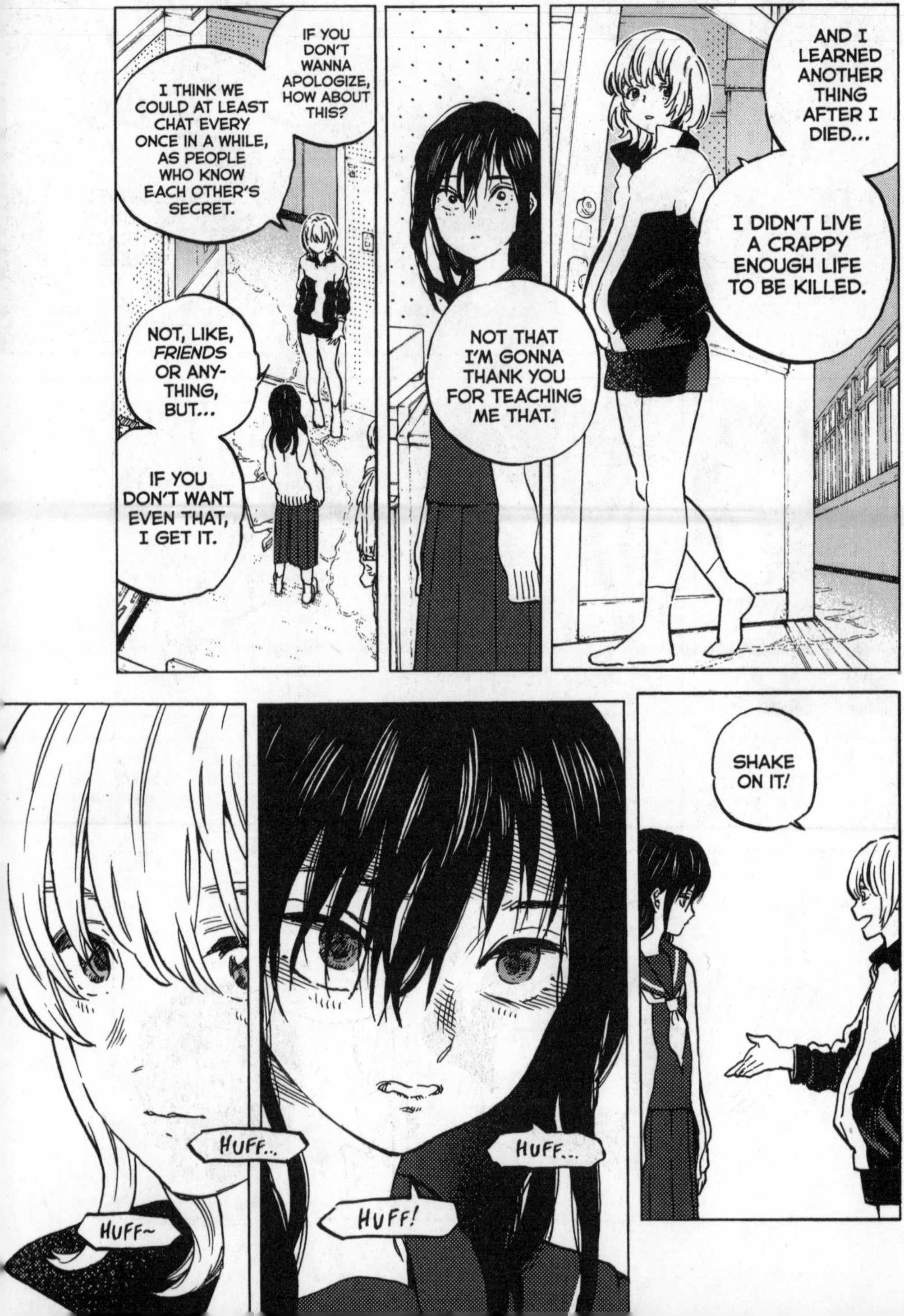
AND I LEARNED ANOTHER THING AFTER I DIED...
I DIDN'T LIVE A CRAPPY ENOUGH LIFE TO BE KILLED.
NOT THAT I'M GONNA THANK YOU FOR TEACHING ME THAT.
IF YOU DON'T WANNA APOLOGIZE, HOW ABOUT THIS?
I THINK WE COULD AT LEAST CHAT EVERY ONCE IN A WHILE, AS PEOPLE WHO KNOW EACH OTHER'S SECRET.
NOT, LIKE, *FRIENDS* OR ANYTHING, BUT...
IF YOU DON'T WANT EVEN THAT, I GET IT.
SHAKE ON IT!
HUFF...
HUFF!
HUFF...
HUFF~

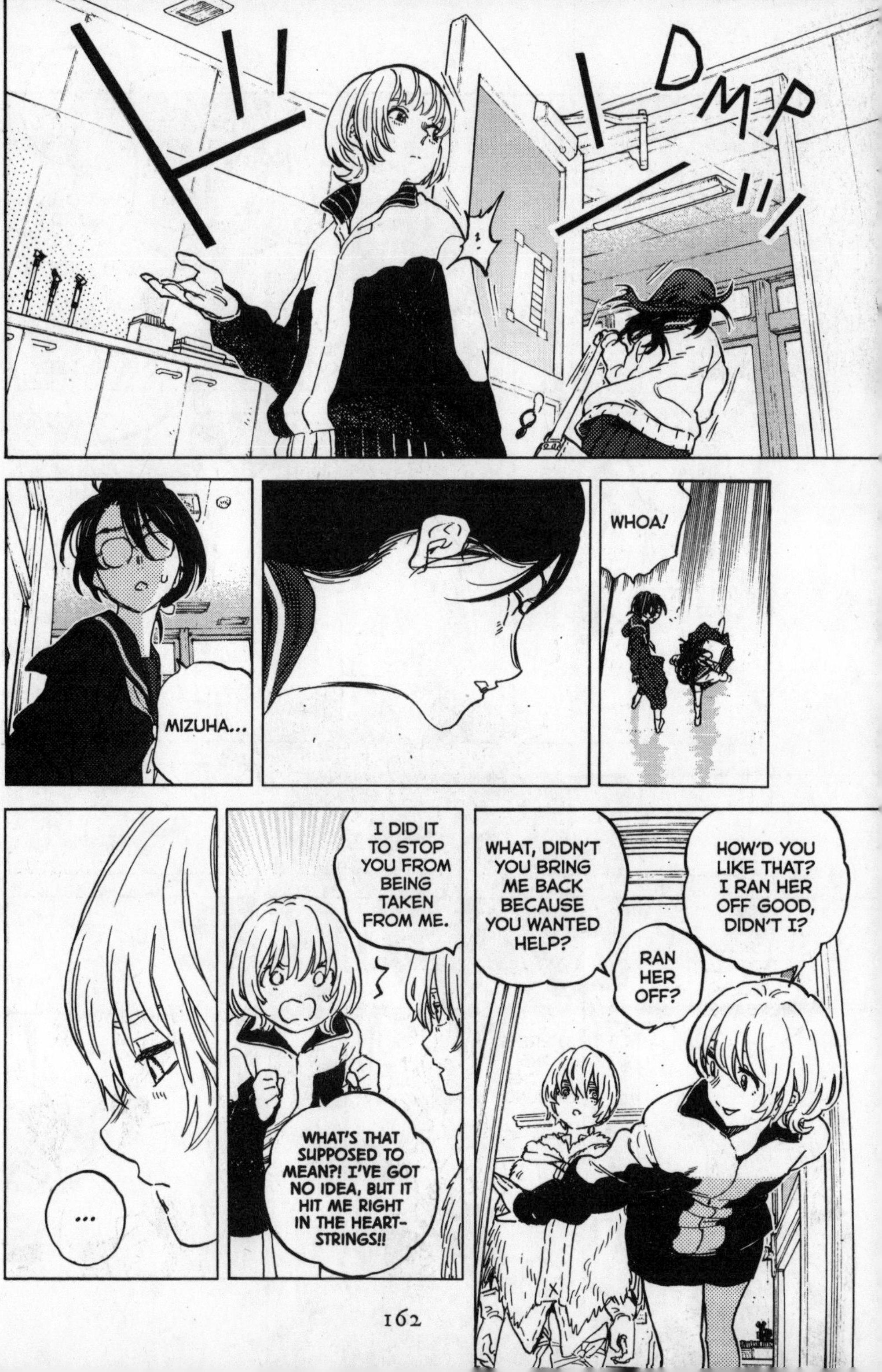
DMP
WHOA!
MIZUHA...
HOW'D YOU LIKE THAT? I RAN HER OFF GOOD, DIDN'T I?
RAN HER OFF?
WHAT, DIDN'T YOU BRING ME BACK BECAUSE YOU WANTED HELP?
I DID IT TO STOP YOU FROM BEING TAKEN FROM ME.
WHAT'S THAT SUPPOSED TO MEAN?! I'VE GOT NO IDEA, BUT IT HIT ME RIGHT IN THE HEART-STRINGS!!
...

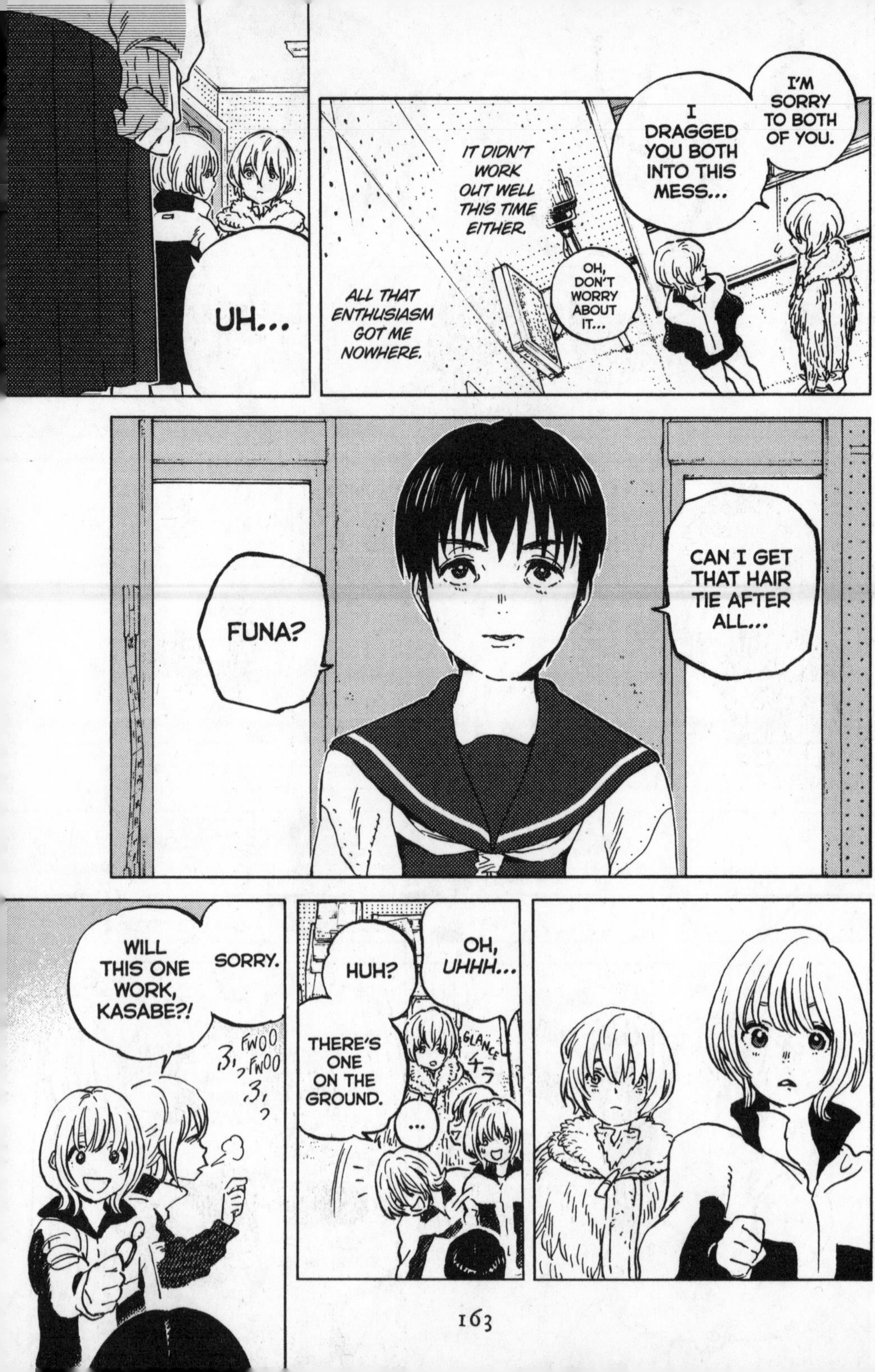
I'M SORRY TO BOTH OF YOU.
I DRAGGED YOU BOTH INTO THIS MESS...
OH, DON'T WORRY ABOUT IT...
IT DIDN'T WORK OUT WELL THIS TIME EITHER.
ALL THAT ENTHUSIASM GOT ME NOWHERE.
UH...
CAN I GET THAT HAIR TIE AFTER ALL...
FUNA?
OH, UHHH...
HUH?
GLANCE
THERE'S ONE ON THE GROUND.
...
SORRY.
WILL THIS ONE WORK, KASABE?!
FWOO
FWOO

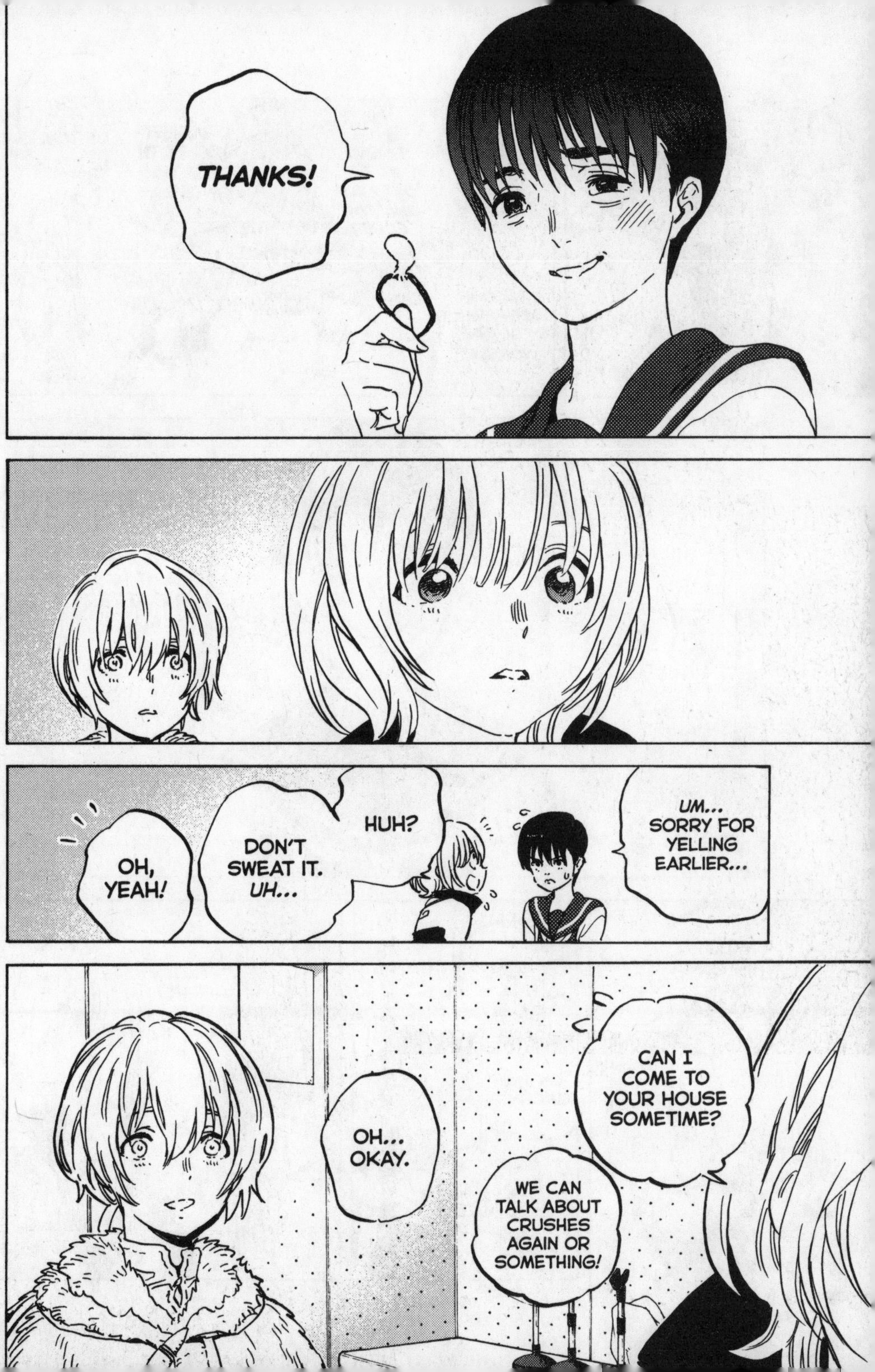
THANKS!
UM... SORRY FOR YELLING EARLIER...
HUH?
DON'T SWEAT IT. UH...
OH, YEAH!
CAN I COME TO YOUR HOUSE SOMETIME?
WE CAN TALK ABOUT CRUSHES AGAIN OR SOMETHING!
OH... OKAY.

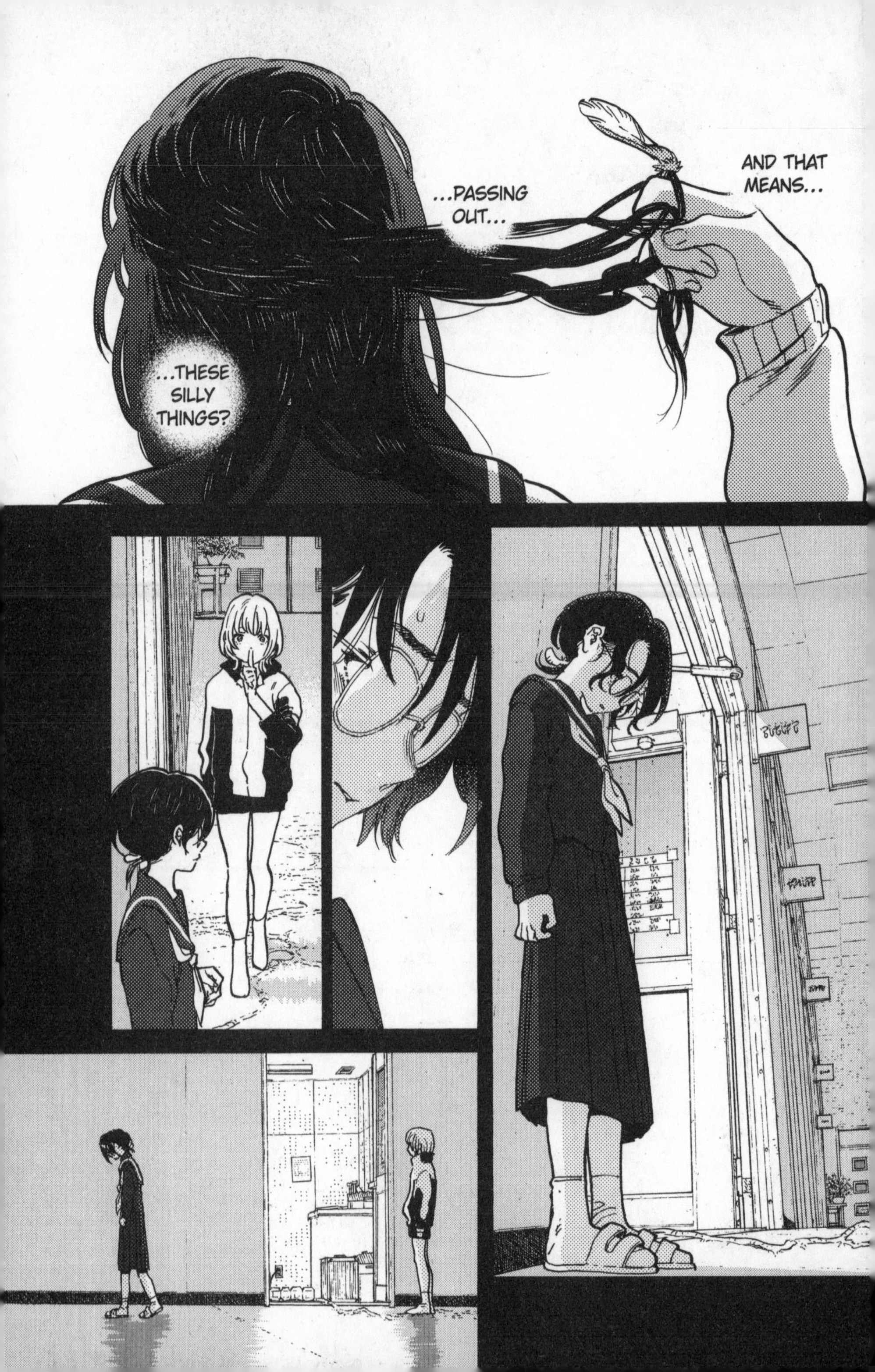
AND THAT MEANS...
...PASSING OUT...
...THESE SILLY THINGS?

#146 Number One

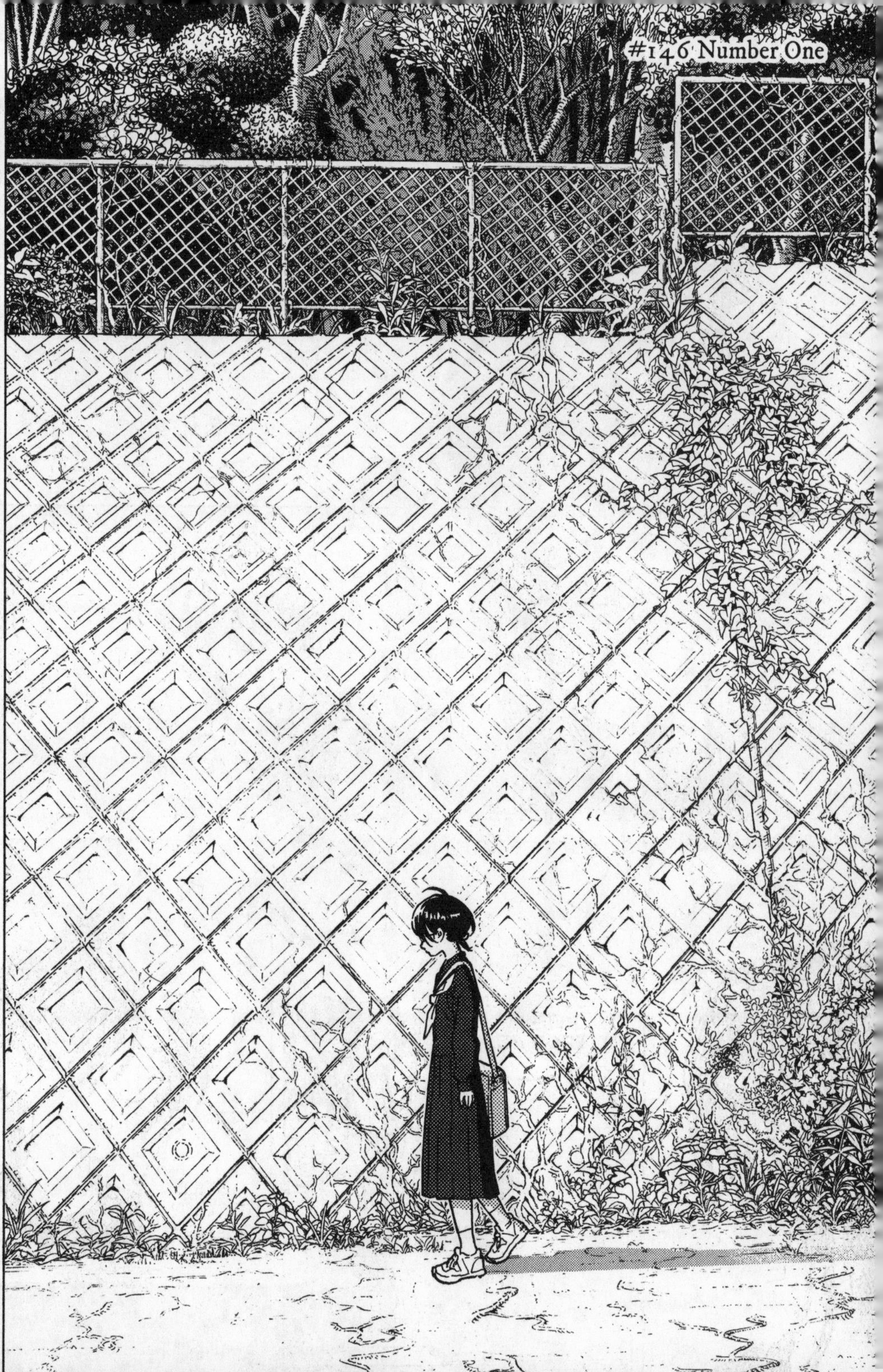

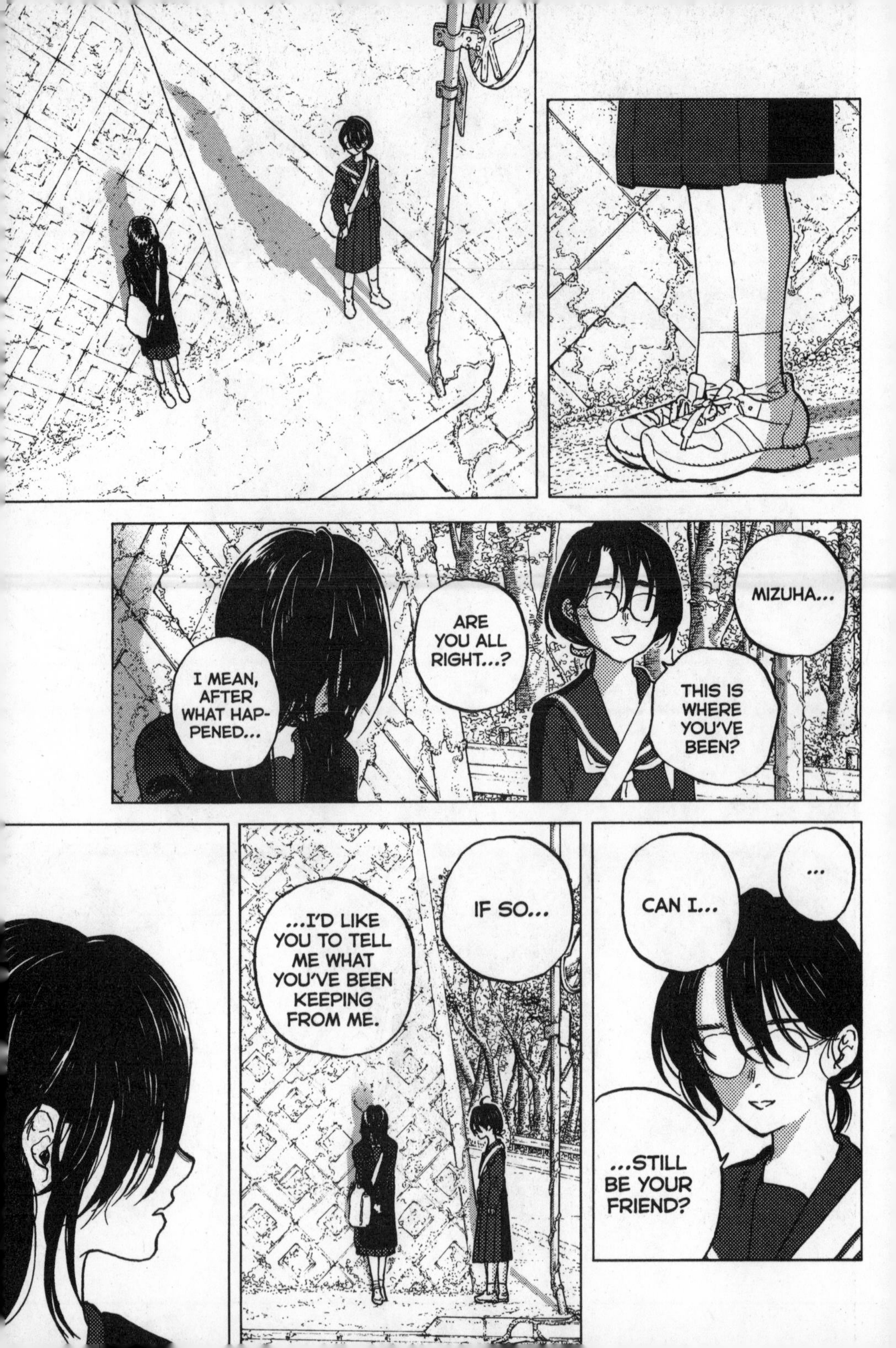
MIZUHA...
THIS IS WHERE YOU'VE BEEN?
ARE YOU ALL RIGHT...?
I MEAN, AFTER WHAT HAP-PENED...
...
CAN I...
...STILL BE YOUR FRIEND?
IF SO...
...I'D LIKE YOU TO TELL ME WHAT YOU'VE BEEN KEEPING FROM ME.

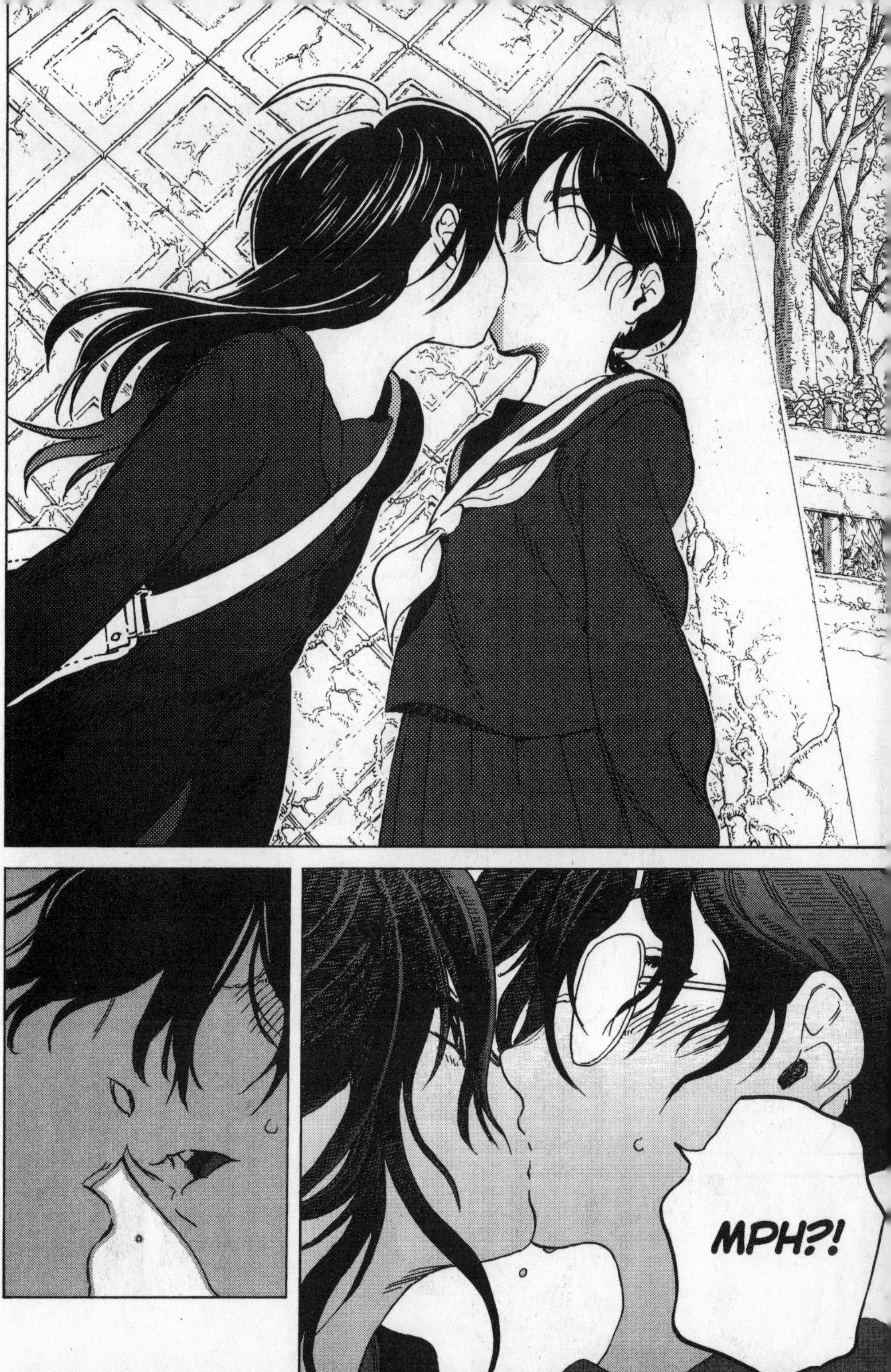
MPH?!

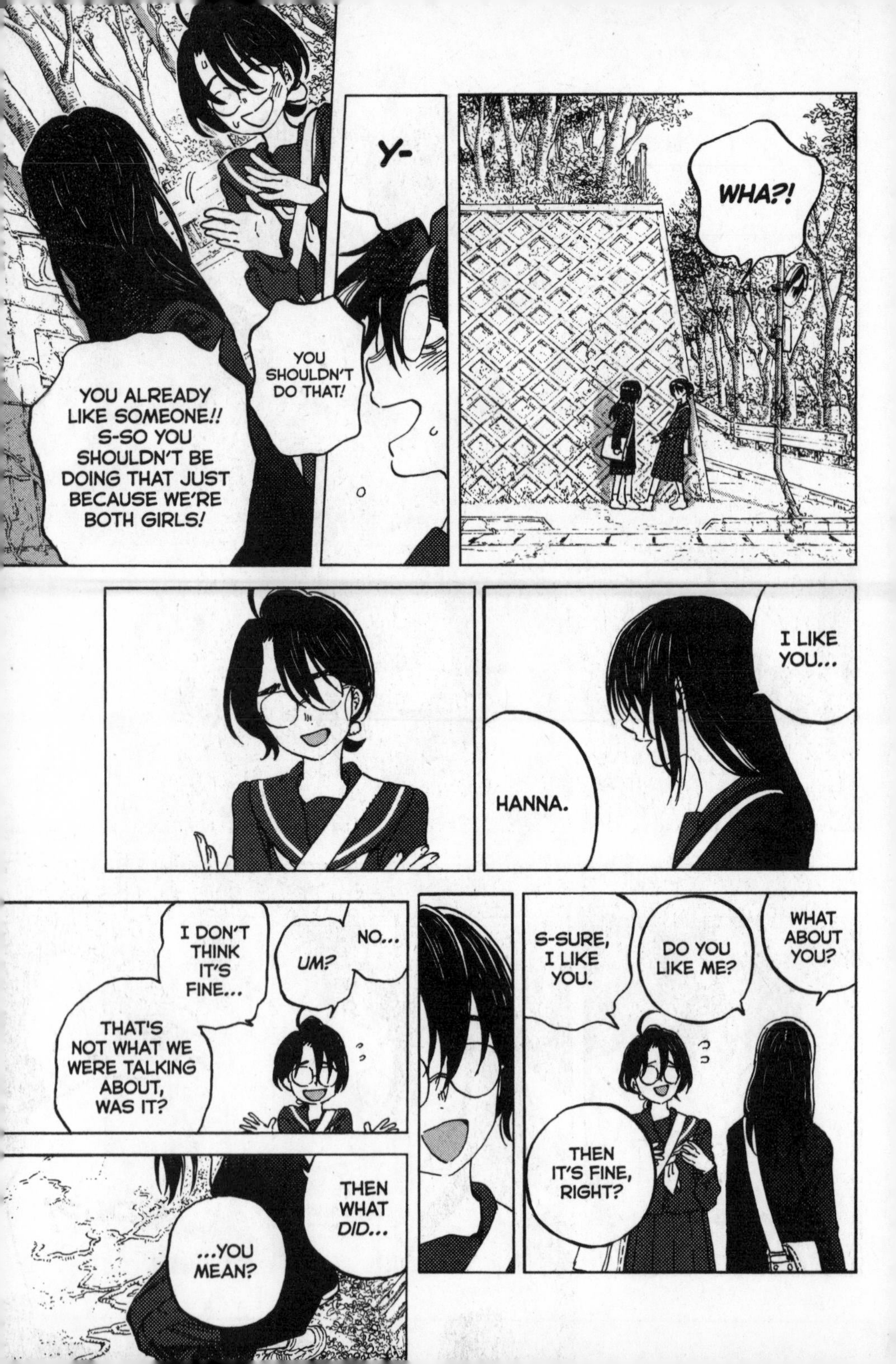
WHA?!
Y-
YOU SHOULDN'T DO THAT!
YOU ALREADY LIKE SOMEONE!! S-SO YOU SHOULDN'T BE DOING THAT JUST BECAUSE WE'RE BOTH GIRLS!
I LIKE YOU...
HANNA.
WHAT ABOUT YOU?
DO YOU LIKE ME?
S-SURE, I LIKE YOU.
THEN IT'S FINE, RIGHT?
NO...
UM?
I DON'T THINK IT'S FINE...
THAT'S NOT WHAT WE WERE TALKING ABOUT, WAS IT?
THEN WHAT DID...
...YOU MEAN?

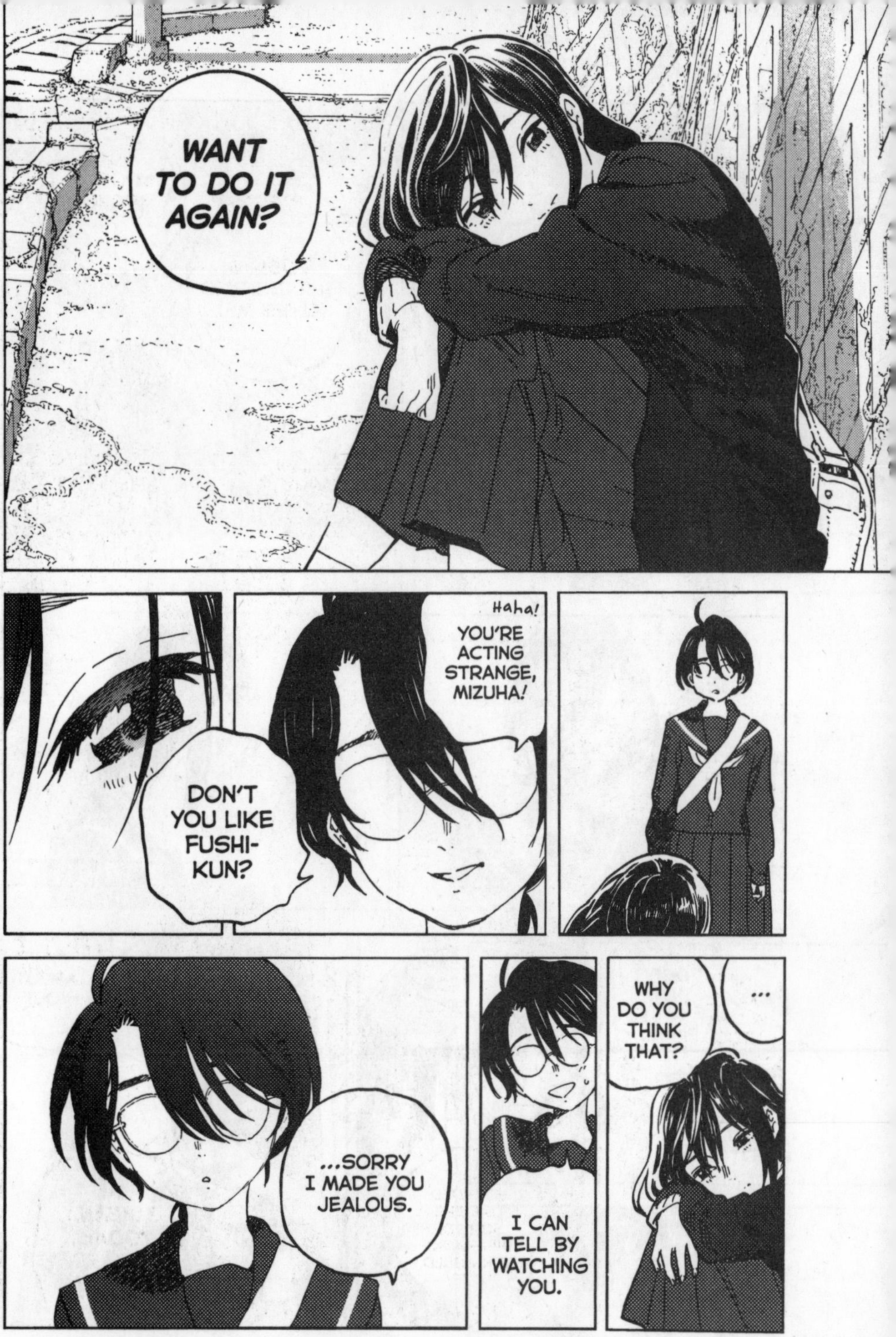
WANT TO DO IT AGAIN?
Haha!
YOU'RE ACTING STRANGE, MIZUHA!
DON'T YOU LIKE FUSHI-KUN?
...
WHY DO YOU THINK THAT?
I CAN TELL BY WATCHING YOU.
...SORRY I MADE YOU JEALOUS.

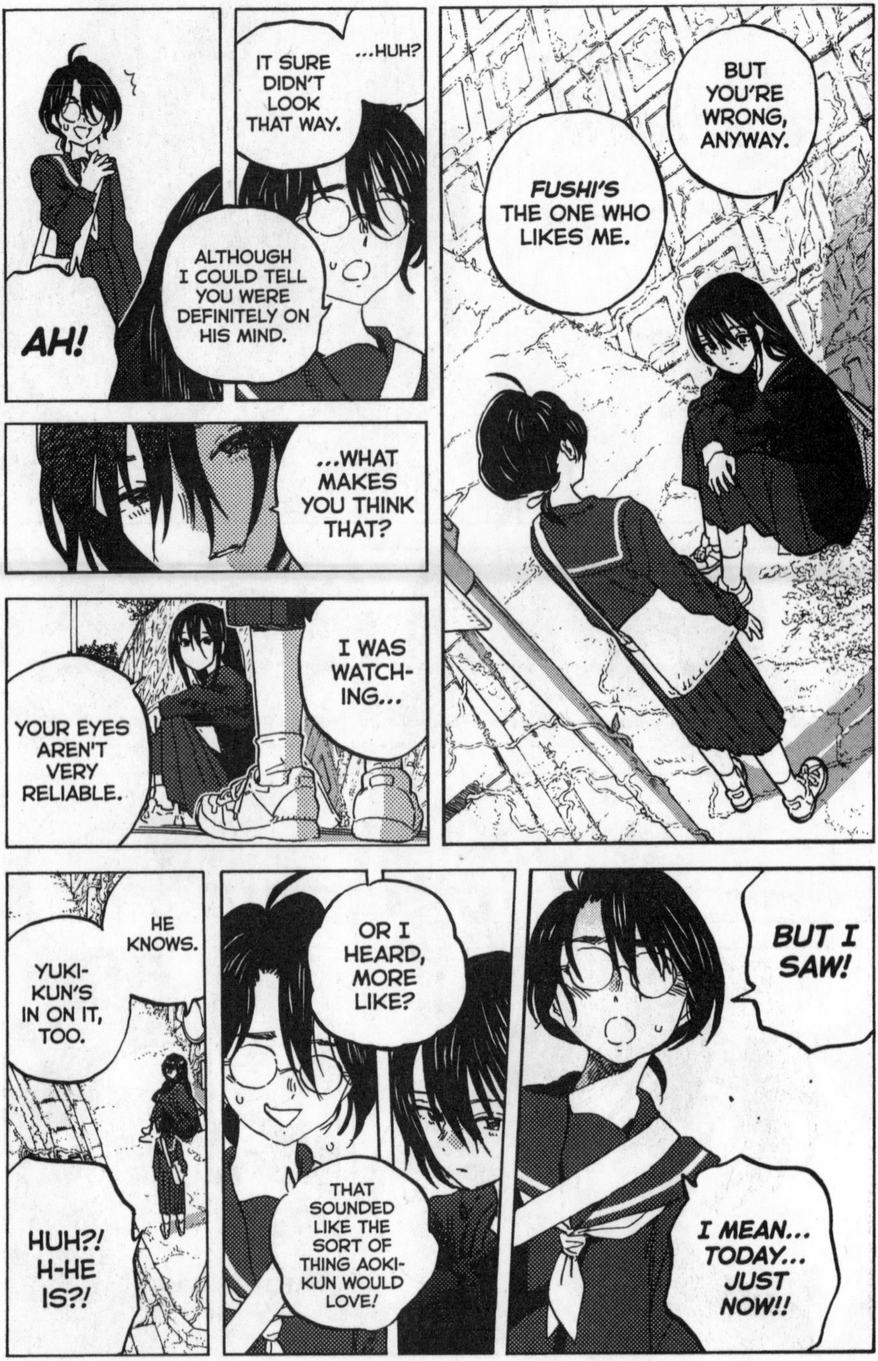
BUT YOU'RE WRONG, ANYWAY.
FUSHI'S THE ONE WHO LIKES ME.
...HUH?
IT SURE DIDN'T LOOK THAT WAY.
ALTHOUGH I COULD TELL YOU WERE DEFINITELY ON HIS MIND.
AH!
...WHAT MAKES YOU THINK THAT?
I WAS WATCHING...
YOUR EYES AREN'T VERY RELIABLE.
BUT I SAW!
I MEAN... TODAY... JUST NOW!!
OR I HEARD, MORE LIKE?
THAT SOUNDED LIKE THE SORT OF THING AOKI-KUN WOULD LOVE!
HE KNOWS.
YUKI-KUN'S IN ON IT, TOO.
HUH?! H-HE IS?!

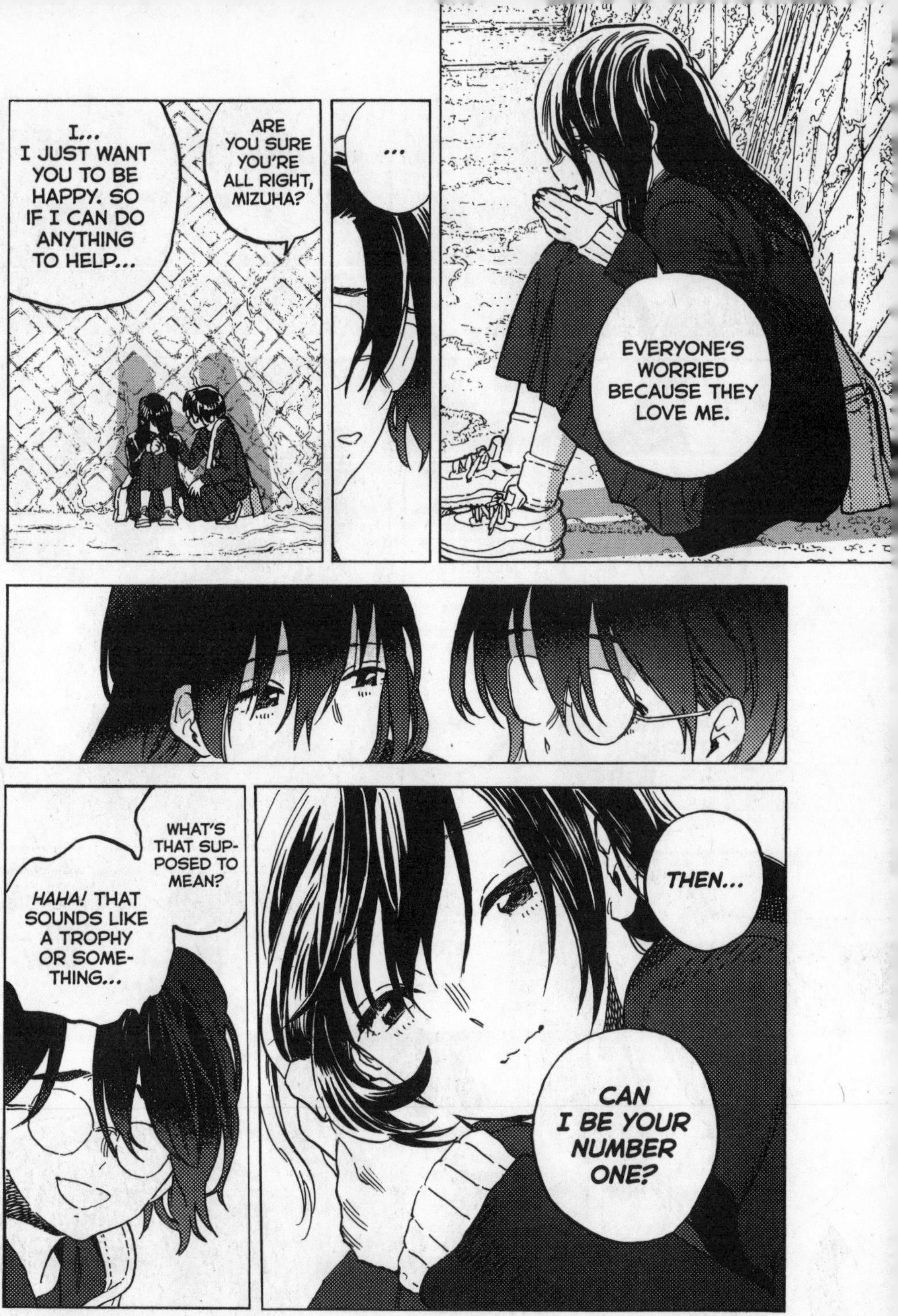
EVERYONE'S WORRIED BECAUSE THEY LOVE ME.
...
ARE YOU SURE YOU'RE ALL RIGHT, MIZUHA?
I... I JUST WANT YOU TO BE HAPPY. SO IF I CAN DO ANYTHING TO HELP...
THEN...
CAN I BE YOUR NUMBER ONE?
WHAT'S THAT SUPPOSED TO MEAN?
HAHA! THAT SOUNDS LIKE A TROPHY OR SOMETHING...

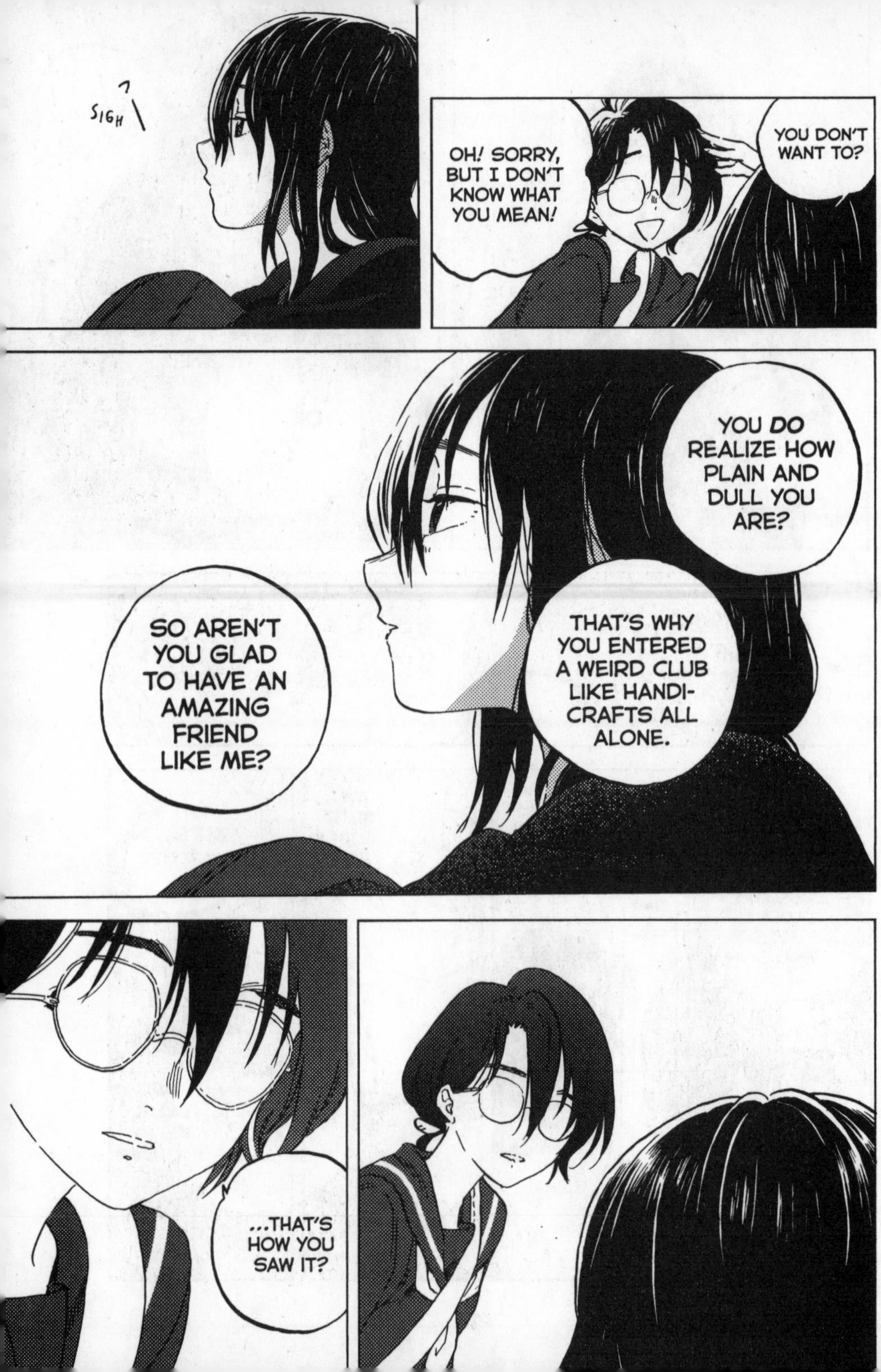
YOU DON'T WANT TO?
OH! SORRY, BUT I DON'T KNOW WHAT YOU MEAN!
SIGH
YOU *DO* REALIZE HOW PLAIN AND DULL YOU ARE?
THAT'S WHY YOU ENTERED A WEIRD CLUB LIKE HANDI-CRAFTS ALL ALONE.
SO AREN'T YOU GLAD TO HAVE AN AMAZING FRIEND LIKE ME?
...THAT'S HOW YOU SAW IT?

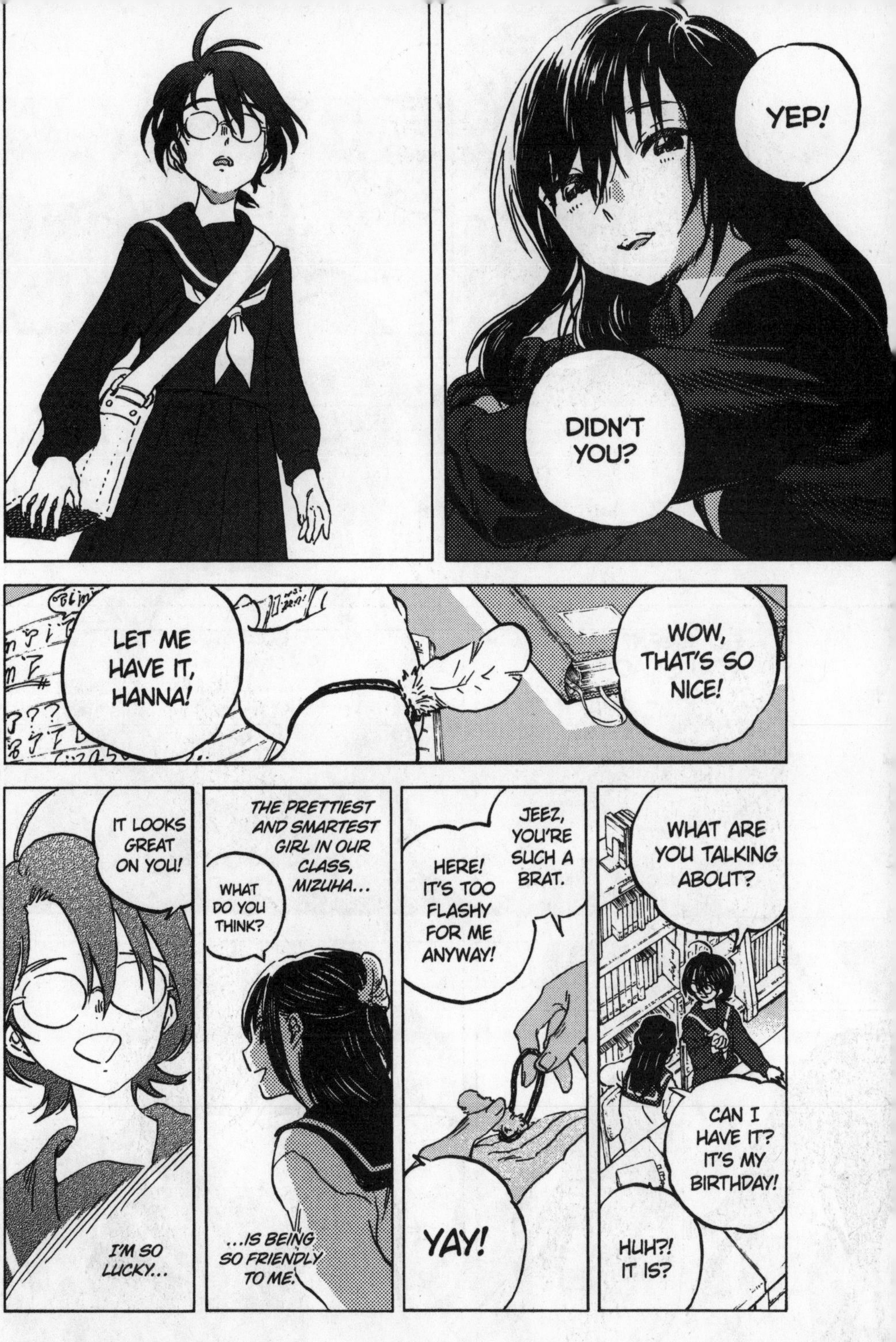
YEP!
DIDN'T YOU?
WOW, THAT'S SO NICE!
LET ME HAVE IT, HANNA!
WHAT ARE YOU TALKING ABOUT?
CAN I HAVE IT? IT'S MY BIRTHDAY!
HUH?! IT IS?
JEEZ, YOU'RE SUCH A BRAT.
HERE! IT'S TOO FLASHY FOR ME ANYWAY!
YAY!
THE PRETTIEST AND SMARTEST GIRL IN OUR CLASS, MIZUHA...
WHAT DO YOU THINK?
...IS BEING SO FRIENDLY TO ME.
IT LOOKS GREAT ON YOU!
I'M SO LUCKY...

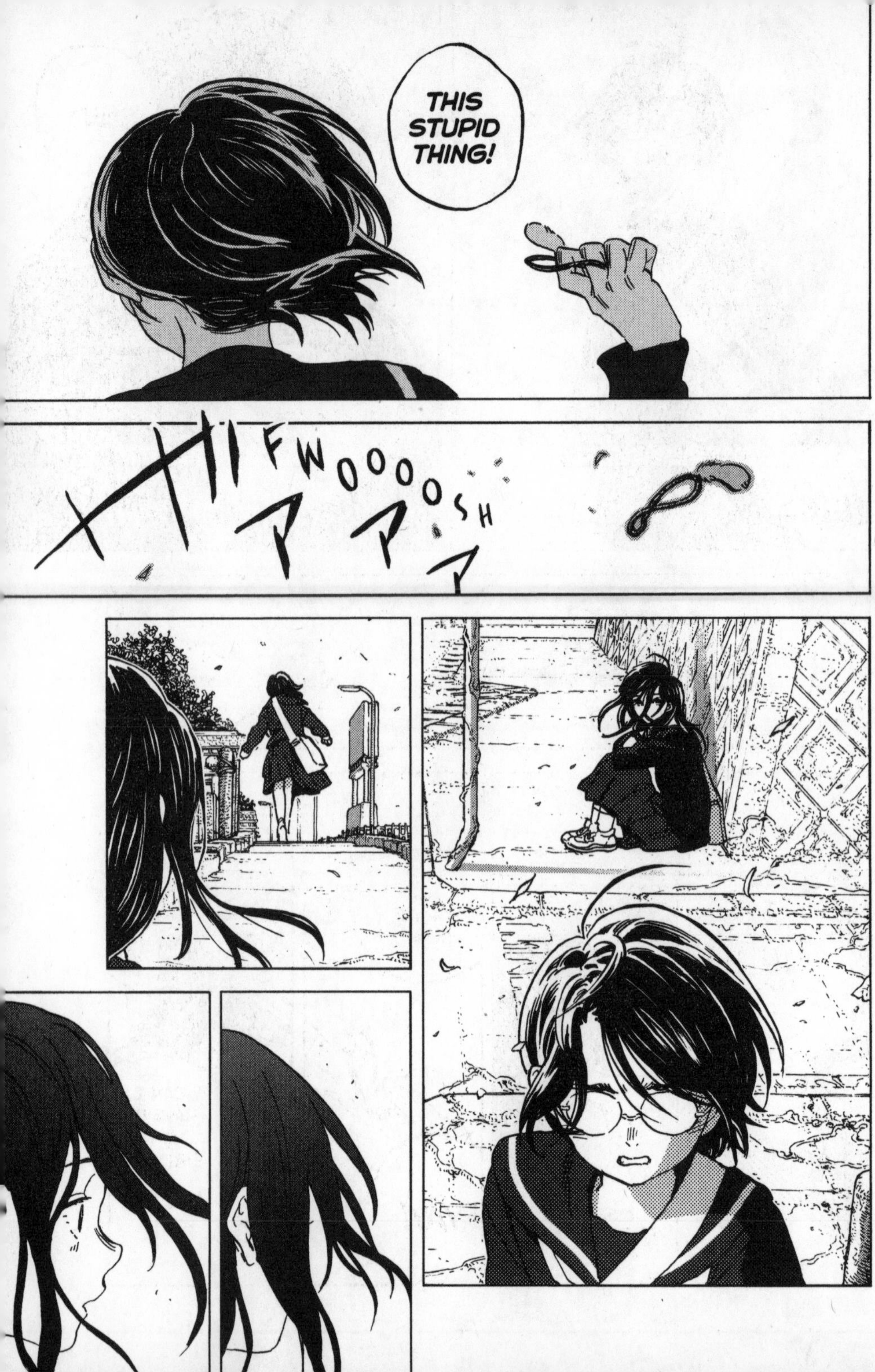
THIS STUPID THING!
FWOOOOSH

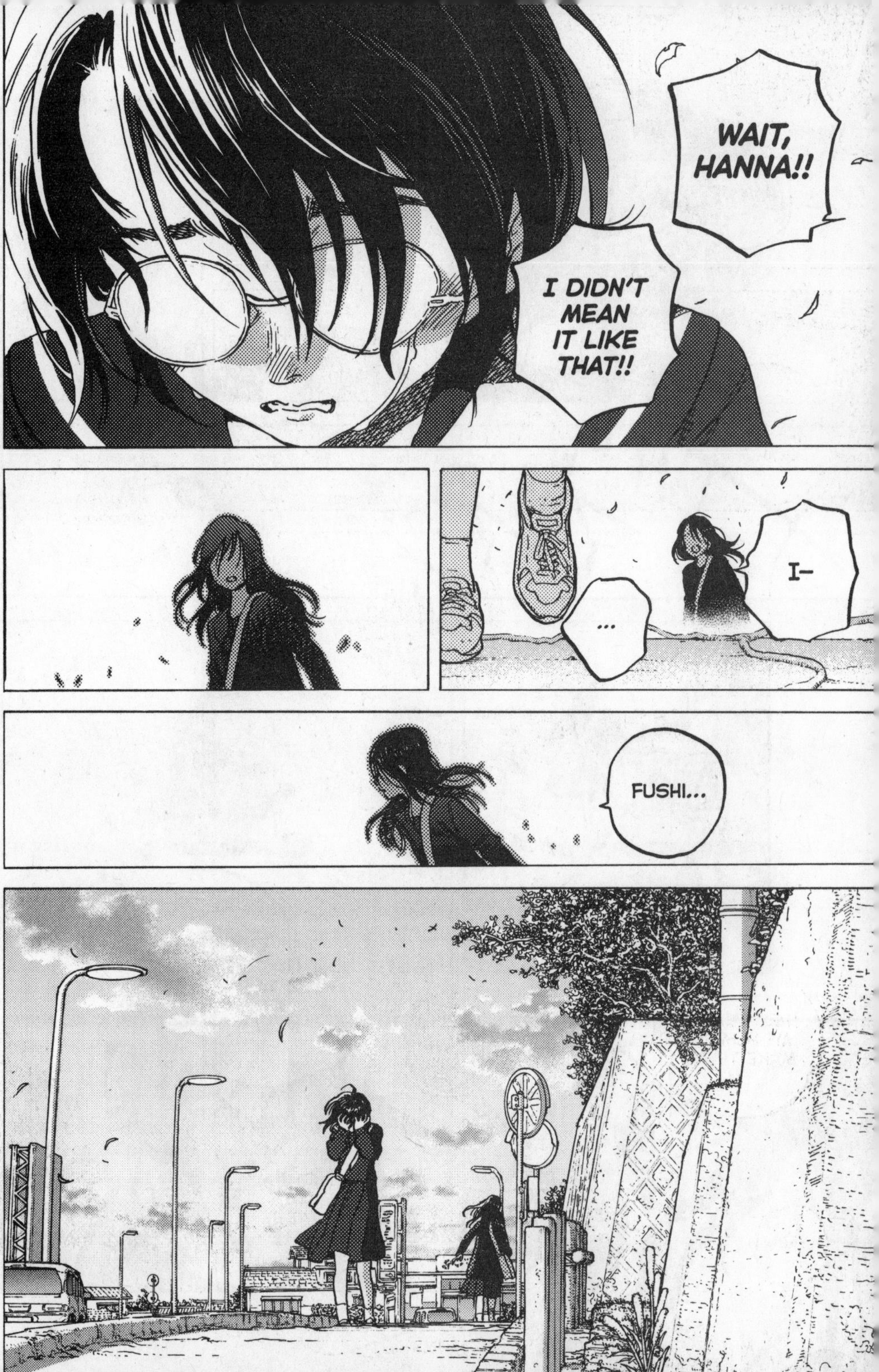
WAIT, HANNA!!
I DIDN'T MEAN IT LIKE THAT!!
I–
...
FUSHI...

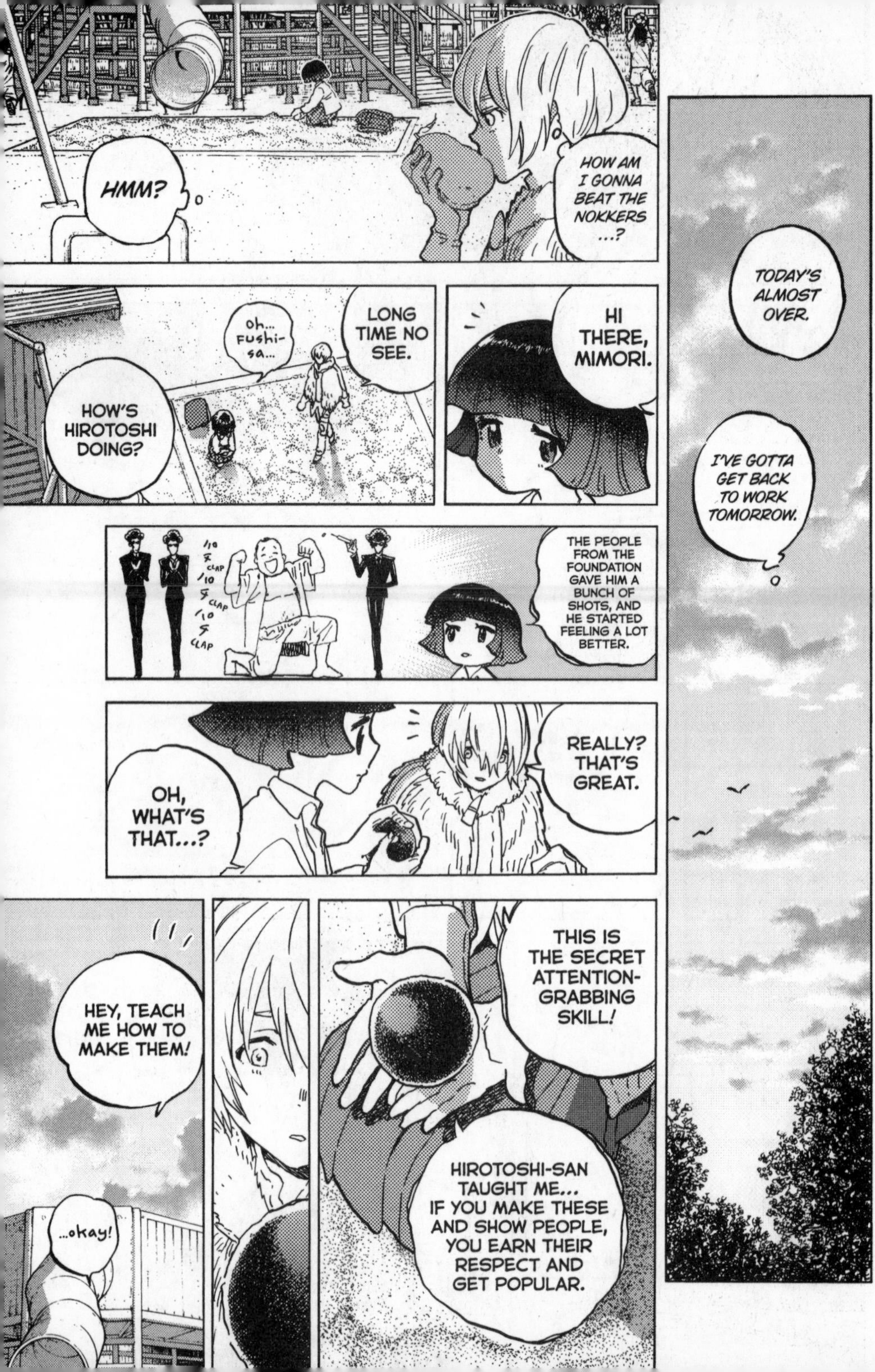
TODAY'S ALMOST OVER.
I'VE GOTTA GET BACK TO WORK TOMORROW.
HOW AM I GONNA BEAT THE NOKKERS ...?
HMM?
HI THERE, MIMORI.
LONG TIME NO SEE.
Oh... Fushi-sa...
HOW'S HIROTOSHI DOING?
THE PEOPLE FROM THE FOUNDATION GAVE HIM A BUNCH OF SHOTS, AND HE STARTED FEELING A LOT BETTER.
CLAP
CLAP
CLAP
REALLY? THAT'S GREAT.
OH, WHAT'S THAT...?
THIS IS THE SECRET ATTENTION-GRABBING SKILL!
HIROTOSHI-SAN TAUGHT ME... IF YOU MAKE THESE AND SHOW PEOPLE, YOU EARN THEIR RESPECT AND GET POPULAR.
HEY, TEACH ME HOW TO MAKE THEM!
...okay!

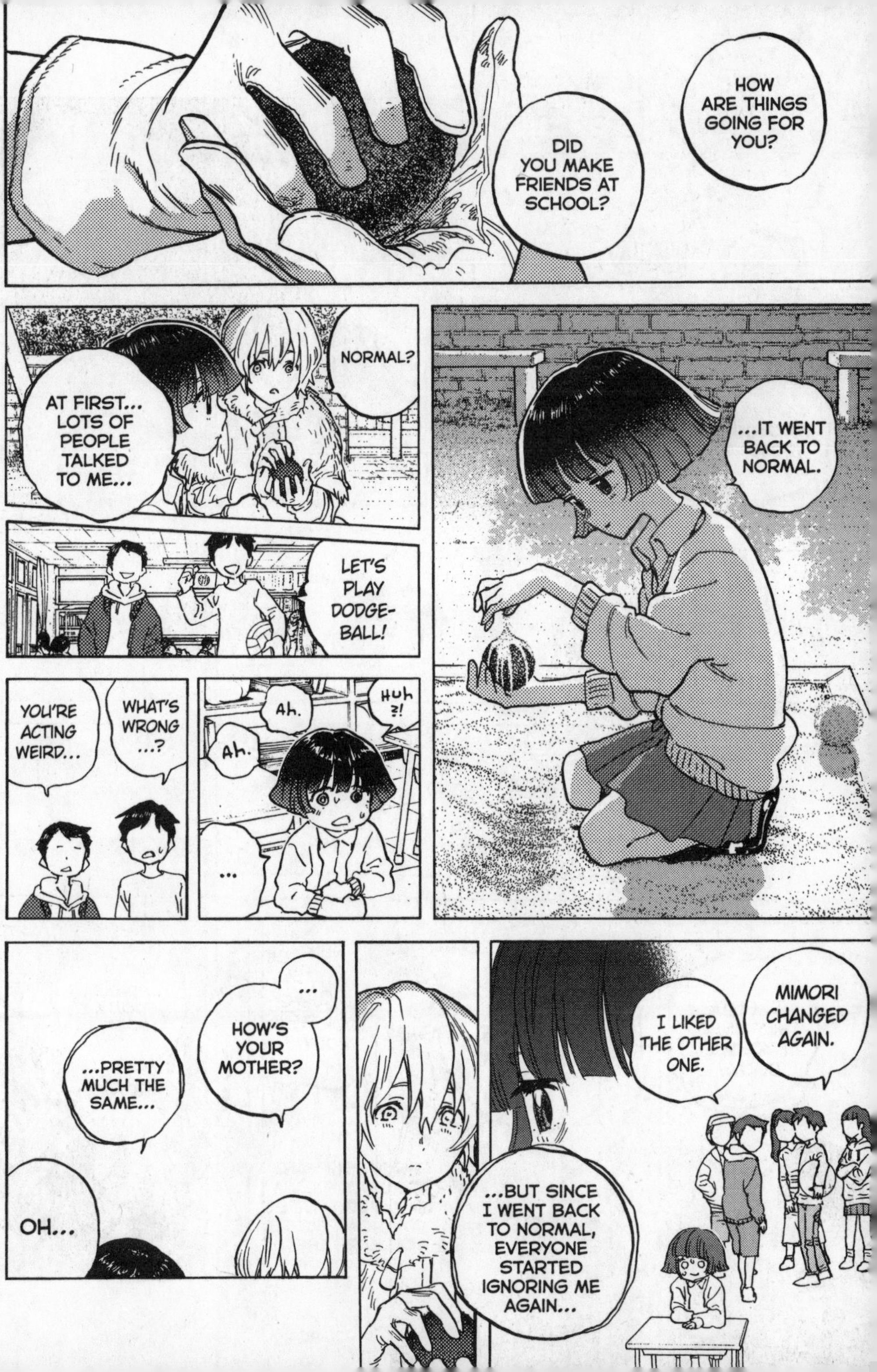

HOW ARE THINGS GOING FOR YOU?
DID YOU MAKE FRIENDS AT SCHOOL?
...IT WENT BACK TO NORMAL.
NORMAL?
AT FIRST... LOTS OF PEOPLE TALKED TO ME...
LET'S PLAY DODGE-BALL!
Huh?!
Ah.
Ah.
...
WHAT'S WRONG ...?
YOU'RE ACTING WEIRD...
MIMORI CHANGED AGAIN.
I LIKED THE OTHER ONE.
...BUT SINCE I WENT BACK TO NORMAL, EVERYONE STARTED IGNORING ME AGAIN...
...
HOW'S YOUR MOTHER?
...PRETTY MUCH THE SAME...
OH...

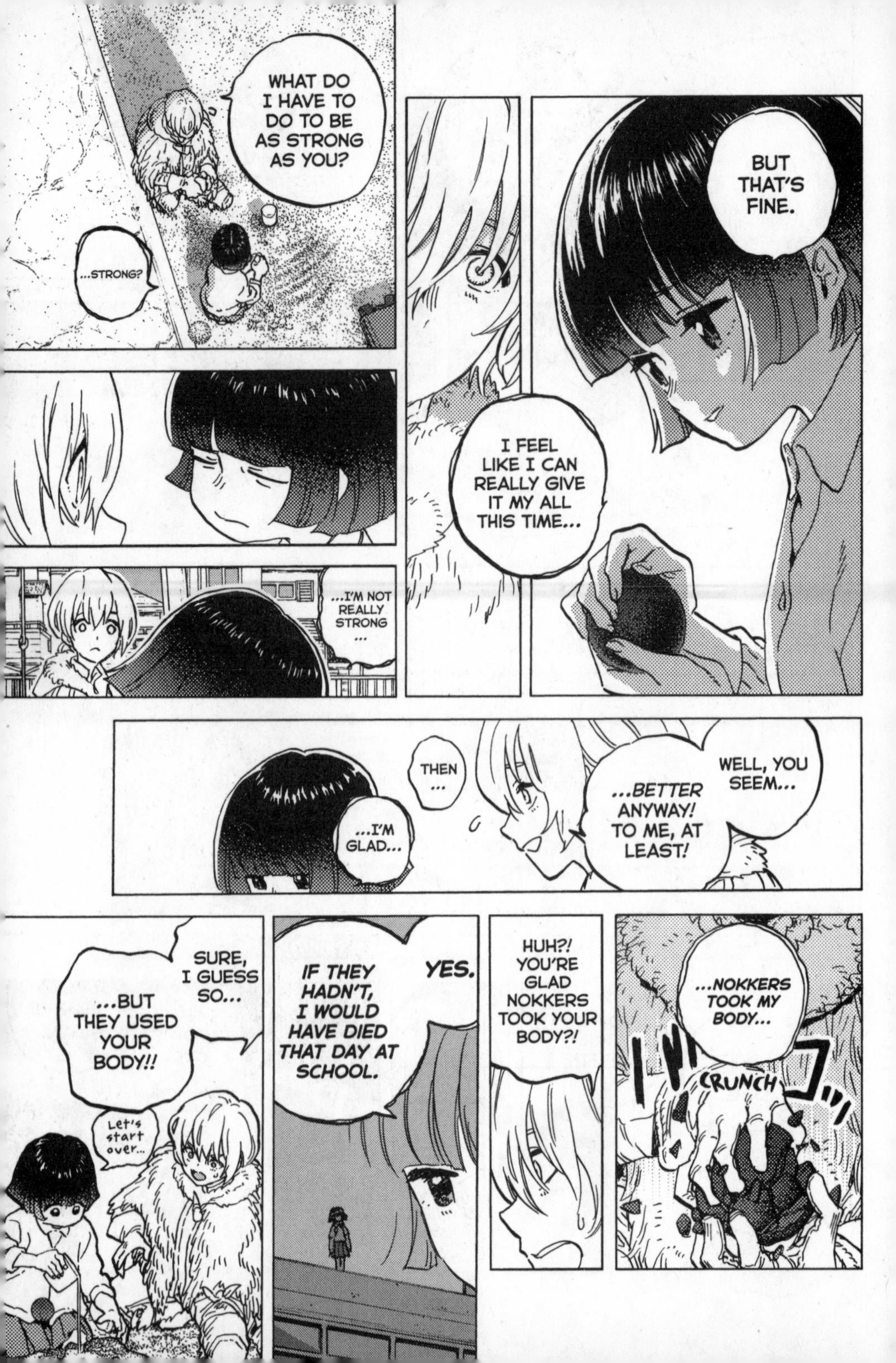
WHAT DO I HAVE TO DO TO BE AS STRONG AS YOU?
...STRONG?
...I'M NOT REALLY STRONG ...
BUT THAT'S FINE.
I FEEL LIKE I CAN REALLY GIVE IT MY ALL THIS TIME...
WELL, YOU SEEM...
...BETTER ANYWAY! TO ME, AT LEAST!
THEN ...
...I'M GLAD...
...NOKKERS TOOK MY BODY...
CRUNCH
HUH?! YOU'RE GLAD NOKKERS TOOK YOUR BODY?!
YES.
IF THEY HADN'T, I WOULD HAVE DIED THAT DAY AT SCHOOL.
SURE, I GUESS SO...
...BUT THEY USED YOUR BODY!!
Let's start over...

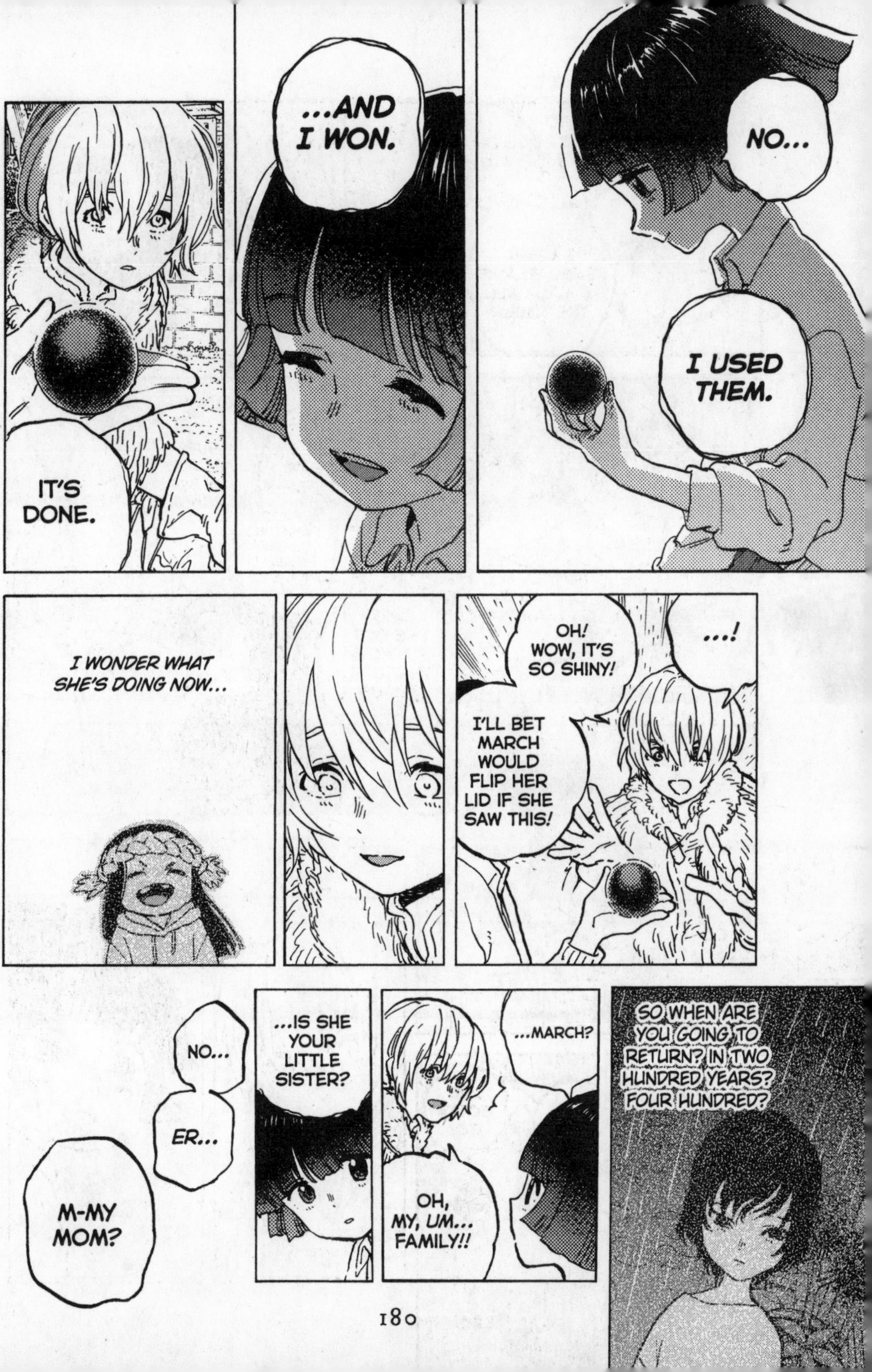
NO...
I USED THEM.
...AND I WON.
IT'S DONE.
...!
OH! WOW, IT'S SO SHINY!
I'LL BET MARCH WOULD FLIP HER LID IF SHE SAW THIS!
I WONDER WHAT SHE'S DOING NOW...
SO WHEN ARE YOU GOING TO RETURN? IN TWO HUNDRED YEARS? FOUR HUNDRED?
...MARCH?
OH, MY, UM... FAMILY!!
...IS SHE YOUR LITTLE SISTER?
NO...
ER...
M-MY MOM?

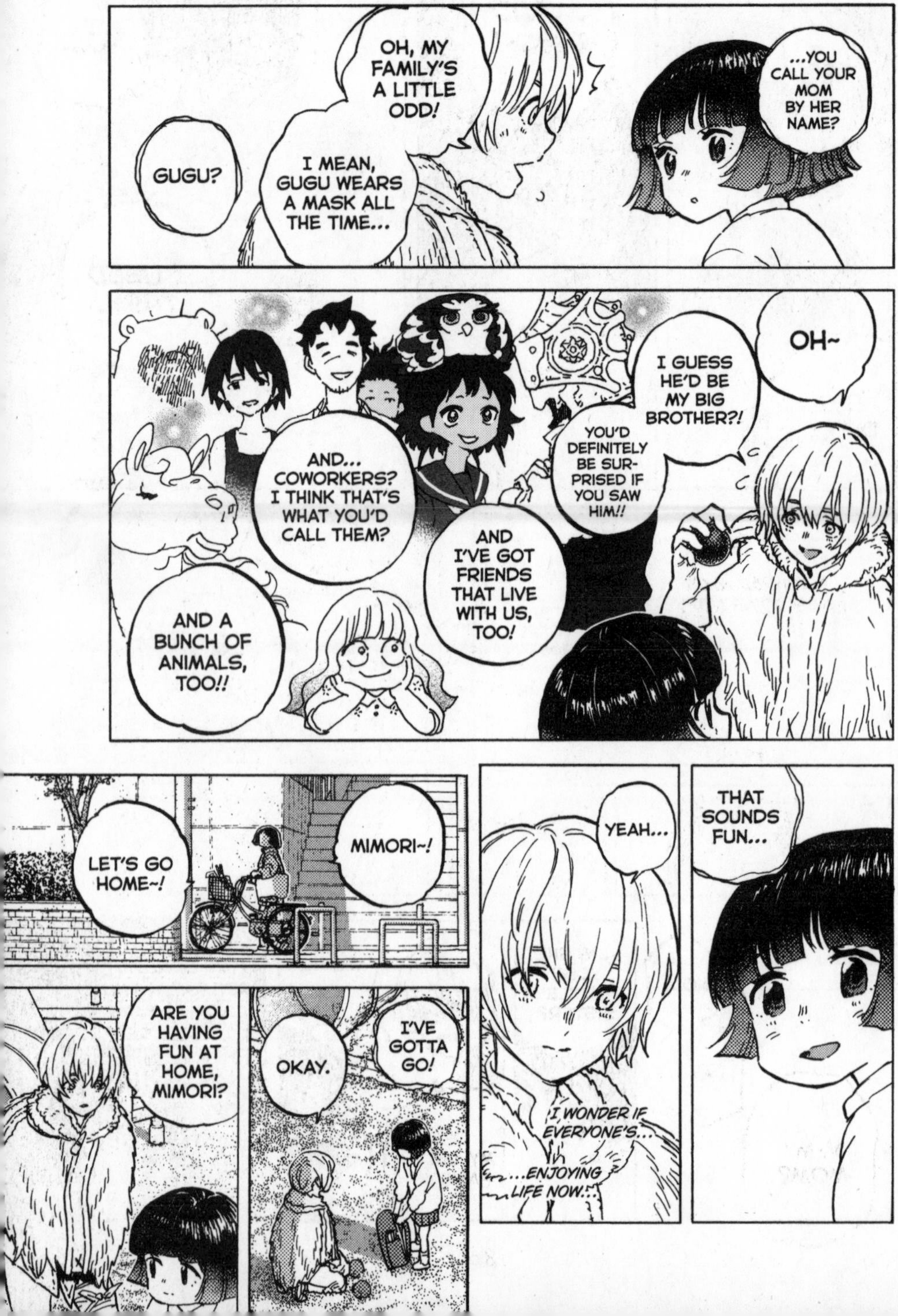
...YOU CALL YOUR MOM BY HER NAME?
OH, MY FAMILY'S A LITTLE ODD!
I MEAN, GUGU WEARS A MASK ALL THE TIME...
GUGU?
OH~
I GUESS HE'D BE MY BIG BROTHER?!
YOU'D DEFINITELY BE SUR-PRISED IF YOU SAW HIM!!
AND... COWORKERS? I THINK THAT'S WHAT YOU'D CALL THEM?
AND I'VE GOT FRIENDS THAT LIVE WITH US, TOO!
AND A BUNCH OF ANIMALS, TOO!!
THAT SOUNDS FUN...
YEAH...
I WONDER IF EVERYONE'S...
...ENJOYING LIFE NOW...
MIMORI~!
LET'S GO HOME~!
I'VE GOTTA GO!
OKAY.
ARE YOU HAVING FUN AT HOME, MIMORI?

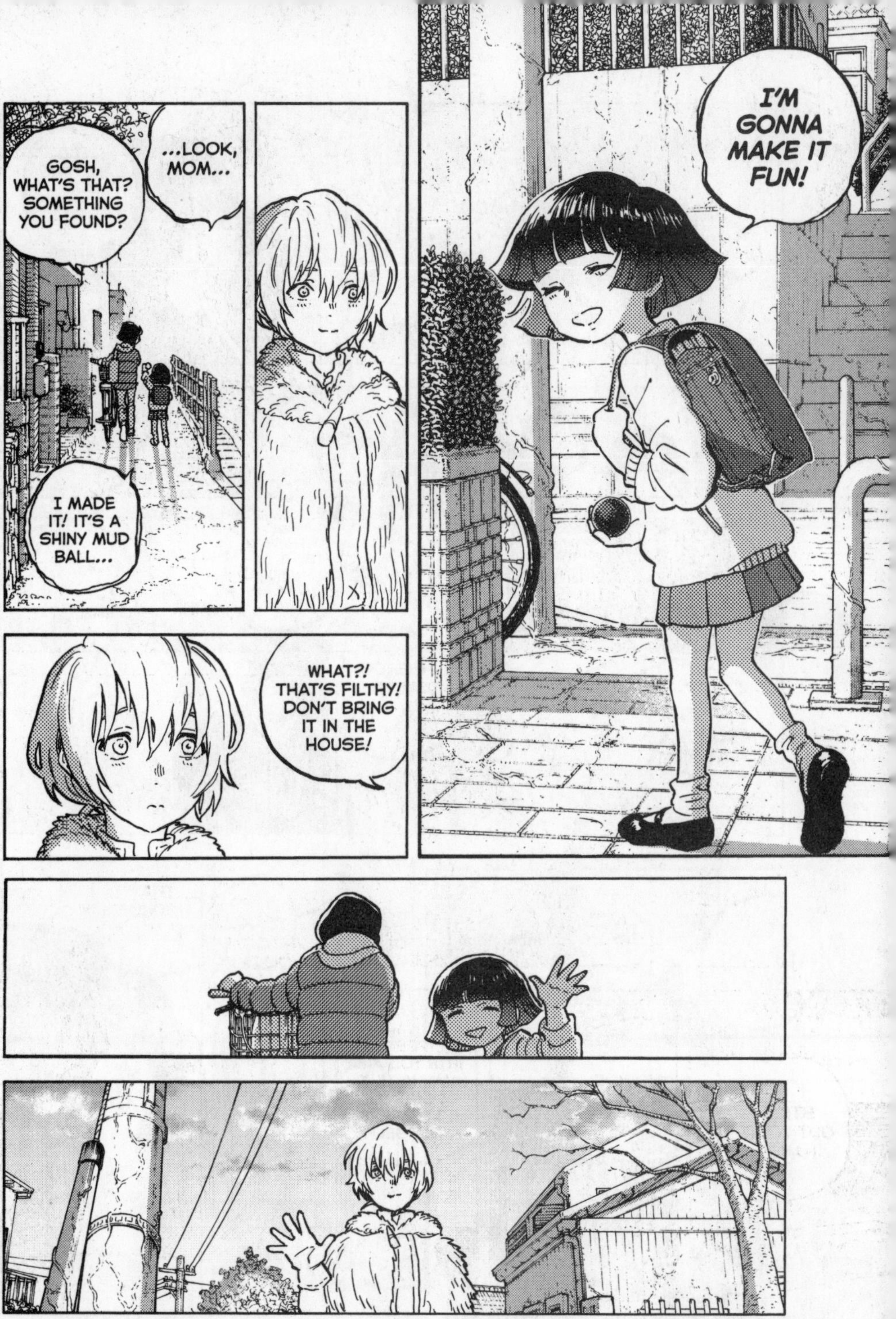

I'M GONNA MAKE IT FUN!
...LOOK, MOM...
GOSH, WHAT'S THAT? SOMETHING YOU FOUND?
I MADE IT! IT'S A SHINY MUD BALL...
WHAT?! THAT'S FILTHY! DON'T BRING IT IN THE HOUSE!

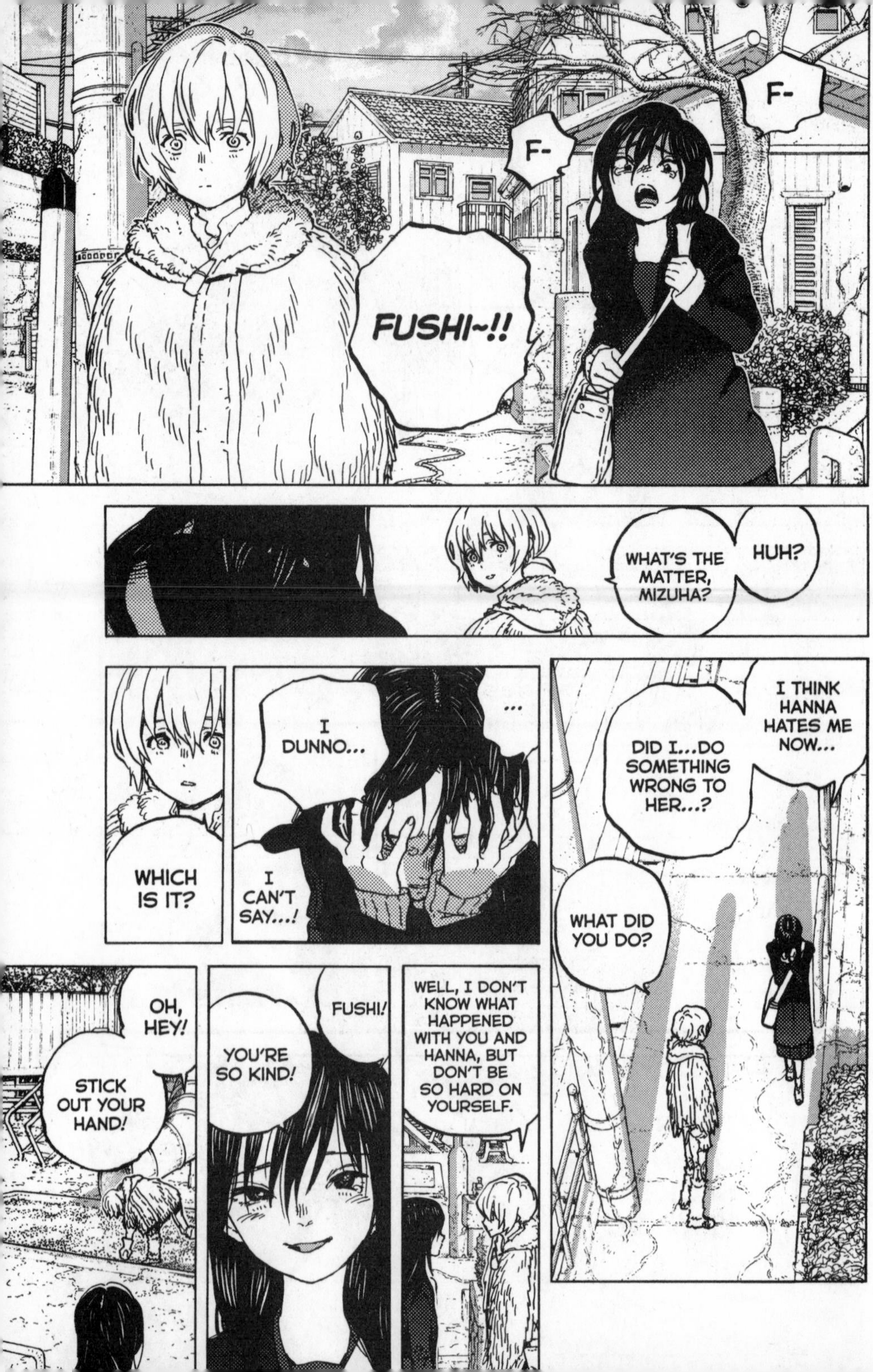
F-
F-
FUSHI~!!
HUH?
WHAT'S THE MATTER, MIZUHA?
I THINK HANNA HATES ME NOW...
DID I...DO SOMETHING WRONG TO HER...?
WHAT DID YOU DO?
...
I DUNNO...
I CAN'T SAY...!
WHICH IS IT?
WELL, I DON'T KNOW WHAT HAPPENED WITH YOU AND HANNA, BUT DON'T BE SO HARD ON YOURSELF.
FUSHI!
YOU'RE SO KIND!
OH, HEY!
STICK OUT YOUR HAND!

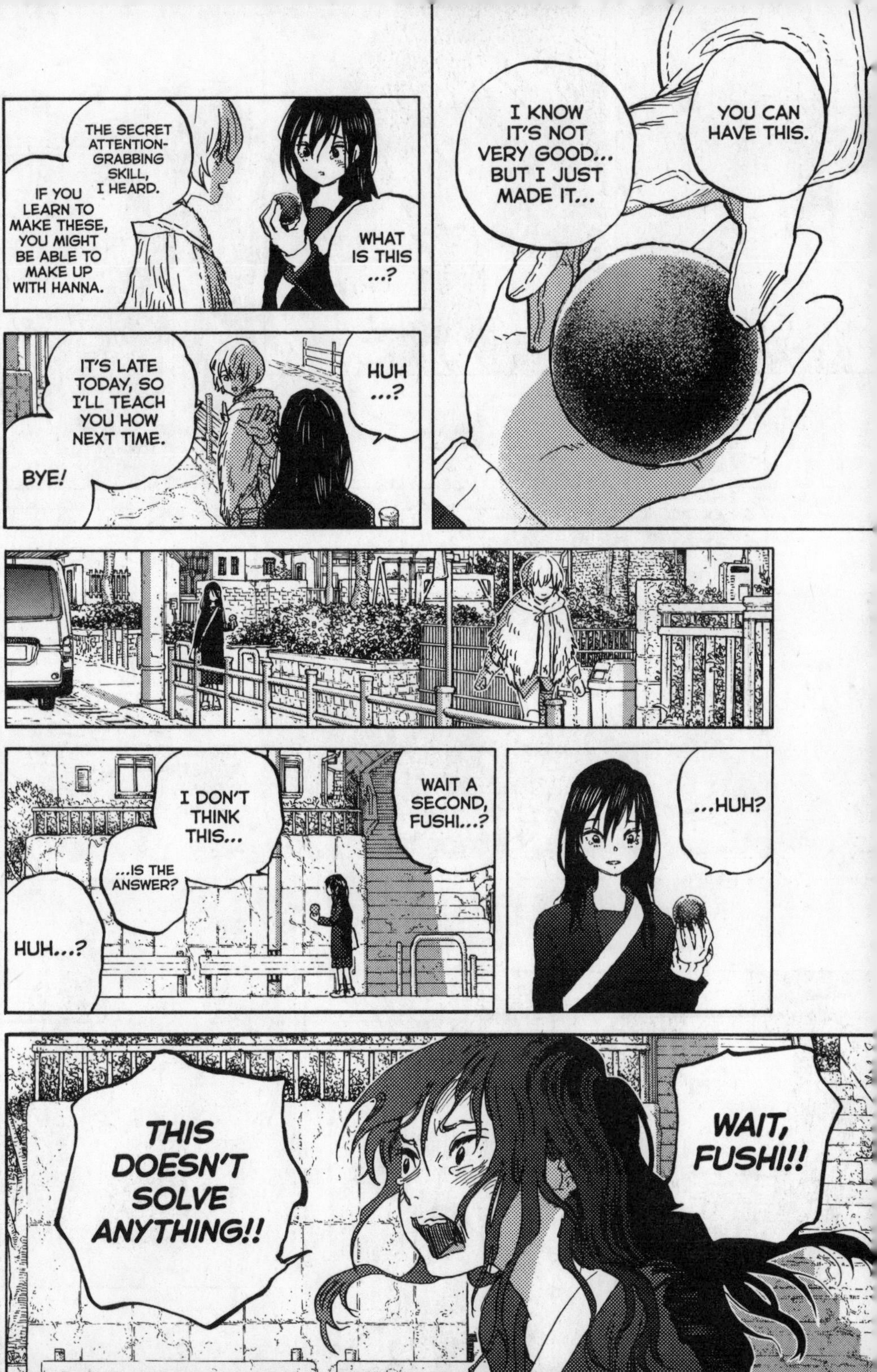
YOU CAN HAVE THIS.
I KNOW IT'S NOT VERY GOOD... BUT I JUST MADE IT...
WHAT IS THIS ...?
THE SECRET ATTENTION-GRABBING SKILL, I HEARD.
IF YOU LEARN TO MAKE THESE, YOU MIGHT BE ABLE TO MAKE UP WITH HANNA.
HUH ...?
IT'S LATE TODAY, SO I'LL TEACH YOU HOW NEXT TIME.
BYE!
...HUH?
WAIT A SECOND, FUSHI...?
I DON'T THINK THIS...
...IS THE ANSWER?
HUH...?
WAIT, FUSHI!!
THIS DOESN'T SOLVE ANYTHING!!

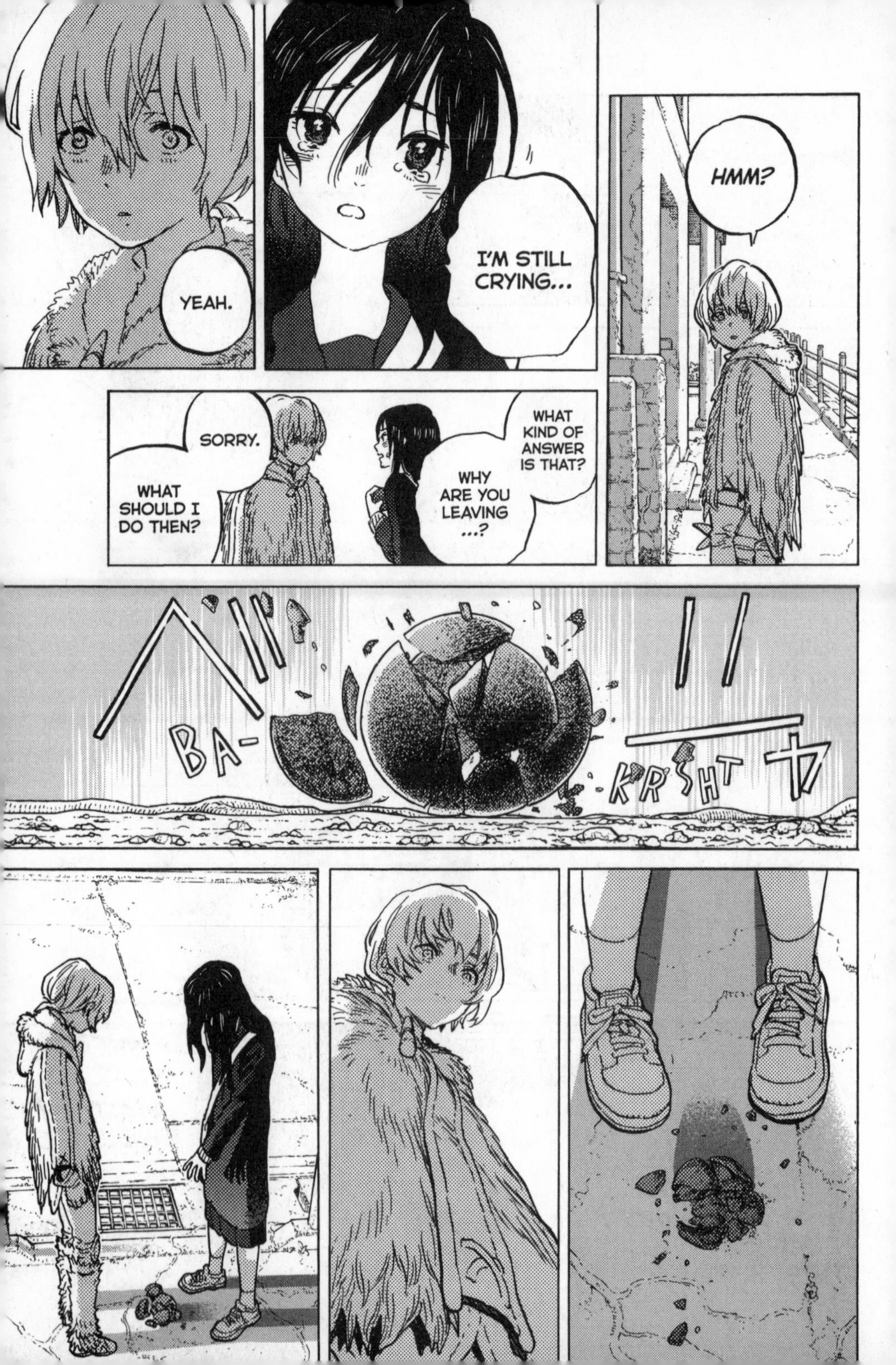
HMM?
I'M STILL CRYING...
YEAH.
WHAT KIND OF ANSWER IS THAT?
WHY ARE YOU LEAVING ...?
SORRY.
WHAT SHOULD I DO THEN?
BA-
KRSHT

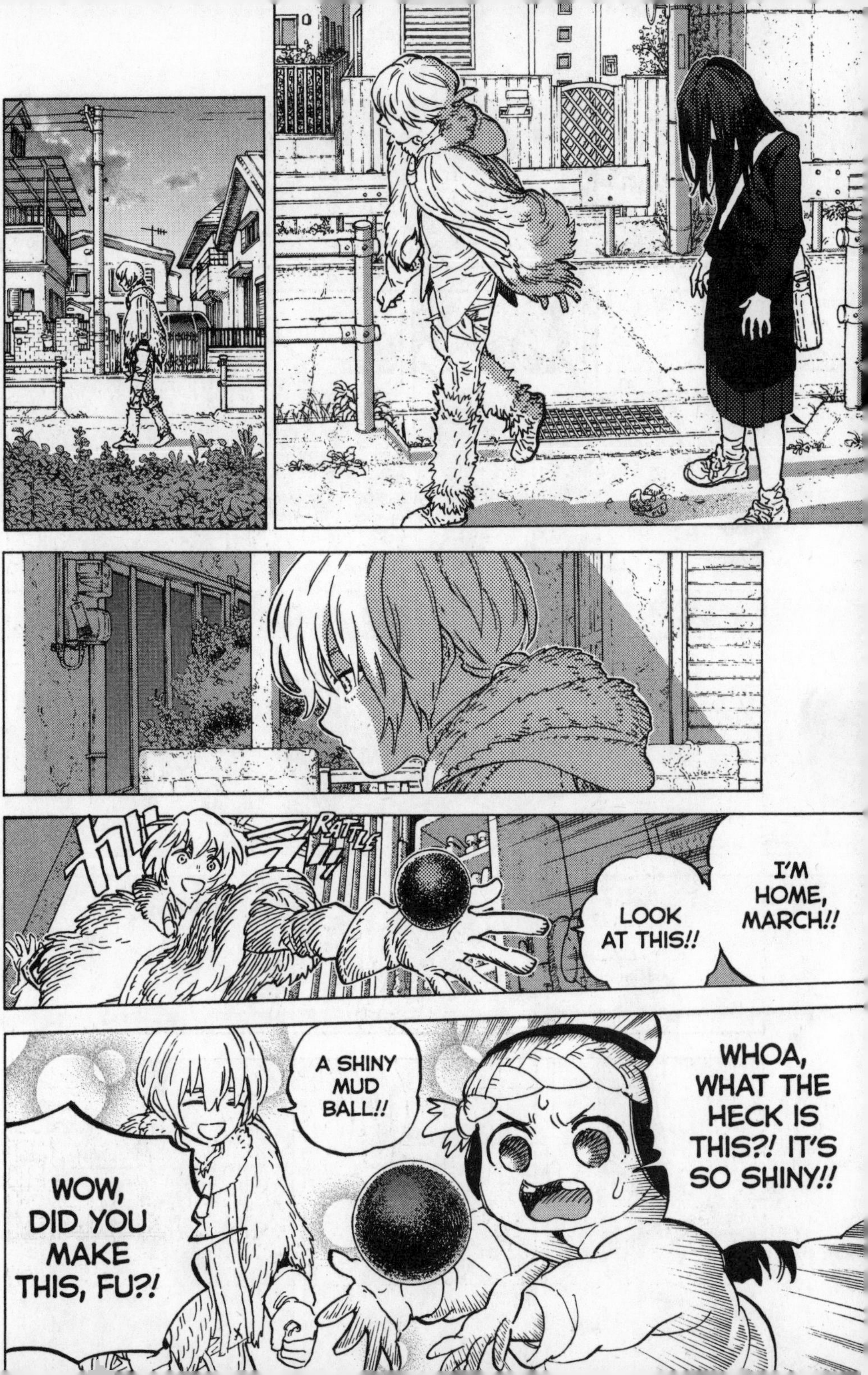
RATTLE
I'M HOME, MARCH!!
LOOK AT THIS!!
WHOA, WHAT THE HECK IS THIS?! IT'S SO SHINY!!
A SHINY MUD BALL!!
WOW, DID YOU MAKE THIS, FU?!

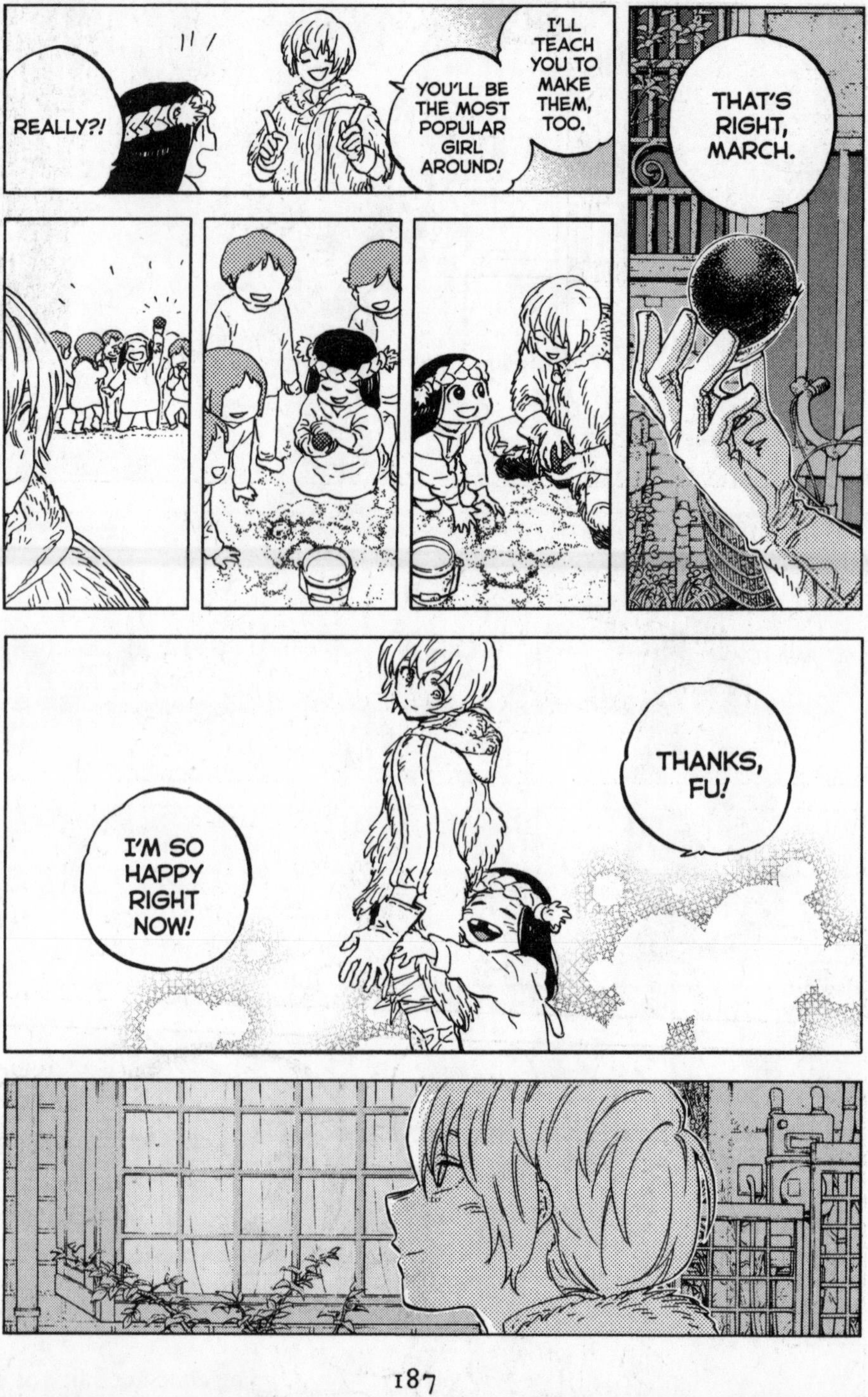
THAT'S RIGHT, MARCH.
I'LL TEACH YOU TO MAKE THEM, TOO.
YOU'LL BE THE MOST POPULAR GIRL AROUND!
REALLY?!
THANKS, FU!
I'M SO HAPPY RIGHT NOW!

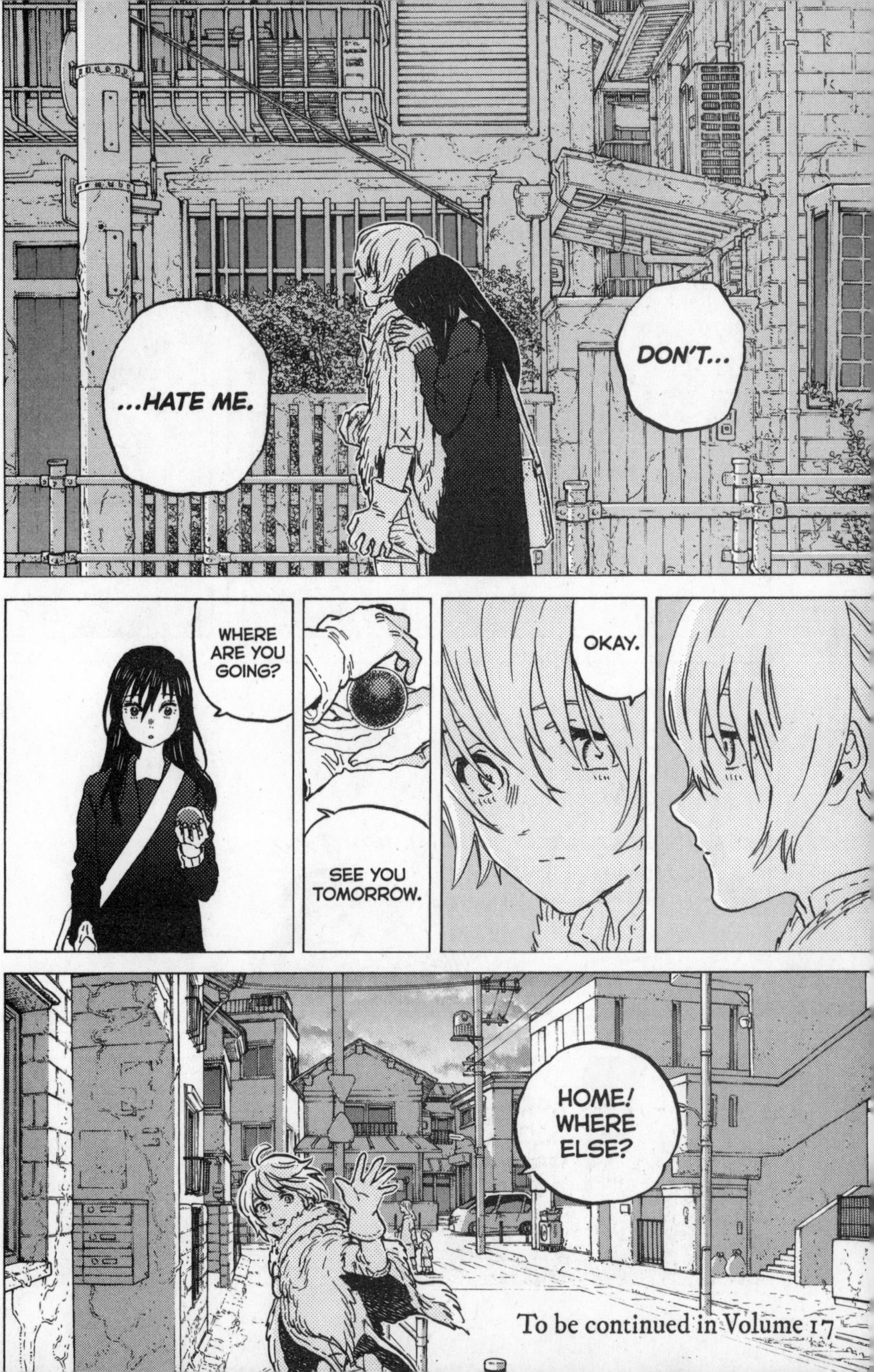
DON'T...
...HATE ME.
OKAY.
SEE YOU TOMORROW.
WHERE ARE YOU GOING?
HOME! WHERE ELSE?

To be continued in Volume 17

TO YOUR ETERNITY

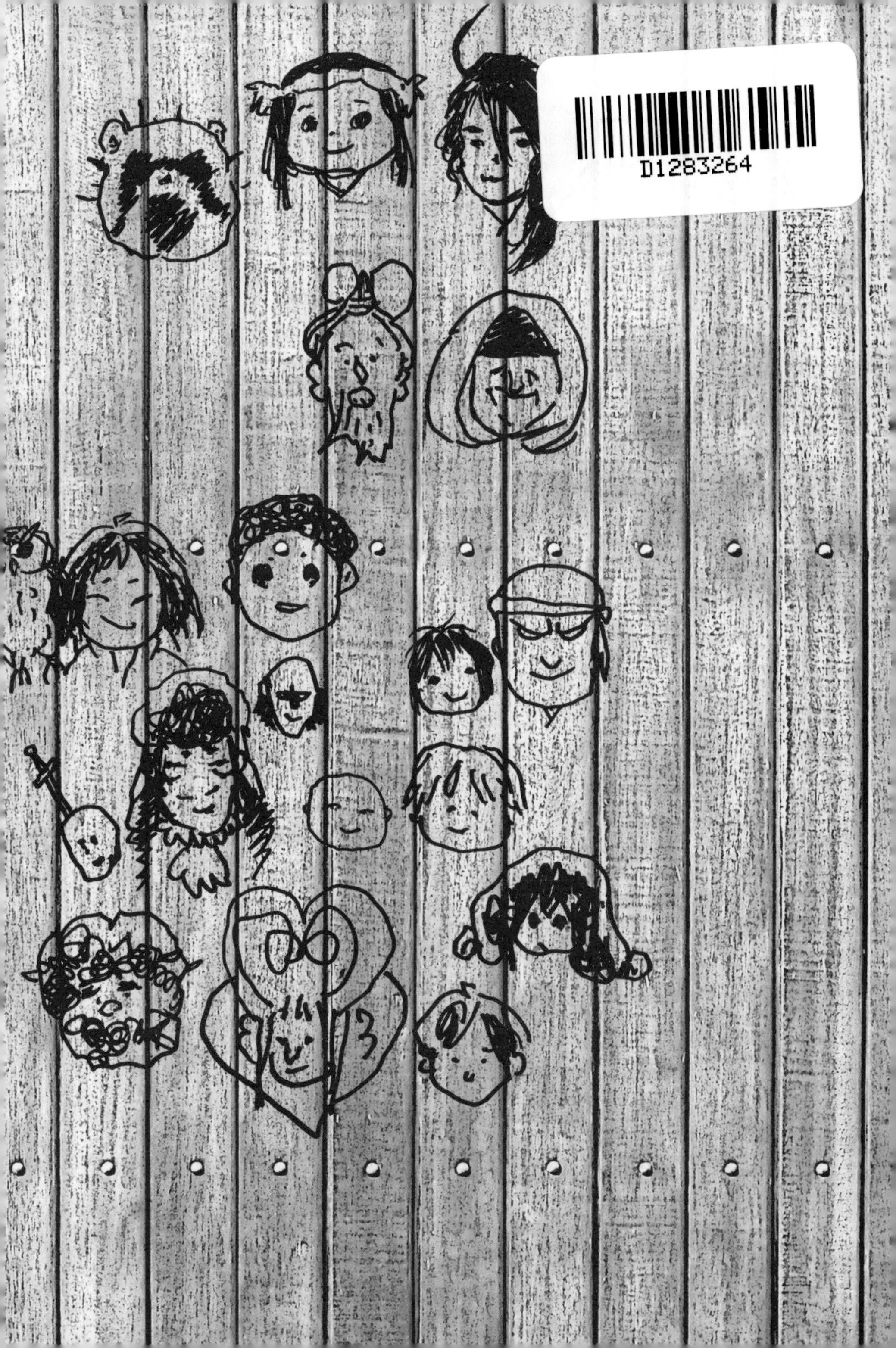